The Song Book
of
The Salvation Army

The Song Book
of
The Salvation Army

Issued by the authority of
THE GENERAL

American Edition
1987
The Salvation Army
National Headquarters

ISBN 0-89216-070-5   (Hard Cover Edition)
ISBN 0-89216-071-3   (Leather Edition)
ISBN 0-89216-073-x   (Compact Edition/ NIV New Testament)

First Printing of Hard Cover Edition - 1987
Second Printing of Hard Cover Edition - 1999
Third Printing of Hard Cover Edition - 2009

The Salvation Army
TERRITORIAL HEADQUARTERS

EASTERN TERRITORY
440 West Nyack Road
West Nyack, NY 10994-1739

CENTRAL TERRITORY
10 W. Algonquin Rd.
Des Plaines, IL 60016-6006

SOUTHERN TERRITORY
1424 Northeast Expressway
Atlanta, GA 30329-2088

WESTERN TERRITORY
108 East Ocean Boulevard
Long Beach, CA 90802-4709

CANADA AND BERMUDA TERRITORY
2 Overlea Blvd., Toronto, Ontario
M4H 1P4 CANADA

Foreword

THIS new edition of *The Song Book of The Salvation Army* is dedicated to the glory of God and the spiritual ministry of Salvationists in various parts of the world. The book is the outcome of thorough world-wide research. It draws upon the treasuries of hymns and songs of many nations and many Christian denominations.

Most of the great traditional Christian hymns included in earlier editions have been retained and to these have been added many others which have gained popularity in recent years. In addition to a large selection of older songs of Salvation Army origin, a number of contemporary songs by Salvationist authors have been included.

It is my hope and desire that the song book will serve many purposes. It will be an effective tool in outreach evangelism, being used in open-air meetings and in many types of gatherings outside our Salvation Army halls. The book will be used to convey the message of salvation and holiness in our regular meetings. The songs of praise will provide individuals and congregations with a medium for expressing their gratitude and thanksgiving to God. The song book will also be used as a manual for private devotion.

General Albert Orsborn wrote in the Foreword to the 1953 edition:

The upward reaching of the soul, the downward reach of the love of God, the incense of devotion, the canticles of praise, are all here.

The song book will also be used in the homes of Salvationists, at family prayers and on occasions when friends and neighbors visit the home.

Our Founder wrote in the Foreword to an early edition of our song book words that are just as appropriate today as when they were penned:

Sing so as to make the world hear. The highest value of our singing after all has not been the mere gladness we have felt because of our salvation, but the joy of pouring out the praises of our God to those who have not known Him, or of rousing them by our singing to new thoughts and a new life.

And sing till your whole soul is lifted up to God, and then sing till you lift the eyes of those who know not God to him who is the fountain of all our joy.

May God bless and use these songs according to his good will.

The GENERAL

International Headquarters
London, England 1986

EXPLANATORY NOTES

FOR easy reference, the songs in each sub-section of the 12 main divisions are set out in alphabetical order and the titles of suitable tunes inserted at the head of each song. A wider choice of tunes may be made by consulting the metrical index. The American Edition adds some tunes from the American Supplement (marked A.S.).

CHORUS SECTION

A selection of old and new choruses are divided under eight headings and arranged alphabetically. Tunes will bear the same number in the chorus section of *The Tune Book of The Salvation Army*. Key signatures are also given for each chorus for the convenience of those musicians who use guitars or pianos.

AUTHORS

Where no reliable information exists concerning the author of a song or chorus, the expression "anon" is used. The abbreviation "alt" before an author's name stands for "altered by"; after the name, that the original work has been altered; "trs" stands for "translated by"; "attr" for "attributed to".

COPYRIGHT

Many of the songs in this book are copyrighted and may not be reprinted by anyone in any form without permission of the publishers or other owners.

INDEX

First lines of all verses and choruses used in the song book are included in the index; first verses are given in bold type, other verses in roman type; choruses in italics.

AMERICAN SUPPLEMENT

There is a requirement by some copyright owners that their songs can only be published with the music in the American Edition. These songs appear in the American Supplement, containing song numbers 963 to 994. The American Supplement also contains patriotic songs of the United States and Canada as well as songs for special occasions.

ACKNOWLEDGMENTS

THE SALVATION ARMY desires to thank those authors, publishers and copyright owners who have kindly granted permission for the inclusion of their songs in this song book.

If any rights have been overlooked or inadvertently infringed, the publishers request that these may be pointed out so that due acknowledgement may be made.

An asterisk denotes that a fee has been paid for permission to print.

Songs in the American Supplement have separate copyright notices where applicable. In such cases a fee has been paid for permission to print.

AUTHOR	OWNER OF COPYRIGHT	NO. OF SONG
Ackley, Alfred H.	The Rodeheaver Co. (A Div. of Word, Inc.)	*334
Bayly, Albert F.	Oxford University Press	*38, *927
Carter, Ruth	Mrs. Bessie Carter	*856
Clayton, Norman J.	Norman Clayton Publishing Co. (A Div. of Word, Inc.).	*349
Cox, Sidney E.	Singspiration Music (A Div. of the Zondervan Corp.)	*227, *340, *347, *384, *386
Dearmer, Percy	Oxford University Press, from *Enlarged Songs of Praise*.	*146
Farjeon, Eleanor	David Higham Associates Ltd.	*35
Fraser, David	David Fraser	851
Herklots, Rosamond	Oxford University Press	*572
Jones, Richard G.	Rev. Richard G. Jones	30
Oxenham, John	Desmond Dunkerly	*615, *826, *827
Peacey, John R.	Mrs. Mildred Peacey	408, 748
Peterson, John W.	John W. Peterson Music Co.	*371
Piggott, William C.	Oxford University Press	*878
Struther, Jan	Oxford University Press	*611
Tucker, Francis Bland	The Church Hymnal Corp.	174
Winslow, John	Mrs. J. Tyrrell	506

CHORUS SECTION

Cox, Sidney E.	Singspiration Music (A Div. of the Zondervan Corp.)	*115, *169
Iverson, Daniel	Moody Bible Institute of Chicago	53

Contents

GOD THE FATHER
Person and Praise

1 Ein' Feste Burg, 640

A MIGHTY fortress is our God,
  A bulwark never failing;
Our helper he, amid the flood,
  Of mortal ills prevailing.
For still our ancient foe
Doth seek to work us woe;
His craft and power are great,
And, armed with cruel hate,
  On earth is not his equal.

2 Did we in our own strength confide,
  Our striving would be losing;
Were not the right man on our side,
  The man of God's own choosing.
Dost ask who that may be?
Christ Jesus, it is he;
Lord Sabaoth his name,
From age to age the same,
  And he must win the battle.

3 And though this world, with demons filled,
  Should threaten to undo us;
We will not fear, for God hath willed
  His truth to triumph through us.
The prince of darkness grim,
We tremble not for him,
His rage we can endure,
For lo! His doom is sure,
  One little word shall fell him!

4 That word above all earthly powers,
  No thanks to them abideth;
The Spirit and the gifts are ours
  Through him who with us sideth.
Let goods and kindred go,
This mortal life also;
The body they may kill;
God's truth abideth still,
  His Kingdom is for ever.
          Martin Luther (1483-1546),
    trs Frederic Henry Hedge (1805-90)

2 St Francis, 45
                              L.M.

A LL creatures of our God and King,
  Lift up your voice and with us sing
    Alleluia, alleluia!
Thou burning sun with golden beam,
Thou silver moon with softer gleam:

O praise him, O praise him,
Alleluia, alleluia, alleluia!

2 Thou rushing wind that art so strong,
Ye clouds that sail in heaven along,
    O praise him, alleluia!
Thou rising morn, in praise rejoice,
Ye lights of evening, find a voice:

3 Thou flowing water, pure and clear,
Make music for thy Lord to hear,
    Alleluia, alleluia!
Thou fire so masterful and bright,
That givest man both warmth and light:

4 Dear mother earth, who day by day
Unfoldest blessings on our way,
    O praise him, alleluia!
The flowers and fruits that in thee grow,
Let them his glory also show:

5 Let all things their Creator bless,
And worship him in humbleness,
    O praise him, alleluia!
Praise, praise the Father, praise the Son,
And praise the Spirit, Three in One:
          Francis of Assisi (1182-1226),
    trs William Henry Draper (1855-1933)

3 Old Hundredth, 38
                              L.M.

A LL people that on earth do dwell,
  Sing to the Lord with cheerful voice;
Him serve with fear, his praise forth tell,
  Come ye before him and rejoice.

2 The Lord, ye know, is God indeed;
  Without our aid he did us make;
We are his flock, he doth us feed,
  And for his sheep he doth us take.

3 O enter then his gates with praise,
  Approach with joy his courts unto;
Praise, laud and bless his name always,
  For it is seemly so to do.

4 For why? The Lord our God is good,
  His mercy is for ever sure;
His truth at all times firmly stood,
  And shall from age to age endure.
                      William Kethe (d 1594)

4 Old Hundredth, 38;
    Sounding Praise, 51   L.M.

B EFORE Jehovah's awful throne,
  Ye nations bow with sacred joy;
Know that the Lord is God alone;
  He can create, and he destroy.

1

God the Father

2 His sovereign power, without our aid,
    Made us of clay, and formed us men;
  And when like wandering sheep we
    strayed,
    He brought us to his fold again.

3 We'll crowd thy gates with thankful songs,
    High as the heavens our voices raise;
  And earth, with her ten thousand tongues,
    Shall fill thy courts with sounding
    praise.

4 Wide as the world is thy command;
    Vast as eternity thy love;
  Firm as a rock thy truth shall stand,
    When rolling years shall cease to move.
            Isaac Watts (1674-1748),
            alt John Wesley (1703-91)

5 Carey's, 489; Eternal God, 492
                8.8.8.8.8.8. Iambic

ETERNAL God, our song we raise
  In thankful, overflowing praise,
For men of faith whose power was thine,
Whose love no barrier could confine;
They humbly offered Christ their bread,
And lo, the multitudes were fed!

2 We thank thee for the fruitful years,
  The sacred gains of toil and tears,
  For mighty works through weakness
    wrought,
  For souls who led in deed and thought;
  They followed Jesus in the light
  And their loud anthems thrilled the night.

3 O may no longing of our own
  Obscure the path by Jesus shown!
  We would not thirst for earth's reward
  And lose the blessing of our Lord:
  His cup of pain and grief and strife
  That yieldeth up the gift of life.

4 Our Father, we beseech thee now:
  Receive again our first pure vow
  To stand though fire and tempest rage,
  Nor fear the terrors of our age,
  To love thee with a constant mind
  And lose ourselves to save mankind.

5 Our great Redeemer liveth still,
  His love sustains us in thy will;
  Because he conquered, we shall win,
  His cross before, his joy within;
  Our cheerful banners are unfurled,
  For Christ has overcome the world.
          Catherine Baird (1895-1984)

6 Alford, 245
               7.6.7.6.D. Iambic

ETERNAL God, unchanging
  Through all the changing years,
Whose hands all things created,
  Who holds the countless stars;
Enthroned in heavenly glory,
  Yet not a God afar;
Thou deignest to have dwelling
  Here where thy people are.

2 Forbid that man's achievements
  Should cause our faith to wane,
  Or seek in human wisdom
  Our spirit to sustain;
  Lord, surely thou art shaping
  All things to thy design,
  And born of this conviction
  Is faith to match our time.

3 And in a world divided
  By selfishness and guile,
  When truth is on the scaffold
  And faith is standing trial,
  Grant us, by inward knowledge
  No learning can bestow,
  A faith that answers firmly:
  These things, these things I know.

4 Though men have wrought confusion
  Thy hand still holds the plan,
  And thou, at length, decideth
  The destiny of man;
  Dominions rise and perish,
  The mighty have their day,
  But still thy word abideth,
  It shall not pass away.
       Albert Ernest Dalziel (1892-1974)

7 Ellacombe, 147; Land of pure delight, 154;
    Materna A.S. 967   D.C.M.

FILL thou my life, O Lord my God,
  In every part with praise,
That my whole being may proclaim
  Thy being and thy ways.
Not for the lip of praise alone,
  Nor e'en the praising heart
I ask, but for a life made up
  Of praise in every part!

2 Praise in the common words I speak,
  Life's common looks and tones,
  In fellowship at hearth and board
  With my belovèd ones;
  Not in the temple crowd alone
  Where holy voices chime,
  But in the silent paths of earth,
  The quiet rooms of time.

Person and Praise

3 Fill every part of me with praise;
  Let all my being speak
Of thee and of thy love, O Lord,
  Poor though I be, and weak.
So shalt thou, Lord, from me, e'en me,
  Receive the glory due;
And so shall I begin on earth
  The song forever new.

4 So shall each fear, each fret, each care
  Be turned into a song,
And every winding of the way
  The echo shall prolong;
So shall no part of day or night
  From sacredness be free;
But all my life, in every step,
  Be fellowship with thee.
Horatius Bonar (1808-89), alt

8 St Denio, 569; Foundation, A.S. 976
11.11.11.11.

IMMORTAL, invisible, God only wise,
  In light inaccessible hid from our eyes,
Most blessèd, most glorious, the Ancient
  of Days,
Almighty, victorious, thy great name we
  praise.

2 Unresting, unhasting, and silent as light,
  Nor wanting, nor wasting, thou rulest in
    might;
Thy justice like mountains high soaring
  above
Thy clouds which are fountains of good-
  ness and love.

3 To all life thou givest, to both great and
  small,
In all life thou livest, the true life of all;
We blossom and flourish as leaves on the
  tree,
And wither and perish; but naught
  changeth thee.

4 Great Father of glory, pure Father of light,
Thine angels adore thee, all veiling their
  sight;
All praise we would render; O help us to
  see
'Tis only the splendor of light hideth thee.
Walter Chalmers Smith (1824-1908)

9 Majesty, 226; St John, 228
6.6.6.6.8.8.

JEHOVAH is our strength,
  And he shall be our song;
We shall o'ercome at length
  Although our foes be strong.
In vain does Satan then oppose,
For God is stronger than his foes.

2 The Lord our refuge is
  And ever will remain;
Since he has made us his
  He will our cause maintain.
In vain our enemies oppose,
For God is stronger than his foes.

3 The Lord our shepherd is;
  He knows our every need,
And since we now are his,
  His care our souls will feed.
In vain do sin and death oppose,
For God is stronger than his foes.

4 Our God our Father is;
  Our names are on his heart;
We ever will be his,
  He ne'er from us will part.
In vain the mightiest powers oppose,
For God is stronger than his foes.
Attr Samuel Barnard (d 1807)

10 Europe, 435
8.7.8.7. D. Troch.

JOYFUL, joyful, we adore thee,
  God of glory, Lord of love;
Hearts unfold like flowers before thee,
  Hail thee as the sun above.
Melt the clouds of sin and sadness,
  Drive the clouds of doubt away;
Giver of immortal gladness,
  Fill us with the light of day.

2 All thy works with joy surround thee,
  Earth and heaven reflect thy rays,
Stars and angels sing around thee,
  Center of unbroken praise;
Field and forest, vale and mountain,
  Bloss'ming meadow, flashing sea,
Chanting bird and flowing fountain
  Call us to rejoice in thee.

3 Thou art giving and forgiving,
    Ever blessing, ever blest,
Wellspring of the joy of living,
    Ocean-depth of happy rest.
Thou the Father, Christ our brother—
    All who live in love are thine;
Teach us how to love each other,
    Lift us to the joy divine.

4 Mortals, join the mighty chorus
    Which the morning stars began;
Father-love is reigning o'er us,
    Brother-love binds man to man.
Ever singing, march we onward,
    Victors in the midst of strife,
Joyful music lifts us sunward
    In the triumph song of life.
Henry van Dyke (1852-1933)

11 Luckington, 727

L ET all the world in every corner sing:
    My God and King!
The heavens are not too high,
    His praise may thither fly;
The earth is not too low,
    His praises there may grow.
Let all the world in every corner sing:
    My God and King!

2 Let all the world in every corner sing:
    My God and King!
The church with psalms must shout,
    No door can keep them out;
But, more than all, the heart
    Must bear the largest part.
Let all the world in every corner sing:
    My God and King!
George Herbert (1593-1633)

12 Now thank we all our God, 752

N OW thank we all our God
    With hearts and hands and voices,
Who wondrous things hath done,
    In whom his world rejoices;
Who from our mothers' arms
    Hath blessed us on our way
With countless gifts of love,
    And still is ours today.

2 O may this bounteous God
    Through all our life be near us,
With ever-joyful hearts
    And blessèd peace to cheer us,

And keep us in his grace,
    And guide us when perplexed,
And free us from all ills
    In this world and the next.

3 All praise and thanks to God
    The Father now be given,
The Son and him who reigns
    With them in highest Heaven.
The one eternal God,
    Whom earth and Heaven adore;
For thus it was, is now,
    And shall be evermore.
Martin Rinkart (1586-1649),
trs Catherine Winkworth (1827-78)

13 St Ann, 127
                                        C.M.

O GOD, our help in ages past,
    Our hope for years to come,
Our shelter from the stormy blast,
    And our eternal home.

2 Under the shadow of thy throne
    Thy saints have dwelt secure;
Sufficient is thine arm alone,
    And our defense is sure.

3 Before the hills in order stood,
    Or earth received her frame,
From everlasting thou art God,
    To endless years the same.

4 A thousand ages in thy sight
    Are like an evening gone,
Short as the watch that ends the night
    Before the rising sun.

5 Time, like an ever-rolling stream,
    Bears all its sons away;
They fly forgotten, as a dream
    Dies at the opening day.

6 O God, our help in ages past,
    Our hope for years to come,
Be thou our guard while life shall last,
    And our eternal home.
Isaac Watts (1674-1748)

14 Richmond, 125; Arnold's, 71;
    Azmon, A.S. 988   C.M.

O LORD, I will delight in thee
    And on thy care depend,
To thee in every trouble flee,
    My best, my only friend.

2 When all created streams are dried,
    Thy fulness is the same;
May I with this be satisfied
    And glory in thy name.

3 No good in creatures can be found
    But may be found in thee;
I must have all things and abound
    While God is God to me.

4 O Lord, I cast my care on thee,
    I triumph and adore;
Henceforth my great concern shall be
    To love and please thee more.
John Ryland (1753-1825)

15 Troyte, 470; Almsgiving, 469
    8.8.8.4.

O LORD of Heaven and earth and sea,
    To thee all praise and glory be;
How shall we show our love to thee,
    Who givest all?

2 For peaceful homes and healthful days,
For all the blessings earth displays,
We owe thee thankfulness and praise,
    Who givest all.

3 Thou didst not spare thine only Son,
But gav'st him for a world undone,
And freely with that blessèd one
    Thou givest all.

4 Thou giv'st the Spirit's blessèd dower,
Spirit of life and love and power,
And dost his sevenfold graces shower
    Upon us all.

5 For souls redeemed, for sins forgiven,
For means of grace and hopes of Heaven,
Father, all praise to thee be given,
    Who givest all.
Christopher Wordsworth (1807-85)

16 Houghton, 533; Hanover, 531; Laudate
    Dominum, 534   10.10.11.11.

O WORSHIP the King, all glorious above;
    O gratefully sing his power and his love;
Our shield and defender, the Ancient of
    Days,
    Pavilioned in splendor and girded with
    praise.

2 O tell of his might, O sing of his grace,
    Whose robe is the light, whose canopy
    space;
His chariots of wrath the deep thunder-
    clouds form,
    And dark is his path on the wings of the
    storm.

3 The earth with its store of wonders untold,
    Almighty, thy power hath founded of old,
Hath stablished it fast by a changeless
    decree,
    And round it hath cast, like a mantle,
    the sea.

4 Thy bountiful care what tongue can
    recite?
    It breathes in the air, it shines in the
    light,
It streams from the hills, it descends to
    the plain,
    And sweetly distils in the dew and the
    rain.

5 Frail children of dust and feeble as frail,
    In thee do we trust, nor find thee to fail;
Thy mercies how tender, how firm to the
    end,
    Our Maker, Defender, Redeemer and
    Friend.

6 O measureless Might! Ineffable Love!
    While angels delight to hymn thee above,
The humbler creation, though feeble their
    lays,
    With true adoration shall sing to thy
    praise.
Robert Grant (1779-1838)

17 Praise, my soul, 422; Triumph, 427
    8.7.8.7.8.7. Troch.

PRAISE, my soul, the King of Heaven,
    To his feet thy tribute bring;
Ransomed, healed, restored, forgiven,
    Who like thee his praise should sing?
    Praise him!
Praise the everlasting King.

2 Praise him for his grace and favor
    To our fathers in distress;
Praise him still the same as ever,
    Slow to chide and swift to bless;
    Praise him!
Glorious in his faithfulness.

God the Father

3 Father-like he tends and spares us;
  Well our feeble frame he knows,
In his hands he gently bears us,
  Rescues us from all our foes.
    Praise him!
  Widely as his mercy flows.

4 Angels in the heights adore him,
  Ye behold him face to face;
Sun and moon bow down before him:
  Dwellers all in time and space,
    Praise him!
  Praise with us the God of grace.
Henry Francis Lyte (1793-1847)

18 Gerontius, 89; Richmond, 125
C.M.

PRAISE to the holiest in the height,
  And in the depth be praise,
In all his words most wonderful,
  Most sure in all his ways.

2 O loving wisdom of our God!
  When all was sin and shame,
A second Adam to the fight
  And to the rescue came.

3 O wisest love! that flesh and blood,
  Which did in Adam fail,
Should strive afresh against their foe,
  Should strive and should prevail.

4 Praise to the holiest in the height,
  And in the depth be praise,
In all his words most wonderful,
  Most sure in all his ways.
John Henry Newman (1801-90)

19 Lobe den Herren, 721

PRAISE to the Lord, the Almighty, the
  King of creation;
O my soul, praise him, for he is thy
  health and salvation;
  All ye who hear,
  Brothers and sisters draw near,
Praise him in glad adoration.

2 Praise to the Lord, who doth prosper thy
  work and defend thee;
Surely his goodness and mercy here daily
  attend thee;
  Ponder anew
  What the Almighty can do,
He who with love doth befriend thee.

3 Praise to the Lord, who, when tempests
  their warfare are waging,
Who, when the elements madly around
  thee are raging,
  Biddeth them cease,
  Turneth their fury to peace,
Whirlwinds and waters assuaging.

4 Praise to the Lord, who, when darkness
  of sin is abounding,
Who, when the godless do triumph, all vir-
  tue confounding,
  Sheddeth his light,
  Chaseth the horrors of night,
Saints with his mercy surrounding.

5 Praise to the Lord! O let all that is in me
  adore him!
All that hath life and breath, come now
  with praises before him!
  Let the amen
  Sound from his people again:
Gladly for aye we adore him.
Joachim Neander (1650-80),
trs Catherine Winkworth (1827-78)
and others

20 Falcon Street, 167
S.M.

STAND up and bless the Lord,
  Ye people of his choice;
Stand up and bless the Lord your God
  With heart and soul and voice.

Praise ye the Lord, hallelujah!

2 Though high above all praise,
  Above all blessing high,
Who would not fear his holy name,
  And laud and magnify?

3 O for the living flame
  From his own altar brought,
To touch our lips, our minds inspire,
  And wing to Heaven our thought!

4 God is our strength and song,
  And his salvation ours;
Then be his love in Christ proclaimed
  With all our ransomed powers.

5 Stand up and bless the Lord,
  The Lord your God adore;
Stand up and bless his glorious name
  Henceforth for evermore.
James Montgomery (1771-1854)

Person and Praise

21 Martyrdom, 113; Irish, 99
C.M.

THROUGH all the changing scenes of life,
   In trouble and in joy,
The praises of my God shall still
   My heart and tongue employ.

2 Of his deliverance I will boast,
   Till all that are distressed
From mine example comfort take,
   And charm their griefs to rest.

3 The hosts of God encamp around
   The dwellings of the just;
Deliverance he affords to all
   Who on his succor trust.

4 O make but trial of his love;
   Experience will decide
How blest they are, and only they,
   Who in his truth confide.

5 Fear him, ye saints, and you will then
   Have nothing else to fear;
Make you his service your delight,
   Your wants shall be his care.
                  Nahum Tate (1652-1715),
                  Nicholas Brady (1659-1726)

22 To God be the glory, 576
11.11.11.11.

TO God be the glory, great things he hath
      done!
So loved he the world that he gave us his
      Son;
Who yielded his life an atonement for sin,
And opened the life gate that all may go
   in.

   Praise the Lord! Praise the Lord!
   Let the earth hear his voice!
   Praise the Lord! Praise the Lord!
   Let the people rejoice!
   O come to the Father through Jesus the
      Son,
   And give him the glory; great things he
      hath done!

2 O perfect redemption, the purchase of
      blood!
To every believer the promise of God;
The vilest offender who truly believes,
That moment from Jesus a pardon
   receives.

3 Great things he hath taught us, great
      things he hath done,
And great our rejoicing through Jesus the
      Son;
But purer and higher and greater will be
Our wonder, our rapture, when Jesus we
   see.
                  Fanny Crosby (1820-1915)

23 Gerontius, 89; Abridge, 69;
Amazing Grace!, 70
C.M.

WHAT shall I render to my God
   For all his mercy's store?
I'll take the gifts he hath bestowed
   And humbly ask for more.

2 The sacred cup of saving grace
   I will with thanks receive,
And all his promises embrace
   And to his glory live.

3 My vows I will to his great name
   Before his people pay,
And all I have, and all I am,
   Upon his altar lay.

4 Thy hands created me, thy hands
   From sin have set me free;
The mercy that hath loosed my bands
   Hath bound me fast to thee.

5 The God of all-redeeming grace,
   My God, I will proclaim,
Offer the sacrifice of praise,
   And call upon his name.
                  Charles Wesley (1707-88)

24 Hanover, 531; Laudate Dominum, 534
10.10.11.11.

YE servants of God, your Master proclaim,
   And publish abroad his wonderful
      name;
The name all-victorious of Jesus extol;
His Kingdom is glorious and rules over
   all.

2 God ruleth on high, almighty to save;
   And still he is nigh, his presence we have;
The great congregation his triumphs shall
   sing,
Ascribing salvation to Jesus our King.

3 Then let us adore and give him his right,
   All glory and power, all wisdom and might;
All honor and blessing, with angels above,
   And thanks never-ceasing and infinite
   love!
                  Charles Wesley (1707-88)

*   *   *

see also: 988 O for a thousand tongues

7

Works

25 All things bright and beautiful, 604;
Royal Oak, 778

ALL things bright and beautiful,
All creatures great and small,
All things wise and wonderful,
The Lord God made them all.

1 Each little flower that opens,
  Each little bird that sings,
He made their glowing colors,
  He made their tiny wings:

2 The purple-headed mountain,
  The river running by,
The sunset, and the morning
  That brightens up the sky:

3 The cold wind in the winter,
  The pleasant summer sun,
The ripe fruits in the garden,
  He made them every one:

4 He gave us eyes to see them,
  And lips that we might tell
How great is God Almighty,
  Who has made all things well:
Cecil Frances Alexander (1818-95)

26 Lydia, 110; Stracathro, 136; Evan, 85
C.M.

BEGIN, my tongue, some heavenly theme,
  Awake, my voice, and sing
The mighty works or mightier name
  Of our eternal King.

2 Tell of his wondrous faithfulness,
  And sound his power abroad;
Sing the sweet promise of his grace,
  The quickening word of God.

3 His every word of grace is strong
  As that which built the skies;
The voice that rolls the stars along
  Speaks all the promises.

4 Now shall my fainting heart rejoice
  To know thy favor sure;
I trust the all-creating voice,
  And faith desires no more.
Isaac Watts (1674-1748)

27 St Stephen, 130; Azmon, A.S. 988
C.M.

BEYOND the farthest bounds of earth,
  Beyond the ocean's line,
Beyond the starlit universe
  We sense a power divine.

2 The lines and circles, planes and arcs
  Which we by science trace
All indicate a master mind,
  Its beauty, truth and grace.

3 Like searching eyes earth's telescopes
  The fiery heavens scan;
And now the music of the spheres
  Is heard by listening man.

4 Lord, as we seek for vaster truth,
  And as our spaceships soar,
Help us to recognize your might
  And praise your mercy more.

5 For you, who set the ordinance
  Of worlds beyond our sight,
Have given us minds desiring truth
  And hearts that know delight.

6 Lord, teach us in your only Son
  To reach the way we dream,
To follow truth as he knew truth,
  And find the life supreme.
Miriam M. Richards (1911-89)

28 Dix, 306; Ratisbon, 313; Coles, 305
7.7.7.7.7.7.

FOR the beauty of the earth,
  For the beauty of the skies,
For the love which from our birth
  Over and around us lies,
Father, unto thee we raise
This our sacrifice of praise.

2 For the beauty of each hour
  Of the day and of the night,
Hill and vale and tree and flower,
  Sun and moon and stars of light,
Father, unto thee we raise
This our sacrifice of praise.

3 For the joy of ear and eye,
  For the heart and mind's delight,
For the mystic harmony
  Linking sense to sound and sight,
Father, unto thee we raise
This our sacrifice of praise.

4 For the joy of human love,
  Brother, sister, parent, child,
Friends on earth, and friends above,
  For all gentle thoughts and mild,
Father, unto thee we raise
This our sacrifice of praise.

Works

5 For each perfect gift of thine
    To our race so freely given,
    Graces human and divine,
      Flowers of earth and buds of Heaven,
    Father, unto thee we raise
    This our sacrifice of praise.
Folliott Sandford Pierpoint (1835-1917)

29 Belmont, 76; French, 88
C.M.

GOD moves in a mysterious way
    His wonders to perform;
He plants his footsteps in the sea
    And rides upon the storm.

2 Deep in unfathomable mines
    Of never-failing skill,
He treasures up his bright designs,
    And works his sovereign will.

3 Ye fearful saints, fresh courage take:
    The clouds ye so much dread
Are big with mercy, and shall break
    In blessings on your head.

4 Judge not the Lord by feeble sense,
    But trust him for his grace;
Behind a frowning providence
    He hides a smiling face.

5 His purposes will ripen fast,
    Unfolding every hour;
The bud may have a bitter taste,
    But sweet will be the flower.

6 Blind unbelief is sure to err
    And scan his work in vain;
God is his own interpreter,
    And he will make it plain.
William Cowper (1731-1800)

30 Minterne, 310; Spanish Chant, 315
7.7.7.7.7.7.

GOD of concrete, God of steel,
    God of piston and of wheel,
God of pylon, God of steam,
God of girder and of beam,
God of atom, God of mine,
All the world of power is thine.

2 Lord of cable, Lord of rail,
    Lord of motorway and mail,
Lord of rocket, Lord of flight,
Lord of soaring satellite,
Lord of lightning's livid line,
All the world of speed is thine.

3 Lord of science, Lord of art,
    God of map and graph and chart,
Lord of physics and research,
Word of Bible, faith of Church,
Lord of sequence and design,
All the world of truth is thine.

4 God whose glory fills the earth,
    Gave the universe its birth,
Loosed the Christ with Easter's might,
Saves the world from evil's blight,
Claims mankind by grace divine,
All the world of love is thine.
Richard Granville Jones

31 Childhood, 471
8.8.8.6.

GOD speaks to us in bird and song,
    In winds that drift the clouds along,
Above the din and toil of wrong,
    A melody of love.

2 God speaks to us in far and near,
    In peace of home and friends most dear,
From the dim past and present clear,
    A melody of love.

3 God speaks to us in darkest night,
    By quiet ways through mornings bright,
When shadows fall with evening light,
    A melody of love.

4 O Voice divine, speak thou to me.
    Beyond the earth, beyond the sea,
First let me hear, then sing to thee
    A melody of love.
Joseph Johnson (1848-1926)

32 Whitechapel, 348
8.5.8.5. D.

GOD who touchest earth with beauty,
    Make my heart anew;
With thy Spirit recreate me
    Pure and strong and true.
Like thy springs and running waters,
    Make me crystal pure;
Like thy rocks of towering grandeur,
    Make me strong and sure.

2 Like thy dancing waves in sunlight,
    Make me glad and free;
Like the straightness of the pine trees
    Let me upright be.
Like the arching of the heavens,
    Lift my thoughts above;
Turn my dreams to noble action,
    Ministries of love.

3 Like the birds that soar while singing,
　　Give my heart a song;
May the music of thanksgiving
　　Echo clear and strong.
God who touchest earth with beauty,
　　Make my heart anew;
Keep me ever by thy Spirit
　　Pure and strong and true.
Mary Susan Edgar (1889-1973)

33 Great is thy faithfulness, 657
**For words and music see Song 983
American Supplement**

34 Monkland, 286; Theodora, 297
7.7.7.7.

LET us with a gladsome mind
　　Praise the Lord, for he is kind:
For his mercies shall endure,
Ever faithful, ever sure.

2 Let us blaze his name abroad,
　　For of gods he is the God:
For his mercies shall endure,
Ever faithful, ever sure.

3 He, with all-commanding might,
　　Filled the new-made world with light:
For his mercies shall endure,
Ever faithful, ever sure.

4 He the golden-tressèd sun
　　Caused all day his course to run:
For his mercies shall endure,
Ever faithful, ever sure.

5 All things living he doth feed,
　　His full hand supplies their need:
For his mercies shall endure,
Ever faithful, ever sure.
John Milton (1608-74)

35 Morning has broken, 735

MORNING has broken
　　Like the first morning,
Blackbird has spoken
　　Like the first bird.
Praise for the singing!
Praise for the morning!
Praise for them, springing
　　Fresh from the Word!

2 Sweet the rain's new fall
　　Sunlit from Heaven,
Like the first dewfall
　　On the first grass.

Praise for the sweetness
Of the wet garden,
Sprung in completeness
　　Where his feet pass.

3 Mine is the sunlight,
Mine is the morning,
Born of the one light
　　Eden saw play.
Praise with elation,
Praise every morning,
God's re-creation
　　Of the new day!
Eleanor Farjeon (1881-1965)

36 Quam Dilecta, 218
6.6.6.6.

O BRIGHT eternal One,
　　Thy voice commanded light
And from the shapeless void
　　Called order and delight!

2 Through thunder, fire and calm
　　Thy secret thoughts have stirred
The hearts of humble men
　　Who waited on thy word.

3 O Word invisible,
　　We see thee now appear
Along the path we tread,
　　For Jesus Christ is here!

4 O loving, living Lord,
　　Thou hast in Jesus given
A purpose and a way
　　For travelers to Heaven!

5 Then let us dwell in him
　　Whose dwelling is above,
And seek until we know,
　　And love until we love.

6 O ever-living Lord,
　　Our hearts and lips shall prove
The beauty of thy house,
　　The glory of thy love!
Catherine Baird (1895-1984)

37 How great thou art! 544
**For words and music see Song 993
American Supplement**

38 Hold thou my hand! 543
11.10.11.10.

O LORD of every shining constellation
That wheels in splendor through the
　　midnight sky,
Grant us your Spirit's true illumination
To read the secrets of your work on high.

2 You, Lord, have made the atom's hidden
        forces,
    Your laws its mighty energies fulfill;
    Teach us, to whom you give such rich
        resources,
    In all we use, to serve your holy will.

3 O Life, awaking life in cell and tissue,
    From flower to bird, from beast to brain
        of man;
    Help us to trace, from birth to final issue,
    The sure unfolding of your age-long plan.

4 You, Lord, have stamped your image on
        your creatures,
    And, though they mar that image, love
        them still;
    Lift up our eyes to Christ, that in his
        features
    We may discern the beauty of your will.

5 Great Lord of nature, shaping and
        renewing,
    You made us more than nature's sons
        to be;
    You help us tread, with grace our souls
        enduing,
    The road to life and immortality.
                Albert Frederick Bayly (1901-84)

39 How great thou art! 544
                                    11.10.11.10.

O MIGHTY GOD! When I thy works
        consider
    Which thou hast formed by thine all-
        wise command;
    And see the care thou to thy works dost
        render,
    That all who live may feed from out thy
        hand:

In songs of praise my heart bursts forth
    to sing:
O mighty God! O mighty God!
In songs of praise my heart bursts forth
    to sing:
O mighty God! O mighty God!

2 When thunders roll, and when the clouds
        are threatening,
    When lightnings flash across the dark-
        ening sky,
    When mighty storms are on my head
        descending,
    And calming rainbows span the heav-
        ens high:

3 When summer winds upon my cheeks are
        breathing,
    And flowers are blooming in the sun-
        light beams;
    When over hill and vale the birds are
        singing,
    And branching willows watch by crystal
        streams:

4 When all that now is real comes to an
        ending,
    And I my faith and hope can see fulfilled;
    When heavenly bells my raptured soul are
        calling,
    To lasting rest, where joys are never
        stilled:
                        Carl Boberg (1859-1940),
                trs Walter Mason Powell (1867-1956)

40 Ruth, 208; Look away to Jesus, 204
                                    6.5.6.5. D.

SUMMER suns are glowing
    Over land and sea,
Happy light is flowing
    Bountiful and free;
Everything rejoices
    In the mellow rays,
All earth's thousand voices
    Swell the psalm of praise.

2 God's free mercy streameth
    Over all the world,
And his banner gleameth
    Everywhere unfurled;
Broad and deep and glorious
    As the heaven above,
Shines in might victorious
    His eternal love.

3 Lord, upon our blindness
    Thy pure radiance pour;
For thy loving kindness
    Make us love thee more.
And when clouds are drifting
    Dark across the sky,
Then, the veil uplifting,
    Father, be thou nigh.

4 We will never doubt thee,
    Though thou veil thy light:
Life is dark without thee;
    Death with thee is bright.
Light of light, shine o'er us
    On our pilgrim way,
Go thou still before us
    To the endless day.
                William Walsham How (1823-97)

God the Father

41
I bring my all to thee, 152; Ellacombe, 147
D.C.M.

THE little cares which fretted me,
I lost them yesterday
Among the fields, above the sea,
Among the winds at play;
Among the lowing of the herds,
The rustling of the trees,
Among the singing of the birds,
The humming of the bees.

2 The foolish fears of what may come,
I cast them all away
Among the clover-scented grass,
Among the new-mown hay;
Among the hushing of the corn,
Where drowsing poppies nod.
Ill thoughts can die, and good be born,
Out in the fields of God.

Elizabeth Barrett Browning (1806-61)

42
Terra Beata, 186
D.S.M.

THIS is my Father's world,
And to my listening ears,
All nature sings and round me rings
The music of the spheres.
This is my Father's world,
I rest me in the thought
Of rocks and trees, of skies and seas;
His hand the wonders wrought.

2 This is my Father's world,
The birds their carols raise,
The morning light, the lily white,
Declare their Maker's praise.
This is my Father's world:
He shines in all that's fair;
In the rustling grass, I hear him pass,
He speaks to me everywhere.

3 This is my Father's world;
O let me ne'er forget
That though the wrong seems oft so
strong,
God is the ruler yet.
This is my Father's world;
The battle is not done;
Jesus who died shall be satisfied,
And earth and Heaven be one.

Maltbie Davenport Babcock (1858-1901)

* * *

see also: 925 Eternal Source of every joy
983 Great is thy faithfulness

Love

43
God is love, 333; Zealley, 338
8.3.8.3.8.8.8.3.

COME, let us all unite to sing:
God is love!
Let Heaven and earth their praises bring,
God is love!
Let every soul from sin awake,
Each in his heart sweet music make,
And sing with us, for Jesus' sake:
God is love!

2 O tell to earth's remotest bound,
God is love!
In Christ we have redemption found,
God is love!
His blood has washed our sins away,
His Spirit turned our night to day,
And now we can rejoice to say:
God is love!

3 How happy is our portion here,
God is love!
His promises our spirits cheer,
God is love!
He is our sun and shield by day,
Our help, our hope, our strength, our stay;
He will be with us all the way;
God is love!

4 In Canaan we will sing again:
God is love!
And this shall be our loudest strain:
God is love!
While endless ages roll along,
We'll triumph with the heavenly throng,
And this shall be our sweetest song:
God is love!

Anon

44
His love remains the same, 668

DON'T assume that God's dismissed you
from his mind,
Don't assume that God's forgotten to be
kind;
For no matter what you do, his love still
follows you;
Don't think that you have left him far
behind.

For his love remains the same,
He knows you by your name,
Don't think because you failed him he
despairs;

12

Love

For he gives to those who ask
His grace for every task,
God plans for you in love for he still
cares.

2 Don't assume that God will plan for you
no more,
Don't assume that there's no future to
explore;
For your life he'll re-design, the pattern be
divine;
Don't think that your repentance he'll
ignore.

3 Don't assume you cannot give what he'll
demand,
Don't assume that God condemns you
out of hand;
For he gives to those who ask his grace
for every task;
Don't think that God will fail to
understand.

John Gowans

45
God gave his Son for me, 188
6.4.6.4.6.6.6.4.

GOD gave his Son for me,
O wondrous love!
From sin to set me free,
O wondrous love!
A guilty rebel I,
Bound and condemned to die,
He did not pass me by;
O wondrous love!

2 There, there at God's right hand,
O wondrous love!
I see my Saviour stand,
O wondrous love!
He makes my nature pure,
In him I am secure,
Whatever I endure;
O wondrous love!

3 He'll give me needful grace,
O wondrous love!
Soon I shall see his face,
O wondrous love!
Join those who've gone before,
Sorrow and pain all o'er,
Heaven, Heaven, for evermore!
O wondrous love!

Charles Fry (1838-82)

46
God loved the world, 90
C.M.

GOD loved the world of sinners lost
And ruined by the fall;
Salvation full, at highest cost,
He offers free to all.

O 'twas love, 'twas wondrous love,
The love of God to me;
It brought my Saviour from above,
To die on Calvary!

2 E'en now by faith I claim him mine,
The risen Son of God;
Redemption by his death I find,
And cleansing through the blood.

3 Love brings the glorious fulness in,
And to his saints makes known
The blessèd rest from inbred sin,
Through faith in Christ alone.

4 Believing souls, rejoicing go;
There shall to you be given
A glorious foretaste, here below,
Of endless life in Heaven.

Martha Matilda Stockton (1821-85)

47
My bonnie lies over the ocean, 738

GOD'S love is as high as the heavens,
God's love is as deep as the sea,
God's love is for all kinds of sinners,
God's love is sufficient for me.

God's love, God's love,
God's love is sufficient for me;
God's love, God's love,
God's love is sufficient for me.

2 God's love is as wide as creation,
God's love is as boundless and free,
God's love, it has brought my salvation,
God's love is sufficient for me.

3 God's love brought his Son down from
Heaven,
God's love let him die on the tree;
God's love, it can never be measured,
God's love is sufficient for me.

Anon

13

God the Father

48 God's love is wonderful, 150;
Faith is the victory, 148   D.C.M.

GOD'S love to me is wonderful,
  That he should deign to hear
The faintest whisper of my heart,
  Wipe from mine eyes the tear;
And though I cannot comprehend
  Such love, so great, so deep,
In his strong hands my soul I trust,
  He will not fail to keep.

God's love is wonderful,
God's love is wonderful,
Wonderful that he should give his Son
  to die for me;
God's love is wonderful!

2 God's love to me is wonderful!
  My very steps are planned;
When mists of doubt encompass me,
  I hold my Father's hand.
His love has banished every fear,
  In freedom I rejoice,
And with my quickened ears I hear
  The music of his voice.

3 God's love to me is wonderful!
  He lights the darkest way;
I now enjoy his fellowship,
  'Twill last through endless day.
My Father doth not ask that I
  Great gifts on him bestow,
But only that I love him too,
  And serve him here below.
Sidney Edward Cox (1887-1975)

49 As high as the sky, 609

HAVE you ever stopped to think how God
  loves you?
It sounds quite incredible, and yet it's
  true.
Nothing on this earth or in the heavens
  above
Is as sure and certain as God's love.

O it's as high as the sky and it's as
  deep as the sea,
And it's as wide as the world, God's love
  for you and for me.
We can't escape his love, or take
  ourselves out of his care,
So where could we hide from his love?
  His love is everywhere.

2 Everything is changing in the world today,
There's one thing reliable in every way,
Other things may alter but it's clear and
  plain
That the love of God is just the same.

3 Wider than the human mind can realize,
His love is unlimited and never dies;
Though we don't deserve it, every day it's
  new;
That's the love of God for me and you.
John Gowans

50 How much more, 25

IF human hearts are often tender,
  And human minds can pity know,
If human love is touched with splendor,
  And human hands compassion show,

Then how much more shall God our
  Father
  In love forgive, in love forgive!
Then how much more shall God our
  Father
  Our wants supply, and none deny!

2 If sometimes men can live for others,
  And sometimes give where gifts are
    spurned,
If sometimes treat their foes as brothers,
  And love where love is not returned,

3 If men will often share their gladness,
  If men respond when children cry,
If men can feel each other's sadness,
  Each other's tears attempt to dry,
John Gowans

51 Love stands the test, 726

LOVE has a language, all its own making,
  Voiced in its giving, love gives its best;
Instant and constant with joy while
  awaking,
  Tells its own story—love stands the test.

Love stands the test,
Love gives its best,
Love planned our life's course,
  designedly blest;
Love won in the garden,
Love climbed the green hill;
Love will live on, for love stands the
  test.

2 Love's life is always all its best giving,
   Giving, it lives, for love thrives on this;
Thus, when the best in this world is
   decaying,
   Love will live on, for love stands the test.

3 Love's gift is God's gift—God is all-loving;
   We can be like him in this blest quest;
Let love's sweet echo in you be
   resounding:
   Love will live on, for love stands the test.
                              Joseph Buck (1889-1945)

52 The wonder of his grace, 826

MANY are the things I cannot under-
   stand,
   All above me mystery I see;
But the gift most wonderful from God's
   own hand
   Surely is his gift of grace to me!

*Higher than the stars that reach
   eternity,
Broader than the boundaries of endless
   space,
Is the boundless love of God that
   pardoned me;
O the wonder of his grace!*

2 When I came to Jesus with my sin and
   shame
   And to him confessed my deepest need,
When by faith I trusted fully in his name,
   God's rich grace was granted me indeed.

3 Passing understanding is his boundless
   love,
   More than I can ever comprehend,
Jesus, in his mercy, left his throne above,
   All to be my Saviour and my friend.
                              Howard Davies

53 Dominus regit me, 353; St Columba, 356
        8.7.8.7. Iambic

THE King of love my Shepherd is,
   Whose goodness faileth never;
I nothing lack if I am his
   And he is mine forever.

2 Where streams of living water flow
   My ransomed soul he leadeth,
And where the verdant pastures grow
   With food celestial feedeth.

3 Perverse and foolish oft I strayed,
   But yet in love he sought me,
And on his shoulder gently laid
   And home rejoicing brought me.

4 In death's dark vale I fear no ill
   With thee, dear Lord, beside me;
Thy rod and staff my comfort still,
   Thy cross before to guide me.

5 And so through all the length of days
   Thy goodness faileth never;
Good Shepherd, may I sing thy praise
   Within thy house forever.
                              Henry Williams Baker (1821-77)

54 Crimond, 82; My Shepherd, 115
                                          C.M.

THE Lord's my Shepherd, I'll not want;
   He makes me down to lie
In pastures green, he leadeth me
   The quiet waters by.

2 My soul he doth restore again,
   And me to walk doth make
Within the paths of righteousness,
   E'en for his own name's sake.

3 Yea, though I walk in death's dark vale,
   Yet will I fear no ill,
For thou art with me, and thy rod
   And staff me comfort still.

4 My table thou hast furnishèd
   In presence of my foes;
My head thou dost with oil anoint,
   And my cup overflows.

5 Goodness and mercy all my life
   Shall surely follow me;
And in God's house for evermore
   My dwelling-place shall be.
                              Scottish Psalter, 1650

55 Stracathro, 136
                                          C.M.

WHAT shall I do my God to love,
   My loving God to praise?
The length and breadth and height to
   prove,
   And depth of sovereign grace?

2 Thy sovereign grace to all extends,
   Immense and unconfined;
From age to age it never ends;
   It reaches all mankind.

3 Throughout the world its breadth is
   known,
   Wide as infinity;
So wide it never passed by one,
   Or it had passed by me.

4 The depth of all-redeeming love,
 What angel tongue can tell?
O may I to the utmost prove
 The gift unspeakable!

5 Come quickly, gracious Lord, and take
 Possession of thine own;
My longing heart vouchsafe to make
 Thine everlasting throne.

Charles Wesley (1707-88)

* * *

see also: 238 Do you sometimes feel that
     no one truly knows
    854 You can't stop rain from falling
     down

THE LORD JESUS CHRIST

Name

56 Miles Lane, 114; Diadem, 83;
Coronation, 352   C.M.

ALL hail the power of Jesus' name!
 Let angels prostrate fall;
Bring forth the royal diadem
 And crown him Lord of all!

2 Let every kindred, every tribe,
 All nations great and small,
To him all majesty ascribe,
 And crown him Lord of all!

3 Ye sinners lost of Adam's race,
 Partakers of the fall,
Come and be saved by Jesus' grace,
 And crown him Lord of all!

4 Crown him, ye martyrs of our God
 Who from his altar call;
Extol the power of Jesus' blood,
 And crown him Lord of all!

5 O that with yonder sacred throng
 We at his feet may fall,
Join in the everlasting song,
 And crown him Lord of all!

Edward Perronet (1759-92), alt

57 Hallelujah to the Lamb, 92;
Nativity New, 117   C.M.

COME, let us join our cheerful songs
 With angels round the throne;
Ten thousand thousand are their tongues,
 But all their joys are one.

Hallelujah to the Lamb,
 Who died on Mount Calvary!
Hallelujah, hallelujah, hallelujah,
 amen!

2 Worthy the Lamb that died, they cry,
 To be exalted thus!
Worthy the Lamb, our hearts reply,
 For he was slain for us!

3 Jesus is worthy to receive
 Honor and power divine;
And blessings more than we can give
 Be, Lord, for ever thine.

4 The whole creation join in one
 To bless the sacred name
Of him that sits upon the throne,
 And to adore the Lamb.

Isaac Watts (1674-1748) (verses)

58 I love the Saviour's name, 98;
St Peter, 129; Lloyd, 107   C.M.

HOW sweet the name of Jesus sounds
 In a believer's ear;
It soothes his sorrows, heals his wounds,
 And drives away his fear.

O how I love the Saviour's name;
So do I; I love the Saviour's name.

2 It makes the wounded spirit whole,
 And calms the troubled breast;
'Tis manna to the hungry soul,
 And to the weary rest.

3 Dear name, the rock on which I build,
 My shield and hiding place,
My never-failing treasury, filled
 With boundless stores of grace.

4 Weak is the effort of my heart,
 And cold my warmest thought,
But when I see thee as thou art,
 I'll praise thee as I ought.

Name

5 Till then I will thy love proclaim
With every fleeting breath;
And may the music of thy name
Refresh my soul in death.
John Newton (1725-1807) (verses)

59 Brantwood, 220; St. John, 228
6.6.6.6.8.8.

I KNOW thee who thou art,
And what thy healing name;
For when my fainting heart
The burden nigh o'ercame,
I saw thy footprints on my road
Where lately passed the Son of God.

2 Thy name is joined with mine
By every human tie,
And my new name is thine,
A child of God am I;
And never more alone, since thou
Art on the road beside me now.

3 Beside thee as I walk,
I will delight in thee,
In sweet communion talk
Of all thou art to me;
The beauty of thy face behold
And know thy mercies manifold.

4 Let nothing draw me back
Or turn my heart from thee,
But by the Calvary track
Bring me at last to see
The courts of God, that city fair,
And find my name is written there.
Albert Orsborn (1886-1967)

60 Hardy Norseman, 93; The Judgment Day,
138; Congress, 80 C.M.

JESUS, the name high over all,
In Hell or earth or sky;
Angels and men before him fall,
And devils fear and fly.

*We have no other argument,
We want no other plea;
It is enough that Jesus died,
And that he died for me.*

2 Jesus, the name to sinners dear,
The name to sinners given;
He scatters all their guilty fear;
He turns their hell to Heaven.

3 Jesus the prisoner's fetters breaks,
And bruises Satan's head;
Power into strengthless souls he speaks,
And life into the dead.

4 O that the world would taste and see
The riches of his grace;
The arms of love that compass me
Would all mankind embrace.

5 His glorious righteousness I show,
His saving truth proclaim;
'Tis all my business here below
To cry: Behold the Lamb!

6 Happy, if with my latest breath
I may but gasp his name,
Preach him to all, and cry in death:
Behold, behold the Lamb!
Charles Wesley (1707-88) (verses)

61 St Agnes, 126; Colne, 79
C.M.

JESUS, the very thought of thee
With sweetness fills my breast;
But sweeter far thy face to see,
And in thy presence rest.

2 Nor voice can sing, nor heart can frame,
Nor can the memory find
A sweeter sound than thy blest name,
O Saviour of mankind.

3 O hope of every contrite heart!
O joy of all the meek!
To those who fall, how kind thou art,
How good to those who seek!

4 But what to those who find? ah! this
Nor tongue nor pen can show;
The love of Jesus, what it is
None but his loved ones know.

5 Jesus, our only joy be thou,
As thou our prize wilt be;
Jesus, be thou our glory now,
And through eternity.
*Attr Bernard of Clairvaux (1091-1153),
trs Edward Caswall (1814-78)*

62 Darwalls, 221; Millenium, 227
6.6.6.6.8.8.

LET earth and Heaven agree,
Angels and men be joined,
To celebrate with me
The Saviour of mankind;
To adore the all-atoning Lamb,
And bless the sound of Jesus' name.

17

The Lord Jesus Christ

2 Jesus, transporting sound,
    The joy of earth and Heaven;
No other help is found,
    No other name is given
By which we can salvation have;
But Jesus came the world to save.

3 His name the sinner hears,
    And is from sin set free;
'Tis music in his ears,
    'Tis life and victory!
New songs do now his lips employ,
And dances his glad heart for joy.

4 O unexampled love!
    O all-redeeming grace!
How swiftly didst thou move
    To save a fallen race:
What shall I do to make it known
What thou for all mankind hast done?

5 O for a trumpet voice
    On all the world to call,
To bid their hearts rejoice
    In him who died for all!
For all my Lord was crucified,
For all, for all my Saviour died.
Charles Wesley (1707-88)

63 Zulu Air, 454; Bethany, 429
8.7.8.7. D. Troch.

NEVER fades the name of Jesus,
    Nor is dimmed by passing time.
Jesus' name is everlasting,
    For its meaning is sublime.
Jesus' name brings joy and gladness,
    Daily sending forth new life;
In his name there's power to gather
    Souls of men from ways of strife.

How I love the name of Jesus!
    He has set my heart aflame!
I have found a great salvation
    Through the merits of his name.

2 Beautiful the name of Jesus;
    Let it echo round the earth,
For to weary, hopeless nations
    Jesus' name has matchless worth.
Hate at last must yield to Jesus,
    Sinfulness before him flee;
Through his name shall truth and justice
    Reign again to make men free.

3 In the night his dear name shineth
    Like a lighthouse evermore,
Guiding lonely shipwrecked seamen
    Safely to salvation's shore.

When the sun's last rays are fading,
    Into darkness spread his fame,
Till the ransomed hosts in Heaven
    Sing the praises of his name.
David Welander (1896-1967),
trs Catherine Baird (1895-1984)

64 Richmond, 125; Grimsby, 91;
Azmon, A.S. 988
C.M.

O FOR a thousand tongues to sing
    My great Redeemer's praise;
The glories of my God and King,
    The triumphs of his grace!

2 My gracious Master and my God,
    Assist me to proclaim,
To spread through all the earth abroad
    The honors of thy name.

3 Jesus! the name that charms our fears,
    That bids our sorrows cease;
'Tis music in the sinner's ears;
    'Tis life and health and peace.

4 He breaks the power of canceled sin,
    He sets the prisoner free;
His blood can make the foulest clean,
    His blood avails for me.
Charles Wesley (1707-88)

65 Annie Laurie, 238
7.6.7.6. Iambic

OF all in earth or Heaven,
    The dearest name to me
Is the matchless name of Jesus,
    The Christ of Calvary.

The Christ of Calvary,
    The dearest name to me
Is the matchless name of Jesus,
    The Christ of Calvary.

2 I cannot help but love him,
    And tell his love to me;
For he became my ransom,
    The Christ of Calvary.

3 I could not live without him,
    His love is life to me;
My blood-bought life I give him,
    The Christ of Calvary.
Nathan Atkinson Aldersley (1826-99)

66 Precious Name, 394
8.7.8.7. Troch.

TAKE the name of Jesus with you,
    Child of sorrow and of woe;
It will joy and comfort give you,
    Take it then where'er you go.

Name

Precious name, O how sweet!
Hope of earth and joy of Heaven.

2 Take the name of Jesus ever
   As a shield from every snare;
   If temptations round you gather,
   Breathe that holy name in prayer.

3 O the precious name of Jesus,
   How it thrills our souls with joy,
   When his loving arms receive us,
   And his songs our tongues employ!

4 At the name of Jesus bowing,
   Falling prostrate at his feet,
   King of kings in Heaven we'll crown him,
   When our journey is complete.

Lydia Baxter (1809-74)

67 The Great Physician, 357
       Dominus regit me, 353   8.7.8.7. Iambic

THE Great Physician now is near,
   The sympathizing Jesus;
He speaks, the drooping heart to cheer;
   O hear the voice of Jesus!

Sweetest note in seraph song,
Sweetest name on mortal tongue,
Sweetest carol ever sung:
Jesus! blessèd Jesus!

2 Your many sins may be forgiven;
   O hear the voice of Jesus!
Go on your way in peace to Heaven,
   And wear a crown with Jesus.

3 All glory to the risen Lamb,
   I now believe in Jesus!
I love the blessèd Saviour's name;
   I love the name of Jesus.

4 His name dispels my guilt and fear;
   No other name but Jesus!
O how my soul delights to hear
   The precious name of Jesus!

William Hunter (1811-77)

68 The name of Jesus, 821

THE name of Jesus is so sweet,
   I love its music to repeat;
It makes my joys full and complete,
   The precious name of Jesus!

Jesus! O how sweet the name!
Jesus! every day the same.
Jesus! let all saints proclaim
   Its worthy praise for ever.

2 I love the name of him whose heart
   Knows all my griefs and bears my part,
   Who bids all anxious fears depart;
   I love the name of Jesus.

3 That name I fondly love to hear,
   It never fails my heart to cheer,
   Its music dries the falling tear;
   Exalt the name of Jesus!

4 No word of man can ever tell
   How sweet the name I love so well;
   O let its praises ever swell!
   O praise the name of Jesus!

W. C. Martin

69 The Saviour's Name, 139; Lydia, 110
                                         C.M.

THERE is a name I love to hear,
   I love to sing its worth;
It sounds like music in mine ear,
   The sweetest name on earth.

O how I love the Saviour's name!
The sweetest name on earth.

2 It tells me of a Saviour's love,
   Who gave his life for me,
That I, and all who come to him,
   From sin may be set free.

3 Jesus, the name I love so well,
   The name I love to hear;
No saint on earth its worth can tell,
   No heart conceive how dear.

4 In Heaven with all the blood-bought throng,
   From sin and sorrow free,
I'll sing the new eternal song
   Of Jesus' love to me.

Frederick Whitfield (1829-1904) (verses)

70 The name of names, 822

THERE is beauty in the name of Jesus,
   Passing time can ne'er extol;
All the splendor of its clear unfolding
   Will eternal years enrol.

In my heart there dwells a song of
      purest beauty,
   Blissful as an echo of the angel-choir
      must be;
Jesus is the wondrous theme its notes
      are weaving.
   Dearest name of names to me.

2 There's salvation in the name of Jesus;
　Trusting in his name alone
We shall find ourselves at last presented
Faultless at his Father's throne.

3 There is comfort in the name of Jesus;
　Comrade, faint amid the strife,
E'en as dew upon the spirit falling,
Jesus is the word of life.

4 There is rapture in the name of Jesus,
　Joy that bears the soul above,
All the wealth of Heaven to earth restoring,
Name of all-redeeming love.

Will J. Brand (1889-1977)

71 No other name, 749

THERE'S no other name but this name,
And no other name will do.
There's no other name but Jesus
For folk like me and you.
For no other name brings pardon
And sets everybody free.
There's no other name but Jesus
For you and me.

1 Say, is there a name to live by?
　Is there a name for joy?
Is there a name to change men,
　Their hate and greed destroy?
Have we a name for healing?
　Have we a name for peace?
Have we a name for freedom,
　Deliverance and release?

2 Say, is there a name for meaning?
　Is there a name for might?
Is there a name for mercy,
　A name for life and light?
Have we a name for laughter?
　Have we a name for grace?
Have we a name for glory,
　Transcending time and space?

3 Say, is there a name for pardon?
　Is there a name for power?
Is there a name to guide us
　Each day and every hour?
Have we a name for cleansing?
　Have we a name for care?
Have we a name for all men
　For always, everywhere?

John Gowans

Birth

72 A child this day is born, 163
S.M.

A CHILD this day is born,
　A child of high renown,
Most worthy of a scepter,
　A scepter and a crown.

Noel, Noel, Noel,
*　Noel, sing all we may,*
Because the King of all kings
*　Was born this blessèd day.*

2 These tidings shepherds heard
　While watching o'er their fold;
'Twas by an angel told them,
　That night revealed and told.

3 They saw a host on high,
　In robes of white arrayed,
Which said: Go ye to Bethlehem,
　And be ye not afraid.

4 This day your Lord is born,
　By name Immanuel,
Whom prophets long ago foretold
　Should ransom Israel.

5 The shepherds joyful sped
　To Bethlehem straightway,
And while with joy they hasten on
　They chant this sacred lay:

6 All glory be to God
　Who reigns enthroned on high,
Goodwill to men and peace on earth.
　O wondrous melody!

Anon

73 All my heart this night rejoices, 602

ALL my heart this night rejoices,
　As I hear, far and near,
Sweetest angel voices;
Christ is born! their choirs are singing,
　Till the air, everywhere,
Now with joy is ringing.

2 Hark! A voice from yonder manger,
　Soft and sweet, doth entreat:
Flee from woe and danger;
Brethren, come; from all doth grieve you
　You are freed; all you need
I will surely give you.

Birth

3 Come then, let us hasten yonder;
  Here let all, great and small,
Kneel in awe and wonder;
Love him who with love is yearning;
Hail the star that from far
Bright with hope is burning.

4 Thee, O Lord, with heed I'll cherish,
  Live to thee, and with thee
Dying, shall not perish,
But shall dwell with thee for ever
Up on high, in the joy
That can alter never.
Paulus Gerhardt (1607-76),
trs Catherine Winkworth (1827-78)

74 Europe, 435
8.7.8.7. D. Troch.

ALL our hearts rejoice this morning,
  On this happy Christmas day;
Praise and joy to God we're sounding,
  Love and peace have come our way.
Jesus Christ, our loving Saviour,
  Came to earth with gifts sublime;
Let us join our voices singing:
  What a glory, he is mine!

2 All the angels told the story
  On the hillside long ago
Of the babe who came from Glory
  Bringing peace in endless flow.
Angels, shepherds, wise men worshiped,
  Bowed before the child sublime;
Let us join our voices singing:
  What a glory, he is mine!

3 Let us hear again the story
  Of the angels' glorious song,
Hear again the message ringing:
  Christ will triumph over wrong.
His salvation freely given
  Is his gift to all mankind;
Let us join our voices singing:
  What a glory, he is mine!
Ernest Henry Parr

75 Regent Square, 423; Iris, 693; Come and worship, 413
8.7.8.7.8.7. Troch.

ANGELS, from the realms of Glory,
  Wing your flight o'er all the earth:
Ye, who sang creation's story,
  Now proclaim Messiah's birth.

  Come and worship,
  Come and worship,
  Worship Christ the new-born King.

2 Shepherds in the field abiding,
  Watching o'er your flocks by night,
God with man is now residing;
  Yonder shines the infant light.

3 Saints before the altar bending,
  Watching long in hope and fear,
Suddenly the Lord, descending,
  In his temple shall appear.

4 Sinners moved by true repentance,
  Doomed for guilt to endless pains,
Justice now revokes the sentence,
  Mercy calls you, break your chains.
James Montgomery (1771-1854)

76 Dix, 306
7.7.7.7.7.7.

AS with gladness men of old
  Did the guiding star behold,
As with joy they hailed its light,
Leading onward, beaming bright,
So, most gracious Lord, may we
Ever more be led to thee.

2 As with joyful steps they sped
  To that lowly manger bed,
There to bend the knee before
Him whom Heaven and earth adore,
So may we with willing feet
Ever seek the mercy seat.

3 As they offered gifts most rare
  At that manger rude and bare,
So may we with holy joy,
Pure and free from sin's alloy,
All our costliest treasures bring,
Christ, to thee, our heavenly King.

4 Holy Jesus! every day
  Keep us in the narrow way;
And, when earthly things are past,
Bring our ransomed souls at last
Where they need no star to guide,
Where no clouds thy glory hide.

5 In the heavenly country bright
  Need they no created light;
Thou its light, its joy, its crown,
Thou its sun which goes not down;
There forever may we sing
Hallelujahs to our King.
William Chatterton Dix (1837-98)

The Lord Jesus Christ

77 Away in a manger, 553; Manger Scene, 564; Come, children, come quickly, 555
11.11.11.11.

AWAY in a manger, no crib for a bed,
The little Lord Jesus laid down his
sweet head;
The stars in the bright sky looked down
where he lay,
The little Lord Jesus asleep on the hay.

2 The cattle are lowing, the baby awakes,
But little Lord Jesus no crying he makes;
I love thee, Lord Jesus; look down from
the sky
And stay by my cradle 'til morning is nigh.

3 Be near me, Lord Jesus; I ask thee to stay
Close by me for ever, and love me, I pray;
Bless all the dear children in thy tender
care,
And fit us for Heaven to live with thee
there.

Attr Martin Luther (1483-1546)

78 Christians Awake, 523
10.10.10.10.10.10.

CHRISTIANS awake, salute the happy
morn
Whereon the Saviour of the world was
born!
Rise to adore the mystery of love,
Which hosts of angels chanted from above;
With them the joyful tidings first begun
Of God incarnate and the Virgin's Son.

2 Then to the watchful shepherds it was told,
Who heard the angelic herald's voice:
Behold,
I bring good tidings of a Saviour's birth
To you and all the nations on the earth;
This day hath God fulfilled his promised
word,
This day is born a Saviour, Christ the Lord!

3 O may we keep and ponder in our mind
God's wondrous love in saving lost
mankind!
Trace we the babe, who hath retrieved our
loss,
From his poor manger to his bitter cross;
Tread in his steps, assisted by his grace,
Till man's first heavenly state again takes
place.

John Byrom (1692-1763)

79 Hyfrydol (2 verses), 438; Sweet chiming
bells, 402; Sardis, 397   8.7.8.7. Troch.

COME, thou long-expected Jesus,
Born to set thy people free;
From our fears and sins release us,
Let us find our rest in thee.

*Sweet chiming bells, O how they ring
To welcome Christ, the new-born
King;
Sweet chiming bells, O how they ring
To welcome Christ, the King.*

2 All thy people's consolation,
Hope of all the earth thou art;
Dear desire of every nation,
Joy of every longing heart.

3 Born thy people to deliver,
Born a child and yet a King,
Born to reign in us for ever,
Now thy gracious Kingdom bring.

4 By thine own eternal Spirit
Rule in all our hearts alone;
By thine all-sufficient merit
Raise us to thy glorious throne.

Charles Wesley (1707-88) (verses)

80 Glory in the highest, 653

DO you know the song that the angels
sang
On that night in the long ago,
When the heavens above with their music
rang
Till it echoed in the earth below?

*All glory in the highest,
Peace on earth, goodwill to men,
Glory in the highest,
Peace, goodwill to men;
Glory in the highest,
Glory in the highest,
Peace on earth, goodwill to men.*

2 Do you know the song that the shepherds
heard
As they watched o'er their flocks by
night,
When the skies bent down, and their hearts
were stirred
By the voices of the angels bright?

Birth

3 Do you know the story that the wise men
learned
  As they journeyed from the East afar,
O'er a pathway plain, for there nightly
burned
  In their sight a glorious guiding star?

A. P. Cobb

81 Joy to the world! 103; Nativity, 116
C.M.

HARK the glad sound! the Saviour comes,
  The Saviour promised long;
Let every heart prepare a throne,
  And every voice a song.

2 He comes, the prisoners to release
  In Satan's bondage held;
The gates of brass before him burst,
  The iron fetters yield.

3 He comes, the broken heart to bind,
  The wounded soul to cure,
And with the treasures of his grace,
  To enrich the humble poor.

4 Our glad hosannas, Prince of Peace,
  Thy welcome shall proclaim,
And Heaven's eternal arches ring
  With thy belovèd name.

Philip Doddridge (1702-51)

82 Hark! the herald angels sing, 322
7.7.7.7.D.

HARK! the herald angels sing:
  Glory to the new-born King;
Peace on earth, and mercy mild,
God and sinners reconciled.
Joyful, all ye nations rise,
Join the triumph of the skies;
With the angelic host proclaim,
Christ is born in Bethlehem.

Hark! the herald angels sing:
Glory to the new-born King.

2 Christ, by highest Heaven adored,
Christ, the everlasting Lord,
Late in time behold him come,
Offspring of a virgin's womb.
Veiled in flesh the Godhead see;
Hail the incarnate Deity!
Pleased as man with man to dwell,
Jesus, our Immanuel.

3 Hail the Heaven-born Prince of Peace!
Hail the Sun of righteousness!
Light and life to all he brings,
Risen with healing in his wings.

Mild he lays his glory by,
Born that man no more may die,
Born to raise the sons of earth,
Born to give them second birth.

Charles Wesley (1707-88)

83 It came upon the midnight clear, 153
D.C.M.

IT came upon the midnight clear,
  That glorious song of old,
From angels bending near the earth
  To touch their harps of gold;
Peace on the earth, goodwill to men,
  From Heaven's all-gracious King!
The world in solemn stillness lay
  To hear the angels sing.

2 Still through the cloven skies they come
  With peaceful wings unfurled,
And still their heavenly music floats
  O'er all the weary world;
Above its sad and lowly plains
  They bend on hovering wing,
And ever o'er its Babel-sounds
  The blessèd angels sing.

3 For lo! the days are hastening on,
  By prophet bards foretold,
When with the ever-circling years
  Comes round the age of gold,
When peace shall over all the earth
  Its ancient splendors fling,
And the whole world give back the song
  Which now the angels sing.

Edmund Hamilton Sears (1810-76)

84 Joy to the world! 103
C.M.

JOY to the world! the Lord is come;
  Let earth receive her King;
Let every heart prepare him room
  And Heaven and nature sing.

2 Joy to the world! the Saviour reigns;
  Let men their songs employ;
While fields and floods, rocks, hills and
plains
  Repeat the sounding joy.

3 He rules the world with truth and grace,
  And makes the nations prove
The glories of his righteousness
  And wonders of his love.

Isaac Watts (1674-1748)

23

The Lord Jesus Christ

85 Adeste Fideles, 552
11.11.11.11.

O COME, all ye faithful,
  Joyful and triumphant,
O come ye, O come ye to Bethlehem;
  Come and behold him
  Born the King of angels:
  O come let us adore him, Christ the Lord!

2   Sing, choirs of angels,
      Sing in exultation,
    Sing, all ye citizens of Heaven above;
      Glory to God
      In the highest:
    O come let us adore him, Christ the Lord!

3   Yea, Lord, we greet thee,
      Born this happy morning;
    Jesus, to thee be glory given;
      Word of the Father,
      Now in flesh appearing:
    O come let us adore him, Christ the Lord!
                        Trs Frederick Oakley (1802-80)

86 Christmas Carol, 146; O little town of Beth-
       lehem, 156; Forest Green, 149   D.C.M.

O LITTLE town of Bethlehem,
  How still we see thee lie!
Above thy deep and dreamless sleep
  The silent stars go by.
Yet in thy dark streets shineth
  The everlasting light;
The hopes and fears of all the years
  Are met in thee tonight.

2   For Christ is born of Mary;
      And, gathered all above,
    While mortals sleep, the angels keep
      Their watch of wondering love.
    O morning stars, together
      Proclaim the holy birth,
    And praises sing to God, the King,
      And peace to men on earth.

3   How silently, how silently
      The wondrous gift is given!
    So God imparts to human hearts
      The blessings of his Heaven.
    No ear may hear his coming;
      But in this world of sin,
    Where meek souls will receive him, still
      The dear Christ enters in.

4   O holy Child of Bethlehem,
      Descend to us, we pray;
    Cast out our sin, and enter in,
      Be born in us today.

We hear the Christmas angels
  The great glad tidings tell;
O come to us, abide with us,
  Our Lord Immanuel.
                        Phillips Brooks (1835-93)

87 Irby, 460
        8.7.8.7.7.7. Troch.

ONCE in royal David's city
  Stood a lowly cattle shed,
Where a mother laid her baby
  In a manger for his bed.
Mary was that mother mild,
Jesus Christ her little child.

2   He came down to earth from Heaven
      Who is God and Lord of all,
    And his shelter was a stable
      And his cradle was a stall;
    With the poor and mean and lowly
    Lived on earth our Saviour holy.

3   And through all his wondrous childhood
      He would honor and obey,
    Love and watch the lowly mother
      In whose gentle arms he lay.
    Christian children all must be
    Mild, obedient, good as he.

4   For he is our childhood's pattern;
      Day by day like us he grew;
    He was little, weak and helpless;
      Tears and smiles like us he knew;
    And he feeleth for our sadness,
    And he shareth in our gladness.

5   And our eyes at last shall see him,
      Through his own redeeming love;
    For that child so dear and gentle
      Is our Lord in Heaven above.
    And he leads his children on
    To the place where he is gone.
                        Cecil Frances Alexander (1818-95)

88 See, amid the winter's snow, 295
        7.7.7.7.

SEE, amid the winter's snow,
  Born for us on earth below,
See the Lamb of God appears
Promised from eternal years.

Hail, thou ever blessèd morn!
Hail, redemption's happy dawn!
Sing through all Jerusalem:
Christ is born in Bethlehem.

Birth

2 Say, ye holy shepherds, say
What your joyful news today;
Wherefore have ye left your sheep
On the lonely mountain steep?

3 As we watched at dead of night,
Lo, we saw a wondrous light;
Angels singing peace on earth
Told us of a Saviour's birth.

4 Sacred Infant, all divine,
What a tender love was thine,
Thus to come from highest bliss
Down to such a world as this!

5 Teach, O teach us, holy Child,
By thy face so meek and mild,
Teach us to resemble thee
In thy sweet humility.
Edward Caswall (1814-78)

89 Stille Nacht, 800

SILENT night! Holy night!
All is calm, all is bright
Round yon virgin mother and Child;
Holy Infant so tender and mild,
Sleep in heavenly peace.

2 Silent night! Holy night!
Shepherds quake at the sight,
Glories stream from Heaven afar,
Heav'nly hosts sing alleluia;
Christ the Saviour is born!

3 Silent night! Holy night!
Son of God, love's pure light,
Radiant beams from thy holy face,
With the dawn of redeeming grace,
Jesus Lord at thy birth.
Joseph Mohr (1792-1848)
trs John F. Young (1820-85)

90 The First Nowell, 816

THE first Noel the angel did say
Was to certain poor shepherds in fields
as they lay;
In fields where they lay keeping their
sheep,
On a cold winter's night that was so deep.

Noel, Noel, Noel, Noel,
Born is the King of Israel.

2 They lookèd up and saw a star,
Shining in the east beyond them far,
And to the earth it gave great light,
And so it continued both day and night.

3 And by the light of that same star,
Three wise men came from country far,
To seek for a king was their intent,
And to follow the star wherever it went.

4 This star drew near to the northwest,
O'er Bethlehem it took its rest,
And there it did both stop and stay
Right over the place where Jesus lay.

5 Then entered in those wise men three,
Fell reverently upon their knee,
And offered there in his presence
Their gold and myrrh and frankincense.

6 Then let us all with one accord
Sing praises to our heavenly Lord,
That hath made Heaven and earth of
naught,
And with his blood mankind hath bought.
Anon

91 Childhood, 471
8.8.8.6.

THEY all were looking for a king
To slay their foes and lift them high;
Thou cam'st a little baby thing
That made a woman cry.

2 O Son of man, to right my lot
Naught but thy presence can avail;
Yet on the road thy wheels are not,
Nor on the sea thy sail.

3 My fancied ways why should'st thou heed?
Thou com'st down thine own secret
stair;
Com'st down to answer all my need,
Yea, every bygone prayer.
George MacDonald (1824-1905)

92 Normandy Carol, 567
11.11.11.11.

WHEN wise men came seeking for Jesus
from far,
With rich gifts to greet him and led by a
star,
They found in a stable the Saviour of men,
A manger his cradle, so poor was he then.

2 Though laid in a manger, he came from a
throne,
On earth though a stranger, in Heaven he
was known.
How lowly, how gracious his coming to
earth!
His love my love kindles to joy in his birth.
Richard Slater (1854-1939), alt

93 Winchester Old, 144; Nativity New, 117
C.M.

WHILE shepherds watched their flocks
  by night
All seated on the ground,
The angel of the Lord came down,
  And glory shone around.

2 Fear not! said he; for mighty dread
  Had seized their troubled mind;
Glad tidings of great joy I bring
  To you and all mankind.

3 To you, in David's town, this day
  Is born, of David's line,
A Saviour, who is Christ the Lord;
  And this shall be the sign:

4 The heavenly Babe you there shall find
  To human view displayed,
All meanly wrapped in swathing bands,
  And in a manger laid.

5 Thus spake the seraph, and forthwith
  Appeared a shining throng
Of angels praising God, and thus
  Addressed their joyful song:

6 All glory be to God on high,
  And to the earth be peace;
Goodwill henceforth from Heaven to men
  Begin and never cease!
Nahum Tate (1652-1715)

Life and Teaching

94 Shall you, shall I? 263; Ewing, 249;
A light came out of darkness, 244
7.6.7.6. D. Iambic

A LIGHT came out of darkness;
  No light, no hope had we,
Till Jesus came from Heaven
  Our light and hope to be.
Oh, as I read the story
  From birth to dying cry,
A longing fills my bosom
  To meet him by and by.

Shall you, shall I, meet Jesus by and
  by?
And when we reach the Glory Land,
We'll swell the song of the angel
  band.
Shall you, shall I, meet Jesus by and
  by?

2 How tender his compassion,
  How loving was his call,
How earnest his entreaty
  To sinners, one and all.
He wooed and won them to him
  By love, and that is why
I long to be like Jesus,
  And meet him by and by.

3 Yet deeper do I ponder,
  His cross and sorrow see,
And ever gaze and wonder
  Why Jesus died for me.
And shall I fear to own him?
  Can I my Lord deny?
No, let me love him, serve him,
  And meet him by and by.
William A. Hawley (1870-1929)

95 Bethany, 429
8.7.8.7. D. Troch.

BLESSÈD are the poor in spirit,
  They the Kingdom shall possess;
Blessèd are the broken-hearted,
  They shall not be comfortless;
Blessèd are the meek and lowly,
  Theirs the earth by right shall be;
Blessèd they who thirst for goodness,
  They shall drink abundantly.

2 Blessèd are the men of mercy,
  They shall fear no threatening rod;
Blessèd are the pure in motive,
  They shall see the face of God;
Blessèd are the peace designers,
  They his children shall be called;
Blessèd are the patient martyrs,
  They in Heaven are now installed.

3 Blessèd are ye, O my people!
  Saith our God's inspiring voice;
When the sons of earth revile you,
  Be exceeding glad—rejoice!
Great is your reward in Heaven,
  For the prophets' marks you bear;
They who suffer persecution
  Shall the prophets' blessings share.
Arch R. Wiggins (1893-1976),
From Matthew 5:3-11

96 Gospel Bells, 253
8.7.8.7. D. Troch.

HAVE you ever heard the story
  Of the Babe of Bethlehem,
Who was worshiped by the angels
  And the wise and holy men?

How he taught the learnèd doctors
  In the temple far away?
O I'm glad, so glad to tell you,
  He is just the same today!

Just the same, just the same
He is just the same today.
Just the same, just the same,
He is just the same today.

2 Have you ever heard the story
    How he walked upon the sea,
  To his dear disciples tossing
    On the waves of Galilee?
  How the waves in angry motion
    Quickly did his will obey?
  O I'm glad, so glad to tell you,
    He is just the same today!

3 Have you ever heard of Jesus
    Praying in Gethsemane,
  And the ever-thrilling story,
    How he died upon the tree,
  Cruel thorns his forehead piercing,
    As his spirit passed away?
  This he did for you, my brother,
    And he's just the same today!

4 Have you ever heard of Jesus
    Who was buried in the tomb,
  And was mourned by his disciples
    In despair, defeat and gloom?
  By the power of God eternal,
    He arose on Easter day,
  And he lives for our salvation:
    He is just the same today!
                S.Z. Kaufman (verses 1-3),
                Gordon Harry Taylor (verse 4)

97 Quem pastores laudavere, 773

JESUS, good above all other,
  Gentle child of gentle mother,
In a stable born our brother,
  Give us grace to persevere.

2 Jesus, cradled in a manger,
  For us facing every danger,
  Living as a homeless stranger,
    Make we thee our King most dear.

3 Jesus, for thy people dying,
  Risen Master, death defying,
  Lord in Heaven, thy grace supplying,
    Keep us to thy presence near.

4 Jesus, who our sorrows bearest,
  All our thoughts and hopes thou sharest;
  Thou to man the truth declarest;
    Help us all thy truth to hear.

5 Lord, in all our doings guide us;
  Pride and hate shall ne'er divide us;
  We'll go on with thee beside us,
    And with joy we'll persevere.
                Percy Dearmer (1867-1936),
                after John Mason Neale (1818-1866)

98 Tell me the old, old story, 265;
      Hosanna, 255   7.6.7.6. D. Iambic

TELL me the old, old story
  Of unseen things above,
Of Jesus and his glory,
  Of Jesus and his love.
Tell me the story simply,
  As to a little child,
For I am weak and weary,
  And helpless and defiled.

Tell me the old, old story,
Tell me the old, old story,
Tell me the old, old story
Of Jesus and his love.

2 Tell me the story slowly,
    That I may take it in,
  That wonderful redemption,
    God's remedy for sin.
  Tell me the story often,
    For I forget so soon;
  The early dew of morning
    Has passed away at noon.

3 Tell me the story softly,
    With earnest tones and grave;
  Remember! I'm the sinner
    Whom Jesus came to save.
  Tell me the story always,
    If you would really be
  In any time of trouble
    A comforter to me.

4 Tell me the same old story
    When you have cause to fear
  That this world's empty glory
    Is costing me too dear.
  Yes, and when that world's glory
    Is dawning on my soul,
  Tell me the old, old story:
    Christ Jesus makes thee whole.
                Arabella Catherine Hankey (1834-1911)

The Lord Jesus Christ

99 Tell me the story of Jesus, 458; Jesus is looking for thee, 457 (verse)

8.7.8.7. D. Dactylic

TELL me the story of Jesus,
　Write on my heart every word;
Tell me the story most precious,
　Sweetest that ever was heard.
Tell how the angels in chorus
　Sang, as they welcomed his birth:
Glory to God in the highest,
　Peace and good tidings to earth!

Tell me the story of Jesus,
Write on my heart every word;
Tell me the story most precious,
Sweetest that ever was heard.

2　Fasting alone in the desert,
　Tell of the days that he passed;
How he was tried and was tempted,
　Yet was triumphant at last.
Tell of the years of his labors,
　Tell of the sorrows he bore;
He was despised and afflicted,
　Homeless, rejected and poor.

3　Tell of the cross where they nailed him,
　Mocking his anguish and pain;
Tell of the grave where they laid him;
　Tell how he liveth again.
Love in that story so tender,
　Clearer than ever I see;
Glory for ever to Jesus,
　He paid the ransom for me.

Fanny Crosby (1820-1915)

100 Martyrdom, 113; Wiltshire, 143

C.M.

THOU art the way: to thee alone
　From sin and death we flee;
And he who would the Father seek,
　Must seek him, Lord, by thee.

2　Thou art the truth; thy word alone
　True wisdom can impart;
Thou only canst inform the mind
　And purify the heart.

3　Thou art the life: the rending tomb
　Proclaims thy conquering arm;
And those who put their trust in thee
　Nor death nor Hell shall harm.

4　Thou art the way, the truth, the life;
　Grant us that way to know,
That truth to keep, that life to win,
　Whose joys eternal flow.

George Washington Doane (1799-1859)

101 Margaret, 112

C.M.

THOU didst leave thy throne and thy
　kingly crown
　When thou camest to earth for me;
But in Bethlehem's home was there found
　no room
　For thy holy nativity.

O come to my heart, Lord Jesus;
There is room in my heart for thee.

2　Heaven's arches rang when the angels
　sang,
　Proclaiming thy royal degree;
But of lowly birth cam'st thou, Lord, on
　earth
　And in great humility.

3　Thou camest, O Lord, with the living word
　That should set thy people free;
But with mocking scorn, and with crown
　of thorn,
　They bore thee to Calvary.

4　When Heaven's arches ring, and her choirs
　shall sing,
　At thy coming to victory,
Let thy voice call me home, saying: Yet
　there is room,
　There is room at my side for thee!

And my heart shall rejoice, Lord Jesus,
When thou comest and callest for me.

Emily Elizabeth Steele Elliott (1836-97)

102 Armadale, 8; Alstone, 4

L.M.

WHEN Christ drew near to dwell with
　men
　And bear with man his earthly lot,
He brought the knowledge of the Lord
　To sinful hearts which knew him not.

2　When Christ drew near with pardoning
　love
　And freed men from remorse and tears,
His triumph over death assured
　Their victory over sins and fears.

3　When Christ draws near his own today,
　The fulness of his power to give,
The Holy Spirit makes him known,
　And by his life we all may live.

4　Draw near, O Christ, unveil thy face,
　The God of glory and of grace;
My heart reveal, with pardon seal,
　And bring me to thy holy place.

Miriam M. Richards (1911-89)

28

Atoning Work

103 Lakeside, 104; Fewster, 86
C.M.

WHEN Jesus looked o'er Galilee,
  So blue and calm and fair,
Upon her bosom, could he see
  A cross reflected there?

2 When sunrise dyed the lovely deeps,
  And sparkled in his hair,
O did the light rays seem to say:
  A crown of thorns he'll wear?

3 When in the hush of eventide,
  Cool waters touched his feet,
Was it a hymn of Calvary's road
  He heard the waves repeat?

4 But when the winds triumphantly
  Swept from the open plain,
The Master surely heard the song:
  The Lord shall live again!
  Catherine Baird (1895-1984)

104 Who is he? 319
7.7.7.7.7.7.

WHO is he in yonder stall,
  At whose feet the shepherds fall?

'Tis the Lord! O wondrous story,
'Tis the Lord, the King of Glory!
At his feet we humbly fall,
Crown him, crown him Lord of all!

2 Who is he in deep distress,
  Fasting in the wilderness?

3 Who is he to whom they bring
  All the sick and sorrowing?

4 Who is he on yonder tree
  Dies in grief and agony?

5 Who is he who from the grave
  Comes to succor, help and save?

6 Who is he who from his throne
  Rules through all the worlds alone?
  Benjamin Russell Hanby (1833-67)

* * *

see also: 304 She only touched the hem of his
        garment
      428 Jesus calls us; o'er the tumult
      558 At even, ere the sun was set
      855 A boy was born in Bethlehem

Atoning Work

105 Remember Me, 122; Irish, 99
C.M.

ALAS! and did my Saviour bleed,
  And did my sovereign die?
Did he devote that sacred head
  For such a worm as I?

Remember me, remember me,
* O Lord, remember me;*
Remember, Lord, thy dying groans,
* And then remember me.*

2 Was it for sins that I have done
  He suffered on the tree?
Amazing pity, grace unknown,
  And love beyond degree!

3 Well might the sun in darkness hide
  And shut his glories in,
When Christ, the mighty maker, died
  For man, the creature's sin.

4 Dear Saviour, I can ne'er repay
  The debt of love I owe!
Here, Lord, I give myself away;
  'Tis all that I can do.
  Isaac Watts (1674-1748) (verses)

106 St John, 228; Hollingsworth, 224;
Darwells, 221
6.6.6.6.8.8.

ARISE, my soul, arise,
  Shake off thy guilty fears;
The bleeding sacrifice
  In my behalf appears;
Before the throne my surety stands,
My name is written on his hands.

2 He ever lives above
  For me to intercede,
His all-redeeming love,
  His precious blood to plead;
His blood atoned for all our race,
And sprinkles now the throne of grace.

3 Five bleeding wounds he bears,
  Received on Calvary;
They pour effectual prayers,
  They strongly plead for me.
Forgive him, O forgive, they cry,
Nor let that ransomed sinner die.

4 The Father hears him pray,
  His dear anointed one;
He cannot turn away
  The presence of his Son;
His Spirit answers to the blood
And tells me I am born of God.

The Lord Jesus Christ

5 My God is reconciled,
   His pardoning voice I hear;
He owns me for his child,
   I can no longer fear;
With confidence I now draw nigh
And Father, Abba Father! cry.

Charles Wesley (1707-88)

107 Behold the Lamb, 330; We're traveling
home, 336   8.3.8.3.8.8.8.3.

BEHOLD! behold the Lamb of God
   On the cross;
For us he sheds his precious blood
   On the cross.
O hear his all-important cry,
Why perish, blood-bought sinner, why?
Draw near and see your Saviour die
   On the cross.

2 Behold his arms extended wide
   On the cross;
Behold his bleeding hands and side
   On the cross.
The sun withholds his rays of light,
The heavens are clothed in shades of night,
While Jesus does with devils fight
   On the cross.

3 Come, sinners, see him lifted up
   On the cross;
He drinks for you the bitter cup
   On the cross.
The rocks do rend, the mountains quake,
While Jesus doth atonement make,
While Jesus suffers for our sake
   On the cross.

4 And now the mighty deed is done
   On the cross;
The battle's fought, the victory's won
   On the cross.
To Heaven he turns his dying eyes;
'Tis finished! now the conqueror cries;
Then bows his sacred head and dies
   On the cross.

5 Where'er I go I'll tell the story
   Of the cross;
In nothing else my soul shall glory
   Save the cross.
Yes, this my constant theme shall be
Through time and in eternity,
That Jesus tasted death for me
   On the cross.

Richard Jukes (1804-67)

108 He wipes the tear, 63;
Sweet hour of prayer, 66   D.L.M.

BEHOLD him now on yonder tree,
   The Prince of Peace, the heavenly King;
O what can his transgression be
   Such shameful punishment to bring?
And lo, a thief hangs on each side;
   Who justly suffers for his crime.
But why should Christ be crucified,
   The one so holy, so divine?

It was for me, yes, even me,
That Jesus died on Calvary;
My soul to cleanse from all its guilt,
His precious blood my Saviour spilt.

2 O sinner, see, for you and me
   He freely suffers in our stead;
And lo, he dies upon the tree;
   Behold, he bows his sacred head!
So pure, yet he has borne our guilt,
   By death our ransom he has paid;
It was for us his blood was spilt,
   Our every sin on him was laid.

3 O loving Saviour, take my heart,
   No longer can I live from thee!
With all unlike thee now I part;
   Thy wondrous love has conquered me.
I yield to thee my little all;
   Accept me now, Lord, as thine own;
I'll be obedient to thy call
   And spend my life for thee alone.

George Samuel Smith (1865-1944)

109 Bethany, 429; Hyfrydol, 438
8.7.8.7. D. Troch.

HAIL, thou once despisèd Jesus,
   Hail, thou Galilean King!
Thou didst suffer to release us;
   Thou didst free salvation bring.
Hail, thou universal Saviour,
   Bearer of our sin and shame!
By thy merits we find favor;
   Life is given through thy name.

2 Precious Lamb by God appointed,
   All our sins on thee were laid;
By almighty love anointed,
   Thou hast full atonement made.
All thy people are forgiven
   Through the virtue of thy blood,
Opened is the gate of Heaven,
   Peace is made 'twixt man and God.

Atoning Work

3 Worship, honor, power and blessing
 Thou art worthy to receive;
Loudest praises without ceasing
 Meet it is for us to give.
Help, ye bright angelic spirits,
 Bring your sweetest, noblest lays;
Help to sing the Saviour's merits,
 Help to chant Immanuel's praise.
John Bakewell (1721-1819) and others

110 St Bees, 293; Hendon, 282
7.7.7.7.

HARK, my soul! it is the Lord;
 'Tis thy Saviour, hear his word;
Jesus speaks, and speaks to thee:
 Say, poor sinner, lov'st thou me?

2 I delivered thee when bound,
 And, when bleeding, healed thy wound;
Sought thee wandering, set thee right,
 Turned thy darkness into light.

3 Can a woman's tender care
 Cease toward the child she bare?
Yes, she may forgetful be;
 Yet will I remember thee.

4 Mine is an unchanging love,
 Higher than the heights above,
Deeper than the depths beneath,
 Free and faithful, strong as death.

5 Thou shalt see my glory soon,
 When the work of grace is done;
Partner of my throne shalt be;
 Say, poor sinner, lov'st thou me?

6 Lord, it is my chief complaint
 That my love is weak and faint;
Yet I love thee, and adore;
 O for grace to love thee more!
William Cowper (1731-1800)

111 The meeting of the waters, 574;
Manger Scene, 564   11.11.11.11.

I MET the good Shepherd
 Just now on the plain,
As homeward he carried
 His lost one again;
I marveled how gently
 His burden he bore,
And as he passed by me
 I knelt to adore.

2 O Shepherd, good Shepherd,
 Thy wounds they are deep;
The wolves have sore hurt thee
 In saving thy sheep.

Thy raiment all over
 With crimson is dyed;
And what is this wound
 They have made in thy side?

3 O Shepherd, good Shepherd,
 And is it for me
This grievous affliction
 Has fallen on thee?
Thy wounds make me love thee,
 My heart shall be thine;
With thee I will journey,
 My shepherd divine.
Edward Caswall (1814-78)

112 St Oswald, 396; Sardis, 397;
Cross of Jesus, 366   8.7.8.7. Troch.

IN the cross of Christ I glory,
 Towering o'er the wrecks of time;
All the light of sacred story
 Gathers round its head sublime.

2 When the woes of life o'ertake me,
 Hopes deceive and fears annoy,
Never shall the cross forsake me;
 Lo! it glows with peace and joy.

3 When the sun of bliss is beaming
 Light and love upon my way,
From the cross the radiance streaming
 Adds more luster to the day.

4 Bane and blessing, pain and pleasure,
 By the cross are sanctified;
Peace is there that knows no measure,
 Joys that through all time abide.

5 In the cross of Christ I glory,
 Towering o'er the wrecks of time;
All the light of sacred story
 Gathers round its head sublime.
John Bowring (1792-1872)

113 St Stephen, 130
C.M.

IT is the blood that washes white,
 That makes me pure within,
That keeps the inward witness right,
 That cleanses from all sin.

2 It is the blood that sweeps away
 The power of Satan's rod,
That shows the new and living way
 That leads to Heaven and God.

3 It is the blood that brings us nigh
 To holiness and Heaven,
The source of victory and joy,
 God's life for rebels given.
William James Pearson (1832-92)

The Lord Jesus Christ

114 Wonderful Love, 864

JESUS came down my ransom to be;
  O it was wonderful love!
For out of the Father's heart he came,
To die for me on a cross of shame,
And from sin's bondage to reclaim;
  O it was wonderful love!

Wonderful, wonderful, wonderful love,
  Coming to me from Heaven above,
Filling me, thrilling me through and
    through;
  O it was wonderful love!

2 Clear to faith's vision the cross reveals
  Beautiful actions of love;
And all that by grace e'en I may be
When saved, to serve him eternally.
He came, he died, for you and me;
  O it was wonderful love!

3 His death's a claim, his love has a plea;
  O it is wonderful love!
Ungrateful was I to slight thy call,
But, Lord, now I come, before thee fall,
I give myself, I give up all,
  All for thy wonderful love.
              Emmanuel Rolfe (1853-1914)

115 Near the cross, 272; Healing Stream, 270
            7.6.7.6. Troch.

JESUS, keep me near the cross;
  There a precious fountain,
Free to all, a healing stream,
  Flows from Calvary's mountain.

In the cross, in the cross, be my glory
    ever;
Till my raptured soul shall find rest
    beyond the river.

2 Near the cross, a trembling soul,
  Love and mercy found me;
There the bright and morning star
  Shed its beams around me.

3 Near the cross! O Lamb of God,
  Bring its scenes before me;
Help me walk from day to day
  With its shadow o'er me.

4 Near the cross I'll watch and wait,
  Hoping, trusting ever,
Till I reach the golden strand
  Just beyond the river.
              Fanny Crosby (1820-1915)

116 Deep Harmony, 16; Arizona, 7
                                    L.M.

JESUS, thy blood and righteousness
  My beauty are, my glorious dress;
'Midst flaming worlds, in these arrayed,
With joy shall I lift up my head.

2 Bold shall I stand in thy great day,
For who aught to my charge shall lay?
Fully absolved through these I am
From sin and fear, from guilt and shame.

3 The holy, meek, unspotted Lamb,
Who from the Father's bosom came,
Who died for me, e'en me, to atone,
Now for my Lord and God I own.

4 Lord, I believe thy precious blood,
Which, at the mercy seat of God,
For ever doth for sinners plead,
For me, e'en for my soul, was shed.

5 When from the dust of death I rise
To claim my mansion in the skies,
E'en then this shall be all my plea,
Jesus hath lived, hath died for me.
        Nicolaus Ludwig von Zinzendorf (1700-60),
                trs John Wesley (1703-91)

117 Lead me to Calvary, 105
       For words and music see Song 985
       American Supplement

118 Man of sorrows! 731

MAN of sorrows! what a name
  For the Son of God, who came
Ruined sinners to reclaim;
  Hallelujah! What a Saviour!

2 Bearing shame and scoffing rude,
In my place condemned he stood,
Sealed my pardon with his blood;
  Hallelujah! What a Saviour!

3 Guilty, vile and helpless we,
Spotless Lamb of God was he;
Full atonement—can it be?
  Hallelujah! What a Saviour!

4 Lifted up was he to die;
It is finished! was his cry;
Now in Heaven, exalted high;
  Hallelujah! What a Saviour!

5 When he comes, our glorious King,
All his ransomed home to bring,
Then anew this song we'll sing:
  Hallelujah! What a Saviour!
              Philip Paul Bliss (1838-76)

119 Mother Machree, 736

MANY thoughts stir my heart as I ponder
alone;
Many places attract me with charms all
their own;
But the thought of all thoughts is of Christ
crucified,
The place of all places, the hill where he
died.

*O the charm of the cross! How I love to
be there!*
*With the love that shines from it, what
love can compare?*
The seal of my ransom in Calvary I see,
*All my sin, O my Saviour, laid upon
thee!*

2 'Tis the end of my sin and the source of
all grace;
'Tis the word of God's love to a prodigal
race;
'Tis the greatest, the grandest gift God
could impart,
Surpassing my reason but winning my
heart.

3 For the sake of the Christ and the love of
his cross
I have yielded my all and not reckoned it
loss;
There's a place in my heart which the Sav-
iour must fill;
No other can take it, and none ever will.
Albert Orsborn (1886-1967)

120 Dennis, 165; No sorrow there, 173
S.M.

NOT all the blood of beasts
On Jewish altars slain,
Could give the guilty conscience peace
Or wash away our stain.

2 But Christ, the heavenly Lamb,
Takes all our sins away,
A sacrifice of nobler name
And richer blood than they.

3 My faith would lay her hand
On that meek head of thine,
While as a penitent I stand
And here confess my sin.

4 My soul looks back to see
The burden thou didst bear,
When hanging on the accursèd tree,
And knows her guilt was there.

5 Believing, we rejoice
To feel the curse remove;
We bless the Lamb with cheerful voice,
And sing his dying love.
Isaac Watts (1674-1748)

121 Warrington, 56; Hursley, 26
L.M.

O COME and look awhile on him,
Whom we have pierced, who for us
died;
Together let us look and mourn,
Jesus, our Lord, is crucified.

2 His willing hands and feet are bound;
His gracious lips with thirst are dried;
His pitying eye is dimmed with woe;
Jesus, our Lord, is crucified.

3 Shall we refuse to hear him speak?
Dare we the sinless one deride?
Surely on him our sins are laid;
Jesus, our Lord, is crucified.

4 His cross of shame is all our hope;
The fountain opened in his side
Shall purge our deepest stains away;
Jesus, our Lord, is crucified.

5 O love of God! O sin of man!
In this dread act your strength is tried;
And victory remains with love,
For he, our Lord, is crucified.

6 A broken and a contrite heart
To none who ask will be denied;
A broken heart love's dwelling is,
The temple of the crucified.
Frederick William Faber (1814-63), alt

122 Mozart, 496
8.8.8.8.8.8. Iambic

O LOVE upon a cross impaled,
My contrite heart is drawn to thee;
Are thine the hands my pride has nailed,
And thine the sorrows borne for me?
Are such the wounds my sin decrees?
I fall in shame upon my knees.

2 'Twere not for sinners such as I
To gaze upon thy sore distress,
Or comprehend thy bitter cry
Of God-forsaken loneliness.
I shelter from such agonies
Beneath thy cross, upon my knees.

3 Forgive! Forgive! I hear thee plead;
  And me forgive! I instant cry.
For me thy wounds shall intercede,
  For me thy prayer shall make reply;
I take the grace that flows from these,
In saving faith, upon my knees.

4 Now take thy throne, O Crucified,
  And be my love-anointed King!
The weapons of my sinful pride
  Are broken by thy suffering.
A captive to love's victories,
I yield, I yield upon my knees.
                    Albert Orsborn (1886-1967)

123 Passion Chorale, 258
            7.6.7.6. D. Iambic

O SACRED head now wounded,
  With grief and pain weighed down,
How scornfully surrounded
  With thorns, thine only crown!
How pale art thou with anguish,
  With sore abuse and scorn!
How does that visage languish
  Which once was bright as morn!

2 O Lord of life and glory,
  What bliss till now was thine!
I read the wondrous story,
  I joy to call thee mine.
Thy grief and thy compassion
  Were all for sinners' gain;
Mine, mine was the transgression,
  But thine the deadly pain.

3 What language shall I borrow
  To thank thee, dearest Friend,
For this thy dying sorrow,
  Thy pity without end?
O make me thine for ever!
  And should I fainting be,
Lord, let me never, never
  Outlive my love to thee.

4 Be near me, Lord, when dying;
  O show thyself to me;
And, for my succor flying,
  Come, Lord, to set me free.
These eyes, new faith receiving,
  From Jesus shall not move;
For he who dies believing,
  Dies safely through thy love.
                Paulus Gerhardt (1607-76)
          (from Bernard of Clairvaux 1091-1153),
          trs James Waddell Alexander (1804-59)

124 The old rugged cross, 585
                          12.9.12.9.

ON a hill far away stood an old rugged
    cross,
  The emblem of suffering and shame,
And I love that old cross where the dearest
    and best
  For a world of lost sinners was slain.

So I'll cherish the old rugged cross
  Till my trophies at last I lay down;
I will cling to the old rugged cross
  And exchange it some day for a
    crown.

2 O that old rugged cross, so despised by
    the world,
  Has a wondrous attraction for me;
For the dear Lamb of God left his glory
    above
  To bear it to dark Calvary.

3 To the old rugged cross I will ever be true,
  Its shame and reproach gladly bear;
Then he'll call me some day to my home
    far away
  Where his glory for ever I'll share.
                    George Bennard (1873-1958)

125 It was on the cross, 28; *Calvary, 14;
          On Calvary's brow, 39   L.M.

ON Calvary's brow my Saviour died,
'Twas there my Lord was crucified;
'Twas on the cross he bled for me,
And purchased there my pardon free.

It was on the cross he shed his blood,
It was there he was crucified;
But he rose again, and he lives in my
    heart
Where all is peace and perfect love.

**O Calvary, dark Calvary,*
  Where Jesus shed his blood for me.
O Calvary, dark Calvary:
  Speak to my heart of Calvary.

2 'Mid rending rocks and darkening skies,
My Saviour bows his head and dies;
The opening veil reveals the way
To Heaven's joys and endless day.

3 O Jesus, Lord, how can it be
That thou shouldst give thy life for me,
To bear the cross and agony
In that dread hour on Calvary?
          William McKendree Darwood (c. 1835-1914)
              John Fairhurst (first chorus)

126
From that sacred hill, 649

ON Calvary's tree the King of Glory
languished,
Held not by nails but by undying love,
Sin's debt to pay, the sting of death remove,
Boundless cleansing to provide,
Mercy's gate open wide.

From that sacred hill
Hope is gleaming still;
Thy shame and grief he bore;
Go in peace, sin no more.

2 His purple robe is parted 'mong the
soldiers,
That scepter-reed discarded where it fell;
Yet, meekly borne, that crown of cruel
thorn
Still attests his royal might,
Fears to quell, wrongs to right.

3 Darkness descends, the cross in mystery
veiling,
Deep thunders roll and lightnings rend
the skies
As Jesus dies, a willing sacrifice;
God's own word by blood is sealed:
By his stripes we are healed.

4 His tender touch can heal the broken-
hearted,
His word dispel the darkness of despair;
Come, bring thy sin, thy sorrow, pain and
care,
And, believing, thou shalt prove
All the strength of his love.
Florence Lilian Pollock (1899-1981)

127
Deep Harmony, 16;
*He wipes the tear, 63   L.M.

ON every hill our Saviour dies,
And not on Calvary's height alone;
His sorrows darken all our skies,
His griefs for all our wrongs atone.

2 Present he is in all our woes,
Upon a world-wide cross is hung;
And with exceeding bitter throes
His world-embracing heart is wrung.

Go! Cry the news from every hill;
Go! Ring the earth with sacred
flame;
To pardon is the Father's will,
And Jesus is the Saviour's name.

3 In us his love invested is,
God cannot pass a suppliant by;
For heard in God's eternities
Our prayers repeat the Saviour's cry.

4 And for the sake of that dear name
With which all hope of good is given,
Our heavy load of sin and shame
The Father clears, and cries: Forgiven!
Albert Orsborn (1886-1967)

128
On the cross of Calvary, 326;
Maidstone, 325   7.7.7.7. D.

ON the cross of Calvary,
Jesus died for you and me;
There he shed his precious blood,
That from sin we might be free.
O the cleansing stream does flow,
And it washes white as snow!
It was for me that Jesus died
On the cross of Calvary.

On Calvary, on Calvary!
It was for me that Jesus died
On the cross of Calvary.

2 O what wondrous, wondrous love
Brought me down at Jesus' feet!
O such wondrous, dying love
Asks a sacrifice complete!
Here I give myself to thee,
Soul and body, thine to be;
It was for me thy blood was shed
On the cross of Calvary.

3 Take me, Jesus, I am thine,
Wholly thine, for evermore;
Blessèd Jesus, thou art mine,
Dwell within for evermore;
Cleanse, O cleanse my heart from sin,
Make and keep me pure within!
It was for this thy blood was shed
On the cross of Calvary.

4 Clouds and darkness veiled the sky
When the Lord was crucified;
It is finished! was his cry
When he bowed his head and died.
With this cry from Calvary's tree
All the world may now go free;
It was for this that Jesus died
On the cross of Calvary.
Sarah Jean Graham (c 1854-c 1889)

35

The Lord Jesus Christ

129 Love's old sweet song, 525
10.10.10.10.10.10.

ONCE, on a day, was Christ led forth to
die,
And with the crowd that pressed on him
joined I.
Slowly they led him, led him to the tree,
And I beheld his hands no more were free.
Bound fast with cords, and this was his
distress,
That men denied those hands out-
stretched to bless.

Sacred hands of Jesus, they were
bound for me;
Wounded hands of Jesus, stretched
upon a tree,
Ever interceding, mercy is their plea.
Their effectual pleading brings grace to
me,
Redeeming grace to me.

2 Hands that were scarred by daily fret and
tear;
Hands quick to soothe the troubled brow
of care;
Hands strong to smite the sins that men
enthrone,
Yet never raised to seek or claim their own:
Dear hands of Christ! and yet men feared
them so
That they must bind them as to death they
go.

3 Hands that still break to men the living
bread;
Hands full of power to raise again the dead,
Potent and healing, eager to reclaim,
Laid in forgiveness on one bowed in
shame;
Say, wouldst thou bind, by pride and
unbelief,
Those hands that compass all thy soul's
relief?

Albert Orsborn (1886-1967)

130 Sunset, 522
10.10.10.10. Iambic

OTHERS he saved, himself he cannot
save,
Railed they against him on the cross
above;
They were the bondsmen by their pride
enslaved:
He was the freeman, bound alone by
love.

2 Others he saved, himself he cannot save;
He was the shepherd, dying for his
sheep.
No man can take it, but his life he gave,
From death returning, all his own to
keep.

3 Others he saved, himself he would not
save,
Though hosts of angels waited his
command;
He marched to victory through an open
grave,
Flung wide life's portals with his mighty
hand.

4 Others he saved, himself he did not save;
Lonely, forsaken, our sinbearer he,
Love to the utmost for my soul he gave;
Lord, by that love I bind myself to thee.

Albert Orsborn (1886-1967)

131 St John, 228; Brantwood, 220
6.6.6.6.8.8.

SILENT and still I stand
Before that weeping tree
Whereon the Son of man
Pours out his life for me.
O sin of man! O love of God!
O cleansing, efficacious flood!

2 The Saviour asks no tears,
Weep not for me, he cries;
Yet all our broken years
Are mirrored in his eyes.
And all our griefs, including mine,
Go surging through that heart divine.

3 Fain would I hide mine eyes
From love so torn with pain;
Yet all within me cries
To look, and look again;
I cannot pierce the mystery,
But this I know: he dies for me.

4 For me, and once for all,
Our Saviour willing dies,
As mercy's tender call
Rings out upon the skies;
O man upon that weeping tree,
In penitence we come to thee!

Albert Orsborn (1886-1967)

132 Fountain, 87; Martyrdom, 113
C.M.

THERE is a fountain filled with blood,
Drawn from Immanuel's veins;
And sinners plunged beneath that flood
Lose all their guilty stains.

Atoning Work

I do believe, I will believe,
That Jesus died for me;
That on the cross he shed his blood,
And now he sets me free.

2 The dying thief rejoiced to see
   That fountain in his day;
   And there have I, as vile as he,
   Washed all my sins away.

3 Dear dying Lamb, thy precious blood
   Shall never lose its power,
   Till all the ransomed host of God
   Be saved, to sin no more.

4 E'er since by faith I saw the stream
   Thy flowing wounds supply,
   Redeeming love has been my theme,
   And shall be till I die.

5 Then in a nobler, sweeter song
   I'll sing thy power to save,
   When this poor lisping, stammering
      tongue
   Lies silent in the grave.
                  William Cowper (1731-1800) (verses)

133 Horsley, 95; Sawley, 132;
       Lloyd, 107   C.M.

THERE is a green hill far away,
   Without a city wall,
Where the dear Lord was crucified
   Who died to save us all.

2 We may not know, we cannot tell
   What pains he had to bear;
But we believe it was for us
   He hung and suffered there.

3 He died that we might be forgiven,
   He died to make us good,
That we might go at last to Heaven,
   Saved by his precious blood.

4 There was no other good enough
   To pay the price of sin;
He only could unlock the gate
   Of Heaven, and let us in.

5 O dearly, dearly, has he loved
   And we must love him too,
And trust in his redeeming blood,
   And try his works to do.
                  Cecil Frances Alexander (1818-95)

134 Calvary, 14; Was it for me? 57
                                        L.M.

WAS it for me, the nails, the spear,
   The cruel thorns, the mocking jeer,
That rugged cross, 'twixt earth and sky—
Was it for me he came to die?

He loved me so! He loved me so!
Dark Calvary he chose to know
To vanquish sin and death and woe;
'Twas all because he loved me so.

2 Was it for me, that opened tomb,
   Dispelling fear and death and gloom?
So vast a truth proclaims to me
That I through him can victor be.

3 Yes, all for me—the cross, the grave,
   A risen Lord with power to save!
My joyful heart is filled with praise
As songs of happiness I raise.
                  Rosina Coull (1876-1957)

135 Turner, 504; Melita, 495
                    8.8.8.8.8.8. Iambic

WE worship thee, O Crucified!
   What glories didst thou lay aside;
What depth of human grief and sin
Didst thou consent to languish in,
That through atoning blood outpoured
Our broken peace might be restored!

2 We mourn that e'er our hearts should be
   One with a world that loves not thee;
That with the crowd we passed thee by
And saw, but did not feel, thee die.
Not till we knew our guilt and shame
Did we esteem the Saviour's name.

3 Though with our shame we shunned the
      light,
   Thou didst not leave us in the night;
We were not left in sin to stray
Unsought, unloved, from thee away;
For from thy cross irradiates
A power that saves and recreates.

4 O loved above all earthly love,
   To thee our hearts adoring move;
Thy boundless mercies yearn to save
And in thy blood sin's wounds to lave.
O speed the day when men shall see
That human hopes are all in thee.
                  Albert Orsborn (1886-1967)

37

The Lord Jesus Christ

136 Rockingham, 43; Deep Harmony, 16
L.M.

WHEN I survey the wondrous cross
  On which the Prince of Glory died,
My richest gain I count but loss,
  And pour contempt on all my pride.

2 Forbid it, Lord, that I should boast
  Save in the death of Christ, my God;
All the vain things that charm me most,
  I sacrifice them to his blood.

3 See, from his head, his hands, his feet,
  Sorrow and love flow mingled down;
Did e'er such love and sorrow meet,
  Or thorns compose so rich a crown?

4 Were the whole realm of nature mine,
  That were a present far too small;
Love so amazing, so divine,
  Demands my soul, my life, my all.
        Isaac Watts (1674-1748)

137 To save a poor sinner, 837

WHEN Jesus was born in the manger
  The shepherds came thither to see,
For the angels proclaimed that a Saviour
    was born
  To save a poor sinner like me.

To save a poor sinner, to save a poor
    sinner,
  To save a poor sinner like me;
For the angels proclaimed that a
    Saviour was born
  To save a poor sinner like me.

2 He was wounded for my transgressions,
  Acquainted with sorrow was he;
In the garden he prayed, and sweat great
    drops of blood,
  To save a poor sinner like me.

3 He was brought to Pilate for judgment,
  He was sentenced to hang on a tree.
It is finished! he cried, when he suffered
    and died
  To save a poor sinner like me.

4 But death and the grave could not hold
    him,
  He burst them asunder for thee.
On the third day he rose, in spite of his
    foes,
  To save a poor sinner like me.

5 I'm fighting my passage to Heaven,
  O'er death I shall conqueror be.
Then to Glory I'll fly, and shout through
    the sky:
  He saved a poor sinner like me.
        John Lawley (1859-1922) (verses 4 and 5)

138 Wareham, 55
L.M.

WITHIN my heart, O Lord, fulfil
  The purpose of thy death and pain,
That all may know thou livest still
  In blood-washed hearts to rule and reign.

2 O Lord, I gaze upon thy face,
  That suffering face so marred for me;
Touched by the wonders of thy grace
  My heart in love goes out to thee.

3 O Saviour, by thy bleeding form
  The world is crucified to me;
Thy loving heart, so rent and torn,
  Thy suffering bids me share with thee.

4 'Twas on the cross thou didst redeem
  My soul from sin and dark despair;
'Tis near the cross I would be seen,
  And welcome every sinner there.
        Herbert Howard Booth (1862-1926)

139 Wonderful story of love, 865

WONDERFUL story of love!
  Tell it to me again;
Wonderful story of love!
  Wake the immortal strain.
Angels with rapture announce it,
Shepherds with wonder receive it;
Sinner, O won't you believe it?
  Wonderful story of love!

Wonderful! Wonderful!
Wonderful story, wonderful story of
  love!

2 Wonderful story of love!
  Though you are far away;
Wonderful story of love!
  Still he doth call today.
Calling from Calvary's mountain,
Down from the crystal bright fountain,
E'en from the dawn of creation;
  Wonderful story of love!

3   Wonderful story of love!
     Jesus provides a rest;
     Wonderful story of love!
     For all the pure and blest;
     Rest in those mansions above us,
     With those who've gone on before us,
     Singing the rapturous chorus;
     Wonderful story of love!
                    John Merritte Driver (1858-1918)

Resurrection and Ascension

141 Camberwell, 201; Princethorpe, 206
                                    6.5.6.5. D.

AT the name of Jesus
     Every knee shall bow,
     Every tongue confess him
     King of Glory now;
'Tis the Father's pleasure
     We should call him Lord,
Who from the beginning
     Was the mighty Word.

2   At his voice creation
     Sprang at once to sight,
     All the angel faces,
     All the hosts of light,
     Thrones and dominations,
     Stars upon their way,
     All the heavenly orders
     In their great array.

140 Sovereignty, 502; Stella, 503
                      8.8.8.8.8.8. Iambic

WOULD Jesus have the sinner die?
     Why hangs he then on yonder tree?
What means that strange expiring cry?
     Sinners, he prays for you and me.
Forgive them, Father, O forgive!
They know not that by me they live!

2   Jesus descended from above
     Our loss of Eden to retrieve;
Great God of universal love,
     If all the world through thee may live,
In me a quickening Spirit be
And witness thou hast died for me!

3   Thou loving, all-atoning Lamb!
     Thee—by thy painful agony,
Thy sweat of blood, thy grief and shame,
     Thy cross and passion on the tree,
Thy precious death and life—I pray,
Take all, take all my sins away.

4   O let me kiss thy bleeding feet,
     And bathe and wash them with my tears;
The story of thy love repeat
     In every drooping sinner's ears,
That all may hear the quickening sound,
Since I, even I, have mercy found.

5   O let thy love my heart constrain,
     Thy love for every sinner free;
That every fallen soul of man
     May taste the grace that found out me,
That all mankind with me may prove
Thy sovereign, everlasting love!
                    Charles Wesley (1707-88)

          *   *   *

see also: 274 He came to give us life
          360 My Saviour suffered on the tree
          985 Lead me to Calvary
          989 Beneath the Cross of Jesus
          990 Victory in Jesus

3   Humbled for a season,
     To receive a name
From the lips of sinners
     Unto whom he came,
Faithfully he bore it
     Spotless to the last,
Brought it back victorious
     When from death he passed.

4   Bore it up triumphant
     With its human light,
Through all ranks of creatures
     To the central height,
To the throne of Godhead,
     To the Father's breast;
Filled it with the glory
     Of that perfect rest.

5   In your hearts enthrone him;
     There let him subdue
All that is not holy,
     All that is not true;
Crown him as your captain
     In temptation's hour;
Let his will enfold you
     In its light and power.
                    Caroline Maria Noel (1817-77)

142 Christ is Alive! (Truro, 54)   L.M.
         For words and music see Song 986
         American Supplement

39

The Lord Jesus Christ

143 Easter Hymn, 281; Llanfair, 271
                                    7.7.7.7.

CHRIST the Lord is risen today,
    Hallelujah!
Sons of men and angels say:
    Hallelujah!
Raise your joys and triumphs high;
    Hallelujah!
Sing, ye heavens; thou earth, reply:
    Hallelujah!

2 Love's redeeming work is done;
  Fought the fight, the battle won;
  Lo! the sun's eclipse is o'er,
  Lo! he sets in blood no more.

3 Vain the stone, the watch, the seal,
  Christ hath burst the gates of Hell;
  Death in vain forbids his rise;
  Christ hath opened Paradise.

4 Lives again our glorious King;
  Where, O death, is now thy sting?
  Once he died our souls to save;
  Where's thy victory, boasting grave?

5 Soar we now where Christ has led,
  Following our exalted head;
  Made like him, like him we rise,
  Ours the cross, the grave, the skies.
                    Charles Wesley (1707-88)

144 And above the rest, 5;
         Morning Hymn, 35   L.M.

I KNOW that my redeemer lives,
    What joy the blest assurance gives!
He lives triumphant o'er the grave,
He lives omnipotent to save.

And above the rest this note shall
        swell,
My Jesus hath done all things well.

2 He lives to bless me with his love,
  He lives to plead my cause above,
  He lives to silence all my fears,
  He lives to wipe away my tears.

3 He lives, my wise and constant friend,
  He lives and loves me to the end,
  He lives my mansion to prepare,
  He lives to guide me safely there.

4 He lives, all glory to his name,
  He lives, eternally the same;
  What joy the sweet assurance gives
  That Jesus, my redeemer, lives!
                Samuel Medley (1738-99) (verses)

145 Maidstone, 325
                                    7.7.7.7. D.

IN the shadow of the cross,
    Side by side with bitter loss,
Bloomed a garden, passing fair,
And they laid the Saviour there.
Sad, they thought his day was done,
But, afar, his rising sun
Flung a quenchless ray across
To the garden near the cross.

2 Not for long the grave prevailed;
  When the dreary night had paled
  Into God's appointed day,
  Angels rolled the stone away.
  Christ, the Lord of truth and might,
  Faring forth in robes of light,
  Drove the fearful shades of loss
  From the garden near the cross.

3 Jesus, give to us to know:
  Though in loneliness we sow,
  We shall pluck the fairest flower
  In the sacrificial hour.
  Sorrow hides beneath her wings
  Recompense for sufferings,
  And the blessing waits for us
  In the garden near the cross.
                    Albert Orsborn (1886-1967)

146 St Francis, 45
                                    L.M.

LET us rejoice, the fight is won,
    Darkness is conquered, death undone,
    Life triumphant! Alleluia!
So age to age each nation grows
More like the heart of him who rose.

    Alleluia, alleluia,
Alleluia, alleluia, alleluia!

2 Joy comes again! all shall be well,
  Friends severed now in Heaven shall dwell
    Reunited! Alleluia!
  The end of all our ways is love,
  Then rise with him to things above.

3 Thou boundless power, thou God on high,
  How could thy children fear to die?
    Joy immortal! Alleluia!
  Thy right rewards, thy love forgives;
  We know that our redeemer lives.
                    Percy Dearmer (1867-1936)

40

Resurrection and Ascension

147
Crown the Saviour, 367; Triumph, 427;
Helmsley, 417   8.7.8.7. Troch.

LOOK, ye saints! The sight is glorious;
See the man of sorrows now,
From the fight returned victorious;
Every knee to him shall bow.
Crown him, crown him!
Crowns become the victor's brow.

2 Crown the Saviour, angels crown him;
Rich the trophies Jesus brings;
In the seat of power enthrone him,
While the vault of Heaven rings.
Crown him, crown him!
Crown the Saviour King of kings!

3 Sinners in derision crowned him,
Mocking thus the Saviour's claim;
Saints and angels crowd around him,
Own his title, praise his name.
Crown him, crown him!
Spread abroad the victor's fame!

4 Hark, those bursts of acclamation!
Hark, those loud triumphant chords!
Jesus takes the highest station;
O what joy the sight affords!
Crown him, crown him!
King of kings and Lord of lords!
Thomas Kelly (1769-1855)

148
Up from the grave he arose, 839

LOW in the grave he lay,
Jesus, my Saviour;
Waiting the coming day,
Jesus, my Lord.

Up from the grave he arose,
With a mighty triumph o'er his foes.
He arose a victor from the dark
domain,
And he lives for ever with his saints to
reign.
He arose! He arose! Hallelujah!
Christ arose!

2 Vainly they watch his bed,
Jesus, my Saviour;
Vainly they seal the dead,
Jesus, my Lord.

3 Death cannot keep his prey,
Jesus, my Saviour;
He tore the bars away,
Jesus, my Lord.
Robert Lowry (1826-99)

149
He Lives, 466   8.8.6.8.8.6.

O JOYFUL sound! O glorious hour
When Christ by his almighty power
Arose and left the grave!
Now let our songs his triumph tell
Who broke the chains of death and Hell,
And ever lives to save.

He lives, he lives,
I know that my redeemer lives.

2 The first-begotten of the dead,
For us he rose, our glorious head,
Immortal life to bring.
What though the saints like him shall die,
They share their leader's victory,
And triumph with their King.

3 No more we tremble at the grave;
For he who died our souls to save
Will raise our bodies too.
What though this earthly house shall fail,
The Saviour's power will yet prevail
And build it up anew.
Thomas Kelly (1769-1855) (verses), alt

150
Winchester New, 61   L.M.

RIDE on, ride on in majesty!
Hark, all the tribes hosanna cry;
Thine humble beast pursues his road
With palms and scattered garments
strowed.

2 Ride on, ride on in majesty!
In lowly pomp ride on to die;
O Christ, thy triumphs now begin
O'er captive death and conquered sin.

3 Ride on, ride on in majesty!
The wingèd squadrons of the sky
Look down with sad and wondering eyes
To see the approaching sacrifice.

4 Ride on, ride on in majesty!
The last and fiercest strife is nigh;
The Father on his sapphire throne
Expects his own anointed Son.

5 Ride on, ride on in majesty!
In lowly pomp ride on to die;
Bow thy meek head to mortal pain,
Then take, O God, thy power, and reign.
Henry Hart Milman (1791-1868)

151 Victory, 840

THE strife is o'er, the battle done;
  Now is the victor's triumph won;
Now be the song of praise begun:
  Alleluia!

2 The powers of death have done their worst,
  But Christ their legions hath dispersed:
Let shouts of holy joy outburst,
  Alleluia!

3 The three sad days have quickly sped;
  He rises glorious from the dead:
All glory to our risen head!
  Alleluia!

4 He closed the yawning gates of Hell;
  The bars from Heaven's high portals fell:
Let hymns of praise his triumphs tell.
  Alleluia!

5 Lord, by the stripes which wounded thee,
  From death's dread sting thy servants free,
That we may live and sing to thee.
  Alleluia!
Symphonia Sirenum Selectarum (1695),
trs Francis Pott (1832-1909), alt

152 Maccabeus, 728

THINE is the glory,
  Risen, conquering Son;
Endless is the victory
  Thou o'er death hast won.
Angels in bright raiment
  Rolled the stone away,
Kept the folded grave clothes
  Where thy body lay.

Thine is the glory,
  Risen, conquering Son;
Endless is the victory
  Thou o'er death hast won.

2 Lo! Jesus meets thee,
  Risen from the tomb;
Lovingly he greets thee,
  Scatters fear and gloom;
Let his Church with gladness
  Hymns of triumph sing,
For her Lord now liveth;
  Death has lost its sting.

3 No more we doubt thee,
  Glorious Prince of Life!
Life is naught without thee;
  Aid us in thy strife;

Make us more than conquerors
Through thy deathless love;
Bring us safe through Jordan
To thy home above.
Edmond Louis Budry (1854-1932),
trs Richard Birch Hoyle (1875-1939)

153 Dutch Carol, 638

THIS joyful Eastertide,
  Away with sin and sorrow,
My love, the crucified,
  Hath sprung to life this morrow:

Had Christ, that once was slain,
Ne'er burst his three-day prison,
Our faith had been in vain:
But now hath Christ arisen.

2 My flesh in hope shall rest,
  And for a season slumber;
Till trump from east to west
  Shall wake the dead in number:

3 Death's flood hath lost his chill,
  Since Jesus crossed the river;
Lover of souls, from ill
  My passing soul deliver.
George Ratcliffe Woodward (1848-1934)

154 Carlisle, 164

S.M.

'TIS good, Lord, to be here,
  Thy glory fills the night;
Thy face and garments, like the sun,
  Shine with unborrowed light.

2 'Tis good, Lord, to be here,
  Thy beauty to behold,
Where Moses and Elijah stood,
  The messengers of old.

3 Fulfiller of the past,
  Promise of things to be,
We hail thy body glorified,
  And our redemption see.

4 Before we taste of death,
  We see thy Kingdom come.
O might we hold the vision bright
And make this hill our home!

5 'Tis good, Lord, to be here,
  Yet we may not remain;
But, since thou bidst us leave the mount,
  Come with us to the plain.
Joseph Armitage Robinson (1858-1933)

155

Forward! be our watchword, 203;
Rachie, 207   6.5.6.5. D.

WELCOME, happy morning,
　Age to age shall say;
Hell today is vanquished,
　Heaven is won today.
Lo! the Christ is living,
　God for evermore!
Him, their true creator,
　All his works adore.

Welcome, happy morning,
Age to age shall say;
Hell today is vanquished,
Heaven is won today.

2 Earth with joy confesses,
　Clothes herself for spring,
Greets with life reviving
　Her returning King.
Bloom in every meadow,
　Leaves on every bough,
Speak his sorrows ended,
　Hail his triumph now.

3 Thou, of life the author,
　Death didst undergo,
Tread the path of darkness,
　Saving strength to show.
Come then, True and Faithful,
　Now fulfil thy word;
'Tis thine own third morning;
　Rise, O buried Lord!

4 Loose the souls long prisoned,
　Bound with Satan's chain;
All that now is fallen
　Raise to life again.
Show thy face in brightness,
　Bid the nations see,
Bring again our daylight,
　Day returns with thee.

Venantius Fortunatus (530-609),
trs John Ellerton (1826-93)

* * *

see also: 134 Was it for me, the nails, the spear
　　　　　242 Have you heard the angels singing
　　　　　986 Christ is alive

for Palm Sunday see:
　　　150 Ride on, ride on in majesty
　　　853 When, his salvation bringing

Kingdom

156

Diademata, 182   D.S.M.

CROWN him with many crowns,
　The Lamb upon his throne;
Hark! how the heavenly anthem drowns
　All music but its own;
　Awake, my soul, and sing
　Of him who died for thee,
And hail him as thy matchless King
　Through all eternity.

2 Crown him the Lord of life,
　Who triumphed o'er the grave,
And rose victorious in the strife
　For those he came to save;
　His glories now we sing
　Who died, and rose on high,
Who died eternal life to bring,
　And lives, that death may die.

3 Crown him the Lord of peace,
　Whose power a sceptre sways
From pole to pole, that wars may cease
　And all be prayer and praise;
　His reign shall know no end,
　And round his piercèd feet
Fair flowers of Paradise extend
　Their fragrance ever sweet.

4 Crown him the Lord of love;
　Behold his hands and side,
Those wounds, yet visible above,
　In beauty glorified;
　All hail, redeemer, hail!
　For thou hast died for me;
Thy praise and glory shall not fail
　Throughout eternity.

Matthew Bridges (1800-94) (verses 1, 3, 4),
Godfrey Thring (1823-1903) (verse 2)

157

Austria, 408; Beautiful Zion, 428
8.7.8.7. D. Troch.

GLORIOUS things of thee are spoken,
　Zion, city of our God;
He whose word cannot be broken
　Formed thee for his own abode.
On the rock of ages founded,
　What can shake thy sure repose?
With salvation's walls surrounded,
　Thou mayest smile at all thy foes.

The Lord Jesus Christ

2 See, the streams of living waters,
　Springing from eternal love,
Well supply thy sons and daughters,
　And all fear of want remove;
Who can faint while such a river
　Ever flows their thirst to assuage;
Grace which, like the Lord, the giver,
　Never fails from age to age?

3 Saviour, if of Zion's city
　I through grace a member am,
Let the world deride or pity,
　I will glory in thy name.
Fading is the worldling's pleasure,
　All his boasted pomp and show;
Solid joys and lasting treasure
　None but Zion's children know.
John Newton (1725-1807)

158 Austria, 408
8.7.8.7. D. Troch.

GOD is with us, God is with us,
　So our brave forefathers sang,
Far across the field of battle
　Loud their holy war cry rang;
Though at times they feared and faltered,
　Never once they ceased to sing:

*God is with us, God is with us,
Christ our Lord shall reign as King!*

2 Great the heritage they left us,
　Great the conquests to be won,
Armèd hosts to meet and scatter,
　Larger duties to be done.
Raise the song they nobly taught us,
　Round the wide world let it ring:

3 Speed the cross through all the nations,
　Speed the victories of love,
Preach the gospel of redemption
　Wheresoever men may move;
Make the future in the present,
　Strong of heart, toil on and sing:
Walter John Mathams (1853-1931), alt

159 Ottawa, 462
8.7.8.7.7.7. Troch.

JESUS comes! Let all adore him!
　Lord of mercy, love and truth,
Now prepare the way before him,
　Make the rugged places smooth;
Through the desert mark his road,
Make a highway for our God.

2 Jesus comes! Reward is with him,
　Let the valleys all be raised,
God's great glory now revealing
　As the mountains are abased.
Lift thy voice and greet the Lord,
Cry to Zion: See thy God!

3 Jesus comes! The Christ is marching
　Through the places waste and wild;
He his Kingdom is enlarging
　Where no verdure ever smiled.
Soon the desert will be glad
And with beauty shall be clad.

4 Jesus comes! Where thorns have
　　flourished
　Trees shall now be seen to grow,
Stablished by the Lord and nourished,
　Strong and fair and fruitful too.
They shall rise on every side,
Spread their branches far and wide.

5 Jesus comes! From barren mountains
　Rivers shall begin to flow,
There the Lord will open fountains
　And supply the plains below;
As he passes, every land
Shall acclaim his powerful hand.
Thomas Kelly (1769-1855), alt

160 Rimington, 42; Duke Street, 17
L.M.

JESUS shall reign where'er the sun
　Doth his successive journeys run;
His Kingdom stretch from shore to shore,
Till suns shall rise and set no more.

2 People and realms of every tongue
　Dwell on his love with sweetest song;
And infant voices shall proclaim
Their young hosannas to his name.

3 Blessings abound where'er he reigns,
　The prisoner leaps to lose his chains,
The weary find eternal rest,
And all the sons of want are blest.

4 Where he displays his healing power,
　Death and the curse are known no more;
In him the tribes of Adam boast
More blessings than their father lost.

5 Let every creature rise and bring
　Peculiar honors to our King;
Angels descend with songs again
And earth prolong the joyful strain.
Isaac Watts (1674-1748)

Kingdom

161 Helmsley, 417; Praise, my soul, 422
8.7.8.7.8.7. Troch.

LO! He comes with clouds descending,
Once for favored sinners slain;
Thousand thousand saints attending,
Swell the triumph of his train;
Hallelujah!
God appears on earth to reign.

2 Every eye shall now behold him
Robed in dreadful majesty;
Those who set at naught and sold him,
Pierced and nailed him to the tree,
Deeply wailing,
Shall the true Messiah see.

3 Those dear tokens of his passion
Still his dazzling body bears;
Cause of endless exultation
To his ransomed worshipers;
With what rapture
Gaze we on those glorious scars!

4 Yea, amen, let all adore thee
High on thy eternal throne;
Saviour, take the power and glory,
Claim the Kingdom for thine own;
Hallelujah!
Everlasting God, come down!
Charles Wesley (1707-88)

162 Battle hymn of the Republic, 614

MINE eyes have seen the glory of the
coming of the Lord;
He is trampling out the vintage where
the grapes of wrath are stored;
He hath loosed the fateful lightning of his
terrible swift sword;
His truth is marching on.

Glory, glory, hallelujah!
Glory, glory, hallelujah!
Glory, glory, hallelujah!
His truth is marching on.

2 I have seen him in the watch-fires of a
hundred circling camps;
They have builded him an altar in the evening dews and damps;
I have read his righteous sentence by the
dim and flaring lamps;
His day is marching on.

3 He has sounded forth the trumpet that
shall never call retreat;
He is sifting out the hearts of men before
his judgment seat;
O be swift, my soul, to answer him, be
jubilant my feet!
Our God is marching on.

4 In the beauty of the lilies Christ was born
across the sea,
With a glory in his bosom that transfig-
ures you and me;
As he died to make men holy, let us live
to make men free,
While God is marching on.
Julia Ward Howe (1819-1910)

163 St John, 228; Skinner, 230
6.6.6.6.8.8.

NOT unto us, O Lord,
But unto thy great name;
Our trumpets are awake,
Our banners are aflame,
We boast no battle ever won;
The victory is thine alone.

2 We were that foolish thing
Unversed in worldly ways,
Which thou didst choose and use
Unto thy greater praise,
Called and commissioned from afar
To bring to naught the things that are.

3 A hundred anthems rise
For every fighting year
Since thou, as Lord of hosts,
Our captain did appear
To sanctify, to take command
And bring us to the promised land.

4 Not yet we hail the day
When all to thee shall yield,
But we behold thee stand
Upon our battlefield.
And this alone shall ever be
Our sign and seal of victory.
Albert Orsborn (1886-1967)

164 Gopsal, 223; Darwalls, 221
6.6.6.6.8.8.

REJOICE, the Lord is King!
Your Lord and King adore;
Soldiers, give thanks, and sing
And triumph evermore:

Lift up your heart, lift up your voice;
Rejoice; again I say, rejoice.

45

2 Jesus the Saviour reigns,
   The God of truth and love;
When he had purged our stains,
   He took his seat above:

3 His Kingdom cannot fail,
   He rules o'er earth and Heaven;
The keys of death and Hell
   Are to our Jesus given:

4 He sits at God's right hand,
   Till all his foes submit,
And bow to his command,
   And fall beneath his feet:

5 He all his foes shall quell,
   Shall all our sins destroy,
And every bosom swell
   With pure seraphic joy:

6 Rejoice in glorious hope;
   Jesus the judge shall come,
And take his servants up
   To their eternal home:

We soon shall hear the archangel's
   voice;
The trump of God shall sound, Rejoice!

Charles Wesley (1707-88)

165 Titchfield, 327
7.7.7.7. D

SEE how great a flame aspires,
   Kindled by a spark of grace!
Jesus' love the nations fires,
   Sets the kingdoms on a blaze.
To bring fire on earth he came;
   Kindled in some hearts it is;
O that all might catch the flame,
   All partake the glorious bliss.

2 When he first the work begun,
   Small and feeble was his day:
Now the word doth swiftly run,
   Now it wins its widening way;
More and more it spreads and grows,
   Ever mighty to prevail;
Sin's strongholds it now o'erthrows,
   Shakes the trembling gates of Hell.

3 Sons of God, your Saviour praise!
   He the door hath opened wide;
He hath given the word of grace,
   Jesus' word is glorified.
Jesus, mighty to redeem,
   He alone the work hath wrought;
Worthy is the work of him,
   Him who spake a world from naught.

4 Saw ye not the cloud arise,
   Little as a human hand?
Now it spreads along the skies,
   Hangs o'er all the thirsty land;
Lo! the promise of a shower
   Drops already from above;
But the Lord will surely pour
   All the Spirit of his love.

Charles Wesley (1707-88)

166 The Glory Song, 529
10.10.10.10.Dact.

SING we the King who is coming to reign,
   Glory to Jesus, the Lamb that was slain,
Life and salvation his empire shall bring
Joy to the nations when Jesus is King.

Come let us sing: Praise to our King,
Jesus our King, Jesus our King;
This is our song, who to Jesus belong:
Glory to Jesus, to Jesus our King.

2 All men shall dwell in his marvelous light,
Races long severed his love shall unite,
Justice and truth from his sceptre shall
      spring,
Wrong shall be ended when Jesus is King.

3 All shall be well in his Kingdom of peace,
Freedom shall flourish and wisdom
      increase,
Foe shall be friend when his triumph we
      sing,
Sword shall be sickle when Jesus is King.

4 Souls shall be saved from the burden of
      sin,
Doubt shall not darken his witness within,
Hell hath no terrors, and death hath no
      sting;
Love is victorious when Jesus is King.

5 Kingdom of Christ, for thy coming we pray,
Hasten, O Father, the dawn of the day
When this new song thy creation shall
      sing,
Satan is vanquished and Jesus is King.

Charles Silvester Horne (1865-1914)

167 Alford, 245

TEN thousand times ten thousand,
   In sparkling raiment bright,
The armies of the ransomed saints
   Throng up the steeps of light;
'Tis finished! all is finished,
   Their fight with death and sin;
Fling open wide the golden gates,
   And let the victors in.

Kingdom

2 What rush of hallelujahs
   Fills all the earth and sky;
What ringing of a thousand harps
   Bespeaks the triumph nigh!
O day, for which creation
   And all its tribes were made!
O joy, for all its former woes
   A thousandfold repaid!

3 Bring near thy great salvation,
   Thou Lamb for sinners slain;
Fulfil thy love's redemptive plan,
   Then take thy power and reign;
Appear, desire of nations,
   Thine exiles long for home;
Show in the heavens thy promised sign;
   Thou Prince and Saviour, come.

Henry Alford (1810-71)

168 St Magnus, 128; Stracathro, 136
C.M.

THE head that once was crowned with thorns
   Is crowned with glory now;
A royal diadem adorns
   The mighty victor's brow.

2 The highest place that Heaven affords
   Is his, is his by right,
The King of kings and Lord of lords
   And Heaven's eternal light.

3 The joy of all who dwell above,
   The joy of all below
To whom he manifests his love,
   And grants his name to know.

4 To them the cross, with all its shame,
   With all its grace, is given,
Their name an everlasting name,
   Their joy the joy of Heaven.

5 They suffer with their Lord below,
   They reign with him above,
Their profit and their joy to know
   The mystery of his love.

6 The cross he bore is life and health,
   Though shame and death to him,
His people's hope, his people's wealth,
   Their everlasting theme.

Thomas Kelly (1769-1855)

169 O the crowning day, 758

THERE is coming on a great day of rejoicing,
   When all the ransomed shall gather,
      their Lord as King to crown;
All earth's sorrow and its sin then disappearing,
   Every heart will the Saviour then own.

*O the crowning day is coming,
   Hallelujah!
O the crowning day is coming,
   Praise the Lord!
For our Saviour-King shall reign,
He shall have his own again,
   Hallelujah! Hallelujah!*

2 From far distant lands battalions now are marching,
   Who will have part in the honors which
      Jesus will bestow;
God be praised for all the souls that now are starting,
   Swelling the hosts that to victory go.

3 Do you, comrades, feel at times a bit downhearted,
   When in the fight all looks dark, and the
      foe seems fierce and strong?
At such times I find my fear has all departed
   When I remember that day coming on.

Richard Slater (1854-1939)

170 They shall come from the east, 831

THEY shall come from the east, they shall
      come from the west,
   And sit down in the Kingdom of God;
Both the rich and the poor, the despised,
      the distressed,
   They'll sit down in the Kingdom of God.
   And none will ask what they have been
   Provided that their robes are clean;
They shall come from the east, they shall
      come from the west,
   And sit down in the Kingdom of God.

2 They shall come from the east, they shall
      come from the west,
   And sit down in the Kingdom of God;
To be met by their Father and welcomed
      and blessed,

The Lord Jesus Christ

And sit down in the Kingdom of God.
The black, the white, the dark, the fair,
Your color will not matter there;
They shall come from the east, they shall
come from the west,
And sit down in the Kingdom of God.

3 They shall come from the east, they shall
come from the west,
And sit down in the Kingdom of God;
Out of great tribulation to triumph and
rest
They'll sit down in the Kingdom of God.
From every tribe and every race,
All men as brothers shall embrace;
They shall come from the east, they shall
come from the west,
And sit down in the Kingdom of God.

John Gowans

171 Diademata, 182

D.S.M.

THINE is the Kingdom, Lord,
Thou art the King of kings;
Thy realm enfolds the universe
And Heaven its tribute brings;
Though evil forces seem
On earth to hold the sway,
Thy loyal peoples wait in faith
To hail thy crowning day.

2 Thine is the power, O Lord,
Nor Heaven nor earth can break;
The oceans move at thy command,
The stars their courses make.
Thou canst the breath of man
Bestow or canst withhold;
Of all the wonders of thy power
No tongue has ever told.

3 Thine is the glory, Lord,
The greatness and the praise,
The final victory over death,
The end of mortal days.
All majesty is thine,
Beyond the poet's pen,
For thou art life, and light and love:
Amen, amen, amen!

Arch R. Wiggins (1893-1976)

172 St Cecilia, 219

6.6.6.6.

THY kingdom come, O God!
Thy rule, O Christ, begin!
Break with thine iron rod
The tyrannies of sin.

2 Where is thy reign of peace,
And purity and love?
When shall all hatred cease,
As in the realms above?

3 When comes the promised time
That war shall be no more,
And lust, oppression, crime,
Shall flee thy face before?

4 We pray thee, Lord, arise,
And come in thy great might;
Revive our longing eyes,
Which languish for thy sight.

5 Men scorn thy sacred name,
And wolves devour thy fold;
By many deeds of shame
We learn that love grows cold.

6 O'er lands both near and far
Thick darkness broodeth yet:
Arise, O morning Star,
Arise, and never set!

Lewis Hensley (1824-1905)

173 Pilgrims, 548

11.10.11.10.

YET once again, by God's abundant
mercy,
We join our song of thankfulness and
praise;
Ever the light of our redeemer's victory
Shineth before us in the world's dark
ways.

Jesus shall conquer, lift up the strain!
Evil shall perish and righteousness
shall reign.

2 O for the time of Christ's completed
mission!
Throbs of its rapture reach us as we
pray;
Gleams of its glory bursting on our vision
Speed us to labor, urge us on our way.

3 Stretch out thy hand, O God, and let the
nations
Feel through thine host the thrill of life
divine;
Grant us, we pray, still greater revelations,
Make of these days an everlasting sign.

Albert Orsborn (1886-1967)

* * *

see also: 84 Joy to the world!
see also: 84 Joy to the world!
147 Look, ye saints! The sight is
glorious
833 We have caught the vision
splendid

Praise and Worship

174 Sine Nomine, 515; St Philip, 514
10.10.10.8.

ALL praise to thee, for thou, O King
divine,
Didst yield the glory that of right was
thine,
That in our darkened hearts thy grace
might shine:
Alleluia! Alleluia!

2 Thou cam'st to us in lowliness of thought;
By thee the outcast and the poor were
sought;
And by thy death was God's salvation
wrought:
Alleluia! Alleluia!

3 Let this mind be in us which was in thee,
Who wast a servant that we might be free,
Humbling thyself to death on Calvary:
Alleluia! Alleluia!

4 Wherefore, by God's eternal purpose, thou
Art high exalted o'er all creatures now,
And given the name to which all knees
shall bow:
Alleluia! Alleluia!

5 Let every tongue confess with one accord
In Heaven and earth that Jesus Christ is
Lord:
And God the Father be by all adored:
Alleluia! Alleluia!
Francis Bland Tucker (1895-1984)

175 Beautiful Christ, 526
10.10.10.10.Dact.

BEAUTIFUL Jesus, bright star of the
earth,
Loving and tender from moment of
birth;
Beautiful Jesus, though lowly thy lot,
Born in a manger, so rude was thy cot.

Beautiful Christ, beautiful Christ,
Fairest of thousands, and pearl of
great price;
Beautiful Christ, beautiful Christ,
Gladly we welcome thee, beautiful
Christ.

2 Beautiful Jesus, what treasure you
brought,
When from Heaven's splendor the earth
first you sought.
Beautiful Jesus, belovèd of God,
Emblem of purity, emblem of good.

3 Beautiful Jesus, so gentle and mild,
Light of the sinner in ways dark and wild;
Beautiful Jesus, O save such just now,
As at thy feet they in penitence bow!
Elizabeth Ashby

176 Warrington, 56; Abends, 2
L.M.

DEEP were the scarlet stains of sin,
Strong were the bonds of fault within;
But now I stand both pure and free,
The blood of Jesus cleanses me.

2 Strong are the foes that round me creep,
Constant the vigil I must keep
But from a secret armory
The grace of Jesus strengthens me.

3 What though the treacherous road may
wind,
Faith in my heart assures my mind;
E'en when his face I do not see,
The hand of Jesus reaches me.

4 This is the lamp to pilgrim given,
This is my passport into Heaven,
Portent of immortality,
That God, through Jesus, dwells in me.
Olive Leah Holbrook (1895-1986)

177 Ascalon, 232
6.6.8.6.6.8.

FAIREST Lord Jesus,
Lord of all nature,
O thou of God and man the Son;
Thee will I cherish,
Thee will I honor,
Thou my soul's glory, joy and crown.

2 Fair are the meadows,
Fairer the woodlands,
Robed in the blooming garb of spring;
Jesus is fairer,
Jesus is purer,
Who makes the woeful heart to sing.

3 Fair is the sunshine,
Fairer the moonlight,
And all the twinkling starry host;
Jesus shines brighter,
Jesus shines purer
Than all the angels Heaven can boast.

4 Beautiful Saviour,
Lord of the nations,
Son of God and Son of man,
Glory and honor,
Praise, adoration,
Now and for evermore be thine.
Anon
v. 4 trs Joseph Augustus Seiss (1823-1904)

The Lord Jesus Christ

178
I love to sing, 678

I LOVE to sing of the Saviour
Who gave his life for me;
He fills my spirit with gladness,
For service sets me free.

How I love to sing,
How I love to sing,
How I love to sing of Jesus!
How I love to sing!

2 I love to sing of his beauty,
His greatness and his love,
A theme that thrills all creation
In earth and Heaven above.

3 I love to sing of his virtue,
His all-transforming might;
To sing of his great salvation
Be all my heart's delight.
Gösta Blomberg (1905-1981)

179
My Saviour's love, 742

I STAND amazed in the presence
Of Jesus the Nazarene,
And wonder how he could love me,
A sinner, condemned, unclean.

How marvelous! How wonderful!
And my song shall ever be:
How marvelous! How wonderful
Is my Saviour's love for me!

2 For me it was in the garden
He prayed: Not my will, but thine;
He had no tears for his own griefs,
But sweat drops of blood for mine.

3 He took my sins and my sorrows,
He made them his very own;
He bore my burden to Calvary,
And suffered and died alone.

4 When with the ransomed in Glory
His face I at last shall see,
'Twill be my joy through the ages
To sing of his love for me.
Charles Hutchinson Gabriel (1856-1932)

180
I will sing of my redeemer, 380
8.7.8.7. Troch.

I WILL sing of my redeemer,
And his wondrous love to me;
On the cruel cross he suffered,
From the curse to set me free.

Sing, O sing of my redeemer!
With his blood he purchased me,
On the cross he sealed my pardon,
Paid the debt and made me free.

2 I will sing the wondrous story,
How my lost estate to save,
In his boundless love and mercy,
He the ransom freely gave.

3 I will praise my dear redeemer,
His triumphant power I'll tell;
How the victory he giveth
Over sin and death and Hell.

4 I will sing of my redeemer
And his heavenly love to me;
He from death to life has brought me,
Son of God, with him to be.
Philip Paul Bliss (1838-76)

181
Bartholomew, 518
10.10.10.10. Iambic

O CHRIST, who came to share our human life,
God's Word made flesh to speak his love for men,
Lead us in service to thy holy cause
Till sons of earth are sons of God again.

2 O Christ, who dared to stand on trial alone
Before the angry mob and Roman might,
We seek thy courage; make it now our own
That we may stand unflinching for thy right.

3 O Christ, who died with arms outstretched in love
For all who lift their faces to thy cross,
Fill, thou, our lives with charity divine,
Till thou and thine are all, and self is loss.

4 O Christ, who rose victorious over death
To loose thy living presence on our earth,
Teach us to feel thy greatness till we know,
In life and death, the soul's enduring worth.
Catherine Bonnell Arnott

50

Praise and Worship

182 Ebenezer, 433; Burning, Burning, 364
8.7.8.7. D. Troch.

O THE deep, deep love of Jesus,
 Vast, unmeasured, boundless, free,
Rolling as a mighty ocean
 In its fulness over me!
Underneath me, all around me,
 Is the current of thy love;
Leading onward, leading homeward,
 To my glorious rest above.

2 O the deep, deep love of Jesus,
 Spread his praise from shore to shore;
How he loveth, ever loveth,
 Changeth never, nevermore;
How he watcheth o'er his loved ones,
 Died to call them all his own;
How for them he intercedeth,
 Watcheth o'er them from the throne.

3 O the deep, deep love of Jesus,
 Love of every love the best;
'Tis an ocean vast of blessing,
 'Tis a haven sweet of rest.
O the deep, deep love of Jesus,
 'Tis a Heaven of heavens to me;
And it lifts me up to Glory,
 For it lifts me up to thee.
*   Samuel Trevor Francis (1834-1925)*

183 Was Lebet, 844

O WORSHIP the Lord in the beauty of
 holiness!
 Bow down before him, his glory
  proclaim;
With gold of obedience, and incense of
 lowliness,
 Kneel and adore him, the Lord is his
  name.

2 Low at his feet lay thy burden of
 carefulness,
 High on his heart he will bear it for thee,
Comfort thy sorrows and answer thy
 prayerfulness,
 Guiding thy steps as may best for thee
  be.

3 Fear not to enter his courts in the
 slenderness
 Of the poor wealth thou wouldst reckon as thine;
Truth in its beauty, and love in its
 tenderness,
 These are the offerings to lay on his
  shrine.

4 These, though we bring them in trembling and fearfulness,
 He will accept for the name that is dear;
Morning of joy give for evenings of
 tearfulness,
 Trust for our trembling, and hope for
  our fear.

5 O worship the Lord in the beauty of
 holiness!
 Bow down before him, his glory
  proclaim;
With gold of obedience, and incense of
 lowliness,
 Kneel and adore him, the Lord is his
  name.
*   John Samuel Bewley Monsell (1811-75)*

184 Praise Him! 771

PRAISE him! Praise him! Jesus, our
 blessèd redeemer!
 Sing, O earth, his wonderful love
  proclaim!
Hail him! Hail him, highest archangels in
 glory;
 Strength and honor give to his holy
  name!
Like a shepherd, Jesus will guard his
 children,
 In his arms he carries them all day long.

Praise him! Praise him!
 Tell of his excellent greatness;
Praise him! Praise him!
 Ever in joyful song.

2 Praise him! Praise him! Jesus, our blessèd
 redeemer!
 For our sins he suffered and bled and
  died;
He our rock, our hope of eternal salvation,
 Hail him! Hail him! Jesus, the crucified!
Sound his praises! Jesus who bore our
 sorrows,
 Love unbounded, wonderful, deep and
  strong.

3 Praise him! Praise him! Jesus, our blessèd
 redeemer!
 Heavenly portals loud with hosannas
  ring!
Jesus, Saviour, reigneth for ever and ever;
 Crown him! Crown him! Prophet and
  priest and King!
Christ is coming, over the world victorious;
 Power and glory unto the Lord belong.
*   Fanny Crosby (1820-1915)*

51

The Lord Jesus Christ

185 Regent Square, 423
8.7.8.7.8.7. Troch.

SON of God! Thy cross beholding,
  Hearing thy expiring cry,
All our guilt and shame unfolding,
  Melt the heart and dim the eye.
    King of Glory,
  Camest thou to earth to die?

2 Is it thus, O Christ eternal,
  Right shall reign and sin shall cease?
Come we to the joy supernal
  By thy dying, Prince of Peace?
    Matchless Jesus,
  Break our bonds and give release.

3 Past the reach of all despising,
  Past man's puny judgment bar,
Now we see thy light arising,
  Hope is singing from afar.
    Hail Immanuel,
  Brighter than the morning star!

4 Lo, we yield thee adoration;
  Glory crowns thy sacred brow,
And the saints of every nation
  At thy feet in reverence bow.
    Hallelujah!
  In thy cross we triumph now.
Albert Orsborn (1886-1967)

186 Wonderful, wonderful Jesus, 866

THERE is never a day so dreary,
  There is never a night so long,
But the soul that is trusting Jesus
  Will somewhere find a song.

Wonderful, wonderful Jesus,
  In the heart he implanteth a song:
A song of deliverance, of courage, of
    strength;
  In the heart he implanteth a song.

2 There is never a cross so heavy,
  There is never a weight of woe,
But that Jesus will help to carry
  Because he loveth so.

3 There is never a care or burden,
  There is never a grief or loss,
But that Jesus in love will lighten
  When carried to the cross.

4 There is never a guilty sinner,
  There is never a wandering one,
But that God can in mercy pardon,
  Through Jesus Christ, his Son.
Anna Belle Russell (1862-1954)

187 Laudes Domini, 714

WHEN morning gilds the skies,
  My heart awaking cries:
    May Jesus Christ be praised!
Alike at work and prayer
To Jesus I repair;
    May Jesus Christ be praised!

2 Whene'er the sweet church bell
Peals over hill and dell,
    May Jesus Christ be praised!
O hark to what it sings,
As joyously it rings,
    May Jesus Christ be praised!

3 Does sadness fill my mind?
A solace here I find,
    May Jesus Christ be praised!
Or fades my earthly bliss?
My comfort still is this:
    May Jesus Christ be praised!

4 In Heaven's eternal bliss
The loveliest strain is this:
    May Jesus Christ be praised!
Let earth and sea and sky
From depth to height reply:
    May Jesus Christ be praised!

5 Be this, while life is mine,
My canticle divine:
    May Jesus Christ be praised!
Be this th' eternal song
Through ages all along:
    May Jesus Christ be praised!
trs Edward Caswall (1814-78)

*   *   *

see also: 38 O Lord of every shining
             constellation
          135 We worship thee, O Crucified
          154 'Tis good, Lord, to be here

THE HOLY SPIRIT
Person and Purpose

188 Holy Spirit, come, O come, 670

ALL the guilty past is washed away,
  From its penalty I'm free;
Holy Spirit, now thy might display,
Lead me on to full salvation.

Holy Spirit, come, O come,
Let thy work in me be done!
All that hinders shall be thrown aside;
Make me fit to be thy dwelling.

2 Come, O Spirit, come to sanctify
  All my body, mind and will;
  Come, O come, and self now crucify,
  Let me henceforth be like Jesus.

3 Make me, Holy Spirit, strong to fight
  For the Lord who died for me;
  Help me point the lost to Calvary's height
  Where for sinners there is mercy.

4 Perfect joy and perfect peace are mine
  For my plea is heard by thee;
  Thou art filling me with grace divine,
  Fitted now for thy indwelling.
                    Richard Slater (1854-1939)

189 Trentham, 180; Carlisle, 164   S.M.

BREATHE on me, Breath of God,
  Fill me with life anew,
That I may love what thou dost love,
And do what thou wouldst do.

2 Breathe on me, Breath of God,
  Until my heart is pure,
  Until with thee I will one will
  To do and to endure.

3 Breathe on me, Breath of God,
  Till I am wholly thine,
  Until this earthly part of me
  Glows with thy fire divine.

4 Breathe on me, Breath of God,
  So shall I never die,
  But live with thee the perfect life
  Of thine eternity.
                    Edwin Hatch (1835-89)

190 Boston, 13; Maryton, 33   L.M.

COME, gracious Spirit, heavenly dove,
  With light and comfort from above,
Be thou our guardian, thou our guide;
O'er every thought and step preside.

2 The light of truth to us display
  That we may know and choose thy way;
  Plant holy fear in every heart
  That we from God may ne'er depart.

3 Lead us to holiness, the road
  That we must take to dwell with God;
  Lead us to God, our final rest,
  To be with him for ever blessed.
                    Simon Browne (1680-1732), alt

191 St Oswald, 396; Sardis, 397;
        Galilee, 371   8.7.8.7. Troch.

COME, thou everlasting Spirit,
  Bring to every thankful mind
All the Saviour's dying merit,
  All his sufferings for mankind.

2 True Recorder of his passion,
  Now the living faith impart;
  Now reveal his great salvation;
  Preach his gospel to my heart.

3 Come, thou Witness of his dying;
  Come, remembrancer divine!
  Let us feel thy power, applying
  Christ to every soul, and mine.

4 Let us groan thine inward groaning,
  Look on him we pierced, and grieve;
  All receive the grace atoning,
  All the sprinkled blood receive.
                    Charles Wesley (1707-88)

192 For the mighty moving of thy Spirit, 646

FOR the mighty moving of thy Spirit
  In our hearts and minds from day to
    day,
For the gentle soothing of thy Spirit,
  When our fears had filled us with
    dismay:

We adore thee, heavenly Father,
And we thank thee, heavenly Father,
And we praise thee, heavenly Father,
  As we pray.

53

The Holy Spirit

2 For the kindly chiding of thy Spirit
   When we thought to find an easier way,
For the gracious guiding of thy Spirit,
   And the strength we needed to obey:

3 For the tender stirring of thy Spirit
   Who recalled us when we went astray,
The persistent spurring of thy Spirit,
   When we hesitated on the way:
         John Gowans

193   Eudoxia, 197; Barnby, 195
                    6.5.6.5.

HOLY Spirit, hear us,
   Help us while we sing;
Breathe into the music
   Of the praise we bring.

2 Holy Spirit, prompt us
   When we kneel to pray;
Nearer come, and teach us
   What we ought to say.

3 Holy Spirit, shine thou
   On the book we read,
Gild its holy pages
   With the light we need.

4 Holy Spirit, give us
   Each a lowly mind;
Make us more like Jesus,
   Gentle, pure and kind.

5 Holy Spirit, help us
   Daily, by thy might,
What is wrong to conquer,
   And to choose the right.
       William Henry Parker (1845-1929)

194   Weber, 301; St Bees, 293
                    7.7.7.7.

HOLY Spirit, truth divine,
   Dawn upon this soul of mine;
Word of God and inward light,
Wake my spirit, clear my sight.

2 Holy Spirit, love divine,
   Glow within this heart of mine;
Kindle every high desire,
Perish self in thy pure fire.

3 Holy Spirit, right divine,
   King within my conscience reign;
Be my Lord, and I shall be
Firmly bound, for ever free.

4 Holy Spirit, peace divine,
   Still this restless heart of mine;
Speak to calm this tossing sea,
Stayed in thy tranquillity.

5 Holy Spirit, joy divine,
   Gladden thou this heart of mine;
In the desert ways I sing,
Spring, O well, for ever spring!
       Samuel Longfellow (1819-92)

195   St John, 228; Southampton, 231
                   6.6.6.6.8.8.

JESUS is glorified
   And gives the Comforter,
His Spirit, to reside
   In all his servants here;
The Holy Ghost to man is given:
Rejoice in God sent down from Heaven.

2 To make an end of sin,
   And Satan's work destroy,
He brings his Kingdom in,
   Peace, righteousness and joy;
The Holy Ghost to man is given:
Rejoice in God sent down from Heaven.

3 The cleansing blood to apply,
   The heavenly life display,
And wholly sanctify
   And seal us to that day;
The Holy Ghost to man is given:
Rejoice in God sent down from Heaven.

4 Sent down to make us meet
   To see his glorious face,
And grant us each a seat
   In that thrice happy place;
The Holy Ghost to man is given:
Rejoice in God sent down from Heaven.
       Charles Wesley (1707-88)

196   St Ethelwald, 174; Franconia, 168;
          Trentham, 180   S.M.

LORD God, the Holy Ghost,
   In this accepted hour,
As on the day of Pentecost,
   Descend with all thy power.

2   We meet with one accord
   In our appointed place,
And wait the promise of our Lord,
   The Spirit of all grace.

3   Like mighty rushing wind
   Upon the waves beneath,
Move with one impulse every mind,
   One soul, one feeling breathe.

4   The young, the old inspire
   With wisdom from above;
And give us hearts and tongues of fire
   To pray and praise and love.

5   Spirit of light explore,
And chase our gloom away,
With luster shining more and more
Unto the perfect day.

6   Spirit of truth, be thou
In life and death our guide;
O Spirit of adoption, now
May we be sanctified.
James Montgomery (1771-1854)

197 Hold the fort, 344; Whitechapel, 348
8.5.8.5.

NEAR thy cross assembled, Master,
At thy feet we fall,
Seeking power to send us faster,
Hear, Lord, while we call.
Soul and body consecrating,
Leaving every sin,
Longing for a full salvation,
Victory we would win.

2   Fire that changes earthly craving
Into pure desire,
Fire destroying fear and doubting,
Fills and saves us higher;
Fire that takes its stand for Jesus,
Seeks and saves the lost;
Fire that follows where he pleases,
Fearless of the cost.

3   Fire that turns men into heroes,
Makes of weakness, might;
Fire that makes us more than conquerors,
Strengthens us to fight.
Crosses bearing, dangers daring,
By the fire set free,
In my Master's suffering sharing,
Send this fire on me.
John Lawley (1859-1922)

198 Pembroke, 467; Praise, 468
8.8.6.8.8.6.

O HOLY Ghost, on thee we wait;
This day in faith we celebrate
Thy coming from on high;
No rushing, mighty wind we hear,
No cloven tongues of fire appear,
Yet we believe thee nigh.

2   Though of a day long past we speak,
We know thou art not far to seek
When faith presents her claim;
We rest on the unbroken word
Of Jesus, our ascended Lord,
From whom the promise came.

3   For not at Pentecost alone
Thy presence and thy power were shown
And many souls were won;
Thou Spirit of the living God,
Thy work through all the earth abroad
From age to age goes on.

4   The works of darkness fail and cease;
The fruits of love and joy and peace,
These flourish and remain;
The meek their heritage possess,
And strength belongs to gentleness
Wherever thou dost reign.

5   We bring the need that makes us bold,
The faith that will not loose its hold
In this most vital hour;
Draw near, O promised Comforter,
And on each waiting soul confer
Thy pentecostal power.
Will J. Brand (1889-1977)

199 Hereford, 23; Whitburn, 58;
Warrington, 56   L.M.

O THOU who camest from above
The pure celestial fire to impart,
Kindle a flame of sacred love
On the mean altar of my heart.

2   There let it for thy glory burn
With inextinguishable blaze,
And trembling to its source return
In humble prayer and fervent praise.

3   Jesus, confirm my heart's desire
To work and speak and think for thee;
Still let me guard the holy fire,
And still stir up thy gift in me.

4   Ready for all thy perfect will,
My acts of faith and love repeat,
Till death thy endless mercies seal,
And make the sacrifice complete.
Charles Wesley (1707-88)

200 St Cuthbert, 779

OUR blest redeemer, ere he breathed
His tender last farewell,
A guide, a Comforter bequeathed
With us to dwell.

2   He came in semblance of a dove,
With sheltering wings outspread,
The holy balm of peace and love
On each to shed.

The Holy Spirit

3 He came in tongues of living flame,
  To teach, convince, subdue;
All-powerful as the wind he came,
  As viewless too.

4 He came sweet influence to impart,
  A gracious, willing guest,
Where he can find one humble heart
  Wherein to rest.

5 And his that gentle voice we hear,
  Soft as the breath of even,
That checks each fault, that calms each
    fear,
  And speaks of Heaven.

6 And every virtue we possess,
  And every victory won,
And every thought of holiness,
  Are his alone.

7 Spirit of purity and grace,
  Our weakness, pitying, see;
O make our hearts thy dwelling-place,
  And worthier thee!
            Henriette Auber (1773-1862)

201 Pour thy Spirit, 393; Govaars, 373
            8.7.8.7. Troch.

PRECIOUS Saviour, we are coming,
  At thy feet just now we fall,
Waiting to receive thy blessing,
  Come and now baptize us all.

  Pour thy Spirit, pour thy Spirit,
  Into this my longing breast,
  And go on from this good hour
  To revive thy work afresh.

2 Mighty Lord, our hearts are open
  To thy penetrating gaze;
Now, O let the fire descending
  Fill our hearts with power and praise.

3 Time and talents I surrender,
  Freely all I give to thee;
Faith lays hold of thy great promise,
  Brings the fire just now on me.

4 Hallelujah! it is falling,
  Burning all my dross and sin,
Purifying all my nature,
  Now I know I'm clean within.
        Thomas McKie (1860-1937) (verses)

202 Arizona, 7; Eden, 18
            L.M.

SPIRIT of God, that moved of old
  Upon the waters' darkened face,
Come, when our faithless hearts are cold,
  And stir them with an inward grace.

2 Thou art the power and peace combined,
  All highest strength, all purest love,
The rushing of the mighty wind,
  The brooding of the gentle dove.

3 Come, give us still thy powerful aid,
  And urge us on, and keep us thine;
Nor leave the hearts that once were made
  Fit temples for thy grace divine.

4 Nor let us quench thy sevenfold light;
  But still with softest breathings stir
Our wayward souls, and lead us right,
  O Holy Ghost, the Comforter.
        Cecil Frances Alexander (1818-95)

203 Tucker, 335; What's the news? 337
            8.3.8.3.8.8.8.3.

THOU Christ of burning, cleansing flame,
  Send the fire!
Thy blood-bought gift today we claim,
  Send the fire!
Look down and see this waiting host,
Give us the promised Holy Ghost,
We want another Pentecost,
  Send the fire!

2 God of Elijah, hear our cry:
  Send the fire!
To make us fit to live or die,
  Send the fire!
To burn up every trace of sin,
To bring the light and glory in,
The revolution now begin,
  Send the fire!

3 'Tis fire we want, for fire we plead,
  Send the fire!
The fire will meet our every need,
  Send the fire!
For strength to ever do the right,
For grace to conquer in the fight,
For power to walk the world in white,
  Send the fire!

4 To make our weak hearts strong and brave,
  Send the fire!
To live a dying world to save,
  Send the fire!
O see us on thy altar lay
Our lives, our all, this very day,
To crown the offering now we pray,
  Send the fire!
        William Booth (1829-1912)

56

Indwelling

204

WHO is it tells me what to do
And helps me to obey?
Who is it plans the route for me
And will not let me stray?
Who is it tells me when to speak
And what I ought to say?

That's the Spirit! Holy Spirit!
That's the Spirit of the Lord in me!

2 Who is it gives me heavy loads
And helps me take the strain?
Who is it calls to sacrifice
And helps me bear the pain?
Who is it sees me when I fall
And lifts me up again?

3 Who is it shows me what to be
And leads me to that goal?
Who is it claims the heart of me
And wants to take control?
Who is it calls to holiness
Of body, mind and soul?

John Gowans

*   *   *

see also: **511** My body, soul and spirit
599 Jesus, stand among us
760 Those first disciples of the Lord

Indwelling

205
Spanish Chant, 315; Wells, 318
7.7.7.7.7.7.

BLESSÈD Lamb of Calvary,
Let thy Spirit fall on me;
Let the cleansing, healing flow
Wash and keep me white as snow,
That henceforth my life may be
Bright and beautiful for thee.

2 Burn out every selfish thought,
Let thy will in me be wrought,
Fan my love into a flame,
Send a pentecostal rain,
That henceforth my life may be
Spent in winning souls for thee.

3 Teach me how to fight and win
Perfect victory over sin;
Give me a compassion deep,
That will for lost sinners weep,
That henceforth my life may prove
That I serve thee out of love.

Barbara Stoddart (1865-1915)

206
Burning, Burning, 364
8.7.8.7. Troch.

BURNING, burning, brightly burning,
Brightly burning Fire divine,
Satisfy my spirit's yearning,
Fill this empty soul of mine.

Burning, burning, always burning,
Holy Spirit, stay with me;
To your will my will is turning,
What you will I want to be.

2 Burning, burning, deeply burning,
Deeply burning holy Fire,
Now, your perfect plan discerning,
Your design is my desire.

3 Burning, burning, gently burning,
Gently burning Fire within,
From your love my love is learning,
Now I feel your work begin.

John Gowans

207
Euphony, 493; Cardiff, 488; Stella, 503
8.8.8.8.8.8. Iambic

COME, Holy Ghost, all-quickening fire,
Come, and in me delight to rest;
Drawn by the lure of strong desire,
O come and consecrate my breast;
The temple of my soul prepare,
And fix thy sacred presence there.

2 If now thy influence I feel,
If now in thee begin to live,
Still to my heart thyself reveal,
Give me thyself, for ever give;
A point my good, a drop my store,
Eager I ask, I pant for more.

3 My peace, my life, my comfort thou,
My treasure and my all thou art;
True witness of my sonship, now
Engraving pardon on my heart,
Seal of my sin in Christ forgiven,
Earnest of love, and pledge of Heaven.

4 Come, then, my God, mark out thine heir;
Of Heaven a larger earnest give;
With clearer light thy witness bear,
More sensibly within me live;
Let all my powers thine entrance feel,
And deeper stamp thyself the seal.

Charles Wesley (1707-88)

The Holy Spirit

208 Arizona, 7; Beethoven, 9
L.M.

COME, Holy Ghost, all sacred fire!
Come, fill this earthly temple now
Emptied of every base desire,
Reign thou within, and only thou.

2 Fill every chamber of my soul;
Fill all my thoughts, my passions fill,
Till under thy supreme control
Submissive rests my cheerful will.

3 'Tis done! Thou dost this moment come;
My longing soul is all thine own,
My heart is thy abiding home;
Henceforth I live for thee alone.

4 The altar sanctifies the gift;
The blood insures the boon divine;
My outstretched hands to Heaven I lift
And claim the Father's promise mine.
Francis Bottome (1823-94)

209 Hail Calvary, 658

COME, Holy Spirit, thou guest of the soul,
Make thine abode in me;
Bring in the calm thy sweet presence
bestows,
Let me thy temple be.
Come to my heart today,
Come to my heart today,
Rekindle the glow and the glory bestow,
Come to my heart today.

2 Come, Holy Spirit, companion divine,
Walk with me in life's way;
By thy rich fellowship confidence give,
Walk thou with me today.
Walk thou with me today,
Walk thou with me today,
Rekindle the glow and the glory bestow,
Walk thou with me today.

3 Come, Holy Spirit, thy guidance we crave;
Speak out thy will we pray;
We would be sensitive to thy control;
Speak to our hearts today.
Speak to our hearts today,
Speak to our hearts today,
Rekindle the glow and the glory bestow,
Speak to our hearts today.
Albert E. Mingay

210 Bethany, 429; Hyfrydol, 438
8.7.8.7. D. Troch.

COME, thou all-inspiring Spirit,
Into every longing heart!
Won for us by Jesus' merit,
Now thy blissful self impart;
Sign our uncontested pardon,
Wash us in the atoning blood;
Make our hearts a watered garden,
Fill our spotless souls with God.

2 If thou gav'st the enlarged desire
Which for thee we ever feel,
Now our panting souls inspire,
Now our canceled sin reveal;
Claim us for thy habitation,
Dwell within our hallowed breast;
Seal us heirs of full salvation,
Fitted for our heavenly rest.

3 Give us quietly to tarry,
Till for all thy glory meet,
Waiting, like attentive Mary,
Happy at the Saviour's feet.
Keep us from the world unspotted,
From all earthly passions free,
Wholly to thyself devoted,
Fixed to live and die for thee.

4 Wrestling on in mighty prayer,
Lord, we will not let thee go
Till thou all thy mind declare,
All thy grace on us bestow;
Peace, the seal of sin forgiven,
Joy and perfect love impart;
Present everlasting Heaven,
All thou hast and all thou art.
Charles Wesley (1707-88)

211 Mozart, 496; St Catherine, 499
8.8.8.8.8.8. Iambic

DESCEND, O Holy Spirit, thou,
In sweet accord we wait for thee;
Our Babel stilled, new words impart
That echo thy divinity;
Love's language by the heart expressed,
By heart received and Spirit blessed.

2 O Sound of mighty, rushing wind,
Wake us, we pray, to larger life;
O Tongue of flame, come, purify
From all that genders inward strife,
The pulse of passion stir again,
Thy power within our lives remain.

3 Breathe in our souls, O Breath divine,
   And sanctify what should'st be thine;
Since gain comes not except by loss,
Empower us to sustain our cross,
And, like thy Spirit, gladly given,
Lead men to truth and joy and Heaven.
Arnold Brown

3 Hearts are open to receive thee
   Though we've grieved thee o'er and o'er;
Holy Ghost, we greatly need thee,
   Come, abide for evermore.
Lelia Naylor Morris (1862-1929)

212 Wells, 318; Ratisbon, 313
7.7.7.7.7.7.

GRACIOUS Spirit, dwell with me;
   I myself would gracious be,
And with words that help and heal
Would thy life in mine reveal;
And with actions bold and meek
Would for Christ, my Saviour, speak.

2 Truthful Spirit, dwell with me;
   I myself would truthful be,
And with wisdom kind and clear
Let thy life in mine appear;
And with actions brotherly
Speak my Lord's sincerity.

3 Tender Spirit, dwell with me;
   I myself would tender be;
Tender in my love for men,
Wooing them to God again;
With compassion pure and sweet
Lead the lost to Jesus' feet.

4 Mighty Spirit, dwell with me;
   I myself would mighty be,
Mighty so as to prevail
Where unaided man must fail;
Ever by a mighty hope
Pressing on and bearing up.

5 Holy Spirit, dwell with me;
   I myself would holy be,
Separate from sin, I would
Choose and cherish all things good;
And whatever I can be
Give to him who gave me thee.
Thomas Toke Lynch (1818-71)

213 Sardis, 397; St Oswald, 396
8.7.8.7. Troch.

HOLY Ghost, we bid thee welcome,
   Source of life and power thou art,
Promise of our heavenly Father,
   Now thrice welcome in our heart.

2 Come like dew from Heaven falling,
   Come like spring's refreshing shower;
Holy Ghost, for thee we're calling,
   Come in all thy quickening power.

214 Mozart, 496; Stella, 503
8.8.8.8.8.8. Iambic

I WANT the gift of power within,
   Of love, and of a healthful mind;
Of power to conquer inbred sin,
   Of love to thee and all mankind,
Of health that pain and death defies,
Most vigorous when the body dies.

2 When shall I hear the inward voice
   Which only faithful souls can hear?
Pardon and peace and heavenly joys
   Attend the promised Comforter;
O come, and righteousness divine
And Christ, and all with Christ, are mine!

3 O that the Comforter would come!
   Nor visit as a transient guest,
But fix in me his constant home
   And take possession of my breast,
And fix in me his loved abode,
The temple of indwelling God.

4 Where is the sure, the certain seal
   That ascertains the Kingdom mine?
The powerful stamp I long to feel,
   The signature of love divine;
O shed it in my heart abroad,
Fulness of love, of Heaven, of God!
Charles Wesley (1707-88)

215 His loving touch, 669
(Introduction each time)

I'VE felt a new and loving touch
   Upon my heart and soul;
I've felt God's love and wondrous power
   Descend and make me whole.

A miracle! Yes, a miracle!
God's Holy Spirit came
And we are not the same,
For he touched us
And filled us with his love.

[Repeat last two lines twice after verse 3]

2 I now have seen his greatness,
  I now can comprehend
The wonders of his matchless love,
  A love that will not end.

3 I can't express by words alone
  What he now means to me;
But O I want to shout to all
  That Christ gives victory!
Iva Lou Samples

216 Silver Hill, 48; Winchester New, 61
L.M.

LORD, we believe to us and ours
  Thy precious promises were given;
We wait the pentecostal powers,
  The Holy Ghost sent down from Heaven.

2 Assembled here with one accord,
  Calmly we wait the promised grace,
The purchase of our dying Lord;
  Come, Holy Ghost, and fill the place.

3 If every one that asks may find,
  If still thou dost on sinners fall,
Come as a mighty rushing wind;
  Great grace be now upon us all.

4 Behold, to thee our souls aspire,
  And languish thy descent to meet;
Kindle in each the living fire,
  And fix in every heart thy seat.
Charles Wesley (1707-88)

217 Irish, 99; Martyrdom, 113
C.M.

SPIRIT divine, attend our prayers,
  And make this house thy home;
Descend with all thy gracious powers;
  O come, great Spirit, come.

2 Come as the light, to us reveal
  Our emptiness and woe;
And lead us in those paths of life
  Where all the righteous go.

3 Come as a fire, and purge our hearts
  Like sacrificial flame;
Let our whole soul an offering be
  To our redeemer's name.

4 Come as the dew, and sweetly bless
  This consecrated hour;
May barrenness rejoice to own
  Thy fertilizing power.

5 Come as the dove, and spread thy wings,
  The wings of peaceful love;
And let thy host on earth become
  Blest as the host above.
Andrew Reed (1787-1862)

218 Spirit Divine, 134
C.M.

SPIRIT divine, come as of old
  With healing in thy train;
Come, as thou did'st, to sanctify;
  Let naught of sin remain.

Come, great Spirit, come,
Make each heart thy home;
Enter every longing soul;
Come, great Spirit, come.

2 Spirit divine, purge thou our hearts,
  Make us to understand
Thy blessèd will concerning us,
  And teach us love's command.

3 Spirit divine, cleanse thou our souls
  With pentecostal flood;
Breathe into us the life that shows
  The Father-love of God.
Brindley Boon

*   *   *

see also: 975 Spirit of God descend

THE TRINITY

219 Harlan, 215; Moscow, 217
6.6.4.6.6.6.4.

COME, thou almighty King,
  Help us thy name to sing,
    Help us to praise;
Father all-glorious,
O'er all victorious,
Come and reign over us,
    Ancient of days.

2 Come, thou incarnate Word,
  Gird on thy mighty sword,
    Our prayer attend;
Come, and thy people bless,
And give thy word success;
Spirit of holiness,
    On us descend.

The Trinity

3 Come, holy Comforter,
  Thy sacred witness bear,
    In this glad hour;
  Thou, who almighty art,
  Now rule in every heart,
  And ne'er from us depart,
    Spirit of power!

4 To the great One in Three,
  Eternal praises be,
    Hence evermore;
  His sovereign majesty,
  May we in glory see,
  And to eternity
    Love and adore.

Anon

220 Nicaea, 748

HOLY, holy, holy, Lord God Almighty!
  Early in the morning our song shall rise
    to thee;
Holy, holy, holy, merciful and mighty,
God in three persons, blessèd Trinity!

2 Holy, holy, holy; all the saints adore thee,
  Casting down their golden crowns around
    the glassy sea;
  Cherubim and seraphim falling down be-
    fore thee,
  Who wert, and art, and evermore shalt be!

3 Holy, holy, holy; though the darkness hide
    thee,
  Though the eye of sinful man thy glory
    may not see,
  Only thou art holy; there is none beside
    thee
  Perfect in power, in love and purity!

4 Holy, holy, holy, Lord God Almighty!
  All thy works shall praise thy name in
    earth and sky and sea;
  Holy, holy, holy, merciful and mighty,
  God in three persons, blessèd Trinity!

Reginald Heber (1783-1826)

221 Hosanna, 255; St Theodulph, 262
7.6.7.6. D. Iambic

O FATHER and Creator,
  Thou God of perfect love,
Come now in all thy fulness,
  Descending from above.
Thou gav'st thy Son to save me,
  To die that I might live;
I humbly kneel before thee,
  My all to thee I give.

2 O Christ, my soul's redeemer,
  Who gave thine all for me,
Thy blood was freely given
  That I might be set free.
Lord, teach me how to give thee
  My body, mind and will;
Then come with grace and beauty
  My emptied heart to fill.

3 O blessèd Holy Spirit,
  Revealer of the right,
I pray thee dwell within me,
  Make of my weakness might.
Within thy light, now streaming,
  The living way is shown;
Abide, O gentle Spirit,
  Till all thy truth I own.

Albert E. Chesham (1886-1971)

222 I Believe, 674

ON God's word relying,
  Every doubt defying,
Faith is heard replying;
  Praise God, I believe!

I believe in God the Father,
I believe in God the Son;
I believe in the Holy Spirit,
Blessèd Godhead, Three in One;
I believe in a full salvation,
In redemption through the blood;
I believe I'll receive a crown of life,
When I hear the Lord's: Well done.

2 Confidence unshaken;
  When bereft, forsaken,
  E'en if life be taken,
    Praise God, I believe!

3 Peace and joy unending
  In my soul are blending,
  Faith on love depending,
    Praise God, I believe!

Arnold Brown

223 Leoni, 717

THE God of Abraham praise,
  Who reigns enthroned above,
Ancient of everlasting days
  And God of love.
Jehovah, great I AM,
  By earth and Heaven confessed,
I bow and bless the sacred name
  Forever blest.

61

2   The God of Abraham praise,
At whose supreme command
From earth I rise, and seek the joys
  At his right hand.
I all on earth forsake,
Its wisdom, fame and power;
And him my only portion make,
  My shield and tower.

3   Before the Saviour's face
The ransomed nations bow,
O'erwhelmed at his almighty grace
  For ever new;
He shows his prints of love,
They kindle to a flame
And sound through all the worlds above:
  Worthy the Lamb.

4   He by himself hath sworn;
I on his oath depend;
I shall, on eagle's wings upborne,
  To Heaven ascend.
I shall behold his face,
I shall his powers adore,
And sing the wonders of his grace
  For evermore.

5   The whole triumphant host
Give thanks to God on high;
Hail Father, Son and Holy Ghost,
  They ever cry.
Hail Abraham's God and mine!
I join the heavenly lays;
All might and majesty are thine,
  And endless praise.

Thomas Olivers (1725-99)

224

Moscow, 217; Light, 216

6.6.4.6.6.6.4.

THOU, whose almighty word
  Chaos and darkness heard,
   And took their flight,
Hear us, we humbly pray,
And where the gospel day
Sheds not its glorious ray
  Let there be light!

2 Thou who didst come to bring
On thy redeeming wing
  Healing and sight,
Health to the sick in mind,
Sight to the inly blind,
O now to all mankind
  Let there be light!

3 Spirit of truth and love,
Life-giving, holy dove,
  Speed forth thy flight;
Move on the waters' face,
Bearing the lamp of grace,
And in earth's darkest place
  Let there be light!

4 Holy and blessèd Three,
Glorious Trinity,
  Wisdom, love, might,
Boundless as ocean tide
Rolling in fullest pride,
Through the world, far and wide,
  Let there be light!

John Marriott (1780-1825)

*   *   *

see also: 569 Eternal Father, strong to save
    870 We praise thee, heavenly Father
    871 What wondrous gifts are in my
    care

THE GOSPEL
Invitation

225

God is near thee, 656

AFAR from Heaven thy feet have
  wandered,
Afar from God thy soul has strayed;
His gifts in sin thy hand has squandered,
  Yet still in love he calls thee home.

God is near thee, tell thy story;
He will hear thy tale of sorrow,
God is near thee, and in mercy
He will welcome thy return.

2 Thy feet have found sin's way is thorny,
  Thy heart has found its pleasures vain,
Thou hast grown weary, and about thee
  The gloom has spread of dark despair.

3 The broken heart the Lord will favor,
  The contrite spirit he will bless;
He came to be the lost one's Saviour,
  He came to be the sinner's friend.

Invitation

4 Tell out thy need, and he'll befriend thee,
  Pour out thy heart's deep grief to him,
  His boundless love, unmeasured mercy,
  His free forgiveness are for thee.
                        Richard Slater (1854-1939)

226 Almost Persuaded, 606

ALMOST persuaded now to believe,
  Almost persuaded Christ to receive,
  Seems now some soul to say:
  Go, Spirit, go thy way,
  Some more convenient day
    On thee I'll call.

2 Almost persuaded, come, come today;
  Almost persuaded, turn not away.
    Jesus invites you here,
    Angels are lingering near,
    Prayers rise from hearts so dear,
      O wanderer, come.

3 Almost persuaded, harvest is past;
  Almost persuaded, doom comes at last.
    Almost cannot avail,
    Almost is sure to fail,
    Sad, sad, that bitter wail,
      Almost—but lost.
                        Philip Paul Bliss (1838-76)

227 Swing wide the door of your heart, 805

ARE you seeking joys that will not fade,
  Lasting pleasure, by God's mercy made?
Christ is waiting, fulness of joy he brings;
Swing wide the door of your heart to the
    King of kings.

*Swing wide the door of your heart to
    the King of kings,
Bid him welcome, for wonderful peace
    he brings,
He will shelter you under his
    outstretched wings;
Swing wide the door of your heart to
    the King of kings.*

2 Are you longing perfect peace to win?
  Turn to Jesus, bid him enter in;
  Peace is found but under his sheltering
    wings;
  Swing wide the door of your heart to the
    King of kings.

3 Now he calls you with his wondrous voice,
  Bid him welcome, make his will your
    choice;
  At his coming heavenly music rings;
  Swing wide the door of your heart to the
    King of kings.
                        Sidney Edward Cox (1887-1975)

228 Bullinger, 342; Stephanos, 343
                                        8.5.8.3.

ART thou weary, art thou languid,
  Art thou sore distressed?
Come to me, saith one, and coming
    Be at rest.

2 Hath he marks to lead me to him
    If he be my guide?
  In his feet and hands are wound-prints,
    And his side.

3 Hath he diadem as monarch
    That his brow adorns?
  Yea, a crown in very surety,
    But of thorns!

4 If I find him, if I follow,
    What my portion here?
  Many a sorrow, many a labor,
    Many a tear.

5 If I still hold closely to him,
    What hath he at last?
  Sorrow vanquished, labor ended,
    Jordan past.

6 If I ask him to receive me,
    Will he say me nay?
  Not till earth and not till Heaven
    Pass away.
                        John Mason Neale (1818-66)

229 Behold me standing at the door, 10;
        Calvary, 14   L.M.

BEHOLD me standing at the door,
  And hear me pleading evermore
With gentle voice: O heart of sin,
May I come in? May I come in?

*Behold me standing at the door,
And hear me pleading evermore:
Say, weary heart, oppressed with sin,
May I come in? May I come in?*

2 I bore the cruel thorns for thee,
  I waited long and patiently;
  Say, weary heart, oppressed with sin,
  May I come in? May I come in?

The Gospel

3 I would not plead with thee in vain;
Remember all my grief and pain;
I died to ransom thee from sin,
May I come in? May I come in?

4 I bring thee joy from Heaven above,
I bring thee pardon, peace and love;
Say, weary heart, oppressed with sin,
May I come in? May I come in?

Fanny Crosby (1820-1915)

230 Guide me, great Jehovah, 415;
Bithynia, 409   8.7.8.7.8.7. Troch.

BOUNDLESS as the mighty ocean,
Rolling on from pole to pole,
Is the boundless love of Jesus
To the weary sinful soul,
Boundless mercy,
Making guilty sinners whole.

2 Boundless as the starry heavens,
Filled with fiery orbs of light,
Are the promises of Jesus
For the soul in nature's night,
Ever shining
Till our faith is changed to sight.

3 Boundless as eternal ages,
As the air we breathe as free,
Is the boundless, full salvation
Jesus purchased on the tree,
Boundless cleansing
From all sin's impurity.

4 Boundless is the grace to save us
From the guilt and power of sin;
Boundless is his power to keep us
Now and every instant clean.
Boundless praises
We our glorious Lord will bring.

Josiah Henry Waller (1865-1938)

231 Only trust him, 120; Evan, 85
C.M.

COME, every soul by sin oppressed,
There's mercy with the Lord,
And he will surely give you rest
By trusting in his word.

Only trust him, only trust him,
Only trust him now!
He will save you, he will save you,
He will save you now!

2 For Jesus shed his precious blood
Rich blessings to bestow;
Plunge now into the crimson flood
That washes white as snow.

3 Yes, Jesus is the truth, the way,
That leads you into rest;
Believe on him without delay
And you are fully blest.

John Hart Stockton (1813-77)

232 Come, O come with me, 632

COME, O come with me where love is
beaming,
Come, O come with me where light is
streaming,
Light and love divine, in Christ revealing
God himself to you and me.

Hallelujah, hallelujah, I love thee, my
Saviour,
Hallelujah, hallelujah, I'll trust but in
thee!

2 Come with all thy sins, although like a
mountain;
Come unto the cross, from whence a
fountain
Flows divinely clear to heal the nations;
Come and wash and make you clean.

3 None can be too vile for love so beaming,
None can be too dark for light so
streaming,
Christ can make you whole through faith
believing,
His salvation give to you.

Anon

233 The Lion of Judah, 573;
The Conquering Saviour, 572
11.11.11.11.

COME, sinners, to Jesus, no longer delay;
A free, full salvation is offered today;
Arise, all ye bondslaves, awake from your
dream;
Believe, and the light and the glory shall
stream.

For the Lion of Judah shall break every
chain,
And give you the victory again and
again.

2 The world will oppose you and Satan will
rage,
To hinder your coming they both will
engage;
But Jesus, your Saviour, hath conquered
for you
And he will assist you to conquer them
too.

Invitation

3 Though rough be the fighting and trou-
　bles arise,
There are mansions of glory prepared in
　the skies;
A crown and a kingdom you shortly shall
　view,
The laurels of victory are waiting for you.
　　　　　　　William Jefferson (1806-70)

234　Harton-Lea, 20; Boston, 13　L.M.

COME, sinners, to the gospel feast,
　Let every soul be Jesus' guest;
Ye need not one be left behind,
For God hath bidden all mankind.

2 Sent by my Lord, on you I call;
The invitation is to all;
Come, all the world; come, sinner, thou!
All things in Christ are ready now.

3 This message as from God receive,
Ye all may come to Christ, and live;
O let his love your hearts constrain,
Nor suffer him to die in vain.

4 His love is mighty to compel;
His conquering love consent to feel;
Yield to his love's constraining power,
And fight against your God no more.
　　　　　　　Charles Wesley (1707-88)

235　Make no delay, 730

COME to the Saviour, make no delay,
　Here in his word he's shown us the way;
Here in our midst he's standing today,
　Tenderly saying: Come!

Joyful, joyful will the meeting be,
When from sin our hearts are pure and
　free,
And we shall gather, Saviour, with thee
　In our eternal home.

2 Come to the Saviour! O hear his voice!
Let every heart leap forth and rejoice,
And let us freely make him our choice;
　Do not delay, but come.

3 Think once again, he's with us today;
Heed now his blest commands, and obey;
Hear now his accents tenderly say:
　Come to your Saviour, come.
　　　　　　　George Frederick Root (1820-95)

236　Come, ye disconsolate, 634

COME, ye disconsolate, where'er ye
　languish,
Come, at the mercy seat fervently kneel;
Here bring your wounded hearts, here tell
　your anguish,
Earth has no sorrow that Heaven can-
　not heal.

2 Joy of the desolate, light of the straying,
Hope of the penitent, advocate sure;
Here speaks the Comforter, tenderly
　saying,
Earth has no sorrow that Heaven can-
　not cure.

3 Here waits the Saviour, gentle and loving,
Ready to meet you, his grace to reveal;
On him your burden cast, trustfully
　coming;
Earth has no sorrow that Heaven can-
　not heal.
　　　　　　　Thomas Moore (1779-1852), alt

237　The wounds of Christ, 575

DARK shadows were falling,
　My spirit appalling,
For hid in my heart sin's deep crimson
　stains lay;
And when I was weeping,
The past o'er me creeping,
I heard of the blood which can wash sin
　away.

The wounds of Christ are open,
　Sinner, they were made for thee;
The wounds of Christ are open,
　There for refuge flee.

2 It soothes all life's sorrows,
It smooths all its furrows,
It binds up the wounds which transgres-
　sion has made;
It turns night to morning,
So truly adorning
The spirit with joy when all other lights
　fade.

3 Come, cast in thy sorrow,
Wait not till tomorrow,
Life's evening is closing, the death-bell will
　toll;
His blood for thee streaming,
His grace so redeeming,
His love intervening will pardon thy soul.
　　　　　　　Evangeline Booth (1865-1950)

65

238 Someone Cares, 792

DO you sometimes feel that no one truly
    knows you,
  And that no one understands or really
    cares?
Through his people, God himself is close
    beside you,
  And through them he plans to answer
    all your prayers.

Someone cares, someone cares,
  Someone knows your deepest need,
    your burden shares;
Someone cares, someone cares,
  God himself will hear the whisper of
    your prayers.

2 Ours is not a distant God, remote,
    unfeeling,
  Who is careless of our loneliness and
    pain,
Through the ministry of men he gives his
    healing,
  In their dedicated hands brings hope
    again.

John Gowans

239 Cwm Rhondda, 414; Face to face, 370
8.7.8.7.8.7. Troch.

HARK! the gospel news is sounding,
  Christ has suffered on the tree;
Streams of mercy are abounding,
  Grace for all is rich and free;
    Now poor sinner,
  Look to him who died for thee.

2 O escape to yonder mountain,
  Refuge find in him today!
Christ invites you to the fountain,
  Come and wash your sins away;
    Do not tarry,
  Come to Jesus while you may.

3 Grace is flowing like a river,
  Millions there have been supplied;
Still it flows as fresh as ever
  From the Saviour's wounded side;
    None need perish,
  All may live for Christ hath died.

4 Christ alone shall be our portion;
  Soon we hope to meet above;
Then we'll bathe in the full ocean
  Of the great redeemer's love;
    All his fulness
  We shall then for ever prove.

Hugh Bourne (1772-1852),
William Sanders (1799-1882)

240 Take Salvation, 426; Mariners, 421
8.7.8.7.8.7. Troch.

HARK! the voice of Jesus calling:
  Come, ye guilty, come to me;
I have rest and peace to offer,
  Rest, thou laboring one, for thee.
    Take salvation,
  Take it now and happy be.

2 Yes, though high in heavenly glory,
  Still the Saviour calls to thee;
Faith can hear his invitation,
  Come, ye laden, come to me,
    Take salvation,
  Take it now and happy be.

3 Soon that voice will cease its calling,
  Now it speaks, and speaks to thee;
Sinner, heed the gracious message,
  To the blood for refuge flee.
    Take salvation,
  Take it now and happy be.

4 Life is found alone in Jesus,
  Only there 'tis offered thee,
Offered without price or money,
  'Tis the gift of God, sent free.
    Take salvation,
  Take it now and happy be.

Albert Midlane (1825-1909)

241 Room for Jesus, 395; Bethany, 429
8.7.8.7. Troch.

HAVE you any room for Jesus,
  He who bore your load of sin?
As he knocks and asks admission,
  Sinner, will you let him in?

Room for Jesus, King of Glory!
Hasten now, his word obey!
Swing your heart's door widely open,
Bid him enter while you may.

2 Room for pleasure, room for business,
  But for Christ, the crucified,
Not a place that he can enter
  In the heart for which he died.

3 Have you any time for Jesus,
  As in grace he calls again?
O today is time accepted,
  Tomorrow you may call in vain.

4 Room and time now give to Jesus,
  Soon will pass God's day of grace;
Soon your heart be cold and silent,
  And your Saviour's pleading cease.

Daniel Webster Whittle (1840-1901)

Invitation

242
Shall we meet? 399; Walk with me, 405
8.7.8.7. Troch.

HAVE you heard the angels singing:
  Christ is risen from the grave?
Have you heard the message ringing:
  Jesus lives to help and save?

Jesus died, O wondrous love!
Jesus died, O wondrous love!
Rose again to bring us freedom,
  Lives to plead our cause above.

2 Have you felt the love he bore you
    When he fought for your release,
  When he trod the way before you,
    Opening thus the paths of peace?

3 Have you heard him interceding
    With his Father for your sin,
  Sorrow, self and shame unheeding
    That his death your life might win?

4 Have you seen the sacred beauty
    Shining from his suffering face,
  Who, in love and not in duty,
    Held our sorrows in embrace?

5 Will you bow your soul before him,
    Will you cast on him your care,
  By your sacrifice adore him
    And as conqueror meet him there?
                        Cornelie Booth (1864-1920)

243
There is a happy land, 235
7.4.7.4.7.7.7.4.

HAVE you seen the crucified?
  O wondrous love!
Do you know for all he died?
  O wondrous love!
Have you seen his thorn-crowned brow?
Have you felt the crimson flow?
Do you his salvation know?
  O wondrous love!

2 Do you know your sins forgiven?
    O wondrous love!
  Have you had a taste of Heaven?
    O wondrous love!
  Has his love cast out your fears?
  Has he wiped away your tears?
  At his word Hell disappears;
    O wondrous love!

3 Is your heart now full of joy?
    O wondrous love!
  Have you peace naught can destroy?
    O wondrous love!

Is not this salvation grand?
May it spread on every hand
E'en to the most distant land;
  O wondrous love!

4 To the north, south, east and west,
    O wondrous love!

  Some have heard, but tell the rest;
    O wondrous love!
  Vast the curse and great the fall,
  Jesus Christ has died for all,
  We will every nation call;
    O wondrous love!
                        John Lawley (1859-1922)

244
If you want it—it's yours, 683

IN your heart of hearts are you a trifle
    weary,
Is there part of you your better self
    deplores?
Do you want the power to be a better
    person?
  If you want it—it's yours!

If you want it—it's yours!
If you want it—it's yours!
Do you want the power to be a better
    person?
If you want it—it's yours!

2 Is your mind mixed up and are your
      thoughts in turmoil?
    Are you tired of fighting, are you sick of
      wars?
  Would you like some peace instead of in-
      ner conflict?
    If you want it—it's yours!

3 Are you somewhat sad and wish that you
      were happy?
    Real contentment has a special set of
      laws;
  Joy is not for sale, it's only found in Jesus;
    If you want it—it's yours!
                        John Gowans

245
Is it nothing to you? 582
12.9.12.9.

IS it nothing to you that one day Jesus
    came
  All our sorrow and suffering to share?
He came as the light of new hope for a
    world
  In the day of its darkest despair.

The Gospel

Is it nothing to you that his cross
    speaks our shame?
*Is it nothing to you, for whose
    cleansing he came,*
*That our guilt made his Calvary and
    pierced his hands through?*
*Is it nothing to you? Is it nothing,
    nothing to you?*

2 Is it nothing to you that one day Jesus
    gave,
Gave in love of his measureless all?
So richly he poured out his limitless life
When he answered our pitiful call.

3 Is it nothing to you that one day Jesus
    died,
    That men mocked him and, heedless,
    passed by?
No sorrow was e'er like the sorrow he bore
    When they scorned him and left him to
    die.

4 Is it nothing to you that today Jesus
    saves?
    Though we stand all condemned before
    God
He carries our sin on his own loving heart,
And he saves by his pardoning blood.

Albert E. Mingay

246   All your anxiety, 605

IS there a heart o'erbound by sorrow?
    Is there a life weighed down by care?
Come to the cross, each burden bearing,
    All your anxiety, leave it there.

All your anxiety, all your care,
    *Bring to the mercy seat, leave it
    there,*
Never a burden he cannot bear,
    Never a friend like Jesus.

2 No other friend so keen to help you;
    No other friend so quick to hear;
No other place to leave your burden;
    No other one to hear your prayer.

3 Come, then, at once; delay no longer;
    Heed his entreaty, kind and sweet;
You need not fear a disappointment;
    You shall find peace at the mercy seat.

Edward Henry Joy (1871-1949)

247   Jesus is looking for thee, 457; Tell me the story of Jesus, 458

8.7.8.7. D. Dact.

IS there a heart that is waiting,
    Longing for pardon today?
Hear the glad message proclaiming
    Jesus is passing this way.
Is there a heart that has wandered?
    Come with thy burden today;
Mercy is tenderly pleading,
    Jesus is passing this way.

Jesus is looking for thee,
Jesus is looking for thee,
Sweet is the message today,
    Jesus is looking for thee.

2 Is there a heart that is broken,
    Weary and sighing for rest?
Come to the Saviour who offers
    Peace to the sad and oppressed.
Come to thy only redeemer,
    Come to his infinite love,
Come to the gate that is leading
    Homeward to mansions above.

Annie L. James (verses),
May Agnew Stephens (chorus)

248   Jesus is calling, 700

JESUS is tenderly calling thee home,
    Calling today, calling today!
Why from the sunshine of love wilt thou
    roam
    Farther and farther away?

Calling today, calling today!
    *Jesus is calling, is tenderly calling
    today!*

2 Jesus is calling the weary to rest,
    Calling today, calling today!
Bring him thy burden and thou shalt be
    blest;
    He will not turn thee away.

3 Jesus is waiting, O come to him now,
    Waiting today, waiting today!
Come with thy sins, at his feet lowly bow;
    Come, and no longer delay!

4 Jesus is pleading, O list to his voice,
    Hear him today, hear him today!
They who believe on his name shall
    rejoice;
    Quickly arise and away.

Fanny Crosby (1820-1915)

Invitation

249
Mighty to save, 734

JOYFUL news to all mankind,
　Jesus is mighty to save!
All who seek shall surely find
　Jesus is mighty to save!
Sinners may relinquish wrong,
Faltering hearts may now be strong;
Sound the tidings right along:
　Jesus is mighty to save!

Jesus is mighty to save!
Jesus is mighty to save!
From the uttermost, to the uttermost,
　Mighty to save!

2 Though as scarlet be the stains,
　　Jesus is mighty to save!
Though as steel the binding chains,
　　Jesus is mighty to save!
His the glorious sacrifice,
His the blood which paid the price,
His the love doth now entice;
　　Jesus is mighty to save!

3 Fearful soul discard thy fears,
　　Jesus is mighty to save!
Seeker haste to dry those tears,
　　Jesus is mighty to save!
With assurance seek his face,
Doubt no more his love and grace,
Give him now his rightful place;
　　Jesus is mighty to save!

4 Since his blood for thee was shed,
　　Jesus is mighty to save!
Since he lives who once was dead,
　　Jesus is mighty to save!
While in conflict we engage,
When the storms around shall rage,
All our earthly pilgrimage,
　　Jesus is mighty to save!
　　　　Charles Coller (1863-1935)

250
While he's waiting, 855

LOVE of love so wondrous,
　Rich and free,
Now the King of Glory
　A pardon offers thee.

While he's waiting, pleading, knocking,
　Let him in.

2 For thy heart he's waited,
　Days and years;
And thy sins, long hated,
　Have caused him bitter tears.

3 Canst thou leave his pardon
　Still unknown,
And forget the mercy
　That unto thee he's shown?

4 Soon the day is coming
　When, alone,
Trembling or rejoicing,
　Thou must his kingship own.

5 Ah! his love, unchanging,
　Calls thee home,
And the gathering shadows
　Bid thee no longer roam.
　　　Herbert Howard Booth (1862-1926)

251
Confidence, 15; Why not tonight? 59
L.M.

O DO not let thy Lord depart,
　And close thine eyes against the light;
Poor sinner, harden not thy heart;
　Thou wouldst be saved, why not
　　tonight?

2 Tomorrow's sun may never rise
　To bless thy long deluded sight;
This is the time, O then, be wise;
　Thou wouldst be saved, why not
　　tonight?

3 Our God in pity lingers still;
　O wilt thou thus his love requite?
Renounce at length thy stubborn will;
　Thou wouldst be saved, why not
　　tonight?

4 Our blessèd Lord refuses none
　Who would to him their souls unite;
Then be the work of grace begun;
　Thou wouldst be saved, why not
　　tonight?
　　　　　Eliza Reed (1794-1867)

252
The Beautiful Stream, 812

O HAVE you not heard of the beautiful
　　stream
　That flows through our Father's land?
Its waters gleam bright in the heavenly
　　light
　And ripple o'er golden sand.

O seek that beautiful stream,
Seek now that beautiful stream!
Its waters so free are flowing for thee;
O seek that beautiful stream!

The Gospel

2 Its fountains are deep, and its waters are
      pure
   And sweet to the weary soul;
   It flows from the throne of Jehovah alone,
   O come where its bright waves roll!

3 This beautiful stream is the river of life,
   It flows for all nations free.
   A balm for each wound in its waters is
      found;
   O sinner, it flows for thee.
                        Richard T. Torrey, Jr.

253 Mercy still for thee, 155
                                        D.C.M.

O WANDERER, knowing not the smile
   Of Jesus' lovely face,
In darkness living all the while,
   Rejecting offered grace;
To thee Jehovah's voice doth sound,
   Thy soul he waits to free;
Thy Saviour hath a ransom found,
   There's mercy still for thee!

   There's mercy still for thee,
   There's mercy still for thee;
   Poor trembling soul, he'll make thee
      whole,
   There's mercy still for thee!

2 For thee, though sunk in deep despair,
   Thy Saviour's blood was shed;
He for thy sins was as a lamb
   To cruel slaughter led,
That thou mayst find, poor sin-sick soul,
   A pardon full and free;
What boundless grace, what wondrous
      love,
   There's mercy still for thee!

3 Though sins of years rise mountains high
   And would thy hopes destroy,
Thy Saviour's blood can wash away
   The stains, and bring thee joy.
Now lift thy heart in earnest prayer,
   To him for safety flee,
While still the angels chant the strain:
   There's mercy still for thee!
                   Herbert Howard Booth (1862-1926)

254 Colne, 79; Amazing Grace! 70
                                        C.M.

O WHAT amazing words of grace
   Are in the gospel found,
Suited to every sinner's case
   Who hears the joyful sound!

2 Poor, sinful, thirsting, fainting souls
   Are freely welcome here;
Salvation like a river rolls
   Abundant, free and clear.

3 This spring with living water flows
   And heavenly joy imparts;
Come, thirsty souls, your wants disclose
   And drink with thankful hearts.

4 Come then, with all your wants and
      wounds,
   Your every burden bring;
Here love, unchanging love, abounds,
   A deep celestial spring.
                        Samuel Medley (1738-99)

255 Only a step, 764

ONLY a step to Jesus!
   Then why not take it now?
Come, and thy sin confessing,
   To him, thy Saviour bow.

   Only a step, only a step! Come, he
      waits for thee;
   Come, and thy sin confessing,
   Thou shalt receive a blessing,
   Do not reject the mercy he freely offers
      thee!

2 Only a step to Jesus!
   Believe, and thou shalt live;
Lovingly now he's waiting
   And ready to forgive.

3 Only a step to Jesus!
   A step from sin to grace;
What has thy heart decided?
   The moments fly apace.

4 Only a step to Jesus!
   O why not come and say:
Gladly to thee, my Saviour,
   I give myself away!
                        Fanny Crosby (1820-1915)

256 Lover of the Lord, 109; Abridge, 69
                                        C.M.

RETURN, O wanderer, return,
   And seek thy Father's face;
Those new desires which in thee burn
   Were kindled by his grace.

   O you must be a lover of the Lord,
   Or you can't go to Heaven when you
      die!

Invitation

2 Return, O wanderer, return,
  He hears thy humble sigh;
He sees thy softened spirit mourn
  When no one else is nigh.

3 Return, O wanderer, return,
  Thy Saviour bids thee live;
Come to his cross, and grateful learn
  How freely he'll forgive.
  William Bengo Collyer (1782-1854) (verses)

257 I know a fount, 545

SAY, are you weary? Are you heavy laden?
  Burdened with sorrow, weighted down
  with care?
Are you in bondage? Do you want
  deliverance?
  Come, then, with me, there is refuge from
  despair.

I know a fount where sins are washed
  away,
I know a place where night is turned
  to day;
Burdens are lifted, blind eyes made to
  see;
There's a wonder-working power in the
  blood of Calvary.

2 Are you still doubting power to keep from
  sinning,
  Power that can change the heart and
  make it new?
Are you still longing for a full salvation?
  You may receive it and live a life that's
  true.

3 Fettered and bound by chains of self-
  indulgence,
  Missing the blessings God on man
  bestows,
Seeking for joy but only sorrow finding?
  Come to the waters where grace and
  mercy flow.

4 Wondrous Deliverer! Sin-forgiving
  Saviour!
  Cleanser of hearts! Unfailing friend and
  guide!
No one has ever trusted unavailing,
  No one has claimed of his love and been
  denied.
  Oliver Cooke (1873-1945)

258 Wonderful words of life, 867

SING them over again to me,
  Wonderful words of life;
Let me more of their beauty see,
  Wonderful words of life.
  Words of life and beauty,
  Teach me faith and duty.

Beautiful words! Wonderful words!
Wonderful words of life!

2 Christ, the blessed one, gives to all
  Wonderful words of life;
Sinner, list to the loving call,
  Wonderful words of life.
  All so freely given,
  Wooing us to Heaven.

3 Sweetly echo the Saviour's call,
  Wonderful words of life;
Offer pardon and peace to all,
  Wonderful words of life.
  Jesus, only Saviour,
  Saves and keeps for ever.
  Philip Paul Bliss (1838-76)

259 O be saved, 390
8.7.8.7. Troch.

SINNER, how thy heart is troubled!
  God is coming very near;
Do not hide thy deep emotion,
  Do not check that falling tear.

O be saved, his grace is free!
O be saved, he died for thee!
O be saved, he died for thee!

2 Jesus now is bending o'er thee,
  Jesus lowly, meek and mild;
To the friend who died to save thee
  Wilt thou not be reconciled?

3 With a lowly, contrite spirit,
  Kneeling at the Saviour's feet,
Thou canst feel this very moment
  Pardon, precious, sure, complete.

4 Let the angels bear the tidings
  Upward to the courts of Heaven;
Let them sing with holy rapture
  O'er another soul forgiven.
  Fanny Crosby (1820-1915)

71

The Gospel

260 Sinner, see yon light, 788

SINNER, see yon light
    Shining clear and bright
From the cross of Calvary
Where the Saviour died,
And from his side
    Flowed the blood that sets us free.

Come away, come away,
    To the cross for refuge flee;
See the Saviour stands
With his outstretched hands;
    Salvation he offers to thee.

2 See, the Saviour stands
    With his wounded hands,
And he calls aloud to thee:
I for thee life gave,
Thy soul to save,
    Now thy heart O give to me!

3 Come away to him
And confess thy sin,
    Come to him who died for thee;
To his feet draw near,
With heart sincere,
    And from sin he'll set thee free.
James Conner Bateman (1854-88)

261 At the cross there's room, 236
    7.5.7.5.7.7.7.5.

SINNER, wheresoe'er thou art,
    At the cross there's room;
Tell the burden of thy heart,
    At the cross there's room.
Tell it in thy Saviour's ear,
Cast away thy every fear,
Only speak, and he will hear,
    At the cross there's room.

2 Haste thee, wanderer, tarry not,
    At the cross there's room;
Seek that consecrated spot,
    At the cross there's room.
Heavy laden, sore oppressed,
Love can soothe thy troubled breast,
In the Saviour find thy rest,
    At the cross there's room.

3 Thoughtless sinner, come today,
    At the cross there's room;
Hark! the bride and Spirit say,
    At the cross there's room.
Now a living fountain see
Opened there for thee and me,
Rich and poor, for bond and free,
    At the cross there's room.

4 Blessèd thought! For everyone
    At the cross there's room;
Love's atoning work is done,
    At the cross there's room.
Streams of boundless mercy flow
Free to all who thither go,
O that all the world might know,
    At the cross there's room.
Fanny Crosby (1820-1915)

262 Christ receiveth sinful men, 277
    7.7.7.7.

SINNERS Jesus will receive;
    Sound this word of grace to all
Who the heavenly pathway leave,
    All who linger, all who fall.

Sing it o'er and o'er again,
    Christ receiveth sinful men;
Make the message clear and plain,
    Christ receiveth sinful men.

2 Come, and he will give you rest;
    Trust him, for his word is plain;
He will take the sinfulest;
    Christ receiveth sinful men.

3 Christ receiveth sinful men,
    Even me with all my sin;
Purged from every spot and stain,
    Heaven with him I enter in.
Erdmann Neumeister (1671-1756),
trs Emma Frances Bevan (1827-1909) (verses),
    alt

263 Hiding in thee, 560; Go, bury thy
    sorrow, 559   11.11.11.11.

SO near to the Kingdom! yet what dost
        thou lack?
So near to the Kingdom! what keepeth
        thee back?
Renounce every idol, though dear it may
        be,
And come to the Saviour now pleading
        with thee!

Calling for thee, calling for thee,
The Saviour is calling, is calling for
        thee.

2 So near, that thou hearest the songs that
        resound
From those who, believing, a pardon have
        found;
So near, yet unwilling to give up thy sin,
When Jesus is waiting to welcome thee
        in.

Invitation

3 To die with no hope! hast thou counted
the cost?
To die out of Christ, and thy soul to be
lost?
So near to the Kingdom! O come, we
implore,
While Jesus is pleading, come enter the
door!
Fanny Crosby (1820-1915)

264 Come Home! 631

SOFTLY and tenderly Jesus is calling,
Calling for you and for me!
Patiently Jesus is waiting and watching,
Watching for you and for me!

Come home, come home!
Ye who are weary, come home!
Earnestly, tenderly, Jesus is calling,
Calling, O sinner, come home!

2 Why should we tarry when Jesus is
pleading,
Pleading for you and for me?
Why should we linger and heed not his
mercies,
Mercies for you and for me?

3 O for the wonderful love he has promised,
Promised for you and for me!
Though we have sinned, he has mercy and
pardon,
Pardon for you and for me!
Will Lamartine Thompson (1847-1909)

265 St Oswald, 396; Jesus, tender shepherd, 384
8.7.8.7. Troch.

SOULS of men! why will ye scatter
Like a crowd of frightened sheep?
Foolish hearts! why will ye wander
From a love so true and deep?

2 Was there ever kindest shepherd
Half so gentle, half so sweet,
As the Saviour who would have us
Come and gather round his feet?

3 There's a wideness in God's mercy
Like the wideness of the sea;
There's a kindness in his justice
Which is more than liberty.

4 There is welcome for the sinner,
And more graces for the good;
There is mercy with the Saviour;
There is healing in his blood.

5 But we make his love too narrow
By false limits of our own;
And we lose the tender shepherd
In the judge upon the throne.

6 For the love of God is broader
Than the measure of man's mind;
And the heart of the eternal
Is most wonderfully kind.
Frederick William Faber (1814-63)

266 Ten thousand souls, 158; The Judgment Day, 138
C.M.

TEN thousand thousand souls there are
Entered within the door;
These countless souls are gathered in,
And yet there's room for more.

Then come, O come, and go with me,
Where pleasure never dies;
And you shall gain the crown of life,
The soul's eternal prize.

2 Room for the lame, the halt, the blind;
Sinner, there's room for thee;
'Twas Christ made room for such poor
souls
By dying on the tree.

3 Room for the chief of sinners still,
Though plagued with unbelief;
That very Christ can save thy soul
Who saved the dying thief.

4 Then sure I am there's room for me,
The worst of Adam's race;
And so I'll sing in songs of praise,
A sinner saved by grace.
Daniel Herbert (1751-1833) (verses), alt

267 St Matthew, 157; Ellacombe, 147
D.C.M.

THE heart that once has Jesus known
And turned away again,
Finds soon the joys of sin are flown
Though sharp the sting remain.
The soul that once has walked with him,
Then left his guiding light,
Can only find earth's glitter dim,
Its promise quenched in night.

73

2 In vain you strive to drown the thought
   Of what you might have been;
Earth's pleasures are too dearly bought,
   Its sorrows all too keen!
Backslider, hear! God speaks your name,
   It is not yet too late;
The Lord in mercy tarries yet,
   He has not closed the gate.

3 We do believe that Jesus can
   Restore his work in you.
His touch will full salvation give;
   He maketh all things new.
O rise at once! delay no more,
   Nor hesitate, nor doubt,
If you but leave your sin and come,
   He will not cast you out.
Mildred Blanche Duff (1860-1932)

268 Better World, 331; Zealley, 338
8.3.8.3.8.8.8.3.

THERE is a better world, they say,
   O so bright!
Where sin and woe are done away,
   O so bright!
And music fills the balmy air,
And angels with bright wings are there,
And harps of gold and mansions fair,
   O so bright!

2 No clouds e'er pass along that sky,
   Happy land!
No tear-drops glisten in the eye,
   Happy land!
They drink the gushing streams of grace,
And gaze upon the Saviour's face
Whose brightness fills the holy place;
   Happy land!

3 And wicked things and beasts of prey
   Come not there!
And ruthless death and fierce decay
   Come not there!
There all are holy, all are good;
But hearts unwashed in Jesus' blood,
And guilty sinners unrenewed,
   Come not there!

4 And though we're sinners every one,
   Jesus died!
And though our crown of peace is gone,
   Jesus died!
We may be cleansed from every stain,
We may be crowned with bliss again,
And in that land of Glory reign;
   Jesus died!
John Lyth (1821-86)

269 Stella, 503; St Matthias, 500
8.8.8.8.8.8. Iambic

THERE is a mercy seat revealed,
   A glorious throne of sovereign grace,
Where broken hearts may all be healed
   And truly feel love's warm embrace.
O trembling soul, dispel thy fear,
By faith through Christ to God draw near.

2 The smoking flax God will not quench,
   Nor will he break the bruisèd reed;
His justice and his love do blend
   When guilty souls for mercy plead.
Come, sinner and backslider, fall
Before his throne, for pardon call.

3 Tears of repentance will not save,
   Nor yet good works for sin atone;
The sacrifice that Jesus gave
   Must be thy plea, and that alone.
No other name, however high,
Can bring thy soul to Heaven nigh.
Arthur Robert Gibby (c 1862-1932)

270 There is a message, 829

THERE is a message, a simple message,
   And it's a message for us all;
There is a Saviour, and what a Saviour!
   There is a Saviour for us all.

*Let's look at Jesus, for he's the
   Saviour,
And he will answer when we call;
Let's look at Jesus, for he's the
   Saviour,
Yes, he's the Saviour for us all.*

2 If you want pardon, then ask for pardon,
   And God's own pardon shall be yours;
For those who seek him are sure to find
   him,
And none who seek him Christ ignores.

3 Though you have failed him, and how
   you've failed him!
Though you have failed him, God loves
   you;
The proof is Jesus, so look at Jesus,
And learn from Jesus God loves you.
John Gowans

Invitation

271

Life for a look, 583

12.9.12.9.

THERE is life for a look at the crucified
one,
There is life at this moment for thee;
Then look, sinner, look unto him and be
saved,
Unto him who was nailed to the tree.

Look, look, look and live;
There is life for a look at the crucified
one,
There is life at this moment for thee.

2 O why was he there as the bearer of sin,
If on Jesus thy sins were not laid?
O why from his side flowed the sin-cleans-
ing blood,
If his dying thy debt had not paid?

3 It is not thy tears of repentance or prayers,
But the blood that atones for the soul;
On him then,who shed it thou mayest at
once
Thy weight of iniquities roll.

4 Then take with rejoicing from Jesus at
once
The life everlasting he gives;
And know, with assurance, thou need'st
never die
Since Jesus, thy righteousness, lives.
Anna Matilda Hull (c 1812-82)

272

Though your sins be as scarlet, 836

THOUGH your sins be as scarlet,
They shall be as white as snow;
Though they be red like crimson,
They shall be as wool.

2 Hear a voice that entreats you,
O return ye unto God!
He is of great compassion
And of wondrous love.

3 He'll forgive your transgressions
And remember them no more.
Look unto me, ye people,
Saith the Lord your God.
Fanny Crosby (1820-1915)

273

For you I am praying, 648

WE have a message, a message from
Jesus,
And time is now speeding, the mo-
ments are few;

The Master is come, O make haste to receive him,
For sinners he waits; he is calling for
you!

For you he is calling, for you he is
calling,
Yes, Jesus is calling, is calling for you.

2 We have a message, a message from Jesus,
A message of hope to the weary of heart;
The love of my Saviour, there's nothing so
precious,
The friendship of Jesus will never
depart.

3 We have a message, a message from Jesus,
A message of love to the poor sinbound
soul;
The love of my Jesus will snap every fetter,
The blood of my Saviour makes per-
fectly whole.

4 We have a message, a message from Jesus:
O do not reject him and forfeit your soul!
The Saviour invites you just now to re-
ceive him,
And in his great love to be made fully
whole.
Rebecca Rhoda Couch (c 1856-1946)

274

He came to give us life, 662

HE came to give us life in all its fullness,
He came to make the blind to see,
He came to banish death and doubt
and darkness,
He came to set his people free.
He liberating love imparted,
He taught men once again to smile;
He came to bind the broken hearted,
And God and man to reconcile.
He came to give us life in all its
fullness,
He came to make the blind to see,
He came to banish death and doubt
and darkness,
He came to set his people free.

(He came to set us free!)
[last chorus only]

1 We wonder why Christ came into the world
A helpless, homeless child;
We wonder why he tolerated men,
The tainted and defiled.
We wonder why! We wonder why!
The Son of God as man came down;
What does this signify?

The Gospel

2 We wonder why Christ came into the world
And let men hurt him so,
We wonder why the Christ should have to
die,
Does anybody know?
We wonder why! We wonder why!
The Son of God as man came down,
What does this signify?

John Gowans

275 We're traveling home, 336; Zealley, 338
8.3.8.3.8.8.8.3.

WE'RE traveling home to Heaven above,
Will you go?
To sing the Saviour's dying love,
Will you go?
Millions have reached that blissful shore,
Their trials and their labors o'er,
And yet there's room for millions more,
Will you go?

2 We're going to see the bleeding Lamb,
Will you go?
In rapturous songs to praise his name,
Will you go?
Our sun will then no more go down,
Our moon no more will be withdrawn,
Our days of mourning ever gone,
Will you go?

3 The way to Heaven is straight and plain,
Will you go?
Repent, believe, be born again,
Will you go?
The Saviour cries aloud to thee:
Take up thy cross and follow me,
And thou shalt my salvation see,
Will you go?

4 O could I hear some sinner say:
I will go!
I'll start this moment, clear the way,
Let me go!
My old companions, fare you well,
I will not go with you to Hell,
I mean with Jesus Christ to dwell,
I will go!

Richard Jukes (1804-67)

276 O Remember, 755

WHAT is the love of Jesus to thee?
Art thou its claims denying?
Dost thou e'er think how he on the tree
Gained thy salvation by dying?

*O remember, O remember
All a loving Saviour bore for thee!
O remember, O remember
Jesus dying on the tree!*

2 What is the call of Jesus to thee?
Say, is thy heart replying?
Henceforth is he thy Master to be?
Wilt thou as rebel defy him?

3 What is his grace, O sinner, to thee?
O 'tis of thanks deserving,
Waiting so long thy soul to set free,
Love in its purpose ne'er swerving.

4 What is the name of Jesus to thee?
Art thou his fame extending?
Dost thou obey? He says: Follow me,
Life in my service be spending.

Richard Slater (1854-1939)

277 Mercy still for thee, 155;
Land of pure delight, 154   D.C.M.

WHO comes to me, the Saviour said,
To him I freely give
Eternal life; though he were dead
Yet henceforth shall he live.
His life shall be with gladness filled,
His treasure is on high,
Bright sunshine shall his pathway gild
And he shall never die.

*The Saviour now will give,
The Saviour now will give,
Eternal life to all who seek,
The Saviour now will give.*

2 Who comes to me, the Saviour said,
That soul will I supply
With portions of that living bread
Which riches cannot buy.
That soul shall never hunger more,
But filled shall ever be
With plenty from the unfailing store
He ever finds in me.

3 Who comes to me, the Saviour said,
Shall constantly partake
The stream that from the fountain-head
Alone his thirst can slake.
Who seeks in faith that fountain pure,
His freshness shall retain,
Shall peace and happiness ensure
And never thirst again.

Invitation

4 Who comes to me, the Saviour said,
　And follows where I lead,
Shall see my light upon him shed
　And in my pastures feed.
No more shall darkness cloud his way,
　My love his fear shall quell,
The gloom that once obscured his day
　My presence shall dispel.
William Kitching (1837-1906)

2 Whosoever cometh need not delay;
　Now the door is open, enter while you may;
　Jesus is the true, the only living way;
　　Whosoever will may come.

3 Whosoever will, the promise is secure;
　Whosoever will, for ever shall endure;
　Whosoever will, 'tis life for evermore;
　　Whosoever will may come.
Philip Paul Bliss (1838-76)

278 Who'll be the next? 859

WHO'LL be the next to follow Jesus?
　Who'll be the next his cross to bear?
Someone is ready, someone is waiting;
　Who'll be the next a crown to wear?

Who'll be the next, who'll be the next?
Who'll be the next to follow Jesus?
Who'll be the next to follow Jesus now?
Follow Jesus now!

2 Who'll be the next to follow Jesus?
　Come and bow at his precious feet;
Who'll be the next to lay every burden
　Down at the Father's mercy seat?

3 Who'll be the next to follow Jesus?
　Who'll be the next to praise his name?
Who'll swell the chorus of free redemption,
　Sing hallelujah, praise the Lamb?

4 Who'll be the next to follow Jesus
　Down through the Jordan's rolling tide?
Who'll be the next to join with the
　ransomed
　Singing upon the other side?
Annie Sherwood Hawks (1835-1918)

279 Whosoever Heareth, 551;
Shout the sound, 550　　11.11.11.7.

WHOSOEVER heareth! shout, shout the
　sound;
Send the blessèd tidings all the world
　around;
Spread the joyful news wherever man is
　found:
　Whosoever will may come.

Whosoever will! Whosoever will!
Send the blessèd tidings over vale and
　hill;
'Tis the loving Father calls the
　wanderer home:
Whosoever will may come.

280 Will your anchor hold? 60

WILL your anchor hold in the storms of
　life,
When the clouds unfold their wings of
　strife?
When the storm tides lift and the cables
　strain,
Will your anchor drift or firm remain?

We have an anchor that keeps the soul
Steadfast and sure while the billows
　roll;
Fastened to the rock which cannot
　move,
Grounded firm and deep in the
　Saviour's love.

2 Will your anchor hold in the straits of fear,
　When the breakers roar and the reef is
　　near?
While the surges rave and the wild winds
　blow,
Shall the angry waves your bark o'erflow?

3 Will your anchor hold in the floods of
　death,
When the waters cold chill your latest
　breath?
On the rising tide you can never fail
While your anchor holds within the veil.

4 Will your eyes behold through the morn-
　ing light
The city of gold and the harbor bright?
Will you anchor safe by the heavenly
　shore,
When life's storms are past for evermore?
Priscilla Jane Owens (1829-1907)

281 Wonder-working power, 868

WOULD you be free from your burden of sin?
There's power in the blood, power in the blood!
Would you o'er evil a victory win?
There's wonderful power in the blood!

There is power, power, wonder-working power,
In the blood of the Lamb.
There is power, power, wonder-working power,
In the precious blood of the Lamb.

2 Would you be free from your passion and pride?
There's power in the blood, power in the blood!
Come then for cleansing to Calvary's tide;
There's wonderful power in the blood!

3 Would you be whiter, yes, whiter than snow?
There's power in the blood, power in the blood!
Sin stains are lost in its life-giving flow;
There's wonderful power in the blood!

4 Would you do service for Jesus your King?
There's power in the blood, power in the blood!
Would you live daily his praises to sing?
There's wonderful power in the blood!

Lewis Edgar Jones (1865-1936)

       ✤   ✤   ✤

see also: 824 All have need of God's salvation
        828 Salvation! Shout salvation
        913 You must have your sins forgiven
        992 The Saviour is waiting

Response

282 O come to my heart, 119; Margaret, 112
                                          C.M.

A NEEDY sinner at thy feet,
With broken heart I bow
For pardon at thy mercy seat;
O Jesus, save me now.

O come to my heart, Lord Jesus,
There is room in my heart for thee.
O come to my heart, Lord Jesus, come,
There is room in my heart for thee.

2 Strong Friend of sinners, hear my cry,
And set my sad heart free;
My sins demand that I should die,
But I believe in thee.

3 To thee, the sinner's changeless friend,
My all I fully give;
The living water, Jesus, send,
O let me drink and live.

Christopher Strang (1854-81) (verses),
Emily Elizabeth Steele Elliott (1836-97)
(chorus)

283 Cardiff, 488; Saved by grace, 47;
       Credo, 490   8.8.8.8.8.8. Iambic

AND can it be that I should gain
An interest in the Saviour's blood?
Died he for me who caused his pain,
For me who him to death pursued?
Amazing love! how can it be
That thou, my God, shouldst die for me?

2 He left his Father's throne above,
So free, so infinite his grace,
Emptied himself of all but love
And bled for Adam's helpless race.
'Tis mercy all, immense and free,
For, O my God, it found out me.

3 Long my imprisoned spirit lay
Fast bound in sin and nature's night;
Thine eye diffused a quickening ray;
I woke; the dungeon flamed with light.
My chains fell off, my heart was free,
I rose, went forth, and followed thee.

4 No condemnation now I dread;
Jesus, and all in him, is mine.
Alive in him, my living head,
And clothed in righteousness divine,
Bold I approach the eternal throne
And claim the crown, through Christ, my own.

Charles Wesley (1707-88)

284 Martyrdom, 113; St Peter, 129
                                          C.M.

APPROACH, my soul, the mercy seat,
Where Jesus answers prayer;
There humbly fall before his feet,
For none can perish there.

2 Thy promise is my only plea,
With this I venture nigh;
Thou callest burdened souls to thee,
And such, O Lord, am I.

3 Bowed down beneath a load of sin,
  By Satan sorely pressed,
By war without and fears within,
  I come to thee for rest.

4 Be thou my shield and hiding-place,
  That, sheltered near thy side,
I may my fierce accuser face
  And tell him thou hast died.

5 O wondrous love, to bleed and die,
  To bear the cross and shame,
That guilty sinners, such as I,
  Might plead thy gracious name!
                John Newton (1725-1807)

285
All through the night, 339
7.4.7.4.7.7.7.4.

AS I am before thy face,
  Saviour, I pray,
Let the merits of thy grace
  Claim me today.
Canst thou my poor treasure take,
And my heart thy temple make,
Can my sins for thy dear sake
  Be washed away?

2 As I am, so tired of strife,
  Lord, I will come.
As I am, for death or life,
  Lord, I will come.
Crowds of fears obstruct my way,
Past defeats would bid me stay,
Yet in childlike faith I pray,
  Lord, let me come.

3 All my past is known to thee,
  Lord, let me come.
All my future thou canst see,
  Lord, let me come.
Take me, I can trust my all
In thy hands whate'er befall,
Then no tempest shall appal,
  Lord, let me come.
                Herbert Howard Booth (1862-1926)

286
Depth of mercy, 280; Hendon, 282;
Worcester, 303   7.7.7.7.

DEPTH of mercy! Can there be
  Mercy still reserved for me?
Can my God his wrath forbear?
Me, the chief of sinners, spare?

God is love, I know, I feel,
Jesus lives and loves me still.
Jesus lives, he lives and loves me still.

2 I have long withstood his grace,
  Long provoked him to his face,
Would not hearken to his calls,
Grieved him by a thousand falls.

3 Whence to me this waste of love?
Ask my advocate above;
See the cause in Jesus' face,
Now before the throne of grace.

4 There for me the Saviour stands,
Shows his wounds, and spreads his hands.
God is love, I know, I feel,
Jesus lives and loves me still.
                Charles Wesley (1707-88) (verses), alt

287
Misericordia, 475; Just as thou art, 474
8.8.8.6.

DRAWN to the cross which thou hast
    blest
With healing gifts for souls distressed;
To find in thee my life, my rest,
  Christ crucified, I come.

2 Stained with the sins which I have wrought
In word and deed and secret thought;
For pardon which thy blood hath bought,
  Christ crucified, I come.

3 To be what thou wouldst have me be,
Accepted, sanctified in thee,
Through what thy grace shall work in me,
  Christ crucified, I come.
                Albert Orsborn (1886-1967)

288
O save me, dear Lord! 756

I BRING thee my cares and my sorrows,
  I bring thee my doubts and my fears,
I bring thee the sins which have burdened
    my soul
  And shadowed my pathway for years.

O save me, dear Lord!
O save me, dear Lord!
I plead by thy mercy,
O save me, dear Lord!

2 O thou who doth know human frailties,
  Prepare me for gain or for loss;
Though born of the dust, Lord, our Father
    art thou,
  The builder of sun and the cross.

3 Forgive all my blindness and folly,
  My prodigal wanderings and shame.
O heed now the outcrying pains of my
    heart!
  I come as the prodigal came.

The Gospel

4 We thank thee we find in life's wilderness
   Established thy gardens of grace,
   In temptation's desert a cool shading rock,
   In darkness the light of thy face.
                        Evangeline Booth (1865-1950)

289 Yes, O yes! 509
                                    9.9.9.9.

I HAVE heard of a Saviour's love,
   And a wonderful love it must be;
But did he come down from above
   Out of love and compassion for me?

   Yes, O yes!
   Out of love and compassion for me!
   Yes, O yes!
   Out of love and compassion for me!

2 I have heard how he suffered and bled,
   How he languished and died on the tree;
But then is it anywhere said
   That he languished and suffered for me?

3 I've been told of a Heaven on high
   Which the soldiers of Jesus shall see;
But is there a place in the sky
   Made ready and furnished for me?

4 Lord, answer these questions of mine;
   To whom shall I go but to thee?
And say, by thy Spirit divine,
   There's a Saviour and Heaven for me.
                Anne Shepherd (1809-57) (verses), alt

290 Chalvey, 181
                                    D.S.M.

I HAVE no claim on grace;
   I have no right to plead;
I stand before my maker's face
   Condemned in thought and deed.
But since there died a Lamb
   Who, guiltless, my guilt bore,
I lay fast hold on Jesus' name,
   And sin is mine no more.

2 From whence my soul's distress
   But from the hold of sin?
And whence my hope of righteousness
   But from thy grace within?
I speak to thee my need
   And tell my true complaint;
Thou only canst convert indeed
   A sinner to a saint.

3 O pardon-speaking blood!
   O soul-renewing grace!
Through Christ I know the love of God
   And see the Father's face.
I now set forth thy praise,
   Thy loyal servant I,
And gladly dedicate my days
   My God to glorify.
                        Albert Orsborn (1886-1967)

291 Take me as I am, 479; Take all my sins
        away, 478   8.8.8.6.

JESUS, my Lord, to thee I cry,
   Unless thou help me I must die;
O bring thy free salvation nigh
   And take me as I am.

   O take me as I am,
   O take me as I am,
   My only plea Christ died for me;
   O take me as I am.

2 Helpless I am and full of guilt,
   But yet for me thy blood was spilt,
And thou canst make me what thou wilt
   And take me as I am.

3 No preparation can I make,
   My best resolves I only break,
Yet save me for thy mercy's sake
   And take me as I am.

4 Behold me, Saviour, at thy feet,
   Deal with me as thou seest meet,
Thy work begin, thy work complete,
   But take me as I am.
                        Eliza Hamilton

292 Nothing but thy blood, 329
                                    7.8.7.8.

JESUS, see me at thy feet,
   Nothing but thy blood can save me;
Thou alone my need canst meet,
   Nothing but thy blood can save me.

   No! no! Nothing do I bring,
   But by faith I'm clinging
   To thy cross, O Lamb of God!
   Nothing but thy blood can save me.

2 See my heart, Lord, torn with grief,
   Nothing but thy blood can save me;
Me unpardoned do not leave,
   Nothing but thy blood can save me.

3 Dark, indeed, the past has been,
   Nothing but thy blood can save me;
Yet in mercy take me in,
   Nothing but thy blood can save me.

Response

4 As I am, O hear me pray,
  Nothing but thy blood can save me;
  I can come no other way,
  Nothing but thy blood can save me.

5 All that I can do is vain,
  Nothing but thy blood can save me;
  I can ne'er remove a stain,
  Nothing but thy blood can save me.

6 Lord, I cast myself on thee,
  Nothing but thy blood can save me;
  From my guilt, O set me free,
  Nothing but thy blood can save me.
                    Richard Slater (1854-1939)

293 Just as thou art, 474; Misericordia, 475
                                        8.8.8.6.

JUST as I am, without one plea,
  But that thy blood was shed for me,
And that thou bid'st me come to thee,
  O Lamb of God, I come!

2 Just as I am, and waiting not
  To rid my soul of one dark blot,
  To thee whose blood can cleanse each spot,
  O Lamb of God, I come!

3 Just as I am, though tossed about
  With many a conflict, many a doubt,
  Fightings within and fears without,
  O Lamb of God, I come!

4 Just as I am, poor, wretchèd, blind;
  Sight, riches, healing of the mind,
  Yea, all I need in thee to find,
  O Lamb of God, I come!

5 Just as I am, thou wilt receive,
  Wilt welcome, pardon, cleanse, relieve,
  Because thy promise I believe,
  O Lamb of God, I come!

6 Just as I am, thy love unknown
  Has broken every barrier down,
  Now to be thine, yea, thine alone,
  O Lamb of God, I come!
                    Charlotte Elliott (1789-1871)

294 Knowing my failings, 711

KNOWING my failings, knowing my fears,
  Seeing my sorrow, drying my tears,
Jesus recall me, me re-ordain;
You know I love you, use me again.

2 I have no secrets unknown to you,
  No special graces, talents are few;
  Yet your intention I would fulfill;
  You know I love you, ask what you will.

3 For the far future I cannot see,
  Promise your presence, travel with me;
  Sunshine or shadows? I cannot tell;
  You know I love you, all will be well.
                    John Gowans

295 Even Me, 369
                              8.7.8.7. Troch.

LORD, I hear of showers of blessing
  Thou art scattering full and free,
Showers, the thirsty land refreshing;
  Let some showers fall on me,
    Even me.

2 Pass me not, O gracious Father,
  Sinful though my heart may be;
  Thou might'st leave me, but the rather
  Let thy mercy light on me,
    Even me.

3 Pass me not, O mighty Spirit,
  Thou canst make the blind to see;
  Witnesser of Jesus' merit,
  Speak the word of power to me,
    Even me.

4 Love of God so pure and changeless,
  Blood of Christ so rich and free,
  Grace of God so strong and boundless,
  Magnify them all in me,
    Even me.
                    Elizabeth Codner (1823-1919)

296 Nearer to thee, 191
                              6.4.6.4.6.6.6.4.

NO, not despairingly
  Come I to thee;
No, not distrustingly
  Bend I the knee.
Sin hath gone over me,
Yet is this still my plea:
Jesus hath died for me,
  Jesus hath died!

2 Ah! mine iniquity
  Crimson hath been,
Infinite, infinite,
  Sin upon sin:
Sin of not loving thee,
Sin of not trusting thee,
Sin of not serving thee,
  Infinite sin.

The Gospel

3 Lord, I confess to thee
    Sadly my sin;
All I am tell I thee,
    All I have been.
Purge thou my sin away,
Wash thou my soul this day,
Now to be pure I pray,
    Lord, make me clean!

4 Faithful and just art thou,
    Forgiving all!
Loving and kind art thou
    When sinners call.
Lord, let the cleansing blood,
Blood of the Lamb of God,
Healing, life-giving flood,
    Pass o'er my soul.

Horatius Bonar (1808-89), alt

297 Dennis, 165; Lascelles, 170
                                     S.M.

NOT what these hands have done
    Can save this guilty soul;
Not what this toiling flesh has borne
    Can make my spirit whole.

2 Not what I feel or do
    Can give me peace with God;
Not all my prayers and sighs and tears
    Can bear my awful load.

3 Thy work alone, O Christ,
    Can ease this weight of sin;
Thy blood alone, O Lamb of God,
    Can give me peace within.

4 Thy love to me, O God,
    Not mine, O Lord, to thee,
Can rid me of this dark unrest
    And set my spirit free.

5 Thy grace alone, O God,
    To me can pardon speak;
Thy power alone, O Son of God,
    Can this sore bondage break.

6 I bless the Christ of God,
    I rest on love divine,
And with unfaltering lip and heart
    I call this Saviour mine.

Horatius Bonar (1808-89)

298 My Jesus, I love thee, 565; Cossar, 556;
     St Denio, 569   11.11.11.11.

O BOUNDLESS salvation! deep ocean of
    love,
O fulness of mercy, Christ brought from
    above,
The whole world redeeming, so rich and
    so free,
Now flowing for all men, come, roll over
    me!

2 My sins they are many, their stains are so
    deep,
And bitter the tears of remorse that I weep;
But useless is weeping; thou great crim-
    son sea,
Thy waters can cleanse me, come, roll over
    me!

3 My tempers are fitful, my passions are
    strong,
They bind my poor soul and they force me
    to wrong;
Beneath thy blest billows deliverance I see,
O come, mighty ocean, and roll over me!

4 Now tossed with temptation, then haunted
    with fears,
My life has been joyless and useless for
    years;
I feel something better most surely would
    be
If once thy pure waters would roll over
    me.

5 O ocean of mercy, oft longing I've stood
On the brink of thy wonderful, life-giving
    flood!
Once more I have reachèd this soul-
    cleansing sea,
I will not go back till it rolls over me.

6 The tide is now flowing, I'm touching the
    wave,
I hear the loud call of the mighty to save;
My faith's growing bolder, delivered I'll be;
I plunge 'neath the waters, they roll over
    me.

7 And now, hallelujah! the rest of my days
Shall gladly be spent in promoting his
    praise
Who opened his bosom to pour out this
    sea
Of boundless salvation for you and for me.

William Booth (1829-1912)

Response

299 Aurelia, 246; Rutherford, 260
7.6.7.6. D. Iambic

O JESUS, thou art standing
  Outside the fast-closed door,
In lowly patience waiting,
  To pass the threshold o'er.
Shame on us, Christian people,
  His name and sign who bear,
O shame, thrice shame upon us,
  To keep him standing there!

2 O Jesus, thou art knocking;
  And lo! that hand is scarred,
And thorns thy brow encircle,
  And tears thy face have marred.
O love that passeth knowledge,
  So patiently to wait!
O sin that hath no equal,
  So fast to bar the gate!

3 O Jesus, thou art pleading
  In accents meek and low:
I died for you, my children,
  And will ye treat me so?
O Lord, with shame and sorrow
  We open now the door;
Dear Saviour, enter, enter,
  And leave us nevermore.
  William Walsham How (1823-97)

300 Out of my bondage, 767

OUT of my bondage, sorrow and night,
  Jesus, I come, Jesus, I come;
Into thy freedom, gladness and light,
  Jesus, I come to thee;
Out of my sickness into thy health,
Out of my want and into thy wealth,
Out of my sin and into thyself,
  Jesus, I come to thee.

2 Out of my shameful failure and loss,
  Jesus, I come, Jesus, I come;
Into the glorious gain of thy cross,
  Jesus, I come to thee;
Out of earth's sorrows into thy balm,
Out of life's storms and into thy calm,
Out of distress to jubilant psalm,
  Jesus, I come to thee.

3 Out of unrest and arrogant pride,
  Jesus, I come, Jesus, I come;
Into thy blessèd will to abide,
  Jesus, I come to thee;

Out of myself to dwell in thy love,
Out of despair into raptures above,
Upward for aye on wings like a dove,
  Jesus, I come to thee.

4 Out of the fear and dread of the tomb,
  Jesus, I come, Jesus, I come;
Into the joy and light of thy home,
  Jesus, I come to thee;
Out of the depths of ruin untold,
Into the peace of thy sheltering fold,
Ever thy glorious face to behold,
  Jesus, I come to thee.
  William True Sleeper (1819-1904)

301 Pass me not, 347; My humble cry, 346
8.5.8.5.

PASS me not, O loving Saviour,
  Hear my humble cry;
And while others thou art calling,
  Do not pass me by.

Saviour! Saviour!
  Hear my humble cry,
And while others thou art calling,
  Do not pass me by.

2 Let me at the throne of mercy
  Find a sweet relief,
Kneeling there in deep contrition;
  Help my unbelief.

3 Trusting only in thy merit,
  Would I seek thy face;
Heal my wounded, broken spirit,
  Save me by thy grace.

4 Thou the spring of all my comfort,
  More than life to me,
Whom have I on earth beside thee?
  Whom in Heaven but thee?
  Fanny Crosby (1820-1915)

302 Norwood, 311; Coles, 305; Toplady, 316
7.7.7.7.7.7.

ROCK of ages, cleft for me,
  Let me hide myself in thee;
Let the water and the blood,
From thy riven side which flowed,
Be of sin the double cure,
Cleanse me from its guilt and power.

2 Not the labors of my hands
  Can fulfil thy law's demands;
Could my zeal no respite know,
Could my tears for ever flow,
All for sin could not atone;
Thou must save, and thou alone.

The Gospel

3 Nothing in my hand I bring,
Simply to thy cross I cling;
Naked, come to thee for dress,
Helpless, look to thee for grace,
Foul, I to the fountain fly;
Wash me, Saviour, or I die.

4 While I draw this fleeting breath,
When mine eyes shall close in death,
When I soar to worlds unknown,
See thee on thy judgment throne,
Rock of ages, cleft for me,
Let me hide myself in thee.
Augustus Montague Toplady (1740-78)

303 The Penitent's Plea, 823

SAVIOUR, hear me while before thy feet
I the record of my sins repeat.
Stained with guilt, myself abhorring,
Filled with grief, my soul outpouring;
Canst thou still in mercy think of me,
Stoop to set my shackled spirit free,
Raise my sinking heart and bid me be
Thy child once more?

Grace there is my every debt to pay,
Blood to wash my every sin away,
Power to keep me spotless day by day,
For me, for me!

2 All the memories of deeds gone by
Rise within me and thy power defy;
With a deathly chill ensnaring,
They would leave my soul despairing.
Saviour, take my hand, I cannot tell
How to stem the tides that round me swell,
How to ease my conscience, or to quell
My flaming heart.

3 Yet why should I fear? Hast thou not died
That no seeking soul should be denied?
To that heart, its sins confessing,
Canst thou fail to give a blessing?
By the love and pity thou hast shown,
By the blood that did for me atone,
Boldly will I kneel before thy throne,
A pleading soul.

4 All the rivers of thy grace I claim,
Over every promise write my name;
As I am I come, believing,
As thou art thou dost, receiving,
Bid me rise a free and pardoned slave,
Master o'er my sin, the world, the grave,
Charging me to preach thy power to save
To sin-bound souls.
Herbert Howard Booth (1862-1926)

304 O touch the hem, 759

SHE only touched the hem of his garment
As to his side she stole,
Amid the crowd that gathered around him,
And straightway she was whole.

O touch the hem of his garment,
And thou, too, shalt be free;
His saving power, this very hour,
Shall give new life to thee!

2 She came in fear and trembling before him,
She knew her Lord had come,
She felt that from him virtue had healed her;
The mighty deed was done.

3 He turned with: Daughter, be of good comfort,
Thy faith hath made thee whole!
And peace that passeth all understanding
With gladness filled her soul.
George Frederick Root (1820-95)

305 Carey's, 489; St Catherine, 499; St Matthias, 500 8.8.8.8.8.8. Iambic

WEARY of wandering from my God
And now made willing to return,
I hear, and bow me to the rod;
For thee, not without hope, I mourn.
I have an advocate above,
A friend before the throne of love.

2 O Jesus, full of truth and grace,
More full of grace than I of sin,
Yet once again I seek thy face,
Open thine arms and take me in,
And freely my backslidings heal
And love the faithless sinner still.

3 Thou knowest the way to bring me back,
My fallen spirit to restore;
O for thy truth and mercy's sake
Forgive, and bid me sin no more!
The ruins of my soul repair
And make my heart a house of prayer.
Charles Wesley (1707-88)

306 Nothing but the blood of Jesus, 328 7.8.7.8.

WHAT can wash away my sin?
Nothing but the blood of Jesus.
What can keep me always clean?
Nothing but the blood of Jesus.

84

Witness

O precious is the flow
That makes me white as snow!
No other fount I know,
    Nothing but the blood of Jesus.

2 For my cleansing this I see,
    Nothing but the blood of Jesus.
For my pardon this my plea,
    Nothing but the blood of Jesus.

3 Nothing can for sin atone,
    Nothing but the blood of Jesus.
Naught of good that I have done,
    Nothing but the blood of Jesus.

4 This is all my hope and peace,
    Nothing but the blood of Jesus.
This is all my righteousness,
    Nothing but the blood of Jesus.
            Robert Lowry (1826-99)

307   Dennis, 165; Southport, 178
                                    S.M.

WHEN shall thy love constrain
    And force me to thy breast?
When shall my soul return again
    To her eternal rest?

2   Thy condescending grace
    To me did freely move;
It calls me still to seek thy face,
    And stoops to ask my love.

3   Lord, at thy feet I fall,
    I long to be set free,
I fain would now obey the call
    And give up all to thee.

4   Nay, but I yield, I yield!
    I can hold out no more,
I sink, by dying love compelled,
    And own thee conqueror.
            Charles Wesley (1707-88)

          *   *   *

see also: 420 I bring my heart to Jesus
         421 I bring my sins to thee

Witness

308   Amazing Grace! 70
                             C.M.

AMAZING grace! how sweet the sound,
    That saved a wretch like me!
I once was lost, but now am found,
    Was blind but now I see.

2 'Twas grace that taught my heart to fear,
    And grace my fears relieved;
How precious did that grace appear
    The hour I first believed!

3 Through many dangers, toils and snares
    I have already come;
'Tis grace hath brought me safe thus far,
    And grace will lead me home.

4 When we've been there ten thousand
      years,
    Bright shining as the sun,
We've no less days to sing God's praise
    Than when we first begun.
      John Newton (1725-1807) (verses 1-3),

309   Before I found salvation, 616

BEFORE I found salvation,
    I was sunk in degradation,
And from my Saviour wandered far astray;
    But I came to Calvary's mountain,
    And plunged into the fountain,
And from my heart the burden rolled away.

'Twas a happy day, and no mistake,
When Jesus from my heart did take
The load of sin that made it ache,
    And filled my soul with joy.

2   Since I have been converted
    And the devil's ranks deserted,
I've had such joy and gladness in my soul.
    For Jesus I've been fighting,
    And in the war delighting,
And now I'm pressing on toward the goal.

3   If faithful to my Saviour,
    I shall enjoy his favor,
And he will keep me safely to the end;
    And when I cross the river,
    I'll live with him forever,
And one eternal day of glory spend.
      William Giles Collins (1854-1931)

310   Blessèd Assurance, 621

BLESSÈD assurance, Jesus is mine;
    O what a foretaste of glory divine!
Heir of salvation, purchase of God,
Born of his Spirit, washed in his blood.

This is my story, this is my song,
Praising my Saviour all the day long.

2 Perfect submission, perfect delight,
  Visions of rapture burst on my sight;
  Angels descending, bring from above
  Echoes of mercy, whispers of love.

3 Perfect submission, all is at rest;
  I, in my Saviour, am happy and blest.
  Watching and waiting, looking above,
  Filled with his goodness, lost in his love.
  Fanny Crosby (1820-1915)

---

311 Carlisle, 164; Shirland, 176
S.M.

COME and rejoice with me,
  For once my heart was poor,
But I have found a treasury
  Of love, a boundless store.

2 Come and rejoice with me;
  I, once so sick at heart,
Have met with one who knows my case,
  And knows the healing art.

3 Come and rejoice with me,
  For I was wearied sore,
But I have found a mighty arm
  Which holds me evermore.

4 Come and rejoice with me,
  For I have found a friend
Who knows my heart's most secret depths,
  Yet loves me without end.
  Elizabeth Rundle-Charles (1828-96)

---

312 Come, comrades dear, 464*;
Praise, 468** 8.8.6.8.8.6.

COME, comrades dear, who love the Lord,
  Who taste the sweets of Jesus' word,
    In Jesus' ways go on;
Our troubles and our trials here
Will only make us richer there,
  When we arrive at home.

2 We feel that Heaven is now begun;
  It issues from the sparkling throne,
    From Jesus' throne on high.
And he will lead his soldiers forth
To living streams of richest worth
  That never will run dry.

3 And then we'll shine and shout and sing,
  And make the heavenly arches ring,
    When all the saints are home.
Come on, come on, my comrades dear,
We soon shall meet together there,
  For Jesus bids us come.

---

4 Amen, amen, my soul replies;
  I'm bound to meet you in the skies,
    And claim a mansion there.
Now, here's my heart and here's my hand,
To meet you in that heavenly land,
  Where we shall part no more.
  Anon

*Repeat lines 3 and 6, then repeat last
2 lines.
**Repeat line 6, then repeat last 3 lines.

---

313 Glory to the Lamb, 372; Bethany, 429
8.7.8.7. Troch.

COME, thou Fount of every blessing,
  Tune my heart to sing thy grace;
Streams of mercy, never ceasing,
  Call for songs of loudest praise.

Glory, glory, Jesus saves me,
Glory, glory to the Lamb!
O the cleansing blood has reached me,
Glory, glory to the Lamb!

2 Here I raise my Ebenezer,
  Hither by thy help I'm come;
And I hope, by thy good pleasure,
  Safely to arrive at home.

3 Jesus sought me when a stranger
  Wandering from the fold of God;
He, to rescue me from danger,
  Interposed his precious blood.

4 O to grace how great a debtor
  Daily I'm constrained to be!
Let that grace, Lord, like a fetter,
  Bind my wandering heart to thee.

5 Prone to wander, Lord, I feel it,
  Prone to leave the God I love;
Here's my heart, Lord, take and seal it,
  Seal it for thy courts above.
  Robert Robinson (1735-90) (verses)

---

314 Diademata, 182; From strength to
strength, 184 D.S.M.

COME, ye that love the Lord,
  And let your joys be known;
Join in a song with sweet accord
  While ye surround his throne;
Let those refuse to sing,
  Who never knew our God,
But soldiers of the heavenly King
  Must speak their joys abroad.

2 There we shall see his face,
  And never, never sin;
There, from the rivers of his grace,
  Drink endless pleasures in;

Yea, and before we rise
  To that immortal state,
The thoughts of such amazing bliss
  Should constant joys create.

3 The men of grace have found
  Glory begun below;
Celestial fruit on earthly ground
  From faith and hope may grow;
Then let our songs abound,
  And every tear be dry;
We're marching through Immanuel's
  ground
To fairer worlds on high.
Isaac Watts (1674-1748)

315 Glory to his name, 654

DOWN at the cross where my Saviour
  died,
Down where for cleansing from sin I cried,
There to my heart was the blood applied,
  Glory to his name!

Glory to his name, glory to his name!
Now to my heart is the blood applied,
  Glory to his name!

2 I am so wondrously saved from sin,
Jesus, my Saviour, abides within;
And, by the cross, I a crown shall win,
  Glory to his name!

3 O precious fountain that saves from sin,
I am so glad I have entered in!
There Jesus saves me and keeps me clean,
  Glory to his name!

4 Come to this fountain, so rich and sweet,
Cast thy poor soul at the Saviour's feet,
Plunge in today and be made complete,
  Glory to his name!
Elisha Albright Hoffman (1839-1929)

316 Sunshine, 803

God is our light and God is our sunshine,
  Lighting our pathway from day unto
  day;
In him we trust when all else seems
  dreary,
  For with his sunshine he brightens our
  way.

Sunshine, sunshine, shining along our
  pathway,
Guiding, guiding, just where the
  Saviour would go;

Shining, shining when all the way
  seems gloomy,
Jesus lights our way up to Glory with
  sunshine rays.

2 Sometimes we're tempted, often grow
  weary,
  'Tis for the sunshine at such times we
  pray;
Then through the dark his bright rays
  come beaming,
Turning our darkness and fears all away.
Richard Nuttall (1891-1946)

317 My sins are under the blood, 743

GOD'S anger now is turned away,
  My sins are under the blood;
My darkness he has changed to day,
  My sins are under the blood.

My sins, my sins are under the blood,
  My guilt is gone and my soul is free,
My peace, my peace is made with God,
  The Lord has pardoned me.

2 How blest the Lord's alone to be,
  My sins are under the blood;
What joy to know he cleanses me,
  My sins are under the blood.

3 When sorrow's waves around me roll,
  My sins are under the blood;
In perfect peace he keeps my soul,
  My sins are under the blood.

4 In every step his hand doth lead,
  My sins are under the blood;
And he supplies my every need,
  My sins are under the blood.
Frederick William Fry (1859-1939)

318 Thou Shepherd of Israel, 487;
The cross now covers my sins, 486
8.8.8.8. D. Amph.

HOW tasteless and tedious the hours
  When Jesus no longer I see;
Sweet prospects, sweet birds and sweet
  flowers
Have lost all their sweetness to me.
The midsummer sun shines but dim,
  The fields strive in vain to look gay;
But when I am happy in him
  December's as pleasant as May.

The Gospel

2 His name yields the richest perfume,
And sweeter than music his voice;
His presence disperses my gloom
And makes all within me rejoice.
I should, were he always thus nigh,
Have nothing to wish or to fear;
No mortal so happy as I,
My summer would last all the year.

3 Content with beholding his face,
My all to his pleasure resigned,
No changes of season or place
Could make any change in my mind.
While blessed with a sense of his love,
A palace a toy would appear;
And prisons would palaces prove
If Jesus would dwell with me there.

4 Dear Lord, if indeed I am thine,
If thou art my sun and my song,
Say why do I languish and pine,
And why are my winters so long?
O drive these dark clouds from my sky!
Thy soul-cheering presence restore,
Or take me to thee up on high
Where winters and clouds are no more.
John Newton (1725-1807)

319 I am amazed, 673

I AM amazed when I think of God's love,
So wonderful, matchless and free;
The love that could see, from eternity,
Something worth saving in sinners like
me.

*I am amazed that the Saviour should
die*
For sinners like me and like you;
*That we may be saved by the work he
has done*
And not by the works that we do.
But it's true, it's true,
*This wonderful story so old, but so
new.*
*I am amazed that the Saviour should
die*
For sinners like me and like you.

2 I am amazed when I think of God's grace,
O word with a heavenly sound!
For sinners condemned, what way could
be found?
More than sufficient God's grace did
abound.

3 I am amazed when I think of God's Son,
From Glory to Calvary he came
To bear in my place sin's darkness and
shame;
O what a Saviour, and Jesus his name!
Sidney Edward Cox (1887-1975)

320 Meet me at the fountain, 440;
Whither pilgrims? 453; The pathway of
duty, 448*   8.7.8.7. D. Troch.

I AM drinking at the fountain
Where I ever would abide,
For I've tasted life's pure river,
And my soul is satisfied.
There's no thirsting for life's pleasure,
Nor adorning, rich and gay,
For I've found a richer treasure,
One that fadeth not away.

Is not this the land of Beulah,
Blessèd, blessèd land of light,
Where the flowers bloom forever
And the sun is always bright?

By the pathway of duty
Flows the river of God's grace;
By the pathway of duty
Flows the river of God's grace.

2 Tell me not of heavy crosses,
Nor of burdens hard to bear,
For I've found this great salvation
Makes each burden light appear.
And I love to follow Jesus,
Gladly counting all but dross,
Worldly honors all forsaking
For the glory of the cross.

3 O the cross has wondrous glory!
Oft I've proved this to be true;
When I'm in the way so narrow
I can see a pathway through;
And how sweetly Jesus whispers:
Take the cross, thou needst not fear,
For I've trod the way before thee
And the glory lingers near.
Anon
Sidney Edward Cox (1887-1975) (2nd chorus)

321 Blessedly Saved, 622

I AM saved, blessedly saved, by the blood,
Ever kept by the power of his might;
I am walking and talking with Jesus, my
Lord,
In his precepts I run with delight.

88

Witness

Blessedly saved, saved by the blood,
Blessedly saved by the blood of the
Lamb;
Happy and free, Jesus with me,
Blessedly saved, blessedly kept, yes,
I am!

2 I was saved years ago by the blood
   After striving and praying with tears;
   But when willing, the Spirit came in like
   a flood,
   And he washed all away sins of years.

3 I've been fighting for God ever since
   In The Salvation Army so brave;
   Where he leads I will follow, I'm at his
   command
   To go forward, poor sinners to save.

4 In this warfare I fight with delight,
   Ever ready for service I am,
   Warning sinners to flee from the wrath
   that's to come,
   And be washed in the blood of the Lamb.
   Edwin Gay (1860-1952)

322   I am saved, 595
12.12.

I AM saved, I am saved,
   Jesus bids me go free;
He has bought with a price
   Even me, even me!

   Hallelujah, hallelujah!
   Hallelujah to my Saviour!
   Hallelujah, hallelujah!
   Hallelujah, amen!

2 Wondrous love, wondrous love,
   Now the gift I receive;
   I have rest in his word,
   I believe, I believe!

3 I am cleansed, I am cleansed,
   I am whiter than snow;
   He is mighty to save,
   This I know, this I know!

4 I was weak, I am strong
   In the power of his might;
   And my darkness he's turned
   Into light, into light!
   Annie Sherwood Hawks (1835-1918)

323   I am so glad, 527
10.10.10.10. Dact.

I AM so glad that our Father in Heaven
   Tells of his love in the book he has given;
Wonderful things in the Bible I see;
This is the dearest, that Jesus loves me.

I am so glad that Jesus loves me,
   Jesus loves me, Jesus loves me,
I am so glad that Jesus loves me,
   Jesus loves even me.

2 Jesus loves me and I know I love him;
   Love brought him down my poor soul to
   redeem,
   Yes, it was love made him die on the tree;
   O I am certain that Jesus loves me!

3 If one should ask of me, how could I tell?
   Glory to Jesus, I know very well;
   God's Holy Spirit with mine doth agree,
   Constantly witnessing Jesus loves me.

4 O if there's only one song I can sing
   When in his beauty I see the great King,
   This shall my song in eternity be:
   O what a wonder that Jesus loves me!

5 In this assurance I find sweetest rest,
   Trusting in Jesus, I know I am blest;
   Satan, dismayed, from my soul now doth
   flee
   When I just tell him that Jesus loves me.
   Philip Paul Bliss (1838-76)

324   Bethany, 429
8.7.8.7. D. Troch.

I BELIEVE that God the Father
   Can be seen in God the Son,
In the gentleness of Jesus
   Love for all the world is shown.
Though men crucify their Saviour,
   And his tenderness rebuff,
God is love, the cross is saying,
   Calvary is proof enough.

2 I believe in transformation,
   God can change the hearts of men,
And refine the evil nature
   Till it glows with grace again.
Others may reject the weakling,
   I believe he can be strong,
To the family of Jesus
   All God's children may belong.

3 In a world of shifting values,
   There are standards that remain,
I believe that holy living
   By God's grace we may attain.
All would hear the Holy Spirit
   If they listen to his voice,
Every Christian may be Christlike
   And in liberty rejoice.

4 All the promises of Jesus
   Are unchanged in every way,
In my yesterdays I proved them,
   I believe them for today.
Still God gives his willing servant
   Full equipment for the task;
Power is found by those who seek it,
   Grace is given to those who ask.
John Gowans

325 Aurelia, 246; Rutherford, 260
                7.6.7.6. D. Iambic

I COULD not do without thee,
   O Saviour of the lost,
Whose precious blood redeemed me
   At such tremendous cost;
Thy righteousness, thy pardon,
   Thy precious blood must be
My only hope and comfort,
   My glory and my plea.

2 I could not do without thee,
   I cannot stand alone,
I have no strength of goodness,
   No wisdom of my own;
But thou, belovèd Saviour,
   Art all in all to me,
And weakness will be power,
   If leaning hard on thee.

3 I could not do without thee;
   No other friend can read
The spirit's strange deep longings,
   Interpreting its need;
No human heart could enter
   Each dim recess of mine,
And soothe and hush and calm it,
   O blessèd Lord, but thine.

4 I could not do without thee,
   For years are fleeting fast,
And soon in solemn loneness
   The river must be passed;
But thou wilt never leave me
   And, though the waves roll high,
I know thou wilt be near me
   And whisper: It is I.
Frances Ridley Havergal (1836-79)

326 I feel like singing, 96;
      Around the throne, 72   C.M.

I FEEL like singing all the time,
   My tears are wiped away,
For Jesus is a friend of mine,
   I'll serve him every day.

Singing glory, glory,
Glory be to God on high.

2 When on the cross my Lord I saw,
   Nailed there by sins of mine,
Fast fell the burning tears; but now
   I'm singing all the time.

3 When fierce temptations try my heart,
   I'll sing: Jesus is mine!
And so, though tears at times may start,
   I'm singing all the time.

4 The wondrous story of the Lamb
   We'll tell in every clime,
Till others, taught the glad new song,
   Go singing all the time.

5 The angels sing a glorious song,
   But not a song like mine,
For I am washed in Jesus' blood,
   And singing all the time.
Edward Payson Hammond (1831-1910)

327 In my heart there rings a melody, 691
   For words and music see Song 984
   American Supplement

328 Saints of God, 781

I HAVE found a great salvation,
   Glory to God!
From my sins I've liberation,
   Glory to God!
   I was sunk in misery,
Bound by Satan's cruel fetters,
   But the Saviour set me free,
   Glory to God!

2 Now my heart is full of singing,
   Glory to God!
I am kept each day from sinning,
   Glory to God!
   O this joy, who can express?
For it never knows an ending;
   I've a life of happiness,
   Glory to God!

3 Sinner, you can have this blessing,
   Glory to God!
Come to Christ, your sins confessing,
   Glory to God!
   Then your life shall happy be,
And in Heaven you'll have a mansion,
   There to live eternally,
   Glory to God!
Thomas William Plant (1865-1944)

Witness

329
A Wonderful Saviour, 599

I HAVE glorious tidings of Jesus to tell,
How he unto me hath done all things well.
And I love him for stooping, in sin when
    I fell,
    Where his strong arm of mercy did reach
    me.

A wonderful Saviour is Jesus,
Cleansing the soul, making it whole;
A wonderful Saviour is Jesus,
I've proved he is mighty to save.

2 I have found that from fear he can free-
        dom bestow,
    And over dark sorrow joy's radiance throw;
    As a friend he can cheer one in grief, this
        I know;
    He indeed is a wonderful Saviour.

3 I am glad that the blessings the Lord gives
        to me
    To all who will ask him are just as free;
    In his pity unmeasured he gracious will
        be
    Unto all who will seek his salvation.
                    Richard Slater (1854-1939)

330
Meet me at the fountain, 440;
Let the lower lights be burning, 386;
The Vacant Chair, 449
                    8.7.8.7. D. Troch.

I HAVE seen his face in blessing
    When my eyes were dimmed with tears;
I have felt his hand caressing
    When my heart was torn by fears.
When the shadows gathered o'er me,
    And the gloom fell deep as night,
In the darkness, just before me,
    There were tokens of his light.

I have victory in temptation,
    Peace amid the tempest's roar;
I abide in his salvation,
    We are one for evermore.

2 I was wandering, and he found me,
    Brought me from the verge of Hell;
I was bruisèd, and he bound me,
    Sick was I, he made me well.
I was wounded, and he healed me
    When a-wearied of the strife;
I was erring, and he sealed me,
    Dead, his Spirit gave me life.

3 By his life's blood he has claimed me
    As a jewel in his sight;
As his own child he has named me,
    Brought me forth to walk in light.
So I'm fighting till he calls me,
    Walking in the path he trod;
And I care not what befalls me
    Living in the life of God.
                William John McAlonan (1863-1925)

331
Those endearing young charms, 541;
The old rustic bridge, 540
                    11.8.11.8. D.

I HEARD of a Saviour whose love was so
        great
    That he laid down his life on the tree;
    The thorns they were pierced on his beau-
        tiful brow
    To pardon a rebel like me.

He pardoned a rebel, a rebel like me,
    He pardoned a rebel like me.
The thorns they were pierced on his
        beautiful brow
    To pardon a rebel like me.

2 They tell me he wept over sinners one day
    Saying: O that your Saviour you knew!
    How oft would I gather you under my wing
    And pardon poor rebels like you.

3 O love so amazing that broke my hard
        heart
    And brought me, dear Jesus, to thee!
    I know, when I came, thou didst not cast
        me out
    But didst pardon a rebel like me.

4 'Tis true that poor sinners of all kinds he
        saves,
    And you he will not cast away;
    He waits in his mercy sweet peace to
        bestow,
    So come to the fountain today.
                            Eliza Read

332
Vox Dilecti, 160; St Matthew, 157
                    D.C.M.

I HEARD the voice of Jesus say:
    Come unto me and rest;
Lay down, thou weary one, lay down
    Thy head upon my breast.
I came to Jesus as I was,
    Weary and worn and sad;
I found in him a resting place,
    And he has made me glad.

The Gospel

2 I heard the voice of Jesus say:
    Behold, I freely give
The living water; thirsty one,
    Stoop down and drink and live.
I came to Jesus, and I drank
    Of that life-giving stream;
My thirst was quenched, my soul revived,
    And now I live in him.

3 I heard the voice of Jesus say:
    I am this dark world's light;
Look unto me, thy morn shall rise,
    And all thy day be bright.
I looked to Jesus, and I found
    In him my star, my sun;
And in that light of life I'll walk
    Till traveling days are done.

Horatius Bonar (1808-89)

333 I bring my heart to Jesus, 675

I LEFT it all with Jesus long ago,
    All my sins I brought him and my woe.
When by faith I saw him on the tree,
Heard his loving whisper: 'Tis for thee;
From my heart the burden rolled away,
    Happy day!

2 I leave it all with Jesus, for he knows
How to steal the bitter from life's woes,
How to gild the teardrop with his smile,
Make the desert garden bloom awhile;
When my weakness leaneth on his might
    All is light!

3 I leave it all with Jesus day by day;
Faith can firmly trust him, come what may;
Hope has dropped her anchor, found her
    rest
In the calm, sure haven of his breast;
Love esteems it Heaven to abide
    At his side.

4 O leave it all with Jesus, needy soul;
Tell not half the story, but the whole.
Worlds on worlds are hanging on his hand,
Life and death are waiting his command;
Yet his tender mercy makes thee room;
    O come home!

Ellen H. Willis

334 I serve a risen Saviour, 681

I SERVE a risen Saviour,
    He's in the world today;
I know that he is living,
    Whatever men may say;
I see his hand of mercy,
    I hear his voice of cheer,
And just the time I need him
    He's always near.

*He lives, he lives,
    Christ Jesus lives today!
He walks with me and talks with me
    Along life's narrow way.
He lives, he lives,
    Salvation to impart!
You ask me how I know he lives?
    He lives within my heart!*

2 In all the world around me
    I see his loving care;
And though my heart grows weary,
    I never will despair;
I know that he is leading
    Through all the stormy blast;
The day of his appearing
    Will come at last.

3 Rejoice, rejoice, O Christian,
    Lift up your voice and sing
Eternal hallelujahs
    To Jesus Christ the King;
The hope of all who seek him,
    The help of all who find;
None other is so loving,
    So good and kind.

Alfred Henry Ackley (1887-1906)

335 This is what the Lord has done, 833

I WANT to tell what God has done
    Through Christ, his well-belovèd Son,
How my poor heart he sought and won;
    Can you wonder that I want to tell it?
I want to tell what God can do
    For sinners lost like me and you,
Of sins washed white and garments new;
    Can you wonder that I want to tell it?

*I want to tell you what the Lord has
    done,
    What the Lord has done for me;
He lifted me from the miry clay;
    O what a happy day!*

92

Witness

I want to tell you what the Lord can do,
What the Lord can do for you:
He can take your life as he did mine,
And make it anew.

2 I want to tell of saving grace,
   Of God's strong arm, his warm embrace,
   Of blood that can all sins erase;
      Can you wonder that I want to tell it?
   I want to tell to sinners lost
      That Christ has paid sin's fearful cost,
   And saves unto the uttermost;
      Can you wonder that I want to tell it?

3 What God has done, he still can do;
   His power can fashion lives anew,
   And all who trust him find him true;
      Can you wonder that I want to tell it?
   I want to tell of that glad day
   For which we watch, for which we pray,
   It must be near, not far away;
      Can you wonder that I want to tell it?
                       Sidney Edward Cox (1887-1975)

336 Love lifted me, 725

I WAS sinking deep in sin,
   Far from the peaceful shore;
Very deeply stained within,
   Sinking to rise no more;
But the Master of the sea
   Heard my despairing cry,
From the waters lifted me;
   Now safe am I.

Love lifted me, love lifted me,
When no one but Christ could help,
   Love lifted me.

2 All my heart to him I give,
      Ever to him I'll cling;
   In his blessèd presence live,
      Ever his praises sing.
   Love so mighty and so true
      Merits my soul's best songs;
   Faithful, loving service, too,
      To him belongs.

3 Souls in danger, look above,
      Jesus completely saves;
   He will lift you by his love
      Out of the angry waves.
   He's the Master of the sea,
      Billows his will obey;
   He your Saviour wants to be,
      Be saved today.
                            James Rowe (1865-1933)

337 I will sing the wondrous story, 381
8.7.8.7. Troch

I WILL sing the wondrous story
   Of the Christ who died for me,
How he left his home in Glory,
   For the cross on Calvary.

Yes, I'll sing the wondrous story
   Of the Christ who died for me;
Sing it with the saints in Glory,
   Gathered by the crystal sea.

2 I was lost, but Jesus found me,
      Found the sheep that went astray,
   Threw his loving arms around me,
      Drew me back into his way.

3 I was bruised, but Jesus healed me,
      Faint was I from many a fall;
   Sight was gone and fears possessed me,
      But he freed me from them all.

4 Days of darkness still come o'er me,
      Sorrow's path I often tread,
   But the Saviour still is with me,
      By his hand I'm safely led.
              Francis Harold Rowley (1854-1952) (verses)

338 I love Jesus, 375; I'm a soldier, 382
8.7.8.7. Troch

I'M a soldier bound for Glory,
   I'm a soldier going home;
Come and hear me tell my story,
   All who love the Saviour, come.

I love Jesus, hallelujah!
   I love Jesus, yes, I do;
I love Jesus, he's my Saviour,
   Jesus smiles and loves me too.

2 I will tell you what induced me
      In the glorious fight to start;
   'Twas the Saviour's loving kindness
      Overcame and won my heart.

3 When I first commenced my warfare
      Many said I'd run away;
   But they all have been deceivèd,
      In the fight I am today.

4 I'm a wonder unto many,
      God alone the change has wrought;
   Here I raise my Ebenezer,
      Hither by his help I'm brought.

5 When to death's dark, swelling river,
      Like a warrior I shall come,
   Then I mean to shout salvation!
      And go singing glory! home.
                          Richard Jukes (1804-67), alt

339 He lifted me, 472

8.8.8.6.

IN loving kindness Jesus came,
My soul in mercy to reclaim,
And from the depths of sin and shame
Through grace he lifted me.

From sinking sand he lifted me;
With tender hand he lifted me;
From shades of night to plains of light,
O praise his name, he lifted me!

2 He called me long before I heard,
Before my sinful heart was stirred;
But when I took him at his word,
Forgiven, he lifted me.

3 His brow was pierced by many a thorn,
His hands by cruel nails were torn,
When from my guilt and grief, forlorn,
In love, he lifted me.

4 Now on a higher plane I dwell,
And with my soul I know 'tis well;
Yet how or why, I cannot tell,
He should have lifted me.

Charlotte G. Homer

340 A melody in my heart, 596

IN my heart there's a gladsome melody,
A song of cheer is ringing clear,
For my heavy burden rolled away,
What a happy, happy day!

In my heart today,
There's a melody in my heart today,
I carried a heavy burden, but it rolled
away;
There's a melody in my heart today.

2 It was love wrought the change so
wonderful,
His love for me, beyond degree,
Found me in the dreary wilderness,
Filled my heart with happiness.

3 And the way grows brighter every day,
What peace is mine! What joy divine!
And the load of sin that burdened me,
Rolled away at Calvary.

Sidney Edward Cox (1887-1975)

341 O what a hiding place, 760

IN the love of Jesus I have found a refuge,
Though the winds may blow, this one
thing I know,
He who never faileth is my shield and
shelter,
And he leads me where still waters flow;
He leads me where still waters flow.

O what a hiding place,
What a precious hiding place,
In the love of Jesus!
In the love of Jesus!
O what a hiding place,
What a precious hiding place,
In the love of Jesus!

2 In his love abiding, in the rock I'm hiding,
Lord of life is he, yet he thinks of me
Oft-times weak and wayward; yet in great
compassion
Jesus watches, O so tenderly,
He watches, O so tenderly!

3 How my soul rejoices in this mighty
Saviour,
His unmeasured grace for a fallen race;
There upon the cross he wrought so great
salvation,
There in love divine, he took my place;
In love divine, he took my place.

Sidney Edward Cox (1887-1975)

342 When his love reached me, 849

IT was love reached me when far away,
The love of my precious Saviour;
He gave himself my debt to pay,
My wonderful, wonderful Saviour.

When his love reached me he set my
heart a-singing,
When his love reached me,
wondrous love reached me;
And the bells of Heaven with harmony
are ringing,
For his love reached me.

2 It is love that keeps me day by day,
The love of my precious Saviour;
He guides me lest my feet should stray,
My wonderful, wonderful Saviour.

3 It is love supplies my every need,
The love of my precious Saviour;
The bread of life my soul to feed,
My wonderful, wonderful Saviour.

Sidney Edward Cox (1887-1975)

Witness

343 Meet me at the fountain, 440;
Let the lower lights be burning, 386
8.7.8.7. D. Troch.

I'VE a friend, of friends the fairest,
  I have known and proved him long;
His is beauty, purest, rarest,
  His is love most true and strong.
Ever since his kindness drew me,
  And my newborn soul found breath,
Jesus has been growing dearer,
  Till to lose him would be death.

Take the world, but give me Jesus,
  He alone can satisfy;
Take the world, but give me Jesus;
  'Neath his cross I'll live and die.

2 When my heart with joy is glowing,
  'Tis of Jesus I would sing,
When my cup is overflowing,
  To his feet my praises bring.
And when care and sorrow meet me,
  Pain and grief and dark distress,
Still I cry: O give me Jesus,
  He alone can help and bless!

3 Would you gain this friend so tender?
  Would you find this faithful guide?
Come then, make a full surrender,
  Yield to Jesus crucified.
Take his easy yoke upon you,
  And his purpose daily learn,
Just to do his will entirely,
  Pleasing him your chief concern.
                    Ruth Tracy (1870-1960)

344 The lily of the valley, 819

I'VE found a friend in Jesus, he's everything to me,
  He's the fairest of ten thousand to my soul;
The lily of the valley, in him alone I see
  All I need to cleanse and make me fully whole.
In sorrow he's my comfort, in trouble he's my stay,
  He tells me every care on him to roll.

He's the lily of the valley, the bright
  and morning star,
He's the fairest of ten thousand to my
  soul.

2 He all my griefs has taken, and all my
    sorrows borne,
  In temptation he's my strong and mighty
    tower;

I've all for him forsaken, I've all my idols
    torn
  From my heart, and now he keeps me
    by his power.
Though all the world forsake me, and
    Satan tempt me sore,
  Through Jesus I shall safely reach
    the goal.

3 He'll never, never leave me, nor yet forsake me here,
  While I live by faith and do his blessèd
    will;
A wall of fire about me, I've nothing now
    to fear,
  With his manna he my hungry soul shall
    fill.
Then sweeping up to Glory, I'll see his
    blessèd face
  Where rivers of delight shall ever flow.
                    Charles Fry (1838-82)

345 I've found a friend, 359
8.7.8.7. D. Iambic

I'VE found a friend, O such a friend!
  He loved me ere I knew him;
He drew me with the cords of love,
  And thus he bound me to him.
And round my heart still closely twine
  Those ties which naught can sever;
For I am his, and he is mine,
  For ever and for ever.

2 I've found a friend, O such a friend!
  He bled, he died to save me;
And not alone the gift of life,
  But his own self he gave me.
Naught that I have my own I call,
  I hold it for the giver;
My heart, my strength, my life, my all
  Are his, and his for ever!

3 I've found a friend, O such a friend!
  All power to him is given
To guard me on my onward course
  And bring me safe to Heaven.
Eternal glories gleam afar
  To nerve my faint endeavor;
So now to watch, to work, to war,
  And then to rest for ever.

95

4 I've found a friend, O such a friend,
So kind, so true and tender,
So wise a counselor and guide,
So mighty a defender!
From him, who loves me now so well,
What power my soul can sever?
Shall life or death? shall earth or Hell?
No! I am his for ever.
James Grindlay Small (1817-88)

346 I've found the pearl, 100;
Nativity New, 117   C.M.

I'VE found the pearl of greatest price,
My heart doth sing for joy;
And sing I must, for Christ I have,
O what a Christ have I!

2 My Christ, he is the Lord of lords,
He is the King of kings,
He is the Sun of righteousness
With healing in his wings.

3 My Christ, he is the tree of life,
Which in God's garden grows,
Whose fruits do feed, whose leaves do heal,
My Christ is Sharon's rose.

4 Christ is my meat, Christ is my drink,
My medicine and health,
My peace, my strength, my joy, my crown,
My glory and my wealth.

5 My Christ, he is the Heaven of heavens,
My Christ, what shall I call?
My Christ is first, my Christ is last,
My Christ is all-in-all.
John Mason (1645-94)

347 This one thing I know, 834

JESUS came to save me
By his precious blood,
Purchased my salvation,
Brought me home to God;
Cleansed my heart as white as snow:
This one thing I know!

This one thing I know!
This one thing I know!
God in great mercy pardoned me,
Snapped sin's fetters and set me free;
Once I was blind but now I see:
This one thing I know!

2 Jesus lives to keep me:
O what wondrous love!
In the Father's presence,
Advocate above;
Keeps me when sin's tempests blow:
This one thing I know!

3 What a precious Saviour,
Of his grace I sing;
Once despised, rejected,
Soon our coming King.
On my path his light doth glow:
This one thing I know!
Sidney Edward Cox (1887-1975)

348 O that's the place, 757;
Where I love to be, 854

JESUS is my Saviour, this I know,
He has given peace to my heart.
When my soul was burdened, filled full of
woe,
Seeking from my sin to part,
Graciously he heard me when I prayed,
Drew me to his riven side,
There by faith I washed, and so was saved,
His blood was there applied.

O that's the place where I love to be,
For mighty wonders there I see.
Would you be blest? Then tarry with me
At the cross of Jesus.

2 There I came to Jesus, bound and sad,
Liberty I claimed from my sin;
Readily he gave it, and O so glad
Was my heart then made by him.
Fetters which had bound me he destroyed;
Blessèd is the spot to me
Where I knelt to thank him, overjoyed
To find my soul was free.

3 Would you know the peace which Jesus
gives?
Would you know the joy he bestows?
Would you know the strength the sinner
receives
When his heart the blood o'erflows?
Come, without delaying, let us go
Where the precious fountain springs
That can make the sinner white as snow,
Removing all his sins.
Richard Slater (1854-1939)

349 Now I belong to Jesus, 751

JESUS my Lord will love me for ever,
From him no power of evil can sever,
He gave his life to ransom my soul,
Now I belong to him.

Now I belong to Jesus,
Jesus belongs to me,
Not for the years of time alone,
But for eternity.

2 Once I was lost in sin's degradation;
Jesus came down to bring me salvation,
Lifted me up from sorrow and shame,
Now I belong to him.

3 Joy floods my soul for Jesus has saved
me,
Freed me from sin that long had enslaved
me,
His precious blood he gave to redeem,
Now I belong to him.
Norman John Clayton

350 Regent Square, 423
8.7.8.7.8.7. Troch.

JESUS saved me! O the rapture
Of that soul-transporting hour,
When in love he stooped to reach me,
Plucked me thence from Satan's power!
O the rapture! O the rapture
Of that soul-transporting hour!

2 Jesus saves me! O the wonder
Of that constant cleansing flow,
Breaking forth from Calvary's mountain,
Making me as white as snow!
O the wonder! O the wonder
Of that constant cleansing flow!

3 He will save me! O what comfort
For unmeasured days to be!
Even when I near the river
He will still be saving me.
O what comfort! O what comfort
He will still be saving me!
Sidney Robert Hubbard (1898-1984)

351 The well is deep, 825

LIFE is a journey; long is the road,
And when the noontide is high
Souls that are weary faint 'neath their load,
Long for the waters, and cry:

The well is deep and I require
A draught of the water of life,
But none can quench my soul's desire
For a draught of the water of life;
Till one draws near who the cry will
heed,
Helper of men in their time of need,
And I, believing, find indeed
That Christ is the water of life.

2 Life is a seeking, life is a quest,
Eager and longing desire;
Unto the true things, unto the best,
Godward our spirits aspire.

3 Life is a finding; vain wand'rings cease
When from the Saviour we claim
All we have longed for, solace and peace,
And we have life in his name.
Albert Orsborn (1886-1967)

352 Armageddon, 200; Rachie, 207
6.5.6.5. D.

LIVING in the fountain,
Walking in the light,
Now and ever trusting
Jesus and his might;
Always realizing
Jesus and his smile
To be ever with me,
In me all the while.

Witnessing for Jesus,
I am fully his;
Everything for Jesus,
O what joy he gives!

2 Having for my portion
Jesus and his joy,
Joy which none can hinder,
Nothing can destroy;
Living and believing,
Saved from every fear,
Working and receiving
Heavenly wages here.

3 Fighting for his glory,
Standing by his cross,
Whether it be profit,
Whether it be loss;
By and by he'll call me:
Lay thy weapons down,
Ended is thy warfare,
Come and take thy crown.
Bramwell Booth (1856-1929)

The Gospel

353 Beethoven, 9; Silver Hill, 48
L.M.

LORD, I was blind! I could not see
In thy marred visage any grace;
But now the beauty of thy face
In radiant vision dawns on me.

2 Lord, I was deaf! I could not hear
The thrilling music of thy voice;
But now I hear thee and rejoice,
And sweet are all thy words and dear.

3 Lord, I was dumb! I could not speak
The grace and glory of thy name;
But now, as touched with living flame,
My lips thine eager praises wake.

4 Lord, I was dead! I could not stir
My lifeless soul to come to thee;
But now, since thou hast quickened me,
I rise from sin's dark sepulchre.

5 For thou hast made the blind to see,
The deaf to hear, the dumb to speak,
The dead to live; and lo! I break
The chains of my captivity.
William Tidd Matson (1833-99)

354 I'm the child of a King, 562
11.11.11.11.

MY Father is rich in houses and lands,
He holdeth the wealth of the world in
his hands;
Of rubies and diamonds, of silver and gold,
His coffers are full, he has riches untold.

I'm the child of a King;
I'm the child of a King;
With Jesus my Saviour,
I'm the child of a King!

2 My Father's own Son, the Saviour of men,
Once wandered on earth as the poorest of
them,
But now he is reigning for ever on high
And will give me a home in Heaven by and
by.

3 I once was an outcast, a stranger on earth,
A sinner by choice, and an alien by birth;
But I've been adopted, my name's written
down
An heir to a mansion, a robe and a crown.

4 A tent or a cottage, why should I care?
They're building a palace for me over there;
Though exiled from home, yet still I may
sing:
All glory to God, I'm the child of a King.
Harriet Eugenia Peck Buell (1834-1910)

355 My God, I am thine, 739;
Harwich New, 532

MY God, I am thine;
What a comfort divine,
What a blessing to know that my Jesus is
mine!

Hallelujah, send the glory! Hallelujah,
amen!
Hallelujah, send the glory! Revive us
again.

2 In the heavenly Lamb
Thrice happy I am,
And my heart it doth dance at the sound
of his name.

3 True pleasures abound
In the rapturous sound,
And whoever has found it hath Paradise
found.

4 My Jesus to know,
And feel his blood flow,
'Tis life everlasting, 'tis Heaven below.

5 Yet onward I haste
To the heavenly feast,
That, that is the fulness, but this is the
taste.

6 And this I shall prove,
Till with joy I remove
To the Heaven of heavens in Jesus' love.
Charles Wesley (1707-88) (verses)

356 Christ for me, 332; God is love, 333;
Zealley, 338
8.3.8.3.8.8.8.3.

MY heart is fixed, eternal God,
Fixed on thee;
And my unchanging choice is made,
Christ for me.
He is my prophet, priest and King,
Who did for me salvation bring,
And while I've breath I mean to sing:
Christ for me.

2 Let others boast of heaps of gold,
Christ for me.
His riches never can be told,
Christ for me.
Your gold will waste and wear away,
Your honors perish in a day,
My portion never can decay,
Christ for me.

3 In pining sickness or in health,
  Christ for me.
In deepest poverty or wealth,
  Christ for me.
And in that all-important day,
When I the summons must obey,
And pass from this dark world away,
  Christ for me.

4 At home, abroad, by night, by day,
  Christ for me.
Where'er I speak, or sing, or pray,
  Christ for me.
Him first and last, him all day long,
My hope, my solace, and my song,
I'll send the ringing cry along:
  Christ for me.
Richard Jukes (1804-67)

357 Unsworth, 577; Flow gently, sweet
Afton, 558   11.11.11.11.

MY Jesus, I love thee, I know thou art
  mine,
For thee all the pleasures of sin I resign;
My gracious Redeemer, my Saviour art
  thou,
If ever I loved thee, my Jesus, 'tis now.

2 I love thee because thou hast first lovèd
  me,
And purchased my pardon on Calvary's
  tree;
I love thee for wearing the thorns on thy
  brow,
If ever I loved thee, my Jesus, 'tis now.

3 I will love thee in life, I will love thee in
  death,
And praise thee as long as thou lendest
  me breath;
And say, when the death-dew lies cold on
  my brow:
If ever I loved thee, my Jesus, 'tis now.

4 In mansions of Glory and endless delight,
I'll ever adore thee and dwell in thy sight;
I'll sing with the glittering crown on my
  brow:
If ever I loved thee, my Jesus, 'tis now.
William Ralph Featherstone (1846-73)

358 Bishopgarth, 358; I've found a friend,
359   8.7.8.7. D. Iambic

MY life flows on in endless song;
  Above earth's lamentation
I hear the sweet though far-off hymn
  That hails a new creation.

Through all the tumult and the strife
  I hear the music ringing;
It finds an echo in my soul;
  How can I keep from singing?

2 What though my joys and comforts die,
  The Lord, my Saviour, liveth!
What though the darkness gather round,
  Songs in the night he giveth!
No storm can shake my inmost calm
  While to that refuge clinging;
Since Christ is Lord of Heaven and earth
  How can I keep from singing?

3 I lift mine eyes, the cloud grows thin,
  I see the blue above it;
And day by day this pathway smooths
  Since first I learned to love it.
The peace of Christ makes fresh my heart,
  A fountain ever springing;
All things are mine since I am his;
  How can I keep from singing?
Anon

359 I've washed my robes, 29
                L.M.

MY robes were once all stained with sin;
  I knew not how to make them clean
Until a voice said, sweet and low:
Go wash, I'll make them white as snow.

*I've washed my robes in Jesus' blood,
And he has made them white as snow.*

2 That promise: Whosoever will,
Included me, includes me still;
I came, and ever since I know
His blood has cleansed me white as snow.

3 I do not doubt, nor do I say:
I hope the stains are washed away;
For in my heart I read it so,
His blood has cleansed me white as snow.

4 O who will come and wash today
Till all their sins are washed away,
Until, by faith, they see and know
Their robes are washed as white as snow?
Edwin Othello Excell (1851-1921)

360 My Saviour suffered on the tree, 741

MY Saviour suffered on the tree,
  Glory to the bleeding Lamb!
O come and praise the Lord with me!
  Glory to the bleeding Lamb!

The Gospel

The Lamb, the Lamb, the bleeding
  Lamb,
I love the sound of Jesus' name,
It sets my spirit all in a flame,
Glory to the bleeding Lamb!

2 He bore my sins and curse and shame,
  Glory to the bleeding Lamb!
And I am saved through Jesus' name,
  Glory to the bleeding Lamb!

3 I know my sins are all forgiven,
  Glory to the bleeding Lamb!
And I am on my way to Heaven,
  Glory to the bleeding Lamb!

4 And this my ceaseless song shall be,
  Glory to the bleeding Lamb!
That Jesus tasted death for me,
  Glory to the bleeding Lamb!
attr Hodgson Casson (1788-1851)

361 My soul is now united, 257;
Missionary, 256   7.6.7.6. D. Iambic

MY soul is now united to Christ, the
  living vine;
His grace I long have slighted, but now I
  feel him mine;
I was to God a stranger till Jesus took me
  in,
He freed my soul from danger and pardoned all my sin.

2 Soon as my all I ventured on the atoning
  blood,
The Holy Spirit entered, and I was born of
  God;
My sins are all forgiven, I feel his blood
  applied,
And I shall go to Heaven if I in Christ abide.

3 By floods and flames surrounded, I still
  my way pursue,
Nor shall I be confounded, with Glory in
  my view;
Still Christ is my salvation; what can I
  covet more?
I fear no condemnation, my Father's wrath
  is o'er.
Hugh Bourne (1772-1852),
William Sanders (1799-1882)

362 Chalvey, 181; Diademata, 182
D.S.M.

NO home on earth have I,
  No nation owns my soul,
My dwelling place is the Most High,
  I'm under his control.
O'er all the earth alike,
  My Father's grand domain,
Each land and sea with him alike
  O'er all he yet shall reign.

2 No place on earth I own,
  No field, no house be mine;
Myself, my all I still disown,
  My God, let all be thine.
Into thy gracious hands
  My life is ever placed;
To die fulfilling thy commands,
  I march with bounding haste.

3 With thee, my God, is home;
  With thee is endless joy;
With thee in ceaseless rest I roam;
  With thee, can death destroy?
With thee, the east, the west,
  The north, the south are one;
The battle's front I love the best,
  And yet: thy will be done.
George Scott Railton (1849-1913)

363 What a Saviour! 406
8.7.8.7. Troch.

NONE the love of Christ can measure,
  None its depths can ever tell,
None can estimate the treasure
  Held by those who with him dwell.

On the cross his life did Jesus give for
  me;
What a Saviour! Hallelujah!
There he died for me who was his
  enemy;
What a Saviour I have found!

2 O how wondrous is the story!
  That his pardon I might claim
Jesus left the realms of Glory
  And on earth a man became.

3 Heavy-laden I approached him,
  Sorrow filled my aching heart,
But the blessèd word was spoken,
  Bidding all my fear depart.

4 Hope each guilty soul may cherish,
  Trembling hearts need not despair,
Jesus died that none might perish,
  He for all sin's curse did bear.
Richard Slater (1854-1939)

100

364 O bliss of the purified, 568;
St Denio, 569;
Foundation, A.S. 976   11.11.11.11.

O BLISS of the purified, bliss of the free!
   I plunge in the crimson tide opened
     for me.
O'er sin and uncleanness exulting I stand,
And point to the print of the nails in his
     hand.

O sing of his mighty love,
Sing of his mighty love,
Sing of his mighty love,
   Mighty to save!

2 O bliss of the purified, Jesus is mine!
   No longer in dread condemnation I pine.
   Quite sure of salvation I sing of his grace,
   Who lifted upon me the smile of his face.

3 O bliss of the purified, bliss of the pure!
   No wound hath the soul that his blood
     cannot cure.
   The sorrowing heart shall in Jesus find
     rest,
   The tears of the mourner be dried on his
     breast.

4 O Jesus the crucified, thee will I sing,
   My blessèd Redeemer, my God and my
     King!
   My soul filled with rapture shall shout o'er
     the grave
   And triumph in death in the mighty to
     save.
                    Francis Bottome (1823-94)

365 O happy day, 37; Morning Hymn, 35
                                    L.M.

O HAPPY day that fixed my choice
   On thee, my Saviour and my God!
Well may this glowing heart rejoice,
   And tell its rapture all abroad.

   Happy day, happy day,
When Jesus washed my sins away!
He taught me how to watch and pray,
And live rejoicing every day;
   Happy day, happy day,
When Jesus washed my sins away.

2 O happy bond that seals my vows
   To him who merits all my love!
   Let cheerful praises fill his house
   While to his blessèd throne I move.

3 'Tis done, the great transaction's done!
   I am my Lord's and he is mine;
   He drew me, and I followed on,
   Charmed to confess the voice divine.
              Philip Doddridge (1702-51) (verses)

366 Down where the living waters flow, 233;
Ascalon, 232   6.6.8.6.6.8.

O HAPPY, happy day
   When old things passed away,
There where the Saviour died for me!
   I knew my sins forgiven
   And had a sight of Heaven,
There where the Saviour died for me.

There where the Saviour died for me;
There where the Saviour died for me;
I saw the cleansing flow
That washes white as snow,
There where the Saviour died for me.

2 I laid my burden down,
   And started for the crown,
There where the Saviour died for me.
   My soul was free at last,
   My sins behind him cast,
There where the Saviour died for me.

3 'Twas there I learned to pray
   And found the narrow way,
There where the Saviour died for me.
   I saw his blessèd face
   And joined the heavenly race,
There where the Saviour died for me.

4 He wiped away my tears
   And drove away my fears,
There where the Saviour died for me.
   He whispered: Go in peace;
   And bade my struggling cease,
There where the Saviour died for me.

5 Though Hell should me assail,
   Through prayer I shall prevail,
There where the Saviour died for me.
   I never need retreat,
   Nor suffer a defeat,
There where the Saviour died for me.
                    John Lawley (1859-1922)

367 We'll all shout hallelujah, 587
                              12.9.12.9.

O HOW happy are they who the Saviour
     obey,
   And have laid up their treasure above.
Tongue can never express the sweet com-
     fort and peace
   Of a soul filled with Jesus' love.

The Gospel

We'll all shout hallelujah
As we march along the way.
We will sing redeeming love
With the shining hosts above,
And with Jesus we'll be happy all the
day.

2 That sweet comfort is mine now the favor
divine
I've received through the blood of the
Lamb;
With my heart I believe, and what joy I
receive,
What a heaven in Jesus' name!

3 'Tis a Heaven below my Redeemer to know,
And the angels can do nothing more
Than to fall at his feet and the story repeat,
And the lover of sinners adore.

4 O the rapturous height of the holy delight
Which I feel in the life-giving blood!
Of my Saviour possessed, I am perfectly
blessed,
As if filled with the Heaven of God.
Charles Wesley (1707-88) (verses), alt

368 The blue bells of Scotland, 813

O JESUS, O Jesus, how vast thy love to
me!
I'll bathe in its full ocean to all eternity;
And wending on to Glory this all my song
shall be:
I was a guilty sinner, but Jesus died for
me.

2 O Calvary, O Calvary, the thorn, the crown,
the spear!
'Tis there thy love, my Jesus, in flowing
wounds appears;
O depths of love and mercy, to those dear
wounds I flee;
I was a guilty sinner, but Jesus died for
me.

3 I'm coming, I'm coming, dear Jesus, to
thy throne,
A few more fleeting hours and I shall be
at home;
And when I reach those pearly gates then
I'll put in this plea:
I was a guilty sinner, but Jesus died for
me.

4 In Glory, in Glory, forever with the Lord,
I'll tune my harp and with the saints will
sing in sweet accord;
And as I strike those golden strings, this
all my theme shall be:
I was a guilty sinner, but Jesus pardoned
me.
Anon

369 Climbing up the golden stair, 629

O MY heart is full of music and of
gladness,
As on wings of love and faith I upward fly;
Not a shadow-cloud my Saviour's face
obscuring,
While I'm climbing to my homestead in
the sky.

O I'm climbing up the golden stair to
Glory,
O I'm climbing with my golden crown
before me,
I am climbing in the light,
I am climbing day and night,
I shall shout with all my might when I
get there!
O I'm climbing up the golden stair to
Glory,
O I'm climbing with my golden crown
before me,
I am climbing in the light,
I am climbing day and night,
I am climbing up the golden stair!

2 Every day it seems I want to love him
better,
Every day it seems I want to serve him
more,
Every day I strive to climb the ladder faster,
Every effort brings me nearer Canaan's
shore.

3 O the joy of getting others to climb with
me!
Lost, despairing, broken-hearted, all may
come;
Calvary-love has made the stair a very wide
one;
Sinners, lay your burden down and hasten home.
Emma Booth-Tucker (1860-1903)

Witness

370 Regent Square, 423; Praise, my soul, 422
8.7.8.7.8.7. Troch.

O THOU God of my salvation,
   My redeemer from all sin,
Moved by thy divine compassion,
   Who hast died my heart to win,
      I will praise thee;
   Where shall I thy praise begin?

2 Though unseen, I love the Saviour;
   He hath brought salvation near,
Manifests his pardoning favor
   And within me doth appear;
      Soul and body
   Then his glorious image bear.

3 While the angel choirs are crying:
   Glory to the great I AM!
I with them will still be vying,
   Glory, glory to the Lamb!
      O how precious
   Is the sound of Jesus' name!

4 Angels now are hovering round us
   Unperceived amid the throng,
Wondering at the love that found us,
   Glad to join our holy song;
      Hallelujah!
   Love and praise to Christ belong.
                    Thomas Olivers (1725-99)

371 Heaven came down, 666

O WHAT a wonderful, wonderful day,
   Day I will never forget!
After I'd wandered in darkness away,
   Jesus my Saviour I met!
O what a tender, compassionate friend,
   He met the need of my heart!
Shadows dispelling, with joy I am telling,
   He made all the darkness depart.

*Heaven came down and Glory filled my
      soul,
When at the cross the Saviour made
      me whole;
   My sins were washed away,
   And my night was turned to day,
Heaven came down and Glory filled my
      soul.*

2 Born of the Spirit with life from above
   Into God's family divine,
Justified fully through Calvary's love,
   O what a standing is mine!

And the transaction so quickly was made
   When as a sinner I came,
Took of the offer of grace he did proffer,
   He saved me, O praise his dear name!

3 Now I've a hope that will surely endure
   After the passing of time,
I have a future in Heaven for sure,
   There in those mansions sublime.
And it's because of that wonderful day,
   When at the cross I believed;
Riches eternal and blessings supernal
   From his precious hand I received.
                    John W. Peterson

372 Hanover, 531; Houghton, 533
10.10.11.11.

O WHAT shall I do my Saviour to praise,
   So faithful and true, so plenteous in
      grace,
So strong to deliver, so good to redeem
The weakest believer that hangs upon
      him?

2 How happy the man whose heart is set
      free,
The people that can be joyful in thee;
Their joy is to walk in the light of thy face,
And still they are talking of Jesus' grace.

3 Their daily delight shall be in thy name,
They shall as their right thy righteous-
      ness claim;
Thy righteousness wearing, and cleansed
      by thy blood,
Bold shall they appear in the presence of
      God.

4 Yes, Lord, I shall see the bliss of thine
      own,
Thy secret to me shall soon be made
      known;
For sorrow and sadness I joy shall receive,
And share in the gladness of all that
      believe.
                    Charles Wesley (1707-88)

373 Open and let the Master in, 765

ONCE I heard a sound at my heart's dark
      door
   And was roused from the slumber of sin;
It was Jesus knocked, he had knocked
      before,
   Now I said: Blessèd Master, come in!

The Gospel

Then open, open, open and let the
    Master in!
For your heart will be bright
With the heavenly light,
If you'll only let the Master in.

2 Then he spread a feast of redeeming love
   And he made me his own happy guest;
   In my joy I thought that the saints above
   Could be hardly more favored or blest.

3 In the holy war with the foes of truth,
   He's my shield, he my table prepares;
   He restores my soul, he renews my youth,
   And gives triumph in answer to prayers.

4 He will feast me still with his presence
       dear,
   And the love he so freely hath given;
   While his promise tells, as I serve him
       here,
   Of the banquet of glory in Heaven.
        Sylvanus Dryden Phelps (1816-95) (verses),
            Robert Lowry (1826-99) (chorus)

374 Down where the living waters flow, 233;
        Ascalon, 232   6.6.8.6.6.8.

ONCE I was far in sin,
    But Jesus took me in,
Down where the living waters flow;
    'Twas there he gave me sight,
    And let me see the light,
Down where the living waters flow.

Down where the living waters flow,
Down where the tree of life does grow;
    I'm living in the light,
    For Jesus now I fight,
Down where the living waters flow.

2   With Jesus at my side,
    I need no other guide,
Down where the living waters flow;
    He is my hope and stay,
    He saves me every day,
Down where the living waters flow.

3   When fighting here is o'er,
    I'll rest for evermore,
Down where the living waters flow;
    I'll join the blood-washed throng,
    And sing the angels' song,
Down where the living waters flow.
        James Conner Bateman (1854-88) (verses),
        Russell Kelso Carter (1849-1926) (chorus)

375 Bound for Canaan's shore, 145

ONCE I was lost, on the breakers tossed,
    And far away from shore;
My drifting bark all in the dark,
    No beacon light before.
I was sinking fast when the lifeboat passed
    And the Captain took me in;
Now the storm is o'er and I fear no more,
    I have perfect peace within.

I'm bound for Canaan's shore,
I'm bound for Canaan's shore,
I'm off for a trip in the gospel ship,
    To Canaan's happy shore.

2 Thank God! 'tis true, my heart's quite new,
   Old things have passed away;
   And now I know the cleansing flow
   Rolls o'er my soul each day.
   'Tis a glorious thing to know the sting
   Of death has been destroyed,
   And that Jesus lives in my heart, and gives
   What can sweetly be enjoyed!

3 And when at last, all dangers past,
   I join the blood-washed throng,
   Though with the least at the heavenly feast,
   I'll sing the glad new song.
   O what bliss complete when my Lord I
       meet
   In the banquet hall on high,
   And with comrades there in love I share
   The joys that never die!
        William Giles Collins (1854-1931), alt

376 When I came to him, 850

ONCE in misery I walked alone,
    Self-sufficient but sad,
But I found a friend to walk with me,
    And I tell you: I'm glad!

When I came to him Christ came to me,
Showed me what he planned that I
        should be;
I was liberated there and then,
O I'll never be the same again!

2 In the ruins of my life I stood,
   I was drowning in tears,
But I found a friend to stand by me,
   And I lost all my fears.

3 Discontented with a pointless life,
   For direction I sighed;
Life has point and purpose now for me,
   Since I made him my guide.
                    John Gowans

Witness

377 All through the night, 339
8.4.8.4.8.8.8.4.

ONE there is above all others,
    O how he loves!
His is love beyond a brother's,
    O how he loves!
Earthly friends may fail or leave us,
One day kind, the next deceive us;
But this friend will never leave us,
    O how he loves!

2 'Tis eternal life to know him,
    O how he loves!
Think, O think how much we owe him,
    O how he loves!
With his precious blood he bought us,
In the wilderness he sought us,
To his fold he safely brought us,
    O how he loves!

3 We have found a friend in Jesus,
    O how he loves!
'Tis his great delight to bless us,
    O how he loves!
How our hearts delight to hear him,
Bid us dwell in safety near him;
Why should we distrust or fear him?
    O how he loves!

4 Blessèd Jesus, wouldst thou know him?
    O how he loves!
Give thyself this moment to him,
    O how he loves!
Best of blessings he'll provide thee,
Naught but good shall e'er betide thee,
Safe to Glory he will guide thee,
    O how he loves!
Mary Ann Nunn (1778-1847)

378 Out of my darkness, 455
8.7.8.7. Dact.

OUT of my darkness God called me,
    Out of the depth of my night,
Out of the shadows of sorrow,
    Into the life of his light.

2 Out of my darkness he called me,
    Out of my doubt, my despair,
Out of the wastes of my winter,
    Into the spring of his care.

3 Out of my darkness he called me
    Into his sunshining day,
Out of my gloom to his glory;
    What could I do but obey?

4 Out of your darkness he calls you,
    Out of your doubt, your despair,
Out of the wastes of your winter,
    Into the spring of his care.
John Gowans

379 Jesus came with peace to me, 699

PLEASURES sought, dearly bought,
    Leading only further from the light;
    Blinded eyes, weary sighs,
Thus grief-laden did I wander in sin's
    night.

Jesus came with peace to me,
His strong arm was stretched to me,
Then my burden took from me—
    My Saviour.

2 Wasted years, doubts and fears,
    I no treasure had in Heaven above;
    Idle hours, misspent powers
Stained my heart, unmoved by Jesus'
    wondrous love.

3 Hollow joys, worldly toys,
    Could not meet my spirit's deep desire;
    Without rest, in my breast
Rose the yearning for the Spirit's
    hallowed fire.

4 Heaven's ray falls today
    On my soul, and makes my pathway
    bright;
    Struggles cease, I have peace,
Walking with my Saviour, trusting in his
    might.
Agnes Parker Heathcote (b 1862)

380 And above the rest, 5; Solid Rock, 501
L.M.

PRAISE God for what he's done for me!
    Once I was blind, but now I see;
I on the brink of ruin fell;
Glory to God, I'm out of Hell!

For what the Lord has done for me,
I'll praise him through eternity.

2 I spurned his grace, I broke his laws,
But Jesus undertook my cause;
Bad as I was he cleansed my soul,
Healed my disease and made me whole.

3 The Lord has pardoned all my sin,
And now to praise him I'll begin;
I never praised the Lord before,
But now I'll praise him more and more.
Anon

The Gospel

381
Saints of God, 781

SAINTS of God, lift up your voices,
    Praise ye the Lord!
While the host of Heaven rejoices,
    Praise ye the Lord!
Praise him as ye onward go
To the realms of endless glory;
Let his praise each heart o'erflow,
    Praise ye the Lord!

2 For the hope of every nation,
    Praise ye the Lord!
He has bought for us salvation,
    Praise ye the Lord!
Jesus died for you and me,
Died for all on Calvary's mountain;
Every sinner may be free,
    Praise ye the Lord!

3 Thousands have in Christ believèd,
    Praise ye the Lord!
And his pardoning love receivèd,
    Praise ye the Lord!
We have joined the happy throng,
God is with us, we're his soldiers;
Jesus shall be all our song,
    Praise ye the Lord!

Anon

382
Lift up the banner, 106; Lydia, 110
C.M.

SALVATION! O the joyful sound!
    What pleasure to our ears!
A sovereign balm for every wound,
    A cordial for our fears.

So we'll lift up the banner on high,
    The salvation banner of love;
We'll fight beneath its colors till we die,
    Then go to our home above.

2 Salvation! let the echo fly
    The spacious earth around;
While all the armies of the sky
    Conspire to raise the sound.

3 Salvation! O thou bleeding Lamb,
    To thee the praise belongs;
Salvation shall inspire our hearts,
    And dwell upon our tongues.
Isaac Watts (1674-1748) (verses 1 and 2),
William Walter Shirley (1725-86) (verse 3),
William Thomas Giffe (b 1848) (chorus)

383
Glory! Glory! 652

SONGS of salvation are sounding
    Joyfully all the time;
Rivers of grace are abounding
    In every land and clime;
Life-giving waters are flowing
    Freely from Calvary;
Heavenly breezes are blowing,
    Fragrance of purity.

Glory! Glory!
Ring all the bells of Heaven!
    Glory! Glory! Praise ye his holy
        name!
Glory! Glory!
Angels and saints are singing,
Sinners to Jesus now clinging;
Gladly his love proclaim.

2 Love in its glory and beauty
    In the Redeemer we see,
Stronger than death, life or duty,
    Dying our souls to free.
Boundless and free as the ocean,
    High as the heavens above,
Sweeter than human devotion
    Is his eternal love.

3 Hearts that were broken and bleeding,
    Torn by remorse and grief,
Came to the mercy seat pleading,
    Finding complete relief.
Love in its fullness is flowing
    Here, where all sins depart,
Pardon and mercy bestowing
    Freely on every heart.
Gustaf Kaleb Johnson (1888-1965)

384
You can tell out the sweet story, 869

TELL out the wonderful story,
    Tell it where'er you go;
Tell of the King and his glory,
    Tell how he loved us so.
This is the story most precious,
Jesus has died to redeem us;
You can tell out the sweet story,
    You, yes, you.

You can tell out the sweet story,
    You, yes, you.
Somebody's life will be brighter,
Somebody's care will be lighter;
You can tell out the sweet story,
    You, yes, you.

2 Never a story so wondrous,
   Tell it to all around;
While we were sinners he loved us,
   Mercy and grace abound.
Wandering and weary he sought us,
Back to the Father he brought us;
You can tell out the sweet story,
   You, yes, you.

3 Wonderful story of Jesus,
   Tell every sin-sick soul;
Wonderful message of mercy,
   Jesus can make them whole.
Still flows the wonderful river,
From every sin to deliver;
You can tell out the sweet story,
   You, yes, you.
                    Sidney Edward Cox (1887-1975)

385 Jesus saves me now, 101
                                C.M.

THE glorious gospel word declares
   That even I may know
Redeeming love, and witness here
   That Jesus saves me now.

   Jesus saves me now!
   Jesus saves me now!
Yes, Jesus saves me all the time,
   Jesus saves me now!

2 God speaks, who cannot lie; why then
   One doubt should I allow?
I doubt him not, but take his word,
   And Jesus saves me now.

3 Temptations here upon me press,
   No strength is mine, I know;
Yet more than conqueror am I
   For Jesus saves me now.

4 Whate'er my future may require,
   His grace will sure allow;
I live a moment at a time
   And Jesus saves me now.
                    Thomas Bowman Stephenson
                         (1839-1912), alt

386 O what a wonderful day, 761

THE Saviour sought and found me,
   Far from the narrow way;
He made my blinded eyes to see
   On that wonderful, wonderful day.

He sought me, he sought me,
   When I was wandering far away;
He found me, he found me,
   O what a wonderful day!

2 He lifted sin's great burden,
   He saw my deep dismay,
And graciously he pardoned me
   On that wonderful, wonderful day.

3 My sin was red like crimson,
   He washed it all away;
He filled my heart with melody
   On that wonderful, wonderful day.
                    Sidney Edward Cox (1887-1975)

387 There is sunshine, 830

THERE is sunshine in my soul today,
   More glorious and bright
Than glows in any earthly sky,
   For Jesus is my light.

   O there's sunshine, blessèd sunshine,
   While the peaceful, happy moments
      roll!
When Jesus shows his smiling face,
   There is sunshine in my soul.

2 There is music in my soul today,
   A carol to my King,
And Jesus, listening, can hear
   The songs I cannot sing.

3 There is gladness in my soul today,
   And hope and praise and love,
For blessings which he gives me now,
   For joys laid up above.
                    Eliza Edmunds Hewitt (1851-1920)

388 He is mine! 664

THERE was a Saviour came seeking his
      sheep,
   He is mine!
Fording the torrent so rushing and deep,
   He is mine!
I was the sheep that had wandered away,
   He is mine!
Me on his shoulder he gently did lay,
   He is mine!

He is mine! He is mine!
   Loving me, seeking me,
   Finding me, keeping me,
   He is mine!

107

The Gospel

2 Steep was the mountain and dark was the
night,
  He is mine!
He came a-seeking, he pitied my plight,
  He is mine!
I could not hope for a happy return,
  He is mine!
But over me his kind Spirit did yearn,
  He is mine!

3 Great was the gladness when he brought
me home,
  He is mine!
Never a murmur and never a frown,
  He is mine!
Showered upon me his pardoning love,
  He is mine!
Told my homecoming to Heaven above,
  He is mine!

4 Say, do you wonder why always I sing,
  He is mine?
Call him my Saviour, my glorious King,
  He is mine?
Would you not like to be able to say
  He is mine?
O he is waiting to be this today,
  Yours and mine!

Edward Henry Joy (1871-1949)

389 In my heart a song is ringing, 690

THERE'S a song that's ringing in my
heart today,
  For I've found a loving friend,
  He'll be with me to the end;
Though the tempter's snares beset my
path below,
He is ever by my side, I know.

In my heart a song is ringing,
* For he pardoned me I know*
Just because he loved me so.
And I'm singing, singing, singing,
* Just because he loved me so.*

2 There's a song that's ringing in my heart
today,
  Jesus' power has set me free,
  And he gives me victory;
All my sin stains vanished in the crimson
flow,
And he'll keep me every hour, I know.

3 There's a song that's ringing in my heart
today,
  For I'll see my Saviour's face
  At the ending of the race;
Wear a spotless robe as white as driven
snow,
Hear the welcome from the King, I know.

Sidney Edward Cox (1887-1975)

390 He keeps me singing, 665

THERE'S within my heart a melody,
  Jesus whispers sweet and low:
Fear not, I am with thee; peace, be still
  In all of life's ebb and flow.

Jesus, Jesus, Jesus,
* Sweetest name I know,*
Fills my every longing,
* Keeps me singing as I go.*

2 All my life was wrecked by sin and strife,
  Discord filled my heart with pain;
Jesus swept across the broken strings,
  Stirred the slumbering chords again.

3 Feasting on the riches of his grace,
  Resting 'neath his sheltering wing,
Always looking on his smiling face;
  That is why I shout and sing.

Luther Burgess Bridgers (1884-1948)

391 Joy without alloy, 345; Whitechapel, 348
8.5.8.5.

THOUGH I wandered far from Jesus
  In the paths of sin,
Yet I heard him gently calling:
  Wanderer, come in.

Yes, he gave me peace and pardon,
* Joy without alloy.*

2 Though my burden pressed me sorely
  And my courage failed,
Christ released me, and his goodness
  O'er my sin prevailed.

3 Now I live for Christ my Saviour,
  Live to do his will;
Though the path be dark and thorny,
  I shall conquer still.

James Conner Bateman (1854-88)

392 Hallelujah! 'tis done, 594
12.12.

'TIS the promise of God full salvation to
give
Unto him who on Jesus, his Son, will
believe.

Hallelujah, 'tis done! I believe on the
   Son;
I am washed in the blood of the
   crucified one.

2 Those redeemed by the blood of their
     Saviour and Lord
  Sing for joy in his presence, in gladsome
     accord:

3 There are loved ones I know in that
     heavenly throng
  Whose sweet voices are raised in the
     triumphant song:

4 There's a place in that Kingdom for you
     and for me,
  And our anthem of praise shall eternally
     be:

          Philip Paul Bliss (1838-76)
          (verse 1 and chorus),
          Brindley Boon (verses 2-4)

393   Jesus Saves! 703

WE have heard the joyful sound:
   Jesus saves!
Tell the message all around:
   Jesus saves!
Bear the news to every land,
Climb the steeps and cross the waves;
Onward! 'tis our Lord's command:
   Jesus saves!

2 Waft it on the rolling tide:
     Jesus saves!
  Say to sinners far and wide:
     Jesus saves!
  Sing, ye islands of the sea,
  Echo back, ye ocean caves;
  Earth shall keep her jubilee:
     Jesus saves!

3 Sing above the toil and strife:
     Jesus saves!
  By his death and endless life
     Jesus saves!
  Sing it softly through the gloom,
  When the heart for mercy craves;
  Sing in triumph o'er the tomb:
     Jesus saves!

4 Give the winds a mighty voice:
     Jesus saves!
  Let the nations now rejoice:
     Jesus saves!
  Shout salvation full and free
  To each land the ocean laves;
  This our song of victory:
     Jesus saves!
        Priscilla Jane Owens (1829-1907)

394   Since Jesus came into my heart, 786

WHAT a wonderful change in my life has
   been wrought
  Since Jesus came into my heart.
I have light in my soul for which long I
   had sought
  Since Jesus came into my heart.

Since Jesus came into my heart,
Since Jesus came into my heart,
Floods of joy o'er my soul
Like the sea billows roll,
Since Jesus came into my heart.

2 I have ceased from my wandering and
     going astray,
  Since Jesus came into my heart.
  And my sins which were many are all
     washed away
  Since Jesus came into my heart.

3 I'm possessed of a hope that is steadfast
     and sure,
  Since Jesus came into my heart.
  And no dark clouds of doubt now my
     pathway obscure,
  Since Jesus came into my heart.

4 I shall go there to dwell in that city I know
  Since Jesus came into my heart.
  I am happy, so happy, as onward I go,
  Since Jesus came into my heart.
       Rufus Henry McDaniel (1850-1940)

395   At the cross, 580   12.9.12.9.

WHEN my heart was so hard
   That I ne'er would regard
The salvation held up to my sight,
   To the cross then I came
   In my darkness and shame,
And 'twas there that I first saw the light.

The Gospel

*At the cross, at the cross, where I first
    saw the light,
And the burden of my heart rolled
    away;
It was there, by faith, I received my
    sight,
And now I am happy all the day.*

2   In my blindness I thought
    That no power could have wrought
Such a marvel of wonder and might;
    But 'twas done, for I felt,
    At the cross as I knelt,
That my darkness was turned into light.

3   Then the gloom had all passed,
    And, rejoicing at last,
I was sure that my soul was made right;
    For my Lord, I could see,
    In his love died for me
On the cross, where I first saw the light.
    Herbert Howard Booth (1862-1926) (verses)

396 Count your blessings, 202
6.5.6.5. D.

WHEN upon life's billows you are
    tempest-tossed,
When you are discouraged, thinking all is
    lost,
Count your many blessings, name them
    one by one,
And it will surprise you what the Lord hath
    done.

*Count your blessings, name them one
    by one,
    Count your blessings, see what God
        hath done.
Count your blessings, name them one
    by one,
    And it will surprise you what the
        Lord hath done.*

2 Are you ever burdened with a load of care?
    Does the cross seem heavy you are called
        to bear?
Count your many blessings, every doubt
    will fly,
And you will keep singing as the days go
    by.

3 So amid the conflict, whether great or
        small,
    Do not be disheartened, God is over all;
Count your many blessings, angels will
    attend,
Help and comfort give you to your jour-
    ney's end.
    Johnson Oatman (1856-1922)

397 Trust and obey, 586
12.9.12.9.

WHEN we walk with the Lord
    In the light of his word,
What a glory he sheds on our way;
    While we do his good will,
    He abides with us still,
And with all who will trust and obey.

*Trust and obey, for there's no other
    way
To be happy in Jesus, but to trust and
    obey.*

2   Not a shadow can rise,
    Not a cloud in the skies,
But his smile quickly drives it away;
    Not a doubt nor a fear,
    Not a sigh nor a tear,
Can abide while we trust and obey.

3   Not a burden we bear,
    Not a sorrow we share,
But our toil he doth richly repay;
    Not a grief nor a loss,
    Not a frown nor a cross,
But is blessed if we trust and obey.

4   But we never can prove
    The delights of his love,
Until all on the altar we lay;
    For the favor he shows,
    And the joy he bestows,
Are for them who will trust and obey.

5   Then in fellowship sweet
    We will sit at his feet,
Or we'll walk by his side in the way;
    What he says we will do,
    Where he sends we will go,
Never fear, only trust and obey.
    John Henry Sammis (1846-1919)

398 I'll serve my Lord alone, 27
L.M.

WHEN wondrous words my Lord would
say,
That I unto his mind may reach,
He chooses out a lowly way,
And robes his thoughts in childlike
speech.

He came right down to me,
He came right down to me,
To condescend to be my friend,
He came right down to me.

2 The voice divine, those accents dear
I languished for, yet had not heard
Till Jesus came with message clear,
And brought to me the living word.

3 Nor could I see my maker's face,
Veiled from my sight his far abode,
Till Christ made known the Father's grace,
And shared with men their heavy load.

4 O Vision clear! O Voice divine!
Dear Son of God and Son of man!
Let all thy gifts of grace be mine;
Complete in me thy perfect plan.
Albert Orsborn (1886-1967)

399 Pleasure in his service, 442;
Bethany, 429   8.7.8.7. D. Troch.

WHERE are now those doubts that
hindered
All his will from being done?
When I saw my Lord they vanished
Like a mist before the sun.
No one now to me is dearer,
Daily I obey his call,
And I've pleasure in his service
More than all.

I have pleasure in his service,
More than all, more than all.

2 What would now be life without him,
I can scarcely dare to think;
Empty, purposeless and worthless,
In despair my heart would sink.
No, I'll never leave my Saviour,
I am his whate'er befall;
And I'll live with him for ever
After all.

3 O the happiness he gives me
Far outweighs the toil and loss!
Sweetest joy I find in leading
Weary sinners to the cross.
Sore temptations may beset me,
Sorrow on my heart may fall;
But there's pleasure in his service
More than all.
Ruth Tracy (1870-1960)

400 Jesus is my light, 701

WHY should life a weary journey seem?
Jesus is my light and song.
Why should I my cross a burden deem?
Jesus is my light and song.
All the way is marked by love divine,
Round my path the rays of glory shine,
Christ himself companion is of mine,
Jesus is my light and song.

Jesus is my light, Jesus is my light,
Jesus is my light and song;
Jesus is my light, I'll serve him with
my might,
Jesus is my light and song.

2 What though foes at every hand I meet?
Jesus is my light and song.
What though snares are ready for my feet?
Jesus is my light and song.
Christ himself was first to lead the way,
He was first to battle in the fray,
Now on him my every hope I stay,
Jesus is my light and song.

3 When my feet shall reach the open door,
Jesus is my light and song.
When life's pilgrimage on earth is o'er,
Jesus is my light and song.
This through countless years my song
shall be,
Love for him who sets the prisoner free,
Love for him who gave his life for me,
Jesus is my light and song.
Emma Johnson

401 Zealley, 338; Christ for me, 332
8.3.8.3.8.8.8.3.

WITH joy of heart I now can sing:
Jesus saves!
He doth to me deliverance bring,
Jesus saves!
I never shall forget the day
Christ saved me, when so far astray,
And sent me singing on my way,
Jesus saves!

2 From sins that filled my life with woe,
    Jesus saves!
Beneath my feet he's put my foe,
    Jesus saves!
From fear of man, from base desire,
From folly's charm, from sin's deep mire,
And from the everlasting fire,
    Jesus saves!

3 I'll shout the news where'er I go:
    Jesus saves!
His blood doth cleanse as white as snow,
    Jesus saves!
I'll sing it when death's flood I see,
I'll sing it then, my joy 'twill be,
I'll sing it in eternity:
    Jesus saves!

Anon

402 Catelinet, 626

WITH my heart so bright in the heavenly
    light,
  I live with Jesus all the time;
And I know I am washed in his blood quite
    white,
  And I am his and he is mine.

My soul is full of joy the devil can't
    destroy,
  I'm serving such a mighty, mighty
    King;
    And it doesn't matter now
    What the world may do or vow,
  While Jesus is my Saviour I can sing.
I've joined the Army of the Lord,
Fighting for the King of kings;
    And it doesn't matter now
    What the world may do or vow,
  While Jesus is my Saviour I can sing.

2 When my heart was dark, and my soul was
    lost,
  My Jesus spoke a pardon free;
And he stilled by his power the ocean that
    tossed
  And bade me go and happy be.

3 By his death he bought me everlasting life,
  By his stripes my soul was healed;
And for my transgression he has borne
    the strife,
  And by his sorrow joy revealed.

Herbert Howard Booth (1862-1926)

403 That means me, 809

WITH stains of sin upon me
  And burdened by my guilt,
I dared not hope that for my soul
  The Saviour's blood was spilt;
But I opened up my Bible
  Where I rejoiced to see
That whosoever will may come,
  And that means me.

That means me, that means me,
Whosoever will may come, that means
  me;
I am so very glad, because the Master
  said:
Whosoever will may come; and that
  means me.

2 I came to him so sinful
  But trusting in his name,
And freely Jesus pardoned me
  And lifted me from shame.
O I'm glad my Lord has offered
  His grace so rich and free
To whosoever comes to him,
  For that means me!

3 O sinner, come to Jesus,
  The promise is for you;
The priceless gift is offered now
  And all you have to do
Is to come this very moment,
  And he will set you free,
For whosoever means you, too,
  As well as me.

Henry Allen (1865-1943), alt

404 This is why, 404; The Reason, 403
8.7.8.7. Troch.

WOULD you know why I love Jesus,
  Why he is so dear to me?
'Tis because my blessèd Saviour
  From my sins has ransomed me.

This is why I love my Jesus,
  This is why I love him so:
He has pardoned my transgressions,
  He has washed me white as snow.

2 Would you know why I love Jesus,
  Why he is so dear to me?
'Tis because the blood of Jesus
  Fully saves and cleanses me.

3 Would you know why I love Jesus,
  Why he is so dear to me?
'Tis because, amid temptation,
  He supports and strengthens me.

4 Would you know why I love Jesus,
   Why he is so dear to me?
   'Tis because in every conflict
   Jesus gives me victory.

5 Would you know why I love Jesus,
   Why he is so dear to me?
   'Tis because my friend and Saviour
   He will ever, ever be.

                                    Anon

405 At Calvary, 611

Y EARS I spent in vanity and pride,
   Caring not my Lord was crucified,
Knowing not it was for me he died
   On Calvary.

*Mercy there was great, and grace was
   free;*
Pardon there was multiplied to me;
There my burdened soul found liberty
   At Calvary.

2 By God's word at last my sin I learned,
   Then I trembled at the law I'd spurned,
Till my guilty soul imploring turned
   To Calvary.

3 Now I've given to Jesus everything,
   Now I gladly own him as my King;
Now my raptured soul can only sing
   Of Calvary.

4 O the love that drew salvation's plan!
   O the grace that brought it down to man!
O the mighty gulf that God did span
   At Calvary!

                  William Reed Newell (1868-1956)

406 Numberless as the sands, 753

Y OU may sing of the joys over Jordan
   And the glories prepared for our sight,
But the soldier of Jesus rejoices
   On the way to that city of light.

*Wonderful is the peace Jesus gives
   me,*
Wonderful is his power full and free;
*No tongue can e'er express all the
   glories I possess;*
*Wonderful is the peace Jesus gives
   me.*

2 You may talk of the harps of the angels,
   Of melodious praises they sing,
But my heart's filled with heavenly music
   While I'm marching to meet the great
      King.

3 You may long for the robes bright and
      shining,
   And the song, and the crown, and the
      palm;
But your heart must be kept pure and
      spotless
   If you'd join in the song of the Lamb.

4 Would you reign with the King in his
      beauty?
   In his cross-bearing now you must
      share;
For none but the soul who has conquered
   May dwell in that land over there.
      Alfred Harmon Saker-Lynne (1867-1948), alt

                  *   *   *

see also: 22 To God be the glory
           65 Of all in earth or Heaven
          116 Jesus, thy blood and
              righteousness
          144 I know that my redeemer lives
          176 Deep were the scarlet stains of
              sin
          283 And can it be that I should gain
          418 Have you on the Lord believed
          730 I know not why God's wondrous
              grace
          969 I love to tell the story
          972 The way of the cross leads home

THE LIFE OF HOLINESS
Challenge

407 Ye banks and braes, 505;
Solid Rock, 501   8.8.8.8.8.8. Iambic

ALL things are possible to him
  That can in Jesus' name believe;
Lord, I no more thy truth blaspheme,
  Thy truth I lovingly receive;
I can, I do believe in thee;
All things are possible to me.

2 The most impossible of all
  Is that I e'er from sin should cease;
Yet shall it be; I know it shall;
  Jesus, look to thy faithfulness!
If nothing is too hard for thee,
All things are possible to me.

3 Though earth and Hell the word gainsay,
  The word of God can never fail;
The Lamb shall take my sins away,
  'Tis certain, though impossible;
The thing impossible shall be,
All things are possible to me.

4 When thou the work of faith hast wrought,
  I here shall in thine image shine,
Nor sin in deed or word or thought;
  Let men exclaim and fiends repine,
They cannot break the firm decree;
All things are possible to me.

5 Thy mouth, O Lord, to me hath sworn
  That I shall serve thee without fear,
Shall find the pearl which others spurn,
  Holy and pure and perfect here;
The servant as his Lord shall be;
All things are possible to me.

6 All things are possible to God,
  To Christ, the power of God in man,
To me, when I am all renewed,
  When I in Christ am formed again,
And witness, from all sin set free,
All things are possible to me.
Charles Wesley (1707-88)

408 Harton-Lea, 20; Duke Street, 17
L.M.

AWAKE, awake! Fling off the night!
  For God has sent his glorious light;
And we who live in Christ's new day
Must works of darkness put away.

2 Awake and rise, like men renewed,
  Men with the Spirit's power endued;
The light of life in us must glow
And fruits of truth and goodness show.

3 Let in the light; all sin expose
  To Christ, whose life no darkness knows.
Before his cross for guidance kneel;
His light will judge and, judging, heal.

4 Awake and rise up from the dead,
  And Christ his light on you will shed;
Its power will wrong desires destroy,
And your whole nature fill with joy.

5 Then sing for joy, and use each day;
  Give thanks for everything alway;
Lift up your hearts; with one accord
Praise God through Jesus Christ our Lord.
John Raphael Peacey (1896-1971)

409 I hear thy welcome voice, 169
S.M.

BEFORE thy face, dear Lord,
  Myself I want to see;
And while I every question sing,
  I want to answer thee.

  While I speak to thee,
  Lord, thy goodness show;
Am I what I ought to be?
O Saviour, let me know.

2 Am I what once I was?
  Have I that ground maintained
Wherein I walked in power with thee,
  And thou my soul sustained?

3 Have I a truthful heart,
  A conscience keen to feel
The baseness of a false excuse,
  The touch of aught unreal?

4 Have I the zeal I had
  When thou didst me ordain
To preach thy word and seek the lost,
  Or do I feel it pain?

5 O Lord, if I am wrong,
  I will not grieve thee more
By doubting thy great love and power
  To make and keep me pure.
Herbert Howard Booth (1862-1926)

Challenge

410 Adeste Fideles, 552
12.11.12.11.

BELIEVE him! Believe him! the holy one
  is waiting
  To perfect within you what grace has
  begun;
God wills for his people an uttermost
  salvation;
  To sanctify you wholly the Spirit will
  come.

2 Surrender! Surrender! Reject the gift no
  longer,
  But say: Blessèd Master, thy will shall
  be done.
I cease from my striving, thy love shall be
  the conqueror;
  To sanctify me wholly, make haste, Lord,
  and come.

3 Salvation! Salvation! O tell to all the story,
  The thraldom of evil is broken and gone!
My sun and my shield, the Lord gives grace
  and glory;
  He sanctifies me wholly; the Spirit has
  come.

Albert Orsborn (1886-1967)

411 Lascelles, 170; Franconia, 168;
Dennis, 165
S.M.

BLEST are the pure in heart,
  For they shall see our God;
The secret of the Lord is theirs;
  Their soul is Christ's abode.

2 The Lord, who left the heavens,
  Our life and peace to bring,
To dwell in lowliness with men,
  Their pattern and their King;

3 Still to the lowly soul
  He doth himself impart,
And for his cradle and his throne
  Chooseth the pure in heart.

4 Lord, we thy presence seek;
  May ours this blessing be;
Give us a pure and lowly heart,
  A temple meet for thee.

John Keble (1792-1866) (verses 1 and 3),
attr William John Hall (1793-1861) (verses 2
and 4)

412 Ramsgate, 312; Rousseau, 314;
Tyndal, 317
7.7.7.7.7.7.

CHRIST, whose glory fills the skies,
  Christ, the true, the only light,
Sun of righteousness arise,
  Triumph o'er the shades of night;
Dayspring from on high, be near;
Daystar, in my heart appear.

2 O disclose thy lovely face!
  Quicken all my drooping powers;
Gasps my fainting soul for grace
  As a thirsty land for showers.
Haste, my Lord, no more delay;
Come, my Saviour, come away.

3 Dark and cheerless is the morn
  Unaccompanied by thee;
Joyless is the day's return
  Till thy mercy's beams I see,
Till thou inward light impart,
Glad my eyes and warm my heart.

4 Visit, then, this soul of mine,
  Pierce the gloom of sin and grief;
Fill me, Radiance divine,
  Scatter all my unbelief;
More and more thyself display,
Shining to the perfect day.

Charles Wesley (1707-88)

413 Calvary's Stream, 247; To the uttermost
he saves, 267*
7.6.7.6. D. Iambic

COME, with me visit Calvary
  Where our redeemer died;
His blood now fills the fountain,
  'Tis deep, 'tis full, 'tis wide.
He died from sin to sever
  Our hearts and lives complete;
He saves and keeps for ever
  Those living at his feet.

Calvary's stream is flowing,
Calvary's stream is flowing,
Flowing so free for you and me;
Calvary's stream is flowing.

To the uttermost he saves,
To the uttermost he saves;
  Dare you now believe
  And his love receive?
To the uttermost he saves.

115

The Life of Holiness

2 God's great, free, full salvation
  Is offered here and now;
Complete blood-bought redemption
  Can be obtained by you.
Reach out faith's hand, now claiming,
  The cleansing flood will flow;
Look up just now, believing,
  His fulness you shall know.

3 I will surrender fully
  And do my Saviour's will;
He shall now make me holy
  And with himself me fill.
He's saving, I'm believing,
  This blessing now I claim;
His spirit I'm receiving,
  My heart is in a flame.

4 I've wondrous peace through trusting,
  A well of joy within;
This rest is everlasting,
  My days fresh triumphs win.
He gives me heavenly measure,
  Pressed down and running o'er;
O what a priceless treasure,
  Glory for evermore!

John Lawley (1859-1922),
James Conner Bateman (1854-88)
(first chorus)

414 Rest, 124; Repton, 123
8.6.8.8.6.

ETERNAL Light! Eternal Light!
  How pure the soul must be,
When, placed within thy searching sight,
It shrinks not, but with calm delight,
  Can live and look on thee.

2 The spirits that surround thy throne
  May bear the burning bliss;
But that is surely theirs alone,
Since they have never, never known
  A fallen world like this.

3 O how shall I, whose native sphere
  Is dark, whose mind is dim,
Before the ineffable appear,
And on my naked spirit bear
  The uncreated beam?

4 There is a way for man to rise
  To that sublime abode;
An offering and a sacrifice,
A Holy Spirit's energies,
  An advocate with God.

5 These, these prepare us for the sight
  Of holiness above;
The sons of ignorance and night
May dwell in the eternal light,
  Through the eternal love.

Thomas Binney (1798-1874)

415 For ever with the Lord, 183; Peace, 185
D.S.M.

FROM every stain made clean,
  From every sin set free;
O blessèd Lord, this is the gift
  That thou hast promised me.
And pressing through the past
  Of failure, fault and fear,
Before thy cross my soul I cast,
  And dare to leave it there.

2 From thee I would not hide
  My sin, because of fear
What men may think; I hate my pride,
  And as I am appear,
Just as I am, O Lord,
  Not what I'm thought to be,
Just as I am, a struggling soul
  For life and liberty.

3 While in thy light I stand,
  My heart, I seem to see,
Has failed to take from thy own hand
  The gifts it offers me.
O Lord, thy plenteous grace,
  Thy wisdom and thy power,
I here proclaim, before thy face,
  Can keep me every hour.

4 Upon the altar here
  I lay my treasure down;
I only want to have thee near,
  King of my heart to crown.
The fire doth surely burn
  My every selfish claim;
And while from them to thee I turn,
  I trust in thy great name.

5 A heart by blood made clean
  In every wish and thought,
A heart that by God's power has been
  Into subjection brought,
To walk, to weep, to sing,
  Within the light of Heaven;
This is the blessing, Saviour-King,
  That thou to me hast given.

Herbert Howard Booth (1892-1926)

116

Challenge

416 Nuttall, 192; Marshall, 189 (verse)
6.4.6.4.6.6.6.4.

GIVE me a holy life,
Spotless and free,
Cleansed by the crystal flow
Coming from thee.
Purge the dark halls of thought,
Here let thy work be wrought,
Each wish and feeling brought
Captive to thee.

2 Cleanse, thou refining Flame,
All that is mine;
Self only may remain
If thou refine.
Fix the intention sure,
Make my desire secure,
With love my heart keep pure,
Rooted in thee.

3 All my best works are naught,
Please they not thee;
Far past my busy hands
Thine eye doth see
Into the depths of mind,
Searching the plan designed,
Gladdened when thou dost find
First of all, thee.

4 Now is my will resigned,
Struggles are quelled;
Clay on the wheel am I,
Nothing withheld.
Master, I yield to thee,
Crumble, then fashion me
Flawless, and fit to be
Indwelt by thee.
Leslie Taylor-Hunt (1901-79)

417 Are you washed? 608

HAVE you been to Jesus for the cleans-
ing power?
Are you washed in the blood of the
Lamb?
Are you fully trusting in his grace this
hour?
Are you washed in the blood of the
Lamb?

Are you washed in the blood,
In the soul-cleansing blood of the
Lamb?
Are your garments spotless? Are they
white as snow?
Are you washed in the blood of the
Lamb?

2 Are you walking daily by the Saviour's
side?
Are you washed in the blood of the
Lamb?
Do you rest each moment in the crucified?
Are you washed in the blood of the
Lamb?

3 Lay aside the garments that are stained
with sin,
And be washed in the blood of the Lamb;
There's a fountain flowing for the soul
unclean,
O be washed in the blood of the Lamb!
Elisha Albright Hoffman (1839-1929)

418 Near the cross, 272; Llanfair, 271
7.6.7.6. Troch.

HAVE you on the Lord believed?
Still there's more to follow;
Of his grace have you received?
Still there's more to follow.

More and more, more and more,
Always more to follow;
O his matchless, boundless love!
Still there's more to follow.

2 Have you felt the Saviour near?
Still there's more to follow;
Does his blessèd presence cheer?
Still there's more to follow.

3 O the grace the Father shows!
Still there's more to follow;
Freely he his grace bestows,
Still there's more to follow.
Philip Paul Bliss (1838-76)

419 Boston 13; Rockingham, 43; Ernan, 19
L.M.

HE wills that I should holy be;
That holiness I long to feel,
That full divine conformity
To all my Saviour's righteous will.

2 On thee, O God, my soul is stayed,
And waits to prove thine utmost will;
The promise, by thy mercy made,
Thou canst, thou wilt in me fulfill.

3 Thy loving Spirit, Christ, alone
Can lead me forth and make me free,
Burst every bond through which I groan
And set my heart at liberty.

4 Now let thy Spirit bring me in,
And give thy servant to possess
The land of rest from inbred sin,
The land of perfect holiness.

5 Lord, I believe thy power the same,
 The same thy grace and truth endure;
 And in thy blessèd hands I am,
 And trust thee for a perfect cure.

6 Come, Saviour, come and make me whole,
 Entirely all my sins remove;
 To perfect health restore my soul,
 To perfect holiness and love.
                    Charles Wesley (1707-88)

420 I bring my heart to Jesus, 675

I BRING my heart to Jesus, with its fears,
 With its hopes and feelings, and its
  tears;
Him it seeks, and finding, it is blest;
Him it loves, and loving, is at rest.
Walking with my Saviour, heart in heart,
 None can part.

2 I bring my life to Jesus, with its care,
And before his footstool leave it there;
Faded are its treasures, poor and dim;
It is not worth living without him.
More than life is Jesus, love and peace,
 Ne'er to cease.

3 I bring my sins to Jesus, as I pray
That his blood will wash them all away;
While I seek for favor at his feet,
And with tears his promise still repeat,
He doth tell me plainly: Jesus lives
 And forgives.

4 I bring my all to Jesus; he hath seen
How my soul desireth to be clean.
Nothing from his altar I withhold
When his cross of suffering I behold;
And the fire descending brings to me
 Liberty.
                    Herbert Howard Booth (1862-1926)

421 Evening, 222; St John, 228
                    6.6.6.6.8.8.

I BRING my sins to thee,
 The sins I cannot count,
That I may cleansèd be
 In thy once opened fount.
I bring them, Saviour, all to thee;
The burden is too great for me.

2 My heart to thee I bring,
 The heart I cannot read;
A faithless, wandering thing,
 An evil heart indeed.
I bring it, Saviour, now to thee
That fixed and faithful it may be.

3 To thee I bring my care,
 The care I cannot flee;
Thou wilt not only share,
 But bear it all for me.
O loving Saviour, now to thee
I bring the load that wearies me.

4 I bring my grief to thee,
 The grief I cannot tell;
No words shall needed be,
 Thou knowest all so well.
I bring the sorrow laid on me,
O suffering Saviour, now to thee.

5 My joys to thee I bring,
 The joys thy love has given,
That each may be a wing
 To lift me nearer Heaven.
I bring them, Saviour, all to thee;
For thou hast purchased all for me.

6 My life I bring to thee,
 I would not be my own;
O Saviour, let me be
 Thine ever, thine alone.
My heart, my life, my all I bring
To thee, my Saviour and my King.
                    Frances Ridley Havergal (1836-79)

422 O Speak, 482
                    8.8.8.8. Amph.

I BRING thee, dear Jesus, my all,
 Nor hold back from thee any part;
Obedient to thy welcome call,
 I yield thee the whole of my heart.

 *O speak, O speak while before thee I
  pray!*
*And, O Lord, just what seemeth thee
  good*
Reveal, and my heart shall obey.

2 Perverse, stubborn once was my will,
 My feet ran in self-chosen ways;
Thy pleasure henceforth to fulfil,
 I'll spend all the rest of my days.

3 The doubts that have darkened my soul,
 The shame and the fears that I hate,
O banish, and bid me be whole,
 A clean heart within me create!

4 O give me a heart that is true,
 Unspotted and pure in thy sight,
A love that would anything do,
 A life given up to the fight!
                    Frederick Booth-Tucker (1853-1929) (verses)

Challenge

423 I hear thy welcome voice, 169

S.M.

I HEAR thy welcome voice
That calls me, Lord, to thee,
For cleansing in thy precious blood
That flowed on Calvary.

I am coming, Lord,
Coming now to thee;
Wash me, cleanse me in thy blood
That flowed on Calvary.

2 Though coming weak and vile,
Thou dost my strength assure;
Thou dost my vileness fully cleanse
Till spotless all and pure.

3 Still Jesus calls me on
To perfect faith and love,
To perfect hope and peace and trust
For earth and Heaven above.

4 'Tis Jesus who confirms
The blessèd work within,
By adding grace to welcomed grace,
Where reigned the power of sin.

5 And he the witness gives
To loyal hearts and free,
That every promise is fulfilled
If faith but brings the plea.
Lewis Hartsough (1828-72)

424 Confidence, 15; Silver Hill, 48

L.M.

I THIRST, thou wounded Lamb of God,
To wash me in thy cleansing blood,
To dwell within thy wounds; then pain
Is sweet, and life or death is gain.

2 Take my poor heart and let it be
For ever closed to all but thee;
Seal thou my breast, and let me wear
That pledge of love for ever there.

3 How blest are they who still abide
Close sheltered in thy bleeding side,
Who life and strength do thence derive,
And for thee fight, and in thee live.

4 O conquering Jesus, Saviour thou,
To thee, lo! all our souls we bow;
To thee our hearts and hands we give;
Thine we will die, thine we will live.
Nicolaus Ludwig von Zinzendorf (1700-60)
(verses 1 and 2),
Johann (1712-83) (verse 3) and Anna
Nitschmann (1715-60) (verse 4),
trs John Wesley (1703-91)

425 Belmont, 76; Colne, 79

C.M.

I WANT a principle within
Of jealous, godly fear,
A sensibility of sin,
A pain to feel it near.

2 I want the first approach to feel
Of pride or fond desire,
To catch the wandering of my will,
And quench the kindling fire.

3 Quick as the apple of an eye,
O God, my conscience make!
Awake my soul when sin is nigh,
And keep it still awake.

4 O may the least omission pain
My well-instructed soul,
And drive me to the blood again
Which makes the wounded whole.
Charles Wesley (1707-88)

426 Begone, vain world, 617

I WANT, dear Lord, a heart that's true and
clean,
A sunlit heart, with not a cloud between;
A heart like thine, a heart divine,
A heart as white as snow;
On me, dear Lord, a heart like this bestow.

2 I want, dear Lord, a love that cares for all,
A deep, strong love that answers every call;
A love like thine, a love divine,
A love to come or go;
On me, dear Lord, a love like this bestow.

3 I want, dear Lord, a soul on fire for thee,
A soul baptized with heavenly energy;
A willing mind, a ready hand
To do whate'er I know,
To spread thy light wherever I may go.
George Galloway Jackson (1866-93)

427 Living beneath the shade
of the cross, 719

IF you want pardon, if you want peace,
If you want sorrow and sighing to cease,
Look up to Jesus who died on the tree
To purchase a full salvation.

Living beneath the shade of the cross,
Counting the jewels of earth but dross,
Cleansed in the blood that flows from
his side,
Enjoying a full salvation.

The Life of Holiness

2 If you want Jesus to reign in your soul,
   Plunge in the fountain and you shall be
      whole,
   Washed in the blood of the crucified one;
      Enjoying a full salvation.

3 If you want boldness, take part in the fight;
   If you want purity, walk in the light;
   If you want liberty, shout and be free;
      Enjoying a full salvation.

4 If you want holiness, cling to the cross,
   Counting the riches of earth as dross;
   Down at his feet you'll be cleansed and
      made free;
      Enjoying a full salvation.
                George Phippen Ewens (1841-1926)

428 Galilee, 371; Cross of Jesus, 366
         8.7.8.7. Troch.

JESUS calls us! O'er the tumult
   Of our life's wild, restless sea,
Day by day his sweet voice soundeth,
   Saying: Christian, follow me.

2 As of old apostles heard it
   By the Galilean lake,
Turned from home and toil and kindred,
   Leaving all for his dear sake.

3 Jesus calls us from the worship
   Of the vain world's golden store,
From each idol that would keep us,
   Saying: Christian, love me more.

4 In our joys and in our sorrows,
   Days of toil and hours of ease,
Still he calls, in cares and pleasures,
   That we love him more than these.

5 Jesus calls us! By thy mercies,
   Saviour, may we hear thy call,
Give our hearts to thy obedience,
   Serve and love thee best of all.
                Cecil Frances Alexander (1818-95)

429 Let the lower lights be burning, 386
         8.7.8.7. Troch.

JESUS, lead me up the mountain,
   Where the whitest robes are seen,
Where the saints can see the fountain,
   Where we may be pure and clean.

*Lead me higher up the mountain,
   Give me fellowship with thee;
In thy light I see the fountain,
   And the blood now cleanses me.*

2 Higher up where light increases,
   Far beyond earth's fading dross,
Where the life of sinning ceases,
   May I choose to gain through loss.

3 Jesus, Light of God, now show me
   Love that shall redeem, refine
All who walk with thee and know thee;
   To thy truth my heart incline.
                William James Pearson (1832-92)

430 Near the cross, 272
         7.6.7.6. Troch.

JESUS, save me through and through,
   Save me from self-mending;
Self-salvation will not do,
   Pass me through the cleansing.

*Through and through, through and
      through,
   Jesus, make me holy;
Save me to the uttermost
   All the way to Glory.*

2 Through temptations save from sin,
   Self and pride subduing;
Save me through and through within,
   Save me by renewing.

3 Through the tempest, through the calm,
   With the Master talking;
On my own belovèd's arm,
   Oft with Jesus walking.

4 Through my thoughts and through my
      heart,
   Through my flesh and spirit;
Save me, Lord, through every part,
   Through thy saving merit.
                William James Pearson (1832-92)

431 Nearer my home, 172;
         No sorrow there, 173   S.M.

JESUS, thy fulness give,
   My soul and body bless;
Cleanse me from sin that I may live
   The life of holiness.

*In white, in white, walking in white;
He makes me worthy through his
      blood
To walk with him in white.*

2 With full salvation might,
   My heart and mind make strong;
Help me to live and do the right
   And part with all that's wrong.

Challenge

3   Give me full joy and peace,
      Eternal inward rest;
   Lead me to Calvary's holy feast,
      There let my soul be blest.

4   Saved from the power of sin,
      Kept by thy grace secure,
   Let all without and all within
      Be pure, as thou art pure.
           William James Pearson (1832-92)

432   Better World, 331; Goldsmith, 334
                        8.3.8.3.8.8.8.3.

JESUS, thy purity bestow
   Through the blood;
The power of perfect cleansing show
   Through the blood.
Take every spot of sin away,
Within my heart for ever stay,
Give me full victory every day,
   Through the blood.

2 Increase the faith that conquers doubt
   Through the blood;
Cast every evil passion out
   Through the blood.
Give me the power to master wrong,
Against the foe to march along,
With holy valor make me strong,
   Through the blood.

3 Give me the love that never dies,
   Through the blood;
That will thy cross and passion prize,
   Through the blood.
Help me to conquer Satan's host,
And keep me faithful at my post,
Anoint me with the Holy Ghost,
   Through the blood.
           William James Pearson (1832-92)

433   Whither Pilgrims? 453; Face to face, 370*
                      8.7.8.7. D. Troch.

JUST outside the land of promise
   You have waited many years,
And your life has been o'erclouded
   With a host of haunting fears.
There is victory in Jesus,
   Come to him without delay;
Seek just now a full salvation
   And the voice of God obey.

*To redeem and make you holy
Jesus left his throne above;
Now believe and take the blessing,
Nothing less than perfect love.*

2 You have long been hesitating,
   Hindered by your unbelief,
And your wilful disobedience
   Oft has caused you bitter grief.
Stay no longer on the threshold,
   Now believe and enter in;
Claim through Christ complete
      deliverance
   From the slavery of sin.

3 Though you know your sins forgiven,
   Greater things await you still;
Freedom here from sin's dominion,
   Power to do the Master's will.
Fear no danger, he is with you,
   Let no foe your steps arrest;
Seek today the Father's blessing,
   Enter now the land of rest.
        Walter Henry Windybank (1872-1952)

434   None of self, 461

LORD, I come to thee beseeching
   For a heart-renewing here;
Up to thee my hands are stretching,
After thee my heart is reaching;
   Saviour, in thy power draw near.

2 Holy Spirit, come revealing
   All I must forsake, confess;
'Tis for light, Lord, I'm appealing;
I am here to seek thy healing,
   Thou art here to save and bless.

3 'Neath the searching light of Heaven,
   Here a deeper truth I see;
Though the past was long forgiven,
One more chain must yet be riven,
   Lord, from self I am not free.

4 Though thy light some pain is bringing,
   Thou art answering my prayer;
To thy promises I'm clinging,
At thy cross myself I'm flinging,
   For the blood is flowing there.

5 'Tis the blood, O wondrous river,
   Now its power has touched my soul!
'Tis the blood from sin can sever,
'Tis the blood that doth deliver,
   Here and now it makes me whole.
               Ruth Tracy (1870-1960)

435   I surrender all, 377
                   8.7.8.7. Troch.

LORD, I pray that I may know thee,
   Risen One, enthroned on high;
Empty hands I'm stretching to thee,
   Show thyself to me, I cry.

The Life of Holiness

Show thyself to me, show thyself to
me,
That I may reveal thy beauty;
Show thyself to me.

2 All that once I thought most worthy,
All of which I once did boast,
In thy light seems poor and passing,
'Tis thyself I covet most.

Give thyself to me, give thyself to me,
That I may show forth thy power;
Give thyself to me.

3 Only as I truly know thee
Can I make thee truly known;
Only bring the power to others
Which in my own life is shown.

Show thy power in me, show thy
power in me,
That I may be used for others;
Show thy power in me.

Ruth Tracy (1870-1960)

436 Lord Jesus, I long, 563; Cossar, 556
11.11.11.11.

LORD JESUS, I long to be perfectly whole,
I want thee for ever to live in my soul;
Break down every idol, cast out every foe,
Now wash me, and I shall be whiter than
snow.

Whiter than snow, yes, whiter than
snow,
Now wash me, and I shall be whiter
than snow.

2 Lord Jesus, let nothing unholy remain,
Apply thine own blood and remove every
stain;
To get this blest washing I all things forgo;
Now wash me, and I shall be whiter than
snow.

3 Lord Jesus, thou seest I patiently wait;
Come now, and within me a new heart
create;
To those who have sought thee thou never
saidst: No!
Now wash me, and I shall be whiter than
snow.

4 The blessing by faith I receive from above.
O glory, my soul is made perfect in love!
My prayer has prevailed, and this moment
I know
The blood is applied, I am whiter than
snow.

James Nicholson (c 1828-76)

437 Long, long ago, 513; Cleansing for
me, 512   10.8.10.8.10.10.10.8.

LORD, through the blood of the Lamb that
was slain,
Cleansing for me;
From all the guilt of my sins now I claim
Cleansing from thee.
Sinful and black though the past may have
been,
Many the crushing defeats I have seen,
Yet on thy promise, O Lord, now I lean,
Cleansing for me.

2 From all the sins over which I have wept,
Cleansing for me;
Far, far away by the blood-current swept,
Cleansing for me.
Jesus, thy promise I dare to believe,
And as I come thou wilt surely receive,
That over sin I may never more grieve,
Cleansing for me.

3 From all the doubts that have filled me
with gloom,
Cleansing for me;
From all the fears that would point me to
doom,
Cleansing for me.
Jesus, although I may not understand,
In childlike faith now I stretch forth my
hand,
And through thy word and thy grace I shall
stand,
Cleansèd by thee.

4 From all the care of what men think or
say,
Cleansing for me;
From ever fearing to speak, sing or pray,
Cleansing for me.
Lord, in thy love and thy power make me
strong
That all may know that to thee I belong;
When I am tempted, let this be my song,
Cleansing for me.

Herbert Howard Booth (1862-1926)

438 Blaenwern, 430; Hyfrydol, 438;
Stainer, 400   8.7.8.7. D. Troch.

LOVE divine, all loves excelling,
Joy of Heaven, to earth come down,
Fix in us thy humble dwelling,
All thy faithful mercies crown.
Jesus, thou art all compassion,
Pure, unbounded love thou art;
Visit us with thy salvation,
Enter every longing heart.

Challenge

2 Come, almighty to deliver,
  Let us all thy grace receive;
Suddenly return, and never,
  Never more thy temples leave.
Thee we would be always blessing,
  Serve thee as thy hosts above;
Pray and praise thee without ceasing,
  Glory in thy perfect love.

3 Finish then thy new creation,
  Pure and spotless let us be;
Let us see thy great salvation,
  Perfectly restored in thee.
Changed from glory into glory,
  Till in Heaven we take our place,
Till we cast our crowns before thee,
  Lost in wonder, love and praise.
                        Charles Wesley (1707-88)

439 Love Divine, 418; Bithynia, 409;
        Cwm Rhondda, 414   8.7.8.7.8.7. Troch.

LOVE divine, from Jesus flowing,
  Living waters rich and free,
Wondrous love without a limit,
  Flowing from eternity;
    Boundless ocean,
    I would cast myself on thee.

2 Love surpassing understanding,
  Angels would the mystery scan,
Yet so tender that it reaches
  To the lowest child of man.
    Let me, Jesus,
    Fuller know redemption's plan.

3 Love that pardons past transgression,
  Love that cleanses every stain,
Love that fills to overflowing
  Yet invites to drink again;
    Precious fountain,
    Which to open Christ was slain.

4 From my soul break every fetter,
  Thee to know is all my cry;
Saviour, I am thine forever,
  Thine I'll live and thine I'll die,
    Only asking
    More and more of love's supply.
              Elizabeth Ann MacKenzie (1853-1943)

440 Mozart, 496; St Catherine, 499
        8.8.8.8.8.8. Iambic

O CHRIST of pure and perfect love,
  Look on this sin-stained heart of mine!
I thirst thy cleansing grace to prove,
  I want my life to be like thine.
O see me at thy footstool bow,
And come and sanctify me now!

2 What is it keeps me out of all
  The love and faith and fire I need?
O drive thy foes from out my soul
  Whate'er it cost, howe'er I bleed!
No sin-cursed thing shall I allow
If thou wilt sanctify me now.

3 In vain my fearful heart points back
  To failures in dark days gone by;
These shall not drive me from the track
  Of heavenly flame once more brought
    nigh.
To keep thy grace thou'lt show me how,
So come and sanctify me now.

4 O pour on me the cleansing flood,
  Nor let thy side be cleft in vain!
'Tis done, I feel the precious blood
  Does purge and keep from every stain.
To all the world I dare avow
That Jesus sanctifies me now.
                        William Booth (1829-1912)

441 I hear thy welcome voice, 169;
        Lascelles, 170   S.M.

O COME and dwell in me,
  Spirit of power within!
And bring the glorious liberty
  From sorrow, fear and sin.

  Hear my pleading, Lord;
  Make my spirit free;
  Fill my soul with perfect love;
  O come and dwell in me!

2 The whole of sin's disease,
    Spirit of health, remove,
Spirit of perfect holiness,
    Spirit of perfect love.

3 I want the witness, Lord,
    That all I do is right,
According to thy will and word,
    Well pleasing in thy sight.

4 I ask no higher state,
    Give me but grace for this;
And then at last, dear Lord, translate
    Me to eternal bliss.
              Charles Wesley (1707-88) (verses)

442 St Agnes, 126; Rest, 124
                                              C.M.

O FOR a closer walk with God,
  A calm and heavenly frame,
A light to shine upon the road
  That leads me to the Lamb!

The Life of Holiness

2 Where is the blessedness I knew
   When first I saw the Lord?
Where is the soul-refreshing view
   Of Jesus and his word?

3 What peaceful hours I once enjoyed;
   How sweet their memory still!
But they have left an aching void
   The world can never fill.

4 Return, O holy Dove, return
   Sweet messenger of rest!
I hate the sins that made thee mourn,
   And drove thee from my breast.

5 The dearest idol I have known,
   Whate'er that idol be,
Help me to tear it from thy throne,
   And worship only thee.

6 So shall my walk be close with God,
   Calm and serene my frame;
So purer light shall mark the road
   That leads me to the Lamb.
William Cowper (1731-1800)

443 O for a heart whiter than snow, 528
10.10.10.10. Dact.

O FOR a heart that is whiter than snow,
   Kept, ever kept 'neath the life-giving flow,
Cleansed from all evil, self-seeking and pride,
Kept pure and holy by Calvary's tide!

O for a heart whiter than snow!
Saviour divine, to whom else shall I go?
Thou who didst die, loving me so,
Give me a heart that is whiter than snow.

2 O for a heart that is whiter than snow,
Calm in the peace that he loves to bestow,
Daily refreshed by the heavenly dews,
Ready for service whene'er he shall choose!

3 O for a heart that is whiter than snow,
With the pure flame of the Spirit aglow,
Filled with the love that is true and sincere,
Love that is able to banish all fear!

4 O for a heart that is whiter than snow,
Then in his grace and his knowledge to grow,
Growing like him who my pattern shall be,
Till in his beauty my King I shall see!
Eliza Edmunds Hewitt (1851-1920)

444 Richmond, 125; Margaret, 112*
C.M.

O FOR a heart to praise my God,
   A heart from sin set free,
A heart that always feels the blood
   So freely spilt for me.

*O come to my heart, Lord Jesus;
There is room in my heart for thee.

2 A heart resigned, submissive, meek,
   My great redeemer's throne;
Where only Christ is heard to speak,
   Where Jesus reigns alone.

3 A humble, lowly, contrite heart,
   Believing, true and clean;
Which neither life nor death can part
   From him that dwells within.

4 A heart in every thought renewed,
   And full of love divine;
Perfect and right, and pure and good,
   A copy, Lord, of thine.

5 Thy nature, gracious Lord, impart,
   Come quickly from above;
Write thy new name upon my heart,
   Thy new best name of love.
Charles Wesley (1707-88) (verses),
Emily Elizabeth Steele Elliott (1836-97)
(chorus)

445 Beethoven, 9; Wareham, 55
L.M.

O FOR a humbler walk with God!
   Lord, bend this stubborn heart of mine;
Subdue each rising, rebel thought,
   And all my will conform to thine.

2 O for a holier walk with God!
   A heart from all pollution free;
Expel, O Lord, each sinful love,
   And fill my soul with love to thee.

3 O for a nearer walk with God!
   Lord, turn my wandering heart to thee;
Help me to live by faith in him
   Who lived and died and rose for me.

Challenge

4 Lord, send thy Spirit from above
   With light and love and power divine;
   And by his all-constraining grace
   Make me and keep me ever thine.

Edward Harland (1810-90)

446 Sagina, 498; Mozart, 496
8.8.8.8.8.8. Iambic

O GOD of light, O God of love,
   Shine on my soul from Heaven above!
Let sin appear in thy pure ray
As black as on the judgment day;
Let perfect love apply the test,
And all that's wrong make manifest.

2 O take thy plummet and thy line,
Apply them to this heart of mine,
And thus reveal each crooked place
By contrast with true righteousness!
Let holy truth condemn each sham;
Show what thou art, and what I am.

3 O smite and spare not, faithful God!
A Father's hand still holds the rod;
O make my sin-stained conscience smart,
And write thy law upon my heart
So plainly, that my will shall bow
In full surrender, here and now!

4 Work on in me thy perfect will,
In me thy promise, Lord, fulfil;
O make me quick to fight for thee,
And set my soul at liberty!
My soul can rest in nothing less
Than in a spotless holiness.

Arthur Sydney Booth-Clibborn (1855-1939)

447 Come on, my partners, 465;
Pembroke, 467; 8.8.6.8.8.6.

O JESUS, Saviour, Christ divine,
   When shall I know and feel thee mine
Without a doubt or fear?
With anxious, longing thirst I come
To beg thee make my heart thy home,
   And keep me holy here.

2 What is there that I will not give
To have thee ever with me live
   A conquering Christ within?
My life, my all, this blessèd day
Down at thy precious feet I lay,
   To be redeemed from sin.

3 O God of pentecostal fame,
Can I not have that living flame
   Burning where'er I go?
From sin and self and shame set free,
Can I not lead lost souls to thee,
   And conquer every foe?

4 I can, I do just now believe,
I do the heavenly grace receive,
   The Spirit makes me clean.
Christ takes the whole of my poor heart,
No sin shall ever from me part
   My Lord who reigns supreme.

William Booth (1829-1912)

448 At thy feet I fall, 613

O LAMB of God, thou wonderful sinbearer,
Hard after thee my soul doth follow on;
As pants the hart for streams in desert
   dreary,
   So pants my soul for thee, O thou life-
   giving one.

At thy feet I fall,
Yield thee up my all,
To suffer, live or die for my Lord
   crucified.

2 I mourn, I mourn the sin that drove thee
   from me,
   And blackest darkness brought into my
   soul;
Now I renounce the cursèd thing that
   hindered,
   And come once more to thee to be made
   fully whole.

3 Descend the heavens, thou whom my soul
   adoreth!
   Exchange thy throne for my poor longing heart.
For thee, for thee I watch as for the
   morning;
   No rest, no joy I find when from thee I'm
   apart.

4 Come, Holy Ghost, thy mighty aid
   bestowing!
   Destroy the works of sin, the self, the
   pride;
Burn, burn in me, my idols overthrowing;
   Prepare my heart for him, for my Lord
   crucified.

Catherine Booth-Clibborn (1858-1955)

449 Saved by grace, 47; He leadeth me! 21
L.M.

O LOVE, revealed on earth in Christ,
   In blindness once I sacrificed
Thy gifts for dross; I could not see,
But Jesus brings me sight of thee.

I come to thee with quiet mind,
Thyself to know, thy will to find;
In Jesus' steps my steps must be,
I follow him to follow thee.

2　O Love, invisible before,
　　I see thee now, desire thee more;
　　When Jesus speaks thy word is clear;
　　I search his face and find thee near.

3　O Love, forever claim my eyes!
　　Thy beauty be my chosen prize;
　　I cast my load on timeless grace
　　That my free soul may run the race.
　　　　　　　　Catherine Baird (1895-1984)

450　Take all my sins away, 478;
　　　　Take me as I am, 479　　　　8.8.8.6.

O SPOTLESS Lamb, I come to thee,
　　From thee no longer can I stay;
Break every chain, now set me free,
　　Take all my sins away.

Take all my sins away,
Take all my sins away;
O spotless Lamb, I come to thee,
Take all my sins away.

2　My hungry soul cries out for thee,
　　Come and for ever seal my breast;
To thy dear arms at last I flee,
　　There only can I rest.

3　Weary I am of inbred sin,
　　O wilt thou not my soul release?
Enter and speak me pure within,
　　Give me thy perfect peace.

4　I plunge beneath thy precious blood,
　　My hand in faith takes hold of thee;
Thy promises just now I claim,
　　Thou art enough for me.
　　　　　Catherine Booth-Clibborn (1858-1955)

451　Thou art enough for me, 53
　　　　　　　　　　　　　　　　L.M.

O THAT in me the mind of Christ
　　A fixed abiding-place may find,
That I may know the will of God,
　　And live in him for lost mankind.

Doing the will of God,
Doing the will of God,
The best thing I know in this world
　　　　below
Is doing the will of God.

2　The suffering servant he became,
　　Yea more; in loneliness and loss
He bore for me in grief and shame,
　　A crown of thorns, a heavy cross.

3　O that in me this mind might be,
　　The will of God be all my joy,
Prepared with him to go or stay,
　　My chief delight his sweet employ.

4　More than all else I would become
　　The servant of my servant-Lord;
My highest glory his reproach,
　　To do his will my best reward.
　　　　　　　Edward Henry Joy (1871-1949)

452　Bethany, 429; Love Divine, 418;
　　　　Austria, 408　　　8.7.8.7. D. Troch.

O THOU God of full salvation,
　　King of righteousness divine,
Author of the new creation,
　　Light of life, within us shine!
　　　　Make us holy;
　　With thy blessing make us thine.

2　From all self and sin deliver,
　　With thy nature make us good;
Make us kings and priests forever,
　　Wash our garments in thy blood.
　　　　O'er our Army
　　Send a great salvation flood.

3　Sun of righteousness arising,
　　Cheer us while we bear the cross,
Living, dying, sacrificing,
　　Purify from sinful dross
　　　　Thy disciples;
　　Teach us how to gain by loss.

4　Thou art love's unfathomed ocean,
　　Wisdom's deepest, clearest sea,
Heaven's and earth's salvation portion,
　　Parent of eternity;
　　　　Grace and glory
　　In abundance flow from thee.
　　　　　　William James Pearson (1832-92)

453　Confidence, 15; Retreat, 41
　　　　　　　　　　　　　　　　L.M.

O THOU to whose all-searching sight
　　The darkness shineth as the light,
Search, prove my heart, it pants for thee;
　　O burst these bonds and set it free!

2　Wash out its stain, refine its dross,
　　Nail my affections to the cross;
Hallow each thought, let all within
　　Be clean, as thou, my Lord, art clean.

3　Saviour, where'er thy steps I see,
　　Dauntless, untired, I'll follow thee;
O let thy hand support me still
　　And lead me to thy holy hill!

Challenge

4 If rough and thorny be the way,
My strength proportion to my day,
Till toil and grief and pain shall cease,
Where all is calm and joy and peace.
Nicolaus Ludwig von Zinzendorf (1700-60),
trs John Wesley (1703-91)

454 Almighty to save, 480
8.8.8.8. Amph.

O WHEN shall my soul find her rest,
My strugglings and wrestlings be o'er?
My heart, by my Saviour possessed,
Be fearing and sinning no more?

2 Now search me, and try me, O Lord!
Now Jesus, give ear to my cry!
See! helpless I cling to thy word,
My soul to my Saviour draws nigh.

3 My idols I cast at thy feet,
My all I return thee, who gave;
This moment the work is complete,
For thou art almighty to save!

4 O Saviour, I dare to believe,
Thy blood for my cleansing I see;
And, asking in faith, I receive
Salvation, full, present and free.

5 O Lord, I shall now comprehend
Thy mercy so high and so deep;
And long shall my praises ascend,
For thou art almighty to keep!
Bramwell Booth (1856-1929)

455 O live thy life in me! 476;
Take me as I am, 479
8.8.8.6.

SAVIOUR, I want thy love to know,
That I in love may be like thee;
O let it now my heart o'erflow,
And live thy life in me!

I give my heart to thee,
Thy dwelling-place to be;
I want thee ever in my heart;
O live thy life in me!

2 I want thy spotless purity
Forever in my heart to be
A reflex of thy holiness;
O live thy life in me!

3 I want thy wisdom from above
That I thy perfect way may see;
To follow thee unblamable,
Live thou thy life in me.

4 I want thy constant presence, Lord,
Then e'en a dark adversity
Will be a blessing in disguise;
Live thou thy life in me.

5 Then to faith's vision thou shalt be
Ever a bright reality,
Keeping my heart in purity,
Living thy life in me.
Harry Anderson

456 Hold thou my hand! 543
11.10.11.10.

SAY but the word, thy servant shall be
healèd,
I shall be loosed from my infirmity;
And, once again, the fount of life unsealèd
Shall upward spring and flow eternally.

2 Vainly I seek a cure for my soul's ailing,
Vainly aspire to reach the life divine;
Slave of myself, myself for ever failing,
Helpless am I until thy grace be mine.

3 I dare not ask as though by right of
pleading;
Only my need lays hold upon thy name;
Yet none can cry and find thy love
unheeding,
And none need fail thy saving grace to
claim.

4 Thine is the name whereon I cry, believing;
Thine is the love that sees and pities
me;
Thine is the power and mine the faith
receiving
Cleansing and healing, life and liberty.
Albert Orsborn (1886-1967)

457 Jesus is looking for thee, 457; Tell me
the story of Jesus, 458
8.7.8.7. D. Dact.

SEND out thy light and thy truth, Lord,
Into my heart let them shine;
Here while I'm waiting in faith, Lord,
Hark to this pleading of mine.
Search now my heart, do not spare it,
Pour in thy Spirit's pure light;
Tell me the truth, I will bear it,
Hide not the worst from my sight.

Saviour, my all I will bring;
How can I offer thee less?
Widely the doors now I fling,
Come and thy temple possess.

2 Send out thy light, let it lead me,
  Bring me to thy holy hill;
When from all sin thou hast freed me,
  I shall delight in thy will.
Jesus, thy wounding is tender,
  Kind is the light that reveals,
Waiting until I surrender,
  Pouring the balm then that heals.

3 Fulness of joy in thy presence,
  Bliss at thy side evermore,
This is the life that I enter,
  Now that my struggles are o'er.
When with thy Spirit's rich treasure
  My earthen vessel is stored,
Mine is the service of pleasure,
  Thine all the glory, dear Lord.
                    Ruth Tracy (1870-1960)

458 Take time to be holy, 571
                              11.11.11.11.

TAKE time to be holy, speak oft with thy
    Lord;
Abide in him always, and feed on his word;
Make friends of God's children; help those
    who are weak;
Forgetting in nothing his blessing to seek.

2 Take time to be holy, the world rushes on;
Spend much time in secret with Jesus
    alone;
By looking to Jesus, like him thou shalt
    be;
Thy friends in thy conduct his likeness
    shall see.

3 Take time to be holy, let him be thy guide,
And run not before him whatever betide;
In joy or in sorrow still follow thy Lord,
And, looking to Jesus, still trust in his
    word.

4 Take time to be holy, be calm in thy soul;
Each thought and each motive beneath
    his control;
Thus led by his Spirit to fountains of love,
Thou soon shalt be fitted for service above.
                William Dunn Longstaff (1822-94)

459 Whiter than the snow, 858

TELL me what to do to be pure
  In the sight of the all-seeing eyes;
Tell me, is there no thorough cure,
  No escape from the sin I despise?

Tell me, can I never be free
  From this terrible bondage within?
Is there no deliverance for me
  From the thraldom of indwelling sin?

*Whiter than the snow! Whiter than the
    snow!*
Wash me in the blood of the Lamb,
And I shall be whiter than snow.

2 Will my Saviour only pass by,
  Only show me how faulty I've been?
Will he not attend to my cry?
  Can I not at this moment be clean?
Blessèd Lord, almighty to heal,
  I know that thy power cannot fail;
Here and now I know, yes, I feel
  The prayer of my heart does prevail.

3 Now I know to me thou wilt show
  What before I never could see;
Now I know in me thou wilt dwell
  And united to thee I shall be.
Surely now thy smile is on me,
  Thy love to my heart is made known.
Now the face of God I shall see,
  And his power in my life shall be shown.
        Samuel Horatio Hodges (1841-1922) (verses),
        Eden Reeder Latta (b. 1839) (chorus)

460 While the Spirit passes by, 857

THERE are wants my heart is telling
  While the Spirit passes by,
And with hope my soul is swelling
  While the Spirit passes by.
O what prospects now I see,
What a life my life must be,
If thy seal is placed on me,
  While the Spirit passes by!

While the Spirit passes by,
While the Spirit passes by;
Let my heart be sealed for thee
While the Spirit passes by.

2 There are sins my lips confessing
  While the Spirit passes by,
Treasures long my heart possessing,
  While the Spirit passes by.
All the world's delight and cheer,
All the things I held so dear,
Ah, how worthless they appear
  While the Spirit passes by.

3 Here I stand, myself disdaining,
　　While the Spirit passes by;
　Stand in faith, thy mercy claiming,
　　While the Spirit passes by;
　Let thy power my soul refine,
　Let thy grace my will incline,
　Take my all and make it thine,
　　While the Spirit passes by.
　　　　　Herbert Howard Booth (1862-1926)

461 Behold the Saviour, 75; Rest, 124
　　　　　　　　　　　　　　　　C.M.

THERE is a holy hill of God,
　Its heights by faith I see;
Now to ascend my soul aspires,
　To leave earth's vanity.

*Lord, cleanse my hands, and cleanse
　　my heart,*
All selfish aims I flee,
My faith reward, thy love impart,
And let me dwell with thee.

2 Though great the world's attractions be,
　I pass contented by;
Gladly I sacrifice their charms
　For those enjoyed on high.

3 I seek the blessing from the Lord
　That humble saints receive,
And righteousness, his own reward
　To all who dare believe.

4 O let me now thy hill ascend,
　Made worthy by thy grace,
There in thy strength to stand and serve
　Within the holy place!
　　　　　William Drake Pennick (1884-1944)

462 The pathway of duty, 448
　　　　　　　　　　8.7.8.7. D. Troch.

THERE'S a path that's sometimes thorny,
　There's a narrow way, and straight;
It is called the path of duty,
　And it leads to Heaven's gate.
While we tread this path of duty,
　We will find our needs supplied
From the river of God's mercy
　That is flowing close beside.

By the pathway of duty
Flows the river of God's grace.
By the pathway of duty
Flows the river of God's grace.

2 'Tis a blessèd way and holy,
　'Tis a path of peace and joy;
Though sometimes the way be stony
　And the cares of life annoy.

But this path that we call duty
　Is the way the Master trod,
And the smile of love and beauty
　Lights the way that leads to God.

3 Let us walk this path of duty
　With our faces to the sun,
Carry all our burdens gladly,
　Finish well what we've begun.
From the river of God's mercy
　That is flowing by the way,
We may drink and find refreshing
　For the burdens of the day.
　　　　　Sidney Edward Cox (1887-1975)

463 South Shields, 444 (repeat second half
　　　　for chorus); The Vacant Chair, 449
　　　　　　　　　　8.7.8.7. D. Troch.

THOU hast called me from the byway
　To proclaim thy wondrous love;
Thou hast placed me on the highway
　That to all men I may prove
There is mission in my living,
　There is meaning in my word;
Saviour, in my daily striving
　May this message yet be heard.

For thy mission make me holy,
For thy glory make me thine,
Sanctify each moment fully,
Fill my life with love divine.

2 Have I lost the sense of mission
　That inspired my early zeal,
When the fire of thy commission
　Did my dedication seal?
Let me hear thy tender pleading,
　Let me see thy beckoning hand,
Let me feel thee gently leading
　As I bow to thy command.

3 Lord, release that latent passion
　Which in me has dormant lain;
Recreate a deep compassion
　That will care and care again.
Needy souls are still my mission,
　Sinners yet demand my love;
This must be my life's ambition,
　This alone my heart shall move.
　　　　　Brindley Boon

464 Walk in the light, 842

'TIS religion that can give—
　In the light, in the light—
Sweetest pleasures while we live
　In the light of God.

The Life of Holiness

Let us walk in the light,
  Walk in the light,
Let us walk in the light,
  In the light of God.

2 'Tis religion must supply—
  In the light, in the light—
Solid comfort when we die
  In the light of God.

3 After death its joys shall be—
  In the light, in the light—
Lasting as eternity,
  In the light of God.

4 Be the living God my friend —
  In the light, in the light—
Then my bliss shall never end,
  In the light of God.

Attr Mary Masters (d. 1759) (verses 1-3),
attr John Rippon (1751-1836) (verse 4)

465 St Agnes, 126; Lloyd, 107
C.M.

WALK in the light: so shalt thou know
  That fellowship of love
His Spirit only can bestow,
  Who reigns in light above.

2 Walk in the light: and thou shalt find
  Thy heart made truly his
Who dwells in cloudless light enshrined,
  In whom no darkness is.

3 Walk in the light: and thou shalt own
  Thy darkness passed away,
Because that light hath on thee shone
  In which is perfect day.

4 Walk in the light: and e'en the tomb
  No fearful shade shall wear;
Glory shall chase away its gloom,
  For Christ hath conquered there.

5 Walk in the light: and thine shall be
  A path, though thorny, bright;
For God, by grace, shall dwell in thee,
  And God himself is light.

Bernard Barton (1784-1849)

466 Turner, 504; Melita, 495
8.8.8.8.8.8. Iambic

WE have not known thee as we ought,
  Nor learned thy wisdom, grace and
    power;
The things of earth have filled our thought,
  And trifles of the passing hour.
Lord, give us light thy truth to see,
And make us wise in knowing thee.

2 We have not feared thee as we ought,
  Nor bowed beneath thine awful eye,
Nor guarded deed and word and thought,
  Remembering that God was nigh.
Lord, give us faith to know thee near,
And grant the grace of holy fear.

3 We have not loved thee as we ought,
  Nor cared that we are loved by thee;
Thy presence we have coldly sought,
  And feebly longed thy face to see.
Lord, give a pure and loving heart
To feel and know the love thou art.

4 We have not served thee as we ought;
  Alas, the duties left undone,
The work with little fervor wrought,
  The battles lost or scarcely won!
Lord, give the zeal, and give the might,
For thee to toil, for thee to fight.

5 When shall we know thee as we ought,
  And fear and love and serve aright?
When shall we, out of trial brought,
  Be perfect in the land of light?
Lord, may we day by day prepare
To see thy face and serve thee there.

Thomas Benson Pollock (1836-96)

467 Jesus is strong to deliver, 702

WHY are you doubting and fearing?
  Why are you still under sin?
Have you not found that his grace doth
    abound?
  He's mighty to save; let him in.

Jesus is strong to deliver,
  Mighty to save! Mighty to save!
Jesus is strong to deliver,
  Jesus is mighty to save.

2 Say, are you weak, are you helpless,
  Trying again and again?
This may be true, but it's not what you
    do,
  'Tis he who is mighty to save.

3 When in my sorrow he found me,
  Found me and bade me be whole;
Turned all my night into heavenly light,
  And from me my burden did roll.

4 When in the tempest he hides me,
  When in the storm he is near;
O'er the long way the Lord is my stay,
  And now I have nothing to fear.

Herbert Howard Booth (1862-1926), alt

Challenge

468 My beautiful home, 36
L.M.

WHY should I be a slave to sin,
To foes without or foes within?
Sometimes I mount, sometimes cast down,
Sometimes all smile, sometimes all frown.

There's victory for me! There's victory for me!
Through the blood of the Lamb there is victory for me;
He came to set his people free
And give them perfect victory.

2 Sin will abound till grace comes in,
Then grace shall triumph over sin;
Just now, dear Saviour, let it be,
Now give me perfect victory.

3 Be thou my strength, be thou my all,
Then surely I shall never fall;
If none can pluck me from thy hand,
I more than conqueror shall stand.

4 'Tis true I have no room to boast;
When most I'm saved I'm humbled most;
Kept low by grace, and not by sin,
My soul shall make her boast in him.
William Baugh (1852-1942)

469 Sweet Heaven, 584; Home on the range, 581
12.9.12.9.

WITH my faint, weary soul to be made fully whole,
And thy perfect salvation to see,
With my heart all aglow to be washed white as snow,
I am coming, dear Saviour, to thee.

I'm coming (*to thee), I'm coming, dear Saviour, to thee,
With my heart all aglow to be washed white as snow,
I'm coming, dear Saviour, to thee.

2 I thy promise believe, that in thee I shall live,
Through thy blood shed so freely for me;
To obtain a pure heart and secure the good part,
I am coming, dear Saviour, to thee.

3 All to thee now I give, thine to die, thine to live,
Crucified to the world e'er to be;
To be dead unto sin, with a new life within,
I am coming, dear Saviour, to thee.

4 To be thine, wholly thine, precious Saviour divine,
With my all consecrated to thee,
To be kept every hour by thy love's wondrous power,
I am coming, dear Saviour, to thee.
W. H. Burrell

470 O Saviour, I am coming, 441
8.7.8.7. D. Troch.

WITH my heart so full of sadness,
I am coming, Lord, to thee;
Coming now to find thy gladness,
And thy grace, so rich and free.
Empty is the world's enjoyment,
Fleeting is its glittering show;
When I see my Saviour's brightness
All is darkness here below.

O Saviour, I am coming,
Coming, coming!
O Saviour, I am coming,
I'm coming now to thee.

2 Coming with my heart of sorrow,
Coming with my life of care,
Coming to the Lord of mercy,
Coming to the God of prayer.
Leaving all the world behind me,
Leaving all my doubts and fears,
Pressing on to find my Saviour,
Who will wipe away my tears.

3 Giving now my soul and body
As an offering, Lord, to thee,
I would follow in thy footsteps,
Living, dying, thine to be.
O in mercy let thy blessing
Fill and overflow my heart!
All my ways and thoughts possessing,
Come, dear Lord, no more to part.
Herbert Howard Booth (1862-1926)

471 Shall we gather at the river? 398
8.7.8.7. Troch.

YES, there flows a wondrous river,
That can make the foulest clean;
To the soul it is the giver
Of the freedom from all sin.

Round us flows the cleansing river,
The holy, mighty, wonder-working river,
That can make a saint of a sinner;
It flows from the throne of God.

2 All who seek this cleansing river
  Have their deepest need supplied;
From all ills its waves deliver
  When for healing they're applied.

3 Have you proved this precious river,
  Perfect cleansing gaining there?
Losing burdens that need never
  Rise again to bring you care?

4 On the margin of this river,
  In your stains, why still delay?
Why not now be free for ever
  And the voice of God obey?
          Richard Slater (1854-1939)

see also: 490 I heard a voice so gently calling
      510 Mine to rise when thou dost
      call me

Consecration and Service

472 Southport, 178; Dennis, 165   S.M.

A CHARGE to keep I have,
  A God to glorify,
A never-dying soul to save,
  And fit it for the sky.

2 To serve the present age,
  My calling to fulfil,
O may it all my powers engage,
  To do my Master's will!

3 Arm me with jealous care,
  As in thy sight to live;
And O thy servant, Lord, prepare
  A strict account to give!

4 Help me to watch and pray,
  And on thyself rely,
Assured, if I my trust betray,
  I shall forever die.
        Charles Wesley (1707-88)

473 All I have I am bringing to thee, 601

ALL I have, by thy blood thou dost claim,
  Blessèd Lord, who for me once was slain;
Now thine own I will give thee,
I know thou wilt take me,
Though long thou hast pleaded in vain.

All I have I am bringing to thee,
All I have I am bringing to thee;
In thy steps I will follow, come joy or
* come sorrow,*
Dear Saviour, I will follow thee.

2 All I have, it shall be nothing less,
All I have thou shalt own, Lord, and bless;
  Loss and pain shall not hinder,
  I'll keep back no longer
From being thine fully, my Lord.

3 Days of darkness there may be for me,
Rough and steep, too, my pathway may be;
  But the joy or the sorrow
  That comes with tomorrow
Will just be the fittest for me.

4 Though by darkness my future is veiled,
Here's my all, for thy love has prevailed;
  I no longer will doubt thee,
  I know thou dost save me,
My life shall be wholly for thee.
    Richard Slater (1854-1939) (verses),
  Herbert Howard Booth (1862-1926) (chorus)

474 I surrender all, 377
        8.7.8.7. Troch.

ALL to Jesus I surrender,
  All to him I freely give;
I will ever love and trust him,
  In his presence daily live.

I surrender all, I surrender all,
All to thee, my blessèd Saviour,
* I surrender all.*

2 All to Jesus I surrender,
  Humbly at his feet I bow,
Worldly pleasures all forsaken;
  Take me, Jesus, take me now.

3 All to Jesus I surrender,
  Make me, Saviour, wholly thine;
Let the Holy Spirit witness,
  I am thine and thou art mine.

4 All to Jesus I surrender,
  Lord, I give myself to thee;
Fill me with thy love and power,
  Let thy blessing rest on me.

5 All to Jesus I surrender,
  Now I feel the sacred flame;
O the joy of full salvation,
  Glory, glory to his name!
    Judson Van de Venter (1855-1939)

475 Slater, 133
      C.M.

AND is it so? A gift from me
  Dost thou, dear Lord, request?
Then speak thy will, whate'er it be:
  Obeying, I am blest.

I have not much to give thee, Lord,
For that great love which made thee
mine:
I have not much to give thee, Lord,
But all I have is thine.

2 And dost thou ask a gift from me:
  The talents I possess?
Such as I have I give to thee
  That others I may bless.

3 And dost thou ask a gift from me:
  The gift of passing time?
My hours I'll give, not grudgingly,
  I feel by right they're thine.

4 And dost thou ask a gift from me:
  A loving, faithful heart?
'Tis thine, for thou on Calvary
  For me with all didst part.
                Richard Slater (1854-1939)

476 Beneath the cross, 618
        See also A.S. 989

BENEATH the cross of Jesus
  I fain would take my stand,
The shadow of a mighty rock
  Within a weary land;
A home within the wilderness,
  A rest upon the way,
From the burning of the noontide heat
  And the burden of the day.

2 Upon that cross of Jesus
  Mine eye at times can see
The very dying form of one
  Who suffered there for me;
And from my smitten heart, with tears,
  Two wonders I confess:
The wonders of his glorious love,
  And my own worthlessness.

3 I take, O cross, thy shadow
  For my abiding place;
I ask no other sunshine than
  The sunshine of his face;
Content to let the world go by,
  To know no gain nor loss,
My sinful self my only shame,
  My glory all the cross.
          Elizabeth Cecilia Clephane (1830-69)

477 Breathe upon me, 363
        8.7.8.7. Troch.

BLESSÈD Saviour, now behold me
  Waiting at thy bleeding feet;
In thy mercy breathe upon me,
  Make me for thyself complete.

Breathe upon me, even me,
Make me what I ought to be;
In thy mercy breathe upon me,
Make me for thyself complete.

2 Take my undivided being,
  Thou hast bought me with thy blood;
All my sins thou hast forgiven;
  Let my future be for God.

3 Should my days be few or many,
  Should my strength be great or small,
Be my talents two or fifty,
  Jesus, thou shalt have them all.

4 While I live be thou my leader,
  When I die be thou my share;
In thy strength I'm bound to conquer
  While for thee my cross I bear.
              William Baugh (1852-1942)

478 Let the lower lights be burning, 386
        8.7.8.7. Troch.

BRIGHTLY beams our Father's mercy
  From his lighthouse evermore;
But to us he gives the keeping
  Of the lights along the shore.

Let the lower lights be burning,
Send a gleam across the wave;
Some poor fainting, struggling seaman
You may rescue, you may save.

2 Dark the night of sin has settled,
  Loud the angry billows roar;
Eager eyes are watching, longing,
  For the lights along the shore.

3 Trim your feeble lamp, my brother;
  Some poor seaman, tempest-tossed,
Trying now to make the harbor,
  In the darkness may be lost.
            Philip Paul Bliss (1838-76)

479 Toplady, 316; Coles, 305
        7.7.7.7.7.7.

CHRIST of Glory, Prince of Peace,
  Let thy life in mine increase;
Though I live may it be shown
'Tis thy life and not my own.
Dwell within, that men may see
Christ, the living Christ, in me.

2 Answer now my soul's desire,
  Purge my heart with holy fire,
Soothe the hurt with gentle balm,
Breathe within my life thy charm,
Fill me now, so shall there be
Christ, the holy Christ, in me.

3 Gracious Lord, thy grace apply,
　Both to save and sanctify;
　All my life wilt thou control,
　Calmly ordering the whole,
　That the world may ever see
　Christ, and only Christ, in me.

Colin Fairclough

480 Maryton, 33; Deep Harmony, 16
L.M.

COME, Saviour Jesus, from above,
　Assist me with thy heavenly grace;
Empty my heart of earthly love,
　And for thyself prepare the place.

2 O let thy sacred presence fill
　And set my longing spirit free,
Which wants to have no other will,
　But day and night to feast on thee!

3 Henceforth may no profane delight
　Divide this consecrated soul;
Possess it thou, who hast the right,
　As Lord and Master of the whole.

4 Wealth, honor, pleasure, and what else
　This short-enduring world can give,
Tempt as ye will, my soul repels;
　To Christ alone resolved to live.

5 Nothing on earth do I desire
　But thy pure love within my breast;
This, only this, do I require,
　And freely give up all the rest.

Antoinette Bourignon (1616-80),
trs John Wesley (1703-91)

481 Coming to the cross, 278; Christ receiveth sinful men, 277
7.7.7.7.

COME, thou burning Spirit, come;
　Lo! we stretch our hands to thee;
From the Father and the Son
　Let us now thy glory see.

Come, O come great Spirit, come!
Let the mighty deed be done;
Satisfy our souls' desire,
Now we trust thee for the fire.

2 On the altar now we lay
　Soul and body, mind and will;
All the evil passions slay,
　Come and every corner fill.

3 Now the sacrifice we make,
　Though as dear as a right eye,
For our blessèd Saviour's sake
　Who for us did bleed and die.

4 Now by faith the gift I claim,
　Bought for me by blood divine,
Through the all-prevailing name
　All the promises are mine.

Charles Fry (1838-82)

482 To the uttermost he saves, 267
7.6.7.6. D. Iambic

DEAR Lord, I do surrender
　Myself, my all, to thee;
My time, my store, my talents,
　So long withheld by me.
I've heard the call for workers,
　The world's great need I see,
O send me to the rescue,
　I'm here, my Lord, send me!

Here am I, my Lord, send me,
Here am I, my Lord, send me,
I surrender all to obey thy call,
Here am I, my Lord, send me.

2 Too long at ease in Zion
　I've been content to dwell,
While multitudes are dying
　And sinking into Hell.
I can no more be careless,
　And say there's naught to do,
The fields are white to harvest
　And laborers are few.

3 O hear, thou God of Heaven,
　The vows that now I make!
To thee my life is given,
　'Tis for the lost world's sake.
To serve thee I am ready,
　Though friends and foes despise,
I now present my body
　A living sacrifice.

W. Walker

483 Follow On, 644

DOWN in the valley with my Saviour I
　　would go,
Where the flowers are blooming and the
　　sweet waters flow;
Everywhere he leads me I would follow,
　　follow on,
Walking in his footsteps till the crown be
　　won.

Follow, follow, I will follow Jesus,
Anywhere, everywhere, I will follow on;
Follow, follow, I will follow Jesus,
Everywhere he leads me I will follow on.

2 Down in the valley with my Saviour I would
   go,
   Where the storms are sweeping and the
   dark waters flow;
   With his hand to lead me I will never, never
   fear;
   Dangers cannot fright me if my Lord is
   near.

3 Down in the valley, or upon the mountain
   steep,
   Close beside my Saviour would my soul
   ever keep;
   He will lead me safely in the path that he
   has trod,
   Up to where they gather on the hills of
   God.
   William Orcutt Cushing (1823-1902)

484 Jesus is calling, 700

EARNESTLY seeking to save and to heal,
   Working for thee, working for thee;
Grant me, O Saviour, the marks of thy zeal,
   Earnestly working for thee.

Working for thee, working for thee,
Earnestly, constantly, faithfully
   working for thee.

2 Constantly working, I will not delay,
   Working for thee, working for thee;
   Keeping my trust through the whole of
   the day,
   Always and only for thee.

3 Faithfully working, my life's purpose
   claimed
   Wholly for thee, wholly for thee,
   That of my work I may not be ashamed
   When I am summoned to thee.
   Albert Orsborn (1886-1967)

485 Spohr, 135
8.6.8.6.8.6.

FATHER, I know that all my life
   Is portioned out for me;
The changes that will surely come,
   I do not fear to see;
I ask thee for a patient mind,
   Intent on pleasing thee.

2 I ask thee for a thoughtful love,
   Through constant watching, wise,
   To meet the glad with joyful smiles,
   And wipe the weeping eyes;
   A heart at leisure from itself,
   To soothe and sympathize.

3 I ask thee for the daily strength
   To none that ask denied,
   A mind to blend with outward life
   While keeping at thy side;
   Content to fill a little space
   If thou be glorified.

4 In service which thy love appoints
   There are no bonds for me;
   My secret heart is taught the truth
   That makes thy children free:
   A life of self-renouncing love
   Is one of liberty.

5 Wherever in the world I am,
   In whatsoe'er estate,
   I have a fellowship with hearts
   To keep and cultivate,
   A work of lowly love to do
   For him on whom I wait.
   Anna Laetitia Waring (1823-1910)

486 I bring thee all, 676

FATHER of love, of justice and of mercy,
   Thou art the dawn, the star at eventide;
Show thou thy face, and light my way to
   Calvary,
   There all my sins in thee to hide.
   I bring thee all my sins,
   None can forgive but thee.

I bring thee all, I bring thee all;
O give thyself to me,
I bring thee all.

2 O thou, of whom the heavens are but a
   symbol,
   Be thou the sun that draws my heart to
   thee;
   Be thou the light the stars at night do
   kindle;
   Thy love is more than all to me.
   I bring thee all my heart,
   None do I love like thee.

3 O Man of sorrows, praying in the garden,
   Thy sweat as blood falls down upon the
   ground.
   In that dark agony my sins are pardoned;
   My solace in thy grief is found.
   I bring thee all my tears,
   None can console like thee.
   Evangeline Booth (1865-1950)

487 Thine own way, Lord, 832

HAVE thine own way, Lord, have thine
own way;
Thou art the potter, I am the clay;
Mold me and make me after thy will,
While I am waiting yielded and still.

2 Have thine own way, Lord, have thine own
way;
Search me and try me, Master, today;
Whiter than snow, Lord, wash me just now,
As in thy presence humbly I bow.

3 Have thine own way, Lord, have thine own
way;
Wounded and weary, help me I pray;
Power, all power, surely is thine,
Touch me and heal me, Saviour divine.

4 Have thine own way, Lord, have thine own
way;
Hold o'er my being absolute sway;
Fill with thy Spirit till all shall see
Christ only, always, living in me.
Adelaide Addison Pollard (1862-1934)

488 Here at the cross, 22; Ernan, 19
L.M.

HOW can I better serve thee, Lord,
Thou who hast done so much for me?
Faltering and weak my labor has been;
O that my life may tell for thee!

Here at the cross in this sacred hour,
Here at the source of reviving power,
Helpless indeed, I come with my need;
Lord, for thy service, fit me I plead.

2 Dull are my ears to hear thy voice,
Slow are my hands to work for thee,
Loath are my feet to conquer the steeps
That lead me to my Calvary.

3 Strength for my weakness, Lord, impart;
Sight for my blindness give to me;
Faith for my doubtings, Lord, I would
crave,
That I may serve thee worthily.
Bramwell Coles (1887-1960)

489 Christ is all, 463
8.8.6.8.8.6.

I BRING to thee my heart to fill;
I feel how weak I am, but still
To thee for help I call.
In joy or grief, to live or die,
For earth or Heaven, this is my cry,
Be thou my all in all.

Christ is all, yes, all in all,
My Christ is all in all.

2 Around me in the world I see
No joy that turns my soul from thee;
Its honors fade and fall;
But with thee, though I mount the cross,
I count it gain to suffer loss,
For thou art all in all.

3 I've little strength to call my own,
And what I've done, before thy throne
I here confess, is small;
But on thy strength, O God, I lean,
And through the blood that makes me
clean,
Thou art my all in all.

4 No tempest can my courage shake,
My love from thee no pain can take,
No fear my heart appall;
And where I cannot see I'll trust,
For then I know thou surely must
Be still my all in all.
Herbert Howard Booth (1862-1926) (verses),
W. A. Williams (chorus)

490 I'll follow thee, 685

I HEARD a voice so gently calling:
Take up thy cross and follow me.
A tempest on my heart was falling,
A living cross this was to be;
I struggled sore, I struggled vainly,
No other light my eyes could see.

I'll follow thee, of life the giver,
I'll follow thee, suffering redeemer,
I'll follow thee, deny thee never,
By thy grace I'll follow thee.

2 I heard his voice unto me saying:
Take up thy cross and follow me.
My heart is thine, now thee obeying,
Speak all thy will, dear Lord, to me.
Make weakness strength, thy power now
give me,
And from this hour I'll follow thee.
Agnes Heathcote

Consecration and Service

491
Pilgrims, 548

11.10.11.10.

I WOULD be true, for there are those who
trust me;
I would be pure, for there are those who
care;
I would be strong, for there is much to
suffer;
I would be brave, for there is much to
dare.

Jesus will help me,
He is my friend;
He'll lead and I will follow
Till life's very end.

2 I would be friend of all—the foe, the
friendless;
I would be giving, and forget the gift;
I would be humble, for I know my
weakness;
I would look up and laugh and love and
lift.

Howard Arnold Walter (1883-1918) (verses)

492
Rousseau, 314; Norwood, 311

7.7.7.7.7.7.

IF so poor a soul as I
May to thy great glory live,
All my actions sanctify,
All my words and thoughts receive;
Claim me for thy service, claim
All I have and all I am.

2 Take my soul and body's powers,
Take my memory, mind and will,
All my goods and all my hours,
All I know and all I feel,
All I think or speak or do;
Take my heart, but make it new!

3 Now, O God, thine own I am,
Now I give thee back thine own;
Freedom, friends and health and fame
Consecrate to thee alone;
Thine I live, thrice happy I,
Happier still if thine I die.

Charles Wesley (1707-88)

493
In deeper consecration, 688

IN the depths of my soul's greatest longing
I am coming, dear Saviour, to thee,
Offering each thought and deed for
refining;
Let thy touch now descend upon me.

Draw me close to thee in deeper
consecration;
Wash me, Lord, and cleanse my soul
from fear and dross;
Sanctify me with the fire of thy
indwelling
As I tarry in the shadow of the cross.

2 Grant me patience to wait love's bestowal
As I seek for that blessing divine;
Quicken each inner wish with thy power
Till my will becomes blended with thine.

3 With the saints, I am now comprehending
Higher heights, deeper depths of thy
love,
Serving thee with a heart of compassion,
Day by day my devotion to prove.

Margaret Lodge MacMillan

494
Chalvey, 181; Peace, 185

D.S.M.

IN their appointed days
All things their maker praise,
For all are lovely in their time
And in their varied ways;
Yet true it is to say,
All beauty fades away
Save that which in the heart resides
And cannot know decay.

2 As gently falling dew
Bids nature smile anew,
So does the beauty of the Lord
True comeliness renew;
It glorifies our Lord,
Shows forth the living word,
So men beholding must confess
The saving grace of God.

3 Come, Saviour, and refine
This sinful heart of mine,
Removing everything that mars
The loveliness divine;
O make and keep me clean,
Spare not one lurking sin,
So shall my life each day proclaim
The Christ who dwells within.

Albert Orsborn (1886-1967)

The Life of Holiness

495 My soul is now united, 257; Aurelia, 246
7.6.7.6. D. Iambic

I'M set apart for Jesus,
  To be a king and priest;
His life in me increases,
  Upon his love I feast.
From evil separated,
  Made holy by his blood,
My all is consecrated
  Unto the living God.

2 I'm set apart for Jesus,
  His goodness I have seen,
He makes my heart his altar,
  He keeps his temple clean.
Our union none can sever,
  Together every hour,
His life is mine for ever
  With resurrection power.

3 I'm set apart for Jesus,
  With him to ever stay,
My spirit he releases,
  He drives my foes away.
He gives full strength for trial
  And shields when darts are hurled;
With him and self-denial
  I overcome the world.
William James Pearson (1832-92)

496 Colne, 79; Bishopthorpe, 77
C.M.

IMMORTAL love, forever full,
  Forever flowing free,
Forever shared, forever whole,
  A never-ebbing sea.

2 Our outward lips confess the name
  All other names above;
Love only knoweth whence it came,
  And comprehendeth love.

3 We may not climb the heavenly steeps
  To bring the Lord Christ down;
In vain we search the lowest deeps,
  For him no depth can drown.

4 In joy of inward peace, or sense
  Of sorrow over sin,
He is his own best evidence,
  His witness is within.

5 For warm, sweet, tender, even yet
  A present help is he;
And faith has still its Olivet,
  And love its Galilee.
John Greenleaf Whittier (1807-92)

497 Weber, 301; Last Hope, 284
7.7.7.7.

JESUS, all-atoning Lamb,
  Thine, and only thine, I am;
Take my body, spirit, soul;
  Only thou possess the whole.

2 Thou my one thing needful be;
  Let me ever cleave to thee;
Let me choose the better part;
  Let me give thee all my heart.

3 Fairer than the sons of men,
  Do not let me turn again,
Leave the fountain-head of bliss,
  Stoop to worldly happiness.

4 All my treasure is above,
  All my riches is thy love;
Who the worth of love can tell?
  Infinite, unsearchable.
Charles Wesley (1707-88)

498 I will follow thee, my Saviour, 378;
Bethany, 429   8.7.8.7. Troch.

JESUS, I my cross have taken,
  All to leave, and follow thee;
Though I be despised, forsaken,
  Thou from hence my all shalt be.

I will follow thee, my Saviour,
  Thou hast shed thy blood for me;
And though all the world forsake thee,
  By thy grace I'll follow thee.

2 Perish every fond ambition,
  All I've sought or hoped or known;
Yet how rich is my condition,
  God and Heaven are still my own.

3 Let the world despise and leave me,
  They have left my Saviour too;
Human hearts and looks deceive me,
  Thou art not like them, untrue.

4 And while thou shalt smile upon me,
  God of wisdom, love and might,
Foes may hate and friends may shun me,
  Show thy face and all is bright.

5 O 'tis not in grief to harm me,
  While thy love is left to me!
O 'twere not in joy to charm me,
  Were that joy not found in thee!
Henry Francis Lyte (1793-1847) (verses),
James Lawson (chorus)

Consecration and Service

499 Anything for Jesus, 199;
Princethorpe, 206   6.5.6.5. D.

JESUS, precious Saviour, thou hast saved
my soul,
From sin's foul corruption made me fully
whole;
Every hour I'll serve thee, whate'er may
befall,
Till in Heaven I crown thee King and Lord
of all.

All my heart I give thee,
Day by day, come what may.
All my life I give thee,
Dying men to save.

2 From the lowly manger I will follow thee,
In the desert and the strife near thee I will
be;
E'en the sufferings of the cross I will gladly
bear,
And with thee in Heaven I a crown shall
wear.

3 In the toils and conflicts faithful I will be,
All things I will gladly bear, they'll be good
for me;
As a savior of mankind, slaves of sin to
bring,
Give me holy courage, mighty, mighty
King.

4 Precious souls are dying, nerve me for the
fight,
Help me spread the glorious news, liberty
and light;
Fiercer gets the contest, Satan's power
shall fall,
Then on earth I'll crown thee glorious Lord
of all.
Harry Davis (1854-1918)

500 Triumph, 427; Bethany, 429
8.7.8.7.8.7. Troch.

KING of love so condescending,
Spurning not our sinful race,
Bearing death, our cause defending,
Lavishing thy gifts of grace,
We adore thee, we adore thee,
And thy Kingdom's cause embrace.

2 Spurning now the world's enticing,
Love of ease and passing show,
Heavenly grace our souls sufficing,
We obey thy word to go
Bearing tidings, precious tidings,
All the world may Jesus know.

3 When the toils of life are over
And the realms of Glory won,
We shall reap in Heaven the harvest,
Hear the Saviour's glad well done.
Hallelujah! Hallelujah!
Jesus' reign has now begun.
William Drake Pennick (1884-1944)

501 Into thy hands, Lord, 692

KNEELING before thee, Lord, I am
praying,
Claiming a closer communion with thee,
Longing to sever from selfish ambition;
Break thou each fetter and set my soul
free.

Into thy hands, Lord, take me and
mold me,
E'en as the potter handles the clay;
Make me a vessel fit for thy service;
Cleanse me and fill me, and use me
today.

2 Fruitless has been the way of my
choosing;
Now I am leaving the future with thee;
Treading the pathway of joyful obedience,
Lord, see me ready thy servant to be.

3 Not in my own strength can I accomplish
All thou art planning for me, day by day;
Owning the limit of human endeavor,
Humbly I seek, Lord, the grace to obey.
Jessie Mountain (1895-1981)

502 Speak, Saviour, speak, 445
8.7.8.7. D. Troch.

LET me hear thy voice now speaking,
Let me hear and I'll obey;
While before thy cross I'm seeking,
O chase my fears away!
O let the light now falling
Reveal my every need,
Now hear me while I'm calling,
O speak, and I will heed!

Speak, Saviour, speak!
Obey thee I will ever,
Now at thy cross I seek
From all that's wrong to sever.

2 Let me hear and I will follow
  Though the path be strewed with thorns;
It is joy to share thy sorrow,
  Thou makest calm the storm.
Now my heart thy temple making,
  In thy fulness dwell with me;
Every evil way forsaking,
  Thine only I will be.

3 Let the blood of Christ forever
  Flood and cleanse my heart within,
That to grieve thee I may never
  More stain my soul with sin.
Farewell to worldly pleasure,
  Farewell to self and pride;
How wondrous is my treasure
  With Jesus at my side.
            Herbert Howard Booth (1862-1926)

503 Let me love thee, 439; Blaenwern, 430
              8.7.8.7. D. Troch.

LET me love thee, thou art claiming
  Every feeling of my soul;
Let that love, in power prevailing,
  Render thee my life, my all.
For life's burdens they are easy,
  And life's sorrows lose their sting,
If they're carried, Lord, to please thee,
  If their pain thy smile should win.

Let me love thee, Saviour,
Take my heart forever;
Nothing but thy favor
My soul can satisfy.

2 Let me love thee, come revealing
  All thy love has done for me.
Help my heart, so unbelieving,
  By the sight of Calvary.
Let me see thy love, despising
  All the shame my sin has brought,
By thy torments realizing
  What a price my pardon bought.

3 Let me love thee, I am gladdest
  When I'm loving thee the best;
For in sunshine or in sadness
  I can find in thee my rest.
Love will soften every sorrow,
  Love will lighten every care,
Love unquestioning will follow,
  Love will triumph, love will dare.
            Herbert Howard Booth (1862-1926)

504 Full Surrender, 650

LORD, I make a full surrender,
  All I have I yield to thee;
For thy love, so great and tender,
  Asks the gift of me.
Lord, I bring my whole affection,
  Claim it, take it for thine own,
Safely kept by thy protection,
  Fixed on thee alone.

Glory, glory, hallelujah!
I have given my all to God;
And I now have full salvation
Through the precious blood.

2 Lord, my will I here present thee
  Gladly, now no longer mine;
Let no evil thing prevent me
  Blending it with thine.
Lord, my life I lay before thee;
  Hear this hour the sacred vow;
All thine own I now restore thee,
  Thine forever now.

3 Blessèd Spirit, thou hast brought me
  Thus my all to thee to give;
For the blood of Christ has bought me,
  And by faith I live.
Show thyself, O God of power,
  My unchanging, loving friend;
Keep me till, in death's glad hour,
  Faith in sight shall end.
            Attr Lowell Mason (1792-1872)

505 Dennis, 165; Silchester, 177
                                    S.M.

LORD, in the strength of grace,
  With a glad heart and free,
Myself, my residue of days,
  I consecrate to thee.

2   Thy ransomed servant, I
    Restore to thee thy own,
And from this moment, live or die
  To serve my God alone.
            Charles Wesley (1707-88)

506 Slane, 789

LORD of creation, to you be all praise;
  Most mighty your working, most won-
    drous your ways;
Your glory and might are beyond us to
    tell,
And yet in the heart of the humble you
    dwell.

2 Lord of all power, I give you my will,
In joyful obedience your tasks to fulfil.
Your bondage is freedom, your service is
song,
And, held in your keeping, my weakness
is strong.

3 Lord of all wisdom, I give you my mind,
Rich truth that surpasses man's knowledge to find.
What eye has not seen and what ear has
not heard
Is taught by your Spirit and shines from
your word.

4 Lord of all bounty, I give you my heart;
I praise and adore you for all you impart:
Your love to inspire me, your counsel to
guide,
Your presence to cheer me, whatever
betide.

5 Lord of all being, I give you my all;
If e'er I disown you I stumble and fall;
But sworn in glad service your word to
obey,
I walk in your freedom to the end of the
way.

John Copley Winslow (1882-1974)

507 O for a heart whiter than snow, 528;
The Glory Song, 529

10.10.10.10. Dact.

LORD, thou art questioning: Lovest thou
me?
Yea, Lord, thou knowest, my answer must
be;
But since love's value is proved by love's
test,
Jesus, I'll give thee the dearest and best.

*All in my heart, Lord, thou canst read;
Master, thou knowest I love thee
indeed.
Ask what thou wilt my devotion to
test,
I will surrender the dearest and best.*

2 How couldst thou smile on me if, in my
heart,
I were unwilling from treasures to part?
Since my redemption cost thee such a
price,
Utmost surrender alone will suffice.

3 Down at thy feet all my fears I let go,
Back on thy strength all my weakness I
throw;
Lord, in my life thou shalt have thine own
way,
Speak but the word, and thy child will
obey.

Ruth Tracy (1870-1960)

508 Chalvey, 181

D.S.M.

MAKE me a captive, Lord,
And then I shall be free;
Force me to render up my sword,
And I shall conqueror be.
I sink in life's alarms
When by myself I stand;
Imprison me within thine arms
And strong shall be my hand.

2 My heart is weak and poor
Until it master find;
It has no spring of action sure,
It varies with the wind.
It cannot freely move
Till thou hast wrought its chain;
Enslave it with thy matchless love
And deathless it shall reign.

3 My will is not my own
Till thou hast made it thine;
If it would reach a monarch's throne
It must its crown resign;
It only stands unbent
Amid the clashing strife,
When on thy bosom it has leant
And found in thee its life.

George Matheson (1842-1906)

509 Sagina, 498; Old 23rd, 497

8.8.8.8.8.8. Iambic

MASTER, I own thy lawful claim,
Thine, wholly thine, I long to be;
Thou seest, at last, I willing am
Where'er thou goest to follow thee;
Myself in all things to deny,
Thine, wholly thine, to live and die.

2 Pleasure and wealth and praise no more
Shall lead my captive soul astray;
These fond pursuits I all give o'er,
Thee, only thee, resolved to obey;
My will in all things to resign,
And know no other will but thine.

3 Wherefore to thee I all resign,
  Being thou art of love and power;
Thy only will be done, not mine;
  Thee, Lord, let Heaven and earth adore;
Flow back the rivers to the sea,
And let my all be lost in thee.
Charles Wesley (1707-88)

510 I will follow thee, my Saviour, 378;
Let the lower lights be burning, 386;
Mine and thine, 388   8.7.8.7. Troch.

MINE to rise when thou dost call me,
  Lifelong though the journey be;
Thine to measure all its windings,
  Leading step by step to thee.

I am thine, O Lord and Master,
  Thine to follow to the end.
Thou art mine, O Christ my Saviour,
  Guide and helper, lover, friend!

2 Mine to follow, even blindly,
  Thine, O Christ, to go before;
Mine to try and scale the barrier,
  Thine to fling an open door.

3 Mine to smile in face of failure,
  Thine to gladden my defeat;
Mine to kneel and drink of Marah,
  Thine to make its waters sweet.

4 Thine the sealing and revealing
  All the outcome of my vow,
As I give thee soul and body,
  Mine no longer, thine just now.
Susie Forrest Swift (1862-1916)

511 My all is on the altar, 242; The Crimson
Stream, 266   7.6.7.6. D. Iambic

MY body, soul and spirit,
  Jesus, I give to thee,
A consecrated offering,
  Thine evermore to be.

My all is on the altar,
  I'm waiting for the fire;
Waiting, waiting, waiting,
  I'm waiting for the fire.

2 O Jesus, mighty Saviour,
  I trust in thy great name;
I look for thy salvation,
  Thy promise now I claim.

3 O let the fire, descending
  Just now upon my soul,
Consume my humble offering,
  And cleanse and make me whole!

4 I'm thine, O blessèd Jesus,
  Washed by thy precious blood;
Now seal me by thy Spirit
  A sacrifice to God.
Mary Dagworthy James (1810-83) (verses)

512 Spohr, 135
8.6.8.6.8.6.

MY life must be Christ's broken bread,
  My love his outpoured wine,
A cup o'erfilled, a table spread
  Beneath his name and sign,
That other souls, refreshed and fed,
  May share his life through mine.

2 My all is in the Master's hands
  For him to bless and break;
Beyond the brook his winepress stands
  And thence my way I take,
Resolved the whole of love's demands
  To give, for his dear sake.

3 Lord, let me share that grace of thine
  Wherewith thou didst sustain
The burden of the fruitful vine,
  The gift of buried grain.
Who dies with thee, O Word divine,
  Shall rise and live again.
Albert Orsborn (1886-1967)

513 Saviour, dear Saviour, draw nearer, 782

MY mind upon thee, Lord, is stayed,
  My all upon thy altar laid,
    O hear my prayer!
And since, in singleness of aim,
I part with all, thy power to gain,
    O God, draw near!

Saviour, dear Saviour, draw nearer,
Humble in spirit I kneel at thy cross;
Speak out thy wishes still clearer,
And I will obey at all cost.

2 By every promise thou hast made
  And by the price thy love has paid
    For my release,
I claim the power to make me whole,
And keep through every hour my soul
    In perfect peace.

3 And now by faith the deed is done,
  And thou again to live hast come
    Within my heart.
And rising now with thee, my Lord,
To lose the world I can afford,
  For mine thou art.
Herbert Howard Booth (1862-1926)

Consecration and Service

514
Not my own, 389
8.7.8.7. Troch.

NOT my own, but saved by Jesus,
  Who redeemed me by his blood;
Gladly I accept the message,
  I belong to Christ the Lord.

Not my own, not my own,
  Saviour, I belong to thee;
All I have and all I hope for,
  Thine for all eternity.

2 Not my own; to Christ my Saviour,
  I, believing, trust my soul,
Everything to him committed,
  While eternal ages roll.

3 Not my own; my time, my talents,
  Freely all to Christ I bring,
To be used in joyful service
  For the glory of my King.

4 Not my own; the Lord accepts me,
  One among the ransomed throng
Who in Heaven shall see his glory,
  And to Jesus Christ belong.
  Daniel Webster Whittle (1840-1901)

515
French, 88; Wiltshire, 143
C.M.

O BLESSÈD Saviour, is thy love
  So great, so full, so free?
Behold we give our thoughts, our hearts,
  Our lives, our all, to thee.

2 We love thee for the glorious worth
  Which in thyself we see;
We love thee for that cross of shame
  Endured so patiently.

3 No man of greater love can boast
  Than for his friend to die;
Thou for thine enemies wast slain;
  What love with thine can vie?

4 Make us like thee in meekness, love,
  And every beauteous grace,
From glory unto glory changed
  Till we behold thy face.
  Joseph Stennett (1663-1713)

516
Euphony, 493; Eaton, 491;
Solid Rock, 501   8.8.8.8.8.8. Iambic

O GOD, what offering shall I give
  To thee, the Lord of earth and skies?
My spirit, soul and flesh receive,
  A holy, living sacrifice;
Small as it is, 'tis all my store,
More shouldst thou have if I had more.

2 Now, O my God, thou hast my soul,
  No longer mine, but thine I am;
Guard thou thine own, possess it whole,
  Cheer it with hope, with love inflame;
Thou hast my spirit, there display
Thy glory to the perfect day.

3 Thou hast my flesh, thy hallowed shrine,
  Devoted solely to thy will;
Here let thy light forever shine,
  This house still let thy presence fill;
O Source of life, live, dwell and move
In me, till all my life be love!

4 Send down thy likeness from above,
  And let this my adorning be;
Clothe me with wisdom, patience, love,
  With lowliness and purity,
Than gold and pearls more precious far,
And brighter than the morning star.

5 Lord, arm me with thy Spirit's might,
  Since I am called by thy great name;
In thee let all my thoughts unite,
  Of all my works be thou the aim;
Thy love attend me all my days,
And my sole business be thy praise.
  Joachim Lange (1670-1744),
  trs John Wesley (1703-91)

517
Holly, 24
L.M.

O LORD, thy heavenly grace impart,
  And fix my frail, inconstant heart!
Henceforth my chief desire shall be
To dedicate myself to thee.

2 Whate'er pursuits my time employ,
  One thought shall fill my soul with joy:
That silent, secret thought shall be
That all my hopes are fixed on thee.

3 Thy glorious eye pervadeth space;
  Thou'rt present, Lord, in every place;
And wheresoe'er my lot may be,
Still shall my spirit cleave to thee.

4 Renouncing every worldly thing,
  Safe 'neath the shelter of thy wing,
My sweetest thought henceforth shall be
That all I want I find in thee.
  John Frederic Oberlin (1740-1826),
  trs Lucy Sarah Wilson (1802-63)

518
Melcombe, 34; Armadale, 8
L.M.

O LORD, whose human hands were quick
  To feed the hungry, heal the sick,
Who love by loving deed expressed,
Help me to comfort the distressed.

The Life of Holiness

2 What is divine about my creed
If I am blind to human need?
For you have said they serve you best
Who serve the helpless and oppressed.

3 Lord, may your love translucent shine
Through every loving deed of mine,
That men may see the works I do
And give the glory all to you.

Malcolm Bale

519 Maryton, 33; Angelus, 6
L.M.

O MASTER, let me walk with thee
In lowly paths of service free;
Tell me thy secret; help me bear
The strain of toil, the fret of care.

2 Help me the slow of heart to move
By some clear, winning word of love;
Teach me the wayward feet to stay,
And guide them in the homeward way.

3 Teach me thy patience; still with thee
In closer, dearer company,
In work that keeps faith sweet and strong,
In trust that triumphs over wrong;

4 In hope that sends a shining ray
Far down the future's broadening way,
In peace that only thou canst give,
For thee, O Master, let me live.

Washington Gladden (1836-1918)

520 Glory to the Lamb, 372;
Denmark Hill, 368   8.7.8.7. Troch.

PRECIOUS Jesus, O to love thee!
O to know that thou art mine!
Jesus, all my heart I give thee
If thou wilt but make it thine.

Glory, glory, Jesus saves me,
Glory, glory to the Lamb!
O the cleansing blood has reached me,
Glory, glory to the Lamb!

2 Take my warmest, best affection,
Take my memory, mind and will;
Then with all thy loving Spirit
All my emptied nature fill.

3 Bold I touch thy sacred garment,
Fearless stretch my eager hand;
Virtue, like a healing fountain,
Freely flows at love's command.

4 O how precious, dear Redeemer,
Is the love that fills my soul!
It is done, the word is spoken:
Be thou every whit made whole.

5 Lo, a new creation dawning!
Lo, I rise to life divine!
In my soul an Easter morning;
I am Christ's and Christ is mine.

Attr Francis Bottome (1823-94)

521 Nearer to thee, 191; Nuttall, 192
6.4.6.4.6.6.6.4.

SAVIOUR, I long to be
Nearer to thee;
In word and deed and thought
Holy to be.
O take this heart of mine
And seal me ever thine,
Fill me with love divine,
For service, Lord!

2 Make me a blazing fire
Where'er I go,
That to a dying world
Thee I may show:
How thou hast bled and died
That none may be denied,
But in thy bleeding side
A refuge find.

3 So shall my moments flow
In praising thee,
For thou hast never failed
To strengthen me.
Filled with the Holy Ghost,
Saved to the uttermost,
In Christ alone I'll boast
And forward go.

Anon

522 The Vacant Chair, 449; Face to face, 370
8.7.8.7. D. Troch.

SAVIOUR, if my feet have faltered
On the pathway of the cross,
If my purposes have altered
Or my gold be mixed with dross,
O forbid me not thy service,
Keep me yet in thy employ,
Pass me through a sterner cleansing
If I may but give thee joy!

All my work is for the Master,
He is all my heart's desire;
O that he may count me faithful
In the day that tries by fire!

2 Have I worked for hireling wages,
Or as one with vows to keep,
With a heart whose love engages
Life or death, to save the sheep?

All is known to thee, my Master,
All is known, and that is why
I can work and wait the verdict
Of thy kind but searching eye.

3 I must love thee, love must rule me,
Springing up and flowing forth
From a childlike heart within me,
Or my work is nothing worth.
Love with passion and with patience,
Love with principle and fire,
Love with heart and mind and utterance,
Serving Christ my one desire.
Albert Orsborn (1886-1967)

523 Lord, with my all I part, 723

SAVIOUR, my all I'm bringing to thee;
Speak, Lord, and I thy voice will obey;
Seal me just now thy servant to be,
For more of thy power, dear Lord, I pray.

Lord, with my all I part,
Closer to thee I'll cling,
All earthly things that bind my heart,
Dear Lord, to thy feet I bring.

2 Give me more love, dear Lord, that I may
Hasten thy blessèd news to proclaim
To all lost sinners, that there's one way
By which they eternal life may obtain.

3 Give me more power, that sinners around
May feel that thou in me now dost live;
Let my light shine that souls who are
bound
May say: To thee, Lord, now myself I give.

4 Sometimes, O Lord, the way may seem
rough;
Then that's the time when thou wilt be
near.
Help me in thee forever to trust,
Then in death's dark valley I'll have no
fear.
Alice Georgina Edwards (1878-1958)

524 Marshall, 189 (verse); Santa Lucia, 194
6.4.6.4.6.6.6.4.

SAVIOUR, thy dying love
Thou gavest me,
Nor should I aught withhold,
My Lord, from thee.
In love my soul would bow,
My heart fulfil its vow,
Some offering bring thee now,
Something for thee.

2 At the blest mercy seat,
Pleading for me,
My feeble faith looks up,
Jesus, to thee.
Help me the cross to bear,
Thy wondrous love declare,
Some song to raise, or prayer,
Something for thee.

3 Give me a faithful heart,
Likeness to thee,
That each departing day
Henceforth may see
Some work of love begun,
Some deed of kindness done,
Some wanderer sought and won,
Something for thee.

4 All that I am and have,
Thy gifts so free,
In joy, in grief, through life,
I yield to thee.
And when thy face I see,
My ransomed soul shall be
Through all eternity
All, all for thee.
Sylvanus Dryden Phelps (1816-95)

525 Nottingham, 289; Randolph, 292;
Consecration Hymn, 279; Hendon, 282
7.7.7.7.

TAKE my life, and let it be
Consecrated, Lord, to thee;
Take my moments and my days,
Let them flow in ceaseless praise.

2 Take my hands, and let them move
At the impulse of thy love;
Take my feet, and let them be
Swift and beautiful for thee.

3 Take my voice, and let me sing
Always, only for my King;
Take my lips, and let them be
Filled with messages from thee.

4 Take my silver and my gold,
Not a mite would I withhold;
Take my intellect, and use
Every power as thou shalt choose.

5 Take my will, and make it thine,
It shall be no longer mine;
Take my heart, it is thine own,
It shall be thy royal throne.

The Life of Holiness

6 Take my love; my Lord, I pour
At thy feet its treasure-store;
Take myself, and I will be
Ever, only, all for thee.
Frances Ridley Havergal (1836-79)

526 Arizona, 7; Accrington, 3
L.M.

THE love of Christ doth me constrain
To seek the wandering souls of men;
With cries, entreaties, tears, to save,
To snatch them from the gaping grave.

2 For this let men revile my name;
No cross I shun; I fear no shame;
All hail reproach, and welcome pain,
Only thy terrors, Lord, restrain.

3 To thee I all my powers present,
That for thy truth they may be spent;
Fulfil thy sovereign counsel, Lord;
Thy will be done, thy name adored.

4 Give me thy strength, O God of power,
Then winds may blow, or thunders roar,
Thy faithful witness will I be;
'Tis fixed, I can do all through thee.
Johann Joseph Winckler (1670-1722),
trs John Wesley (1703-91)

527 The old rustic bridge, 540
11.8.11.8. D.

THE Saviour of men came to seek and to
save
The souls who were lost to the good;
His Spirit was moved for the world which
he loved
With the boundless compassion of God.
And still there are fields where the labor-
ers are few,
And still there are souls without bread,
And still eyes that weep where the dark-
ness is deep,
And still straying sheep to be led.

Except I am moved with compassion,
How dwelleth thy Spirit in me?
In word and in deed
Burning love is my need;
I know I can find this in thee.

2 O is not the Christ 'midst the crowd of
today
Whose questioning cries do not cease?
And will he not show to the hearts that
would know
The things that belong to their peace?

But how shall they hear if the preacher
forbear
Or lack in compassionate zeal?
Or how shall hearts move with the Mas-
ter's own love,
Without his anointing and seal?

3 It is not with might to establish the right,
Nor yet with the wise to give rest;
The mind cannot show what the heart
longs to know
Nor comfort a people distressed.
O Saviour of men, touch my spirit again,
And grant that thy servant may be
Intense every day, as I labor and pray,
Both instant and constant for thee.
Albert Orsborn (1886-1967)

528 Denmark Hill, 368; Govaars, 373
8.7.8.7. Troch.

THOU art holy, Lord of Glory,
From thy altar blessings flow;
I, unworthy, kneel before thee,
Cleanse from sin and peace bestow.

Come, O Lord, with tender healing,
Touch my lips with living coal;
Sanctify each human feeling,
Speak and make me fully whole.

2 If my strength is at its weakest
And my weariness brings pain,
With my spirit at its meekest,
Thou canst lift me up again.

3 Thou hast touched me, I am fitted
For the task that thou hast given;
In thy ministry committed,
Wayward men to lead to Heaven.

4 I will go where thou canst use me;
Help me see my mission plain;
Ask, for I cannot refuse thee;
Lose I all, the crown I'll gain.
Brindley Boon

529 Finlandia, 643; Thou art the way, 835

THOU art the way, none other dare I
follow;
Thou art the truth, and thou hast made
me free;
Thou art the life, the hope of my tomorrow;
Thou art the Christ who died for me.
This is my creed, that 'mid earth's sin and
sorrow,
My life may guide men unto thee.

Consecration and Service

2 Hold thou my feet, let there be no returning
 Along the path which thou hast bid me tread;
 Train thou my mind, I would be ever learning
 The better way thy fame to spread;
 Keep thou my heart ablaze with holy burning
 That love for souls may ne'er be dead.

3 I would bring peace to lives now torn asunder,
 Ease aching hearts with words that soothe and heal;
 I would bring peace when, breaking like the thunder,
 Men rise in war, and hatred feel.
 Peacemaker, Lord! Now I am stirred to wonder;
 O take me, and my calling seal!
 Arch R. Wiggins (1893-1976)

530 The greatest of these, 817

THOUGH in declaring Christ to the sinner,
 I may all men surpass,
If love impassioned seal not the message,
 I am naught but sounding brass.

Love suffereth patiently;
Love worketh silently;
 Love seeketh not her own.
Love never faileth;
Love still prevaileth;
 Lord, in me thy love enthrone!

2 Though I have wisdom lighting all mysteries;
 Though I may all things know;
Though great my faith be, removing mountains,
 Without love 'tis empty show.

3 Though I distribute all my possessions;
 Though as a martyr die;
My sacrifices profit me nothing,
 Unless love doth sanctify.
 Arch R. Wiggins (1893-1976)

531 In me, Lord, 383
8.7.8.7. Troch.

TOUCH me with thy healing hand, Lord,
 Take the life I fully yield,
Teach thy word and tell thy will, Lord,
 Test the heart that thou hast sealed.

In me, Lord, in me, Lord,
Thy will fulfil in me, Lord.

2 Melt the hardness and the coldness,
 Mold the life I yield to thee,
Mark for pureness and for boldness,
 Make thy presence felt in me.

3 Show me how to win the lost ones,
 Send me where I ought to go,
Satisfy my deepest longings,
 Sanctifying power bestow.

4 Feed me with the bread of Heaven,
 Fill me with thy love divine,
Fit me for yet wider service,
 Finish, Lord, this work of thine.
 Hugh Sladen (1878-1962)

532 Maidstone, 325; Holy Spirit, faithful guide, 324
7.7.7.7. D.

UNTO thee, O Saviour-King,
 Our allegiance now we bring,
Body, soul and spirit, all
 In obedience to thy call.
Naught have we thou didst not give,
 By thy life and grace we live,
Selfish aims do we forsake,
 Service with our Lord to take.

2 We are with thee 'gainst thy foe,
 Fighting for his overthrow;
Though the fight be doubly fierce,
 Though the venomed dart should pierce,
Satan never shall prevail,
 Thou, O Christ, shalt never fail;
We who fight with thee shall win,
 Conquer over Hell and sin.

3 We are with thee 'neath the cross,
 Henceforth earthly things are dross;
Thine, resigned to mortal ill,
 Thine to die if thou shouldst will.
Thou who hast the winepress trod,
 Reconciling us to God,
Help us each returning day,
 Be thou with us all the way.

4 We are with thee, Christ of love,
 Thou who camest from above,
Thou whose blood was spilt to save,
 Thou whose might burst e'en the grave.
From thy throne again come down;
 Take thy Kingdom, take thy crown;
Hear us as with joy we sing:
 We are with thee, Saviour-King.
 Charles Coller (1863-1935)

533 Warrington, 56; Boston, 13
L.M.

WHAT shall we offer to our Lord
  In gratitude for all his grace?
Fain would we his great name record
  And worthily set forth his praise.

2 O thou, who callest forth our love,
    To whom our more than all we owe,
  Open the fountain from above,
    And let thy love our souls o'erflow.

3 So shall our lives thy power proclaim,
    Thy grace for every sinner free,
  Till all mankind shall learn thy name,
    Shall all stretch out their hands to thee.

4 Open a door which earth and Hell
    May strive to shut, but strive in vain;
  Let thy word richly in us dwell,
    And let our gracious fruit remain.

5 We all, in perfect love renewed,
    Shall know the greatness of thy power,
  Stand in the temple of our God
    As pillars, and go out no more.
            August Gottlieb Spangenberg (1704-92),
            trs John Wesley (1703-91)

534 Trust in God, 838

WHEN from sin's dark hold thy love had
    won me,
  And its wounds thy tender hands had
    healed,
As thy blest commands were laid upon
    me,
  Growing light my growing need revealed.
Thus I sought the path of consecration
  When to thee, dear Lord, my vows were
    given;
And the joy which came with full salvation
  Winged my feet and filled my heart with
    Heaven.

By the love that never ceased to hold
    me,
By the blood which thou didst shed for
    me,
While thy presence and thy power
    enfold me,
  I renew my covenant with thee.

2 But my heart at times with care is
    crowded,
  Oft I serve with weak, o'erladen hands,
And that early joy grows dim and clouded
  As each day its heavy toll demands.

Have I ceased from walking close beside
    thee?
  Have I grieved thee with an ill-kept vow?
In my heart of hearts have I denied thee?
  Speak, dear Lord, O speak and tell me
    now.

3 By the love that never ceased to hold me
    In a bond nor life nor death shall break,
  As thy presence and thy power enfold me,
    I would plead fresh covenant to make.
From before thy face, each vow renewing,
  Strong in heart, with purpose pure and
    deep,
I will go henceforth thy will pursuing,
  With my Lord unbroken faith to keep.
            Will J. Brand (1889-1977)

                    ※   ※   ※

see also: 23 What shall I render to my God
         136 When I survey the wondrous
             cross
         706 What can I say to cheer a world of
             sorrow
         720 Give me the faith which can
             remove
         786 I would be thy holy temple
         788 Jesus, thou hast won us
         789 Lord of life and love and power
         832 We are witnesses for Jesus
         862 O Jesus, I have promised
         978 Take up thy cross

Praise and Thanksgiving

535 Thou Shepherd of Israel, 487; The cross
now covers my sins, 486
8.8.8.8. D. Amph.

ALL glory to Jesus be given
  That life and salvation are free;
And all may be washed and forgiven
  For Jesus has cleansed even me.

Yes, Jesus is mighty to save,
  And all full salvation may know;
Come, plunge in the sin-cleansing
    wave,
  His blood washes whiter than snow.

2 From darkness, from sin and despair,
    Out into the light of his love
  He brought me, and made me an heir
    To kingdoms and mansions above.

3 O rapturous heights of his love!
    O measureless depths of his grace!
  My soul all his fulness would prove,
    And live in his loving embrace.

4 In him all my wants are supplied,
   His love makes my Heaven below;
And freely his blood is applied,
   And makes my heart whiter than snow.
Annie Turner Wittenmyer (1827-1900)

536 At peace with God, 612

A^T peace with God! How great the
     blessing
   In fellowship with him to be,
   And from all stains of sin set free;
How rich am I such wealth possessing!

My soul has found a resting place,
And I am now, through heavenly
     grace,
At peace with God, at peace with God.

2 The fear of death has gone forever,
   No more to cause my heart to grieve;
   There is a place, I dare believe,
In Heaven for me beyond the river.

3 At peace with God! No change can harm
   me
   Whichever way my course may run;
   One wish alone, God's will be done,
I seek, since I have known his mercy.
Richard Slater (1854-1939)

537 Be glad in the Lord, 481
8.8.8.8. Amph.

B^E glad in the Lord and rejoice,
   All ye that are upright in heart;
And ye that have made him your choice,
   Bid sadness and sorrow depart.

Rejoice, rejoice! Be glad in the Lord and
   rejoice!

2 What though in the conflict for right
   Your enemies almost prevail,
   God's armies, just hid from your sight,
   Are more than the foes which assail.

3 Though darkness surround you by day,
   Your sky by the night be o'ercast,
   Let nothing your spirit dismay,
   But trust till the danger is past.

4 Be glad in the Lord and rejoice,
   His praises proclaiming in song;
Acclaim him with trumpet and voice,
   The loud hallelujahs prolong.
Mary Elizabeth Servoss (b 1849)

538 Thou art a mighty Saviour, 298
7.7.7.7.

B^{LESSÈD} Lamb of Calvary,
   Thou hast done great things for me,
Thou didst leave thy throne above,
Thou didst suffer out of love.

Thou art a mighty Saviour,
Thy love doth never waver,
Thou shalt be mine forever,
And thine alone I'll be.

2 Thou wast to the slaughter led,
   Thou didst bow thy sacred head,
   'Twas for me thy blood was spilt
That I might be cleansed from guilt.

3 In thy mercy, rich and free,
   Thou hast pardoned even me;
   Thou dost keep me every hour,
By thy Holy Spirit's power.

4 Draw me closer, Lord, to thee;
   May my life a blessing be;
   May it be a life of love;
Lord, supply me from above.

5 Now, Lord, let my light so shine
   That the world may know I'm thine;
   May I bear much fruit in thee
That will stand eternally.
George Samuel Smith (1865-1944)

539 Ellan Vannin, 434; Salvator, 443
8.7.8.7. D. Troch.

F^{ROM} the heart of Jesus flowing,
   Cometh Heaven's peace to me,
Ever deeper, richer growing,
   Through the cross of Calvary.
Passing mortal understanding,
   Yet to seeking ones made known,
And, for all the race expanding,
   Gift of God unto his own.

2 To the heart where strife was reigning,
   Jesus spake, dissension ceased;
From the bonds, so long enchaining,
   I was instantly released.
Pardon for all past transgression,
   Grace for every time of need;
With such treasure in possession,
   Happy is my lot indeed.

The Life of Holiness

3 Undisturbed, throughout the ages,
  Heaven's peace is in God's will,
Present though the conflict rages,
  Blessing me through good or ill.
Jesus, source of calm unfailing,
  With his peace my heart has filled,
He abides, o'er all prevailing,
  And, in him, life's storms are stilled.
Charles Coller (1863-1935)

540 Bithynia, 409; Vesper Hymn, 450; Guide
me, great Jehovah, 415
8.7.8.7.8.7. Troch.

FULL salvation, full salvation,
  Lo! the fountain, opened wide,
Streams through every land and nation
  From the Saviour's wounded side!
Full salvation, full salvation,
  Streams an endless crimson tide.

2 O the glorious revelation!
  See the cleansing current flow,
Washing stains of condemnation
  Whiter than the driven snow.
Full salvation, full salvation,
  O the rapturous bliss to know!

3 Love's resistless current sweeping
  All the regions deep within,
Thought and wish and senses keeping
  Now, and every instant, clean.
Full salvation, full salvation,
  From the guilt and power of sin.

4 Life immortal, Heaven descending,
  Lo! my heart the Spirit's shrine;
God and man in oneness blending,
  O what fellowship is mine!
Full salvation, full salvation,
  Raised in Christ to life divine.

5 Care and doubting, gloom and sorrow,
  Fear and shame are mine no more;
Faith knows naught of dark tomorrow,
  For my Saviour goes before.
Full salvation, full salvation,
  Full and free for evermore.
Francis Bottome (1823-94)

541 Jesus is good to me, 473 (verse);
Childhood, 471
8.8.8.6.

I SOUGHT for love and strength and light,
  For grace and power to win the fight;
And prayed that Christ would come in
    might
  Within my heart to reign.

2 I saw the treasure I might win,
  Freedom from self, from inbred sin;
A holy fire to burn within,
  If Christ came in to reign.

3 O wondrous change, there's victory within,
  All fear cast out, the soul kept clean;
Joy, peace and rest, and hatred of sin,
  Now Christ has come to reign.

4 Now Christ is King, my heart his throne,
  He reigns in love, he reigns alone;
O wondrous grace that he should come,
  King of my heart to reign.
Alfred Humphrey (1864-1933)

542 The cross now covers my sins, 486;
Crugybar, 507
9.8.9.8. D.

I STAND all bewildered with wonder
  And gaze on the ocean of love,
And over its waves to my spirit
  Comes peace like a heavenly dove.

The cross now covers my sins,
  The past is under the blood;
I'm trusting in Jesus for all,
  My will is the will of my God.

2 I struggled and wrestled to win it,
  The blessing that setteth me free;
But, when I had ceased from my
    struggling,
  His peace Jesus gave unto me.

3 He laid his hand on me and healed me,
  And bade me be every whit whole;
I touched but the hem of his garment,
  And glory came thrilling my soul.

4 The Prince of my peace is now passing,
  The light of his face is on me;
But listen, belovèd, he speaketh:
  My peace I will give unto thee.
Wilbur Fisk Crafts (1850-1922)

543 Cleansing for me, 512; Long, long
ago, 513
10.8.10.8.10.10.10.8.

JESUS, my Lord, through thy triumph I
    claim
  Victory for me, victory for me;
Lover of souls, by thy conquering name,
  Victory for me, victory for me.
Canst thou not save a poor sinner like
    me?
Didst thou not suffer my soul to set free?
Thou didst provide by thy death on the
    tree
  Victory for me, victory for me.

150

Praise and Thanksgiving

2 Here, Lord, I yield thee the whole of my
   heart,
      Victory for me, victory for me;
   From all that hinders at last I will part;
      Victory for me, victory for me.
   Called to thy service, I gladly obey,
   Humbly my all at thy feet now I lay,
   Trusting and fighting till life's latest day;
      Victory for me, victory for me.

3 Singing, I feel I shall conqueror be,
      Victory for me, victory for me;
   Boundless salvation is coming to me,
      Victory for me, victory for me.
   Cleansed by thy blood I shall walk in the
      light,
   Held in thine arms I shall live in thy sight,
   Filled with thy love I shall win in the fight;
      Victory for me, victory for me.

4 Finished my work, I shall mount to the
      skies,
      Victory for me, victory for me;
   Comrades and kindred will shout as I rise,
      Victory for me, victory for me.
   Then saints and angels their welcomes will
      sing,
   Then in his glory I'll see my great King,
   Then in loud rapture I'll make Heaven ring;
      Victory for me, victory for me.
           William Booth (1829-1912)

544   Life is great! (Praise, my soul, 422)
       For words and music see Song 987
       American Supplement

545   Ramsgate, 312; Titchfield, 327
                 7.7.7.7.D.

L OVED with everlasting love,
   Led by grace that love to know;
Spirit, breathing from above,
   Thou hast taught me this is so.
O this full and perfect peace!
   O this transport all divine!
In a love which cannot cease
   I am his and he is mine.

2 Heaven above is softer blue,
   Earth around is sweeter green;
Something lives in every hue,
   Christless eyes have never seen;
Birds with gladder songs o'erflow,
   Flowers with deeper beauties shine,
Since I know, as now I know,
   I am his and he is mine.

3 His for ever, only his;
   Who the Lord and me shall part?
Ah! with what a rest of bliss
   Christ can fill the loving heart.
Heaven and earth may fade and flee,
   First-born light in gloom decline,
But, throughout eternity,
   I am his and he is mine.
        George Wade Robinson (1838-77)

546   Llanfair, 271
                7.6.7.6. D. Troch.

N OW I feel the sacred fire,
   Kindling, flaming, glowing,
Higher still, and rising higher,
   All my soul o'erflowing.
Life immortal I receive,
   O the wondrous story!
I was dead, but now I live,
   Glory, glory, glory!

2 Now I am from bondage freed,
   Every bond is riven,
Jesus makes me free indeed,
   Just as free as Heaven.
'Tis a glorious liberty,
   O the wondrous story!
I was bound, but now I'm free,
   Glory, glory, glory!

3 Let the glorious message roll,
   Roll through every nation,
Witnessing from soul to soul
   This immense salvation.
Now I know 'tis full and free,
   O the wondrous story!
For I feel 'tis saving me,
   Glory, glory, glory!
                 Anon

547   None but Christ can satisfy, 118;
       Covenant, 81   C.M.

O CHRIST, in thee my soul hath found,
   And found in thee alone,
The peace, the joy, I sought so long,
   The bliss till now unknown.

Now none but Christ can satisfy,
   No other name for me;
There's love and life and lasting joy,
   Lord Jesus, found in thee.

2 I sighed for rest and happiness,
   I yearned for them, not thee;
But while I passed my Saviour by,
   His love laid hold on me.

3 I tried the broken cisterns, Lord,
   But, ah! the waters failed;
E'en as I stooped to drink they fled,
And mocked me as I wailed.

4 The pleasures lost I sadly mourned,
   But never wept for thee,
Till grace my sightless eyes received,
Thy loveliness to see.

B. E.

548 None of self, 461

O THE bitter shame and sorrow
   That a time could ever be
When I let the Saviour's pity
Plead in vain, and proudly answered:
All of self and none of thee!

2 Yet he found me; I beheld him
   Bleeding on th' accursèd tree,
Heard him pray: Forgive them, Father!
And my wistful heart said faintly:
Some of self and some of thee!

3 Day by day his tender mercy,
   Healing, helping, full and free,
Sweet and strong and, ah! so patient,
Brought me lower, while I whispered:
Less of self and more of thee!

4 Higher than the highest Heaven,
   Deeper than the deepest sea,
Lord, thy love at last has conquered;
Grant me now my spirit's longing:
None of self and all of thee!
Theodore Monod (1836-1921)

549 O the peace, 391; Walk with me, 405
8.7.8.7. Troch.

ONCE I thought I walked with Jesus,
   Yet such changeful feelings had,
Sometimes trusting, sometimes doubting,
Sometimes joyful, sometimes sad.

O the peace my Saviour gives,
   Peace I never knew before!
And my way has brighter grown
   Since I learned to trust him more.

2 But he called me closer to him,
   Bade my doubts and fears all cease,
And, when I had fully yielded,
Filled my soul with perfect peace.

3 Now I'm trusting every moment,
   Nothing less can be enough;
And my Saviour bears me gently
O'er the places once so rough.
Francis Augustus Blackmer (1855-1930)

550 Ring the bells of Heaven, 777

RING the bells of Heaven, there is joy
   today
For a soul returning from the wild!
See, the Father meets him out upon the
   way,
Welcoming his weary, wandering child.

Glory, glory, how the angels sing!
   Glory, glory, how the loud harps ring!
'Tis the ransomed army, like a mighty
   sea,
Pealing forth the anthem of the free.

2 Ring the bells of Heaven, there is joy today
For the wanderer now is reconciled!
Yes, a soul is rescued from his sinful way,
And is born anew, a ransomed child.

3 Ring the bells of Heaven, spread the feast
   today;
Angels, swell the glad, triumphant
   strain!
Tell the joyful tidings, bear them far away,
For a precious soul is born again.
William Orcutt Cushing (1823-1902)

551 St Matthew, 157; Behold the Saviour, 75
D.C.M.

SHOW me thy face, one transient gleam
   Of loveliness divine,
And I shall never think or dream
   Of other love save thine;
All lesser light will darken quite,
   All lower glories wane,
The beautiful of earth will scarce
   Seem beautiful again.

2 Show me thy face, I shall forget
   The weary days of yore,
The fretting ghosts of vain regret
   Shall haunt my soul no more.
All doubts and fears for future years
   In quiet trust subside,
And naught but blest content and calm
   Within my breast abide.

3 Show me thy face, the heaviest cross
   Will then seem light to bear,
There will be gain in every loss,
   And peace with every care.
With such light feet the years will fleet,
   Life seem as brief as blest,
Till I have laid my burden down,
   And entered into rest.

Anon

Praise and Thanksgiving

552 Tack, min Gud, 447; He the pearly gates will open, 436   8.7.8.7. D. Troch.

THANK you, Lord, for all your goodness:
  Through the years of yesterday;
Thank you, too, for present mercies
  And your blessing on my way.
Thank you for each revelation,
  And for what you choose to hide;
Thank you, Lord, for grace sustaining
  As I in your love abide.

2 Thank you, Lord, for sunlit pathways,
    Thank you, too, for byways rough;
  Thank you for the fruitful summers
    Also for the winters tough.
  Thank you, Lord, for fragrant flowers
    Growing right amid the weeds;
  Thank you for the peace you give me
    Even when my spirit bleeds.

3 Thank you, Lord, for wayside roses,
    Even for the thorns beside;
  Thank you for the prayers you granted
    And for those that you denied;
  Thank you, Lord, for precious comfort
    In my hours of grief and pain;
  Thank you for your gracious promise
    Life eternal I shall gain.
        August Ludvig Storm (1862-1914),
                    trs Flora Larsson

553 Crugybar, 507; The cross now covers my sins, 486   9.8.9.8. D.

WHEN Jesus from Calvary called me,
  Unfolding its meaning to me,
The life which he offered enthralled me,
  Abundant, enduring and free.
I hungered to make a beginning
  My meeting with Jesus to show,
And, ceasing that moment from sinning,
  Salvation's full measure to know.

2 But oh, as the journey grew longer,
    Temptations my pathway beset;
  When I, self-deceiving, felt stronger,
    Then only with failure I met.
  But troubled with much condemnation,
    And weakened by many a wound,
  In seeking for God's full salvation
    The secret of victory I found.

3 For, held by my halting behavior,
    No progress I truly had gained;
  How greatly I needed the Saviour,
    How rooted my weakness remained.

And so, my unworthiness pressing,
  I yielded, my will to resign,
And as I reached out for the blessing,
  That moment the blessing was mine.

4 Now daily the Saviour is showing
    How gracious his presence can be;
  The life which he promised is growing
    And finding fulfilment in me.
  Engaged in his sacred employment
    And furnished with all that I need,
  In him I have fullest enjoyment,
    In him perfect friendship indeed.
                    Will J. Brand (1889-1977)

554 St Oswald, 396; Galilee, 371   8.7.8.7. Troch.

WHO shall dare to separate us
  From the love of Christ, our Lord?
Neither pain nor tribulation,
  Persecution, want nor sword.

2 Nay in all things that may hurt us
    We shall more than conquerors be,
  Through the Christ who proved he loved
      us
    By his dying on the tree.

3 Neither death, nor life, nor angels,
    Principalities nor powers,
  Nor things present, nor things future
    Can disturb this faith of ours.

4 Height, nor depth, nor any creature—
    'Tis the promise of his word—
  Shall have power to separate us
    From the love of Christ, our Lord.
                    Arch R. Wiggins (1893-1976)

555 Bethany, 429; Austria, 408   8.7.8.7. D. Troch.

WHO the child of God shall sever
  From the faith in which he stands?
Who shall wound or who shall pluck him
  From the careful shepherd's hands?
Not distress or persecution,
  Neither peril nor the sword;
For in days of tribulation
  Shines the glory of the Lord.

2 His abundant grace is given
    To the heart resigned and meek,
  Mercy moves the King of Heaven
    To the penitent and weak;
  Lowly paths our Lord has taken,
    And he proved by word and deed,
  For the lonely and forsaken
    There is grace beyond all need.

The Life of Holiness

3 Faith is not afraid of darkness,
  Hope will triumph over loss,
Love is not afraid of hardness,
  Patience helps to bear the cross;
These are all the gifts of Heaven,
  Beautiful are they and free,
Graces that the Lord has given;
  O that they may shine in me!

4 Works or wealth can never buy them,
  Nor a single grace impart;
God himself has sanctified them
  In the meek and lowly heart;

All besides is vain endeavor,
  Failure every work of mine;
Saviour, let thy grace for ever
  Cleanse and blend my will with thine.

Albert Orsborn (1886-1967)

* * *

see also: 59 I know thee who thou art
       616 My maker and my King
       970 We gather together
       982 Rejoice, ye pure in heart
       984 In my heart there rings a melody

MEANS OF GRACE

Prayer

556 Warrington, 56; Abends, 2; Alstone, 4
L.M.

ALL scenes alike engaging prove
  To souls impressed with sacred love;
Where'er they dwell, they dwell in thee,
In Heaven, in earth, or on the sea.

2 To me remains nor place nor time,
My country is in every clime;
I can be calm and free from care
On any shore, since God is there.

3 While place we seek, or place we shun,
The soul finds happiness in none;
But with my God to guide my way
'Tis equal joy to go or stay.

4 My dwelling place art thou alone;
No other can I claim or own,
The point where all my wishes meet,
My law, my love, life's only sweet.

5 Then let me to thy throne repair
And never be a stranger there;
There love divine shall be my guard,
And peace and safety my reward.

Jeanne de la Mothe Guyon (1648-1717),
trs William Cowper (1731-1800)

557 Spohr, 135; Stracathro, 136
C.M.

AS pants the hart for cooling streams,
  When heated in the chase,
So longs my soul, O Lord, for thee,
And thy refreshing grace.

2 For thee, my God, the living God,
My thirsty soul doth pine;
O when shall I behold thy face,
Thou majesty divine?

3 I sigh to think of happier days,
  When thou, O Lord, wast nigh,
When every heart was tuned to praise,
And none more blest than I.

4 Why restless, why cast down, my soul?
  Hope still, and thou shalt sing
The praise of him who is thy God,
Thy health's eternal spring.

Nahum Tate (1652-1715),
Nicholas Brady (1659-1726)

558 Angelus, 6; Abends, 2
L.M.

AT even, ere the sun was set,
  The sick, O Lord, around thee lay;
O in what divers pains they met!
O with what joy they went away!

2 Once more 'tis eventide, and we,
Oppressed with various ills, draw near;
What if thy form we cannot see!
We know and feel that thou art here.

3 O Saviour Christ, our woes dispel,
For some are sick and some are sad,
And some have never loved thee well,
And some have lost the love they had.

4 O Saviour Christ, thou too art man;
Thou hast been troubled, tempted, tried,
Thy kind but searching glance can scan
The very wounds that shame would hide.

5 Thy touch has still its ancient power;
No word from thee can fruitless fall;
Hear in this solemn evening hour,
And in thy mercy heal us all.

Henry Twells (1823-1900)

154

Prayer

559
Morning Hymn, 35; Duke Street, 17
L.M.

AWAKE, our souls; away, our fears!
    Let every trembling thought be gone;
Awake, and run the heavenly race,
    And put a cheerful courage on.

2 True, 'tis a strait and thorny road,
    And mortal spirits tire and faint;
But they forget the mighty God
    That feeds the strength of every saint.

3 O mighty God, thy matchless power
    Is ever new, and ever young,
And firm endures, while endless years
    Their everlasting circles run.

4 From thee, the ever-flowing spring,
    Our souls shall drink a fresh supply;
While such as trust their native strength
    Shall melt away and droop and die.

5 Swift as the eagle cuts the air
    We'll mount aloft to thine abode;
On wings of love our souls shall fly,
    Nor tire along the heavenly road.
                        Isaac Watts (1674-1748)

560
Silchester, 177; Downham, 166
S.M.

BEHOLD the throne of grace,
    The promise calls me near;
There Jesus shows a smiling face
    And waits to answer prayer.

2 My soul, ask what thou wilt,
    Thou canst not be too bold;
Since his own blood for thee he spilt,
    What else can he withhold?

3 Beyond thy utmost wants
    His love and power can bless;
To praying souls he always grants
    More than they can express.

4 Thine image, Lord, bestow,
    Thy presence and thy love;
I ask to serve thee here below,
    And reign with thee above.

5 Teach me to live by faith;
    Conform my will to thine;
Let me victorious be in death,
    And then in Glory shine.
                        John Newton (1725-1807)

561
Harlan, 215; Moscow, 217
6.6.4.6.6.6.4.

BLESSÈD and glorious King,
    To thee our praise we bring
        In this glad hour.
Thou God of peace and love,
Thou Christ enthroned above,
Spirit whose fruit is love,
    Display thy power.

2 Come to our hearts and bless,
    Give strength and happiness,
        And every good.
Direct and safely lead,
Supply each daily need
For thought and word and deed,
    Most gracious God.

3 Grant to thy people all
    Thy grace for every call,
        In this their day;
That heart and life may be
In joyful harmony,
United, Lord, with thee,
    Life, truth and way.

4 Help by thy Spirit's sword,
    The true and living word,
        Souls to inspire.
With lips now touched by thee,
And hearts from sin set free,
Let us forever be
    All flames of fire.
                Thomas Hodgson Mundell (1849-1934)

562
Diademata, 182; Chalvey, 181
D.S.M.

COME in, my Lord, come in
    And make my heart thy home;
Come in and cleanse my soul from sin,
    And dwell with me alone.
        Thyself to me be given,
        In fulness of thy love;
Thyself alone wilt make my Heaven
    Though all thy gifts remove.

2 Come in, my Lord, come in,
    Show forth thy saving power;
Restore, renew, release from sin,
    O save this very hour!
        Thy promise now I claim,
        By faith put in my plea,
And trust in that almighty name,
    Immanuel and thee.

3 My Lord, thou dost come in,
   I feel it in my soul;
I hear thy words, my Saviour-King:
   Be every whit made whole.
Glory to God on high!
Let Heaven and earth agree
My risen Christ to magnify,
   For lo! he lives with me.
Bramwell Booth (1856-1929)

563 Newton, 288; Last Hope, 284
                      7.7.7.7.

COME, my soul, thy suit prepare,
   Jesus loves to answer prayer;
He himself has bid thee pray,
Therefore will not say thee nay.

2 Thou art coming to a King,
Large petitions with thee bring,
For his grace and power are such
None can ever ask too much.

3 With my burden I begin:
Lord, remove this load of sin;
Let thy blood, for sinners spilt,
Set my conscience free from guilt.

4 Lord, I come to thee for rest,
Take possession of my breast,
Then thy blood-bought right maintain,
And without a rival reign.

5 While I am a soldier here,
Let thy love my spirit cheer;
As my guide, my guard, my friend,
Lead me to my journey's end.
John Newton (1725-1807)

564 Sunset, 522; Bartholomew, 518
                10.10.10.10. Iambic

COME ye yourselves apart and rest
   awhile,
   Weary, I know it, of the press and throng;
Wipe from your brow the sweat and dust
   of toil,
   And in my quiet strength again be
      strong.

2 Come ye aside from all the world holds
   dear,
   For converse which the world has never
      known,
Alone with me and with my Father here,
   With me and with my Father not alone.

3 Come, tell me all that ye have said and
   done,
   Your victories and your failures, hopes
      and fears;
I know how hardly souls are wooed and
   won;
   My choicest laurels are bedewed with
      tears.

4 Then fresh from converse with your Lord,
   return
   And work till daylight softens into even;
The brief hours are not lost in which you
   learn
   More of your Master, and his rest in
      Heaven.
Edward Henry Bickersteth (1825-1906)

565 Bishopthorpe, 77; Irish, 99; Evan, 85
                        C.M.

COMPARED with Christ, in all beside
   No fairer charm I see;
The one thing needful, dearest Lord,
   Is to be one with thee.

2 The knowledge of thy dying love
   Into my soul convey;
Thyself bestow; for thee alone,
   My all-in-all, I pray.

3 Less than thyself will not suffice
   My comfort to restore;
More than thyself I cannot have,
   And thou canst give no more.

4 Whate'er conforms not to thy love,
   O teach me to resign!
I'm rich to all intents of bliss
   If thou, O Christ, art mine.
Augustus Montague Toplady (1740-78), alt

566 Last Hope, 284; Weber, 301
                      7.7.7.7.

DAY by day the manna fell;
   O to learn this lesson well!
Still, by constant mercy fed,
Give me, Lord, my daily bread.

2 Day by day, the promise reads,
Daily strength for daily needs;
Cast foreboding fears away,
Take the manna of today.

3 Lord, my times are in thy hand;
All my sanguine hopes have planned
To thy wisdom I resign,
And would make thy purpose mine.

4 Thou my daily task shalt give,
Day by day to thee I live;
So shall added years fulfil
Not my own, my Father's will.

5 O to live exempt from care
By the energy of prayer;
Strong in faith, with mind subdued,
Yet elate with gratitude!
Josiah Conder (1789-1855)

567 Repton, 123; Rest, 124
8.6.8.8.6.

D EAR Lord and Father of mankind,
Forgive our foolish ways;
Reclothe us in our rightful mind;
In purer lives thy service find,
In deeper reverence, praise.

2 In simple trust like theirs who heard,
Beside the Syrian sea,
The gracious calling of the Lord,
Let us, like them, without a word
Rise up and follow thee.

3 O Sabbath rest by Galilee!
O calm of hills above,
Where Jesus knelt to share with thee
The silence of eternity,
Interpreted by love!

4 Drop thy still dews of quietness
Till all our strivings cease;
Take from our souls the strain and stress,
And let our ordered lives confess
The beauty of thy peace.

5 Breathe through the heats of our desire
Thy coolness and thy balm;
Let sense be dumb, let flesh retire;
Speak through the earthquake, wind and
fire,
O still small voice of calm!
John Greenleaf Whittier (1807-92)

568 Diademata, 182; Terra Beata, 186
D.S.M.

E QUIP me for the war,
And teach my hands to fight,
My simple, upright heart prepare,
And guide my words aright;
Control my every thought,
The whole of sin remove;
Let all my works in thee be wrought,
Let all be wrought in love.

2 O arm me with the mind,
Meek Lamb, which was in thee,
And let my earnest zeal be found
With perfect charity!
With calm and tempered zeal,
Let me enforce thy call,
And vindicate thy gracious will
Which offers life to all.

3 O may I love like thee,
In all thy footsteps tread!
Thou hatest all inquity,
But nothing thou hast made.
O may I learn the art
With meekness to reprove,
To hate the sin with all my heart,
But still the sinner love!
Charles Wesley (1707-88)

569 Melita, 495
8.8.8.8.8.8. Iambic

E TERNAL Father, strong to save,
Whose arm hath bound the restless
wave,
Who bidd'st the mighty ocean deep
Its own appointed limits keep:
O hear us when we cry to thee
For those in peril on the sea.

2 O Saviour, whose almighty word
The winds and waves submissive heard,
Who walkedst on the foaming deep,
And calm amid its rage didst sleep:
O hear us when we cry to thee
For those in peril on the sea.

3 O Holy Spirit, who didst brood
Upon the chaos dark and rude,
And bid its angry tumult cease,
And give, for wild confusion, peace:
O hear us when we cry to thee
For those in peril on the sea.

4 O Trinity of love and power,
Our brethren shield in danger's hour;
From rock and tempest, fire and foe,
Protect them wheresoe'er they go:
And ever let there rise to thee
Glad hymns of praise from land and sea.
William Whiting (1825-78)

570 St Oswald, 396; Stainer, 400; Galilee, 371
8.7.8.7. Troch.

F ATHER, hear the prayer we offer;
Not for ease that prayer shall be,
But for strength that we may ever
Live our lives courageously.

2 Not for ever in green pastures
    Do we ask our way to be;
  But the steep and rugged pathway
    May we tread rejoicingly.

3 Be our strength in hours of weakness,
    In our wanderings be our guide,
  Through endeavor, failure, danger,
    Father, be thou at our side.
                    Love Maria Willis (1824-1908)

571 Harlan, 215; Moscow, 217
                    6.6.4.6.6.6.4.

FIRM in thy strong control,
    O Father, hold my soul
      Faithful to thee!
If e'er I fear to fall,
Then let me hear thee call:
I am thy all in all,
      Trust thou in me.

2 A revelation new
  Of what thy grace can do,
      O God, be mine!
  The need is all my own,
  The grace is thine alone,
  Grace, deep as need, made known,
      Thy grace divine.

3 A power within reveal,
  Thy power to help and heal,
      Strong, changeless, free.
  O by temptations sore,
  By sorrows that he bore,
  Who loves me evermore,
      Give victory!

4 A freeman, once a slave,
  Freedom to serve I crave,
      To serve but thee.
  Blessing and being blest,
  Be this my only quest,
  How I may serve thee best,
      Till thee I see.

                          Anon

572 Gerontius, 89; Irish, 99; St Peter, 129
                                C.M.

FORGIVE our sins as we forgive,
    You taught us, Lord, to pray;
  But you alone can grant us grace
    To live the words we say.

2 How can your pardon reach and bless
    The unforgiving heart
  That broods on wrongs, and will not let
    Old bitterness depart?

3 In blazing light your cross reveals
    The truth we dimly knew;
  How small the debts men owe to us,
    How great our debt to you!

4 Lord, cleanse the depths within our souls
    And bid resentment cease;
  Then reconciled to God and man,
    Our lives will spread your peace.
            Rosamond Eleanor Herklots (1905-87)

573 Retreat, 41; Hursley, 26
                            L.M.

FROM every stormy wind that blows,
  From every swelling tide of woes,
  There is a calm, a sure retreat;
  'Tis found beneath the mercy seat.

2 There is a place where Jesus sheds
  The oil of gladness on our heads,
  A place than all besides more sweet;
  It is the blood-stained mercy seat.

3 There is a scene where spirits blend,
  And friend holds fellowship with friend;
  Though sundered far, by faith they meet
  Around one common mercy seat.

4 There, there on eagle wings we soar,
  And time and sense seem all no more;
  And Heaven comes down our souls to
      greet,
  And glory crowns the mercy seat.

5 O let my hand forget her skill,
  My tongue be silent, cold and still,
  This throbbing heart forget to beat,
  If I forget the mercy seat!
                    Hugh Stowell (1799-1865)

574 Silchester, 177; Southport, 178
                                S.M.

GIVE me a restful mind,
    One that in calm repose,
  Safe in thy love though tempests rage,
    Peace and refreshment knows.

2 Give me a trustful mind
    When doubts and fears assail;
  Help me confide in thee, assured
    Thy grace can never fail.

3 Give me an earnest mind,
    Set thou my zeal aflame,
  So that with willing service here
    I may extol thy name.

Prayer

4   Give me a steadfast mind,
     Firm as a rock, and sure;
    Unswerving, loyal, I would stand
    And to the end endure.

5   Give me a thankful mind,
     So that in full accord,
    Mind, heart and voice shall ever sing
    Glad praise to Christ, my Lord.
           Frederick George Hawkes (1869-1959)

575

To the uttermost he saves, 267
7.6.7.6. D. Iambic

GIVE us a day of wonders,
  Jehovah, bare thine arm;
Pour out thy Holy Spirit,
  Make known thy healing balm;
Give blessings without number,
  Supply us from thy store;
Dear Saviour, richly bless us,
  Baptize us more and more.

Lord, hear us while we pray!
Lord, hear us while we pray!
Now thy Spirit give, let the dying live,
And bless us here today.

2 We offer thee this temple,
   With power, Lord, enter in
And teach us when we worship
   Or wage the war with sin.
O may the sinner find thee
   Within these hallowed walls,
Here may young, eager spirits
   Obey when Jesus calls!

3 Give courage for the battle,
   Give strength thy foes to slay;
Give light to cheer the darkness,
   Give grace from day to day;
Give rest amidst life's conflict,
   Give peace when lions roar;
Give faith to fight with patience
   Till fighting days are o'er.
           John Lawley (1859-1922)

576

South Shields, 444; Bethany, 429
8.7.8.7. D. Troch.

GOD of comfort and compassion,
  God of wisdom, grace and power,
Hear our earnest intercession
  In this quiet evening hour.
Strengthen all who fight thy battles
  In this land and lands afar,
Be companion, friend and shepherd
  Whereso'er thy children are.

2 Some we love bear heavy burdens,
   Some have wandered from the way;
Be their guide, and their Deliverer,
   Heavenly Father, now we pray.
O'er our world so filled with sorrow,
   Fear and hunger, pain and strife,
Shed thy light of hope and mercy,
   Gift of love, eternal life.

3 Sovereign Lord, we bow before thee,
   Thou art merciful and kind;
Our petitions now presenting,
   All we need in thee we find.
Lord, we seek thy strength, thy guidance,
   And the Holy Spirit's dower;
Grant thy fortitude and courage
   In temptation's threatening hour.

4 May thy grace and peace o'ershadow
   Those for whom we pray tonight;
May thy mighty arm uphold them;
   They are precious in thy sight.
Lord, for answered prayer we thank thee,
   Thou art good in all thy ways;
With thanksgiving we adore thee,
   Fill our hearts with love and praise.
           Doris N. Rendell (1896-1990)

577

Regent Square, 423
8.7.8.7.8.7. Troch.

GOD of grace and God of glory,
  On thy people pour thy power;
Now fulfil thy Church's story,
  Bring her bud to glorious flower.
Grant us wisdom, grant us courage,
  For the facing of this hour.

2 Lo, the hosts of evil round us
   Scorn thy Christ, assail his ways;
From the fears that long have bound us
   Free our hearts to faith and praise.
Grant us wisdom, grant us courage,
   For the living of these days.

3 Cure thy children's warring madness,
   Bend our pride to thy control;
Shame our wanton, selfish gladness,
   Rich in goods and poor in soul.
Grant us wisdom, grant us courage,
   Lest we miss thy Kingdom's goal.

4 Set our feet on lofty places,
   Gird our lives that they may be
Armored with all Christlike graces
   In the fight to set men free.
Grant us wisdom, grant us courage,
   That we fail not man nor thee.
       Harry Emerson Fosdick (1878-1969)

Means of Grace

578 Bread of Heaven, 411; Cwm Rhondda, 414; Calabar, 431   8.7.8.7.8.7. Troch.

GUIDE me, O thou great Jehovah,
  Pilgrim through this barren land;
I am weak, but thou art mighty;
  Hold me with thy powerful hand.
    Bread of Heaven,
    Feed me now and evermore.

2 Open thou the crystal fountain
  Whence the healing stream shall flow;
Let the fiery, cloudy pillar
  Lead me all my journey through.
    Strong Deliverer,
    Be thou still my strength and shield.

3 When I tread the verge of Jordan,
  Bid my anxious fears subside;
Death of death and Hell's destruction,
  Land me safe on Canaan's side.
    Songs of praises
    I will ever give to thee.
                William Williams (1717-91)

579 Blacklands, 591; The Ash Grove, 592
                              12.11.12.11.

HE giveth more grace as our burdens
    grow greater,
  He sendeth more strength as our labors
    increase,
To added afflictions he addeth his mercy,
To multiplied trials he multiplies peace.

2 When we have exhausted our store of
    endurance,
  When our strength has failed ere the day
    is half done,
When we reach the end of our hoarded
    resources
Our Father's full giving is only begun.

3 His love has no limits, his grace has no
    measure,
  His power no boundary known unto
    men;
For out of his infinite riches in Jesus
He giveth, and giveth, and giveth again.
                Annie Johnson Flint (1866-1932)

580 Sunset, 522; Ellers, 519
                          10.10.10.10. Iambic

HE walks with God who speaks to God
    in prayer,
And daily brings to him his daily care;
Possessing inward peace, he truly knows
A heart's refreshment and a soul's repose.

2 He walks with God who, as he onward
    moves,
Follows the footsteps of the Lord he loves,
And keeping him forever in his view,
His Saviour sees and his example too.

3 He walks with God who turns his face to
    Heaven,
And keeps the blest commands by Jesus
    given;
His life upright, his end untroubled peace,
Whom God will crown when all his labors
    cease.
                Dorothy Ann Thrupp (1779-1847), alt

581 Wareham, 55; Benediction, 11
                                      L.M.

HERE, Lord, assembled in thy name
  Thy work to do, thy help we claim,
And pray for grace that we may be
Inspired by purest love to thee.

2 Not might, nor power, thyself hast said,
  Can vice destroy or virtue spread;
Thy Spirit, Lord, this work must do,
Who only can our hearts renew.

3 Come, then, to us reveal thy love,
  And pour the Spirit from above,
That we with holy motives may
The impulse of his will obey.

4 O touch our lips, that we may speak
  To guard the tempted, help the weak,
And guide the wandering to retrace
Their steps, and seek a Father's face!
                Edward Boaden (1827-1913)

582 Bullinger, 342; Stephanos, 343
                                    8.5.8.3.

HOLY Father, in thy mercy
  Hear our anxious prayer;
Keep our loved ones, now far distant,
  'Neath thy care.

2 Jesus, Saviour, let thy presence
  Be their light and guide;
Keep, O keep them, in their weakness,
  At thy side.

3 When in sorrow, when in danger,
  When in loneliness,
In thy love look down and comfort
  Their distress.

4 May the joy of thy salvation
  Be their strength and stay;
May they love and may they praise thee
  Day by day.

Prayer

5 Holy Spirit, let thy teaching
   Sanctify their life;
Send thy grace that they may conquer
   In the strife.
Isabel Stephana Stevenson (1843-90)

583 Ellers, 519; Sunset, 522
10.10.10.10. Iambic

HOW wonderful it is to walk with God
  Along the road that holy men have trod;
How wonderful it is to hear him say:
Fear not, have faith, 'tis I who lead the
    way!

2 How wonderful it is to talk with God
When cares sweep o'er my spirit like a
   flood;
How wonderful it is to hear his voice,
For when he speaks the desert lands
   rejoice!

3 How wonderful it is to praise my God,
Who comforts and protects me with his
   rod;
How wonderful to praise him every hour,
My heart attuned to sing his wondrous
   power!

4 How wonderful it is to fight for God,
And point poor sinners to the precious
   blood;
How wonderful it is to wield his sword
'Gainst sin, the enemy of Christ, my Lord!

5 How wonderful 'twill be to live with God
When I have crossed death's deep and
   swelling flood;
How wonderful to see him face to face
When I have fought the fight and won the
   race!
Theodore Hopkins Kitching (1866-1930)

584 I am praying, blessèd Saviour, 374
8.7.8.7. D. Troch.

I AM praying, blessèd Saviour,
  To be more and more like thee;
I am praying that thy Spirit
  Like a dove may rest on me.

Thou who knowest all my weakness,
  Thou who knowest all my care,
While I plead each precious promise,
  Hear, O hear, and answer prayer!

2 I am praying to be humbled
  By the power of grace divine;
To be clothed upon with meekness
  And to have no will but thine.

3 I am praying, blessèd Saviour,
  And my constant prayer shall be
For a perfect consecration
  That shall make me more like thee.
Fanny Crosby (1820-1915)

585 Draw me nearer, 637

I AM thine, O Lord; I have heard thy voice,
  And it told thy love to me;
But I long to rise in the arms of faith,
  And be closer drawn to thee.

Draw me nearer, nearer, nearer, blessèd
   Lord,
  To the cross where thou hast died;
Draw me nearer, nearer, nearer, blessèd
   Lord,
  To thy precious bleeding side.

2 Consecrate me now to thy service, Lord,
  By the power of grace divine;
Let my soul look up with a steadfast hope,
  And my will be lost in thine.

3 O the pure delight of a single hour
  That before thy throne I spend,
When I kneel in prayer, and with thee, my
   God,
  I commune as friend with friend!

4 There are depths of love that I cannot
   know
  Till I cross the narrow sea;
There are heights of joy that I may not
   reach
  Till I rest in peace with thee.
Fanny Crosby (1820-1915)

586 For ever with the Lord, 183; Chalvey, 181
D.S.M.

I DO not ask thee, Lord,
  That all my life may be
An easy, smooth and pleasant path;
  'Twould not be good for me.
  But O I ask today
  That grace and strength be given
To keep me fighting all the way
  That leads to God and Heaven!

2 I do not ask thee, Lord,
  That tears may never flow,
Or that the world may always smile
  Upon me as I go.
  From thee fell drops of blood;
  A thorn-crown pressed thy brow;
Thy suffering brought thee victory then,
  And thou canst help me now.

Means of Grace

3   And what if strength should fail,
And heart more deeply bleed?
Or what if dark and lonely days
Draw forth the cry of need?
That cry will bring thee down
My needy soul to fill,
And thou wilt teach my yearning heart
To know and do thy will.

Fannie Jolliffe (1862-1943)

587 I need thee, 680

I NEED thee every hour,
Most gracious Lord,
No tender voice like thine
Can peace afford.

*I need thee, O I need thee,
Every hour I need thee;
O bless me now, my Saviour,
I come to thee.*

2 I need thee every hour,
Stay thou near by;
Temptations lose their power
When thou art nigh.

3 I need thee every hour,
In joy or pain;
Come quickly and abide,
Or life is vain.

4 I need thee every hour,
Teach me thy will,
And thy rich promises
In me fulfil.

*Annie Sherwood Hawks (1835-1918) (verses),
Robert Lowry (1826-99) (chorus)*

588 Carlisle, 164; St Michael, 175;
Trentham, 180   S.M.

I OFTEN say my prayers;
But do I ever pray?
And do the wishes of my heart
Go with the words I say?

2 I may as well kneel down
And worship gods of stone,
As offer to the living God
A prayer of words alone.

3 For words without the heart
The Lord will never hear;
Nor will he to those lips attend
Whose prayers are not sincere.

4   Lord, show me what I need,
And teach me how to pray;
Nor let me ask thee for thy grace,
Not feeling what I say.

John Burton, Jr. (1803-77)

589 O Speak, 482
8.8.8.8. Amph.

I WANT that adorning divine
Thou only, my God, canst bestow;
I want in those garments to shine
Which mark out thy household below.

*O speak, O speak while before thee I
pray!
And, O Lord, just what seemeth thee
good
Reveal, and my heart shall obey.*

2 I want, O I want to attain
More likeness, my Saviour, to thee;
That longed-for resemblance to gain,
Thy comeliness put upon me!

3 I want to be marked for thine own,
Thy seal in my forehead to wear,
Each talent and grace thine alone,
Each act thy approval to bear.

4 I want every moment to feel
Thy Spirit indwelling my heart,
Thy power ever present to heal
And newness of life to impart.

5 I want, and this sums up my prayer,
To glorify thee till I die;
Then yield up my soul to thy care,
And breathe out in faith my last sigh.

Charlotte Elliott (1789-1871) (verses)

590 Behold the Saviour, 75
D.C.M.

IN days long past the mercy seat
Was made of purest gold;
'Twas placed upon the sacred ark,
Love's meaning to unfold.
Within the holiest place God planned
Redemption's grace to show;
More sacred now is Calvary's hill
Where healing waters flow.

2 Thy blood, O Jesus, spotless Lamb,
Once lifted up to die,
Was shed to cleanse our fallen race
And lead to realms on high.
No one too sinful, or too low,
Too desolate, too blind,
But here before the mercy seat
Can full deliverance find.

Prayer

3 O hallow now our mercy seat,
  Thou Son of God most high!
Here may the lame man leap for joy,
  The dumb sound joyful cry,
The sin-sick soul, though wearied sore,
  By evil power possessed,
The halt, the blind, the great, the small,
  Find peace from sins confessed.

4 We seek the healing of thy cross,
  The mercy of thy grace;
Here at this sacred mercy seat
  May we behold thy face;
Here may we glimpse thy holiness,
  Here on our souls descend,
Here may we meet, and talk with thee,
  Our Master and our friend.

Doris N. Rendell (1896-1990)

591
The Vacant Chair, 449
8.7.8.7. D. Troch.

IN the secret of thy presence,
  Where the pure in heart may dwell,
Are the springs of sacred service
  And a power that none can tell.
There my love must bring its offering,
  There my heart must yield its praise,
And the Lord will come, revealing
  All the secrets of his ways.

In the secret of thy presence,
  In the hiding of thy power,
Let me love thee, let me serve thee,
  Every consecrated hour.

2 More than all my lips may utter,
  More than all I do or bring,
Is the depth of my devotion
  To my Saviour, Lord and King.
Nothing less will keep me tender;
  Nothing less will keep me true;
Nothing less will keep the fragrance
  And the bloom on all I do!

3 Blessèd Lord, to see thee truly,
  Then to tell as I have seen,
This shall rule my life supremely,
  This shall be the sacred gleam.
Sealed again is all the sealing,
  Pledged again my willing heart,
First to know thee, then to serve thee,
  Then to see thee as thou art.

Albert Orsborn (1886-1967)

592
Eden, 18; Holly, 24
L.M.

JESUS, and shall it ever be
  A sinful man ashamed of thee?
Ashamed of thee, whom angels praise,
Whose glory shines through endless
  days?

2 Ashamed of Jesus! that dear friend
  On whom my hopes of Heaven depend?
Whene'er I blush, be this my shame,
That I no more revere his name.

3 Ashamed of Jesus! Yes, I may,
  When I've no sin to wash away,
No tears to wipe, no good to crave,
And no immortal soul to save.

4 Till then, nor is the boasting vain,
  Till then, I'll boast the Saviour slain;
And O may this my glory be,
That Christ is not ashamed of me.

Joseph Grigg (c 1728-68)

593
Guide me, great Jehovah, 415;
Bithynia, 409   8.7.8.7.8.7. Troch.

JESUS, give thy blood-washed Army
  Universal liberty;
Keep us fighting, trusting calmly
  For a world-wide jubilee.
    Hallelujah!
  We shall have the victory.

2 Thou hast bound brave hearts together,
  Clothed us with the Spirit's might,
Made us warriors forever,
  Sent us in the field to fight.
    In the Army
  We will serve thee day and night.

3 'Neath thy scepter foes are bending,
  And thy name makes devils fly;
Captives' fetters thou art rending,
  And thy blood doth sin destroy.
    For thy glory
  We will fight until we die.

4 Lift up valleys, cast down mountains,
  Make all evil natures good;
Wash the world in Calvary's fountain,
  Send a great salvation flood.
    All the nations
  We shall win with fire and blood.

William James Pearson (1832-92)

594 St Michael, 175; Franconia, 168; Dennis, 165   S.M.

JESUS, I fain would find
  Thy zeal for God in me,
Thy yearning pity for mankind,
  Thy burning charity.

2 In me thy Spirit dwell,
    In me thy mercies move,
  So shall the fervor of my zeal
    Be the pure flame of love.
Charles Wesley (1707-88)

595 Beautiful Zion, 428; Salvator, 443
     8.7.8.7. D. Troch.

JESUS, Lord, we come to hail thee,
  Love of God to us made known,
From thy lips his word is spoken,
  Through thy life, his life is shown;
We are come to seek the Father,
  Come with burdens, joy and care;
Lead us to his holy presence
  Through the open door of prayer.

2 Loving Friend, we stand before thee
    Without merit or pretence;
  Teach us, guide us as we follow,
    Trusting in thy sure defense;
  We would contemplate thy goodness,
    Finding fortitude and grace,
  Learning of our Father's mercy
    In the beauty of thy face.

3 Saviour-King, we wait beside thee,
    When earth's deepening shades
      descend,
  Still with thee in faith abiding
    While the storms of trial rend;
  Drawing closer as thou prayest:
    Father, let thy will be done;
  Sharing in the new communion
    When the victory is won.
Catherine Baird (1895-1984)

596 Chalvey, 181; For ever with the Lord, 183
     D.S.M.

JESUS, my strength, my hope,
  On thee I cast my care,
With humble confidence look up,
  And know thou hearest prayer.
Give me on thee to wait,
  Till I can all things do,
On thee, almighty to create,
  Almighty to renew.

2 I want a sober mind,
    A self-renouncing will,
That tramples down and casts behind
  The baits of pleasing ill;
A soul inured to pain,
  To hardship, grief and loss,
Bold to take up, firm to sustain,
  The consecrated cross.

3 I want a godly fear,
    A quick-discerning eye,
That looks to thee when sin is near,
  And sees the tempter fly;
A spirit still prepared
  And armed with jealous care,
Forever standing on its guard,
  And watching unto prayer.

4 I rest upon thy word;
    The promise is for me;
My succor and salvation, Lord,
  Shall surely come from thee.
But let me still abide,
  Nor from my hope remove,
Till thou my patient spirit guide
  Into thy perfect love.
Charles Wesley (1707-88)

597 Carlisle, 164; St Ethelwald, 174; Silchester, 177   S.M.

JESUS, my truth, my way,
  My sure, unerring light,
On thee my feeble steps I stay,
  Which thou wilt guide aright.

2 My wisdom and my guide,
    My Counselor thou art;
  O never let me leave thy side,
    Or from thy paths depart!

3 Teach me the happy art
    In all things to depend
  On thee; O never, Lord, depart,
    But love me to the end!

4 Let me thy witness live,
    When sin is all destroyed;
  And then my spotless soul receive,
    And take me home to God.
Charles Wesley (1707-88)

598 Jesus, Saviour, pilot me, 309; Toplady, 316   7.7.7.7.7.7.

JESUS, Saviour, pilot me
  Over life's tempestuous sea;
Unknown waves before me roll,
Hiding rocks and treacherous shoal;
Chart and compass come from thee,
Jesus, Saviour, pilot me.

2 As a mother stills her child,
Thou canst hush the ocean wild.
Raging waves obey thy will,
When thou say'st to them: Be still.
Wondrous Sovereign of the sea,
Jesus, Saviour, pilot me.

3 When at last I near the shore,
And the fearful breakers roar
'Twixt me and the peaceful rest,
Then, while leaning on thy breast,
May I hear thee say to me:
Fear not, I will pilot thee.
Edward Hopper (1818-88)

599
Eudoxia, 197; Barnby, 195
6.5.6.5.

JESUS, stand among us
In thy risen power;
Let this time of worship
Be a hallowed hour.

2 Breathe the Holy Spirit
Into every heart;
Bid the fears and sorrows
From each soul depart.

3 Thus with quickened footsteps
We'll pursue our way,
Watching for the dawning
Of eternal day.
William Pennefather (1816-73)

600
Jesus, thou art everything to me, 705

JESUS, tender lover of my soul,
Pardoner of my sins, and friend indeed,
Keeper of the garden of my heart,
Jesus, thou art everything to me.

Jesus, thou art everything to me,
Jesus, thou art everything to me,
All my lasting joys are found in thee;
Jesus, thou art everything to me.

2 What to me are all the joys of earth?
What to me is every sight I see,
Save the sight of thee, O Friend of mine?
Jesus, thou art everything to me.

3 Here I lay me at thy bleeding feet,
Deepest homage now I give to thee;
Hear thy whispered love within my soul;
Jesus, thou art everything to me.
Edward Henry Joy (1871-1949) (verses),
Arthur Smith Arnott (1870-1941) (chorus)

601
Mozart, 496; St Catherine, 499
8.8.8.8.8.8. Iambic

JESUS, the gift divine I know;
The gift divine I ask of thee;
That living water now bestow,
Thy Spirit and thyself, on me;
Thou, Lord, of life the fountain art,
Now let me find thee in my heart.

2 Thee let me drink, and thirst no more
For drops of finite happiness;
Spring up, O Well, in heavenly power,
In streams of pure perennial peace,
In joy that none can take away,
In life which shall for ever stay.

3 Father, on me the grace bestow,
And make me blameless in thy sight,
Whence all the streams of mercy flow;
Mercy, thine own supreme delight,
To me, for Jesus' sake impart,
And plant thy nature in my heart.
Charles Wesley (1707-88)

602
Maryton, 33; Harton-Lea, 20; Boston, 13
L.M.

JESUS, thou joy of loving hearts,
Thou fount of life, thou light of men,
From the best bliss that earth imparts
We turn unfilled to thee again.

2 Thy truth unchanged hath ever stood;
Thou savest those that on thee call;
To them that seek thee thou art good,
To them that find thee, all in all.

3 Our restless spirits yearn for thee,
Where'er our changeful lot is cast;
Glad when thy gracious smile we see,
Blest when our faith can hold thee fast.

4 O Jesus, ever with us stay,
Make all our moments calm and bright!
Chase the dark night of sin away,
Shed o'er the world thy holy light.
Attr Bernard of Clairvaux (1091-1153),
trs Ray Palmer (1808-87)

603
Dennis, 165; St Michael, 175
S.M.

JESUS, we look to thee,
Thy promised presence claim;
Thou in the midst of us shalt be,
Assembled in thy name.

2 Thy name salvation is,
Which here we come to prove;
Thy name is life and health and peace
And everlasting love.

3 We meet, the grace to take
   Which thou hast freely given;
   We meet on earth for thy dear sake
   That we may meet in Heaven.

4 Present we know thou art;
   But, O thyself reveal!
   Now, Lord, let every waiting heart
   Thy mighty comfort feel!

5 O may thy quickening voice
   The death of sin remove,
   And bid our inmost souls rejoice
   In hope of perfect love!
                    Charles Wesley (1707-88)

604 Warrington, 56; Harton-Lea, 20
                                    L.M.

JESUS, where'er thy people meet,
   There they behold the mercy seat;
Where'er they seek thee thou art found,
And every place is hallowed ground.

2 For thou, within no walls confined,
   Inhabitest the humble mind;
   Such ever bring thee where they come,
   And going take thee to their home.

3 Here may we prove the power of prayer
   To strengthen faith and sweeten care,
   To teach our faint desires to rise,
   And bring all Heaven before our eyes.

4 Lord, we are few, but thou art near,
   Nor short thine arm, nor deaf thine ear;
   O rend the heavens, come quickly down,
   And make a thousand hearts thine own!
                    William Cowper (1731-1800)

605 Penitence, 193; Nuttall, 192
                              6.4.6.4.6.6.6.4.

KNEELING in penitence I make my
      prayer,
Owning my weaknesses and my despair;
   Failure I cannot hide,
   Broken my selfish pride,
   Pardon thou dost provide,
      Pardon declare.

2 Nothing can I achieve, nothing attain;
   He that without thee builds, labors in vain;
   Shatter my own design,
   Shaping a plan divine,
   Come to this heart of mine,
      Saviour, again.

3 Though few the gifts I have that thou canst
      use,
   Make thy demands on me; I'll not refuse;
   Take all there is of me,
   Take what I hope to be;
   Thy way at last I see,
      Thy way I choose.
                    John Gowans

606 Sandon, 511; Lux Benigna, 510
                              10.4.10.4.10.10.

LEAD, kindly Light, amid the encircling
      gloom,
   Lead thou me on!
The night is dark, and I am far from home;
   Lead thou me on!
Keep thou my feet; I do not ask to see
The distant scene: one step enough for
      me.

2 I was not ever thus, nor prayed that thou
      Shouldst lead me on.
   I loved to choose and see my path; but
      now
      Lead thou me on!
   I loved the garish day and, spite of fears,
   Pride ruled my will: remember not past
      years.

3 So long thy power hath blest me, sure it
      still
      Will lead me on
   O'er moor and fen, o'er crag and torrent,
      till
      The night is gone;
   And with the morn those angel faces smile
   Which I have loved long since, and lost
      awhile.
                    John Henry Newman (1801-90)

607 Mannheim, 419; Praise, my soul, 422
                              8.7.8.7.8.7. Troch.

LEAD us, heavenly Father, lead us
   O'er the world's tempestuous sea;
Guard us, guide us, keep us, feed us,
   For we have no help but thee,
Yet possessing every blessing
   If our God our Father be.

2 Saviour, breathe forgiveness o'er us;
   All our weakness thou dost know;
Thou didst tread this earth before us;
   Thou didst feel its keenest woe;
Lone and dreary, faint and weary,
   Through the desert thou didst go.

3 Spirit of our God, descending,
   Fill our hearts with heavenly joy,
Love with every passion blending,
   Pleasure that can never cloy;
Thus provided, pardoned, guided,
Nothing can our peace destroy.
James Edmeston (1791-1867)

608 Long, long ago, 513; Cleansing for me, 512   10.8.10.8.10.10.10.8.

LORD, for a mighty revival we plead,
   Lord, give us souls, Lord, give us souls;
Thy saving power in this meeting we need,
   Lord, give us souls; Lord, give us souls.
Quicken our hearts by the Holy Ghost's power,
Pour out thy Spirit, a great, mighty shower,
Of sin the sinner convict, Lord, this hour,
   Lord, give us souls; Lord, give us souls.

2 Let every heart on this object be set,
   Lord, give us souls, Lord, give us souls;
Help us to pray till the answer we get,
   Lord, give us souls; Lord, give us souls.
Give us the faith that will not let thee go,
Faith that says, yes, though the devil says, no;
Lord, thy salvation in this meeting show,
   Lord, give us souls; Lord, give us souls.

3 Lord, we believe thou art going to save,
   Lord, we believe, Lord, we believe;
Floods of salvation and power we shall have,
   Lord, we believe; Lord, we believe.
Souls shall be truly converted to thee,
From all the bondage of Satan be free,
Made into soldiers to fight well for thee,
   Lord, we believe; Lord, we believe.
Harry Davis (1854-1918)

609 Praise, 468; Pembroke, 467; He Lives, 466   8.8.6.8.8.6.

LORD, give me more soul-saving love,
   Send a revival from above,
      Thy mighty Spirit pour.
The Army of salvation bless
With righteousness and holiness,
      Pressed down and running o'er.

2 Spread Calvary's great salvation fame,
   Make every tongue a living flame,
      Soul-saving truth inspire.
With zeal inflame thy fighting host,
Baptize us with the Holy Ghost,
      And set us all on fire.

3 Give power to speak thy conquering word,
To wield the Spirit's two-edged sword,
   And all Hell's legions rout.
O touch us with the living coal,
And kindle fire in every soul
   That never will die out!
William James Pearson (1832-92)

610 Wonderful Healer, 863

LORD, here today my great need I am feeling;
   Wilt thou not visit my soul once again?
I long to feel thy sweet touch and its healing;
   Wonderful Healer, touch me again.

Touch me again, touch me again,
Wonderful Healer, touch me again.

2 Often I've pressed through the throng for the blessing
   Which, through my doubting, I've failed to obtain;
Here once again to thy feet I am pressing;
   Wonderful Healer, touch me again.

3 Only in thee can I find liberation,
   Cleansing and freedom from sin's hidden stain;
Only in thee can I find full salvation,
   Wonderful Healer, touch me again.
William Henry Woulds (1874-1940)

611 Slane, 789

LORD of all hopefulness, Lord of all joy,
   Whose trust, ever childlike, no cares could destroy,
Be there at our waking, and give us, we pray,
Your bliss in our hearts, Lord, at the break of the day.

2 Lord of all eagerness, Lord of all faith,
   Whose strong hands were skilled at the plane and the lathe,
Be there at our labors, and give us, we pray,
Your strength in our hearts, Lord, at the noon of the day.

3 Lord of all kindliness, Lord of all grace,
   Your hands swift to welcome, your arms to embrace,
Be there at our homing, and give us, we pray,
Your love in our hearts, Lord, at the eve of the day.

Means of Grace

4 Lord of all gentleness, Lord of all calm,
  Whose voice is contentment, whose pres-
    ence is balm,
  Be there at our sleeping, and give us, we
    pray,
  Your peace in our hearts, Lord, at the end
    of the day.

  Jan Struther (1901-53)

612 Maryton, 33; Beethoven, 9
  L.M.

LORD, speak to me, that I may speak
  In living echoes of thy tone;
As thou hast sought, so let me seek
  Thy erring children lost and lone.

2 O lead me, Lord, that I may lead
    The wandering and the wavering feet;
  O feed me, Lord, that I may feed
    Thy hungering ones with manna sweet.

3 O strengthen me, that while I stand
    Firm on the rock, and strong in thee,
  I may stretch out a loving hand
    To wrestlers with the troubled sea.

4 O teach me, Lord, that I may teach
    The precious things thou dost impart;
  And wing my words, that they may reach
    The hidden depths of many a heart.

5 O give thine own sweet rest to me,
    That I may speak with soothing power
  A word in season, as from thee,
    To weary ones in needful hour.

6 O fill me with thy fulness, Lord,
    Until my very heart o'erflow
  In kindling thought and glowing word,
    Thy love to tell, thy praise to show.

7 O use me, Lord, use even me,
    Just as thou wilt and when and where,
  Until thy blessèd face I see,
    Thy rest, thy joy, thy glory share.

  Frances Ridley Havergal (1836-79)

613 St Catherine, 499; Make me aware
  of thee, 494   8.8.8.8.8.8. Iambic

MAKE me aware of thee, O Lord,
  As in thy temple I give praise;
Attentive to thy holy word,
  Or in glad song my voice to raise.
That I may feel thy Spirit's power,
O come, invade my soul this hour.

2 Make me aware of thee, O Lord,
    As supplicant, I bow the knee.
  My faith, though small, wilt thou reward
    That contact I may make with thee
  And thus obtain that inward calm
  That makes of life a living psalm.

3 Make me aware of thee, O Lord,
    As with thy children I unite
  To share that wondrous heritage
    Of Calvary and Easter light.
  O Master, let thy people be
  Consistently aware of thee.

  Victor Ottaway (1892-1968)

614 Ottawa, 462; Govaars, 373
  8.7.8.7.7.7.

MASTER, speak: thy servant heareth,
  Waiting for thy gracious word,
Longing for thy voice that cheereth;
  Master, let it now be heard.
I am listening, Lord, for thee;
What hast thou to say to me?

2 Speak to me by name, O Master,
    Let me know it is to me.
  Speak, that I may follow faster,
    With a step more firm and free,
  Where the shepherd leads the flock
  In the shadow of the rock.

3 Master, speak: though least and lowest,
    Let me not unheard depart.
  Master, speak! for O thou knowest
    All the yearning of my heart,
  Knowest all its truest need;
  Speak! and make me blest indeed.

4 Master, speak: and make me ready,
    When thy voice is truly heard,
  With obedience glad and steady
    Still to follow every word.
  I am listening, Lord, for thee;
  Master, speak: O speak to me!

  Frances Ridley Havergal (1836-79)

615 Colne, 79; Lloyd, 107
  C.M.

'MID all the traffic of the ways,
  Turmoils without, within,
Make in my heart a quiet place,
  And come and dwell therein:

2 A little shrine of quietness,
    All sacred to thyself,
  Where thou shalt all my soul possess,
    And I may find myself:

3 A little place of mystic grace,
  Of self and sin swept bare,
Where I may look into thy face,
  And talk with thee in prayer.

4 Come, occupy my silent place,
  And make thy dwelling there!
More grace is wrought in quietness
  Than any is aware.
                    John Oxenham (1852-1941)

616 Downham, 166; No sorrow there, 173;
I hear thy welcome voice, 169   S.M.

MY Maker and my King,
  To thee my all I owe;
Thy constant goodness is the spring
  Whence all my blessings flow.

2 The creature of thy hand,
  On thee alone I live;
Thy countless benefits demand
  More praise than I can give.

3 O let thy grace inspire
  My soul with strength divine!
Let all my powers to thee aspire,
  And all my days be thine.
                    Anne Steele (1716-78)

617 Nearer, my God, to thee, 190;
Horbury, 187   6.4.6.4.6.6.6.4.

NEARER, my God, to thee,
  Nearer to thee!
E'en though it be a cross
  That raiseth me;
Still all my song shall be,
Nearer, my God, to thee,
  Nearer to thee.

2 Though like a wanderer,
  The sun gone down,
Darkness be over me,
  My rest a stone,
Yet in my dreams I'd be
Nearer, my God, to thee,
  Nearer to thee.

3 There let my way appear
  Steps unto Heaven;
All that thou sendest me
  In mercy given;
Angels to beckon me
Nearer, my God, to thee,
  Nearer to thee.

4 Then with my waking thoughts
  Bright with thy praise,
Out of my stony griefs
  Bethel I'll raise;
So by my woes to be
Nearer, my God, to thee,
  Nearer to thee.

5 Or if on joyful wing,
  Cleaving the sky,
Sun, moon and stars forgot,
  Upward I fly,
Still all my song shall be,
Nearer, my God, to thee,
  Nearer to thee.
                    Sarah Fuller Adams (1805-48)

618 He wipes the tear, 63;
Saved by grace, 47   D.L.M.

NOT only, Lord, on that great day
  When men before thy throne shall stand
I ask that thou my judge shalt be,
  With every thought and motive scanned;
But in the midst of common days,
  O let me know that thou art nigh,
And teach me, Lord, to meet thy gaze
  With frank and unaverted eye!

O Saviour, search my heart today
  And tell me all thou findest there!
I must more closely dwell with thee;
  O grant me this, my earnest prayer!

2 I would not meet at life's far end
  Thy final judgment with dismay;
I need thy keen appraisal now
  That I may live, from day to day,
A life that only seeks thy ways,
  A life more closely linked with thee
Who art the Christ of working days,
  The man who walked by Galilee.

3 And if thy judgments make me quail
  And give me cause for grief and pain,
Yet shall thy love uphold me still
  And bid my spirit rise again;
And so, with eyes that see anew
  The task that thou to me hast given,
Let me my covenant renew
  And bring a worthier gift to Heaven.
                    Miriam M. Richards (1911-89)

619 French, 88; St Ann, 127
                                C.M.

O GOD, if still the holy place
  Is found of those in prayer,
By all the promises of grace
  I claim an entrance there.

Means of Grace

2 Give me a self-denying soul,
  Enlarged and unconfined;
  Abide within me, and control
  The wanderings of the mind.

3 Give me the strength of faith that dares
  To die to self each day,
  That bravely takes the cross, nor cares
  To find an easier way.

4 Help me to make more sacrifice,
  To walk where Christ would lead,
  That in my life he may arise
  To hallow every deed.
                    Albert Orsborn (1886-1967)

620 St Catherine, 499; Stella, 503
8.8.8.8.8.8. Iambic

O JESUS, Saviour, hear my cry,
  And all my need just now supply!
New power I want, and strength and light,
That I may conquer in the fight.
O let me have, where'er I go,
Thy strength to conquer every foe!

2 I need thy love my heart to fill,
  To tell to all thy blessèd will,
  And to the hopeless souls make known
  The power that dwells in thee alone;
  And then wherever I shall go
  Thy power shall conquer every foe.

3 O make my life one blazing fire
  Of pure and fervent heart-desire
  The lost to find, the low to raise,
  And give them cause thy name to praise,
  Because wherever I may go
  I show thy power to every foe!

4 Let love be first, let love be last,
  Its light o'er all my life be cast;
  Come now, my Saviour, from above
  And deluge all my soul with love,
  So that wherever I may go
  Thy love shall conquer every foe.
                    Thomas Charles Marshall (1854-1942)

621 St Margaret, 477
8.8.8.6.

O LOVE that wilt not let me go,
  I rest my weary soul in thee;
I give thee back the life I owe,
That in thine ocean depths its flow
  May richer, fuller be.

2 O Light that followest all my way,
  I yield my flickering torch to thee;
My heart restores its borrowed ray,
That in thy sunshine's blaze its day
  May brighter, fairer be.

3 O Joy that seekest me through pain,
  I cannot close my heart to thee;
I trace the rainbow through the rain
And feel the promise is not vain,
  That morn shall tearless be.

4 O cross that liftest up my head,
  I dare not ask to fly from thee;
I lay in dust life's glory dead,
And from the ground there blossoms red
  Life that shall endless be.
                    George Matheson (1842-1906)

622 Austria, 408; Regent Square, 423
8.7.8.7.8.7. Troch.

O THOU God of every nation,
  We now for thy blessing call;
Fit us for full consecration,
  Let the fire from Heaven fall.
Bless our Army! Bless our Army!
  With thy power baptize us all.

2 Fill us with thy Holy Spirit;
  Make our soldiers white as snow;
Save the world through Jesus' merit,
  Satan's kingdom overthrow.
Bless our Army! Bless our Army!
  Send us where we ought to go.

3 Give us all more holy living,
  Fill us with abundant power;
Give the Army more thanksgiving,
  Greater victories every hour.
Bless our Army! Bless our Army!
  Be our rock, our shield, our tower.

4 Bless our General, bless our leaders,
  Bless our officers as well.
Bless our converts, bless our soldiers;
  Speed the war 'gainst sin and Hell.
Bless our Army! Bless our Army!
  We will all thy goodness tell.
                    William James Pearson (1832-92)

623 Calabar, 431; Morning has broken, 735

O TO be like thee! blessèd Redeemer,
  This is my constant longing and prayer,
Gladly I'll forfeit all of earth's treasures,
  Jesus, thy perfect likeness to wear.

Prayer

O to be like thee! O to be like thee,
  Blessèd Redeemer, pure as thou art!
Come in thy sweetness, come in thy
    fulness;
  Stamp thine own image deep on my
    heart.

2 O to be like thee! full of compassion,
  Loving, forgiving, tender and kind,
Helping the helpless, cheering the fainting,
  Seeking the wandering sinner to find.

3 O to be like thee! lowly in spirit,
  Holy and harmless, patient and brave;
Meekly enduring cruel reproaches,
  Willing to suffer, others to save.

4 O to be like thee! while I am pleading,
  Pour out thy Spirit, fill with thy love;
Make me a temple meet for thy dwelling,
  Fit me for life and Heaven above.
Thomas Obediah Chisholm (1866-1960)

624 Salzburg, 131; Fewster, 86   C.M.

OUR Father, who in Heaven art,
  All hallowed be thy name,
Thy Kingdom come to every heart
  To light the holy flame.

2 Help us on earth to do thy will
  As angels do in Heaven,
And may to us in good and ill
  Thy gracious gifts be given.

3 Our trespasses, O Lord, forgive,
  And grant us grace to show
To all with whom we move and live
  The grace thou dost bestow.

4 Be near us in temptation's hour,
  Let strength divine abound;
Deliver by thy mighty power
  When evil shall surround.

5 The kingdoms of the world are thine,
  Thine too the praise shall be;
Grant us to worship at thy shrine
  To all eternity.
Charles Coller (1863-1935)

625 St Agnes, 126; Bedford, 74   C.M.

PRAYER is the soul's sincere desire
  Uttered or unexpressed,
The motion of a hidden fire
  That trembles in the breast.

2 Prayer is the burden of a sigh,
  The falling of a tear,
The upward glancing of an eye
  When none but God is near.

3 Prayer is the simplest form of speech
  That infant lips can try;
Prayer the sublimest strains that reach
  The majesty on high.

4 Prayer is the contrite sinner's voice
  Returning from his ways,
While angels in their songs rejoice
  And cry: Behold, he prays!

5 Prayer is the Christian's vital breath,
  The Christian's native air,
His watchword at the gates of death;
  He enters Heaven with prayer.

6 O thou by whom we come to God,
  The life, the truth, the way!
The path of prayer thyself hast trod:
  Lord, teach us how to pray!
James Montgomery (1771-1854)

626 Chalvey, 181; Peace, 185   D.S.M.

REVIVE thy work, O Lord,
  Thy mighty arm make bare;
Speak with the voice that wakes the dead,
  And make thy people hear.
Revive thy work, O Lord,
  While here to thee we bow;
Descend, O gracious Lord, descend!
  O come and bless us now.

2 Revive thy work, O Lord,
  Create soul-thirst for thee;
And hungering for the bread of life
  O may our spirits be!
Revive thy work, O Lord,
  Exalt thy precious name;
And by the Holy Ghost, our love
  For thee and thine inflame.

3 Revive thy work, O Lord,
  Give power unto thy word;
Grant that thy blessèd gospel may
  In living faith be heard.
Revive thy work, O Lord,
  And give refreshing showers;
The glory shall be all thine own,
  The blessing shall be ours.
Albert Midlane (1825-1909)

Means of Grace

627 Saviour, lead me, 294

7.7.7.7.

SAVIOUR, lead me, lest I stray,
  Gently lead me all the way;
I am safe when by thy side,
I would in thy love abide.

Lead me, lead me,
Saviour, lead me, lest I stray,
Gently down the stream of time;
Saviour, lead me all the way.

2 Thou the refuge of my soul
  When the stormy billows roll;
  I am safe when thou art nigh,
  On thy mercy I rely.

3 Saviour, lead me, lead at last,
  When the storm of life is past,
  To the land of endless day,
  Where all tears are wiped away.
                    Frank M. Davis (1839-96)

628 O Man of Galilee, 754

SAVIOUR of light, I look just now to thee;
  Brighten my path, so only shall I see
Thy footprints, Lord, which mark the way
    for me;
Light of my life, so surely thou wilt be,
    O Man of Galilee!

O Man of Galilee,
Stay with and strengthen me;
Walk thou through life with me,
O Man of Galilee!

2 Another touch, I ask another still,
  That daily, hourly, I may do thy will;
  Healer of wounds and bearer of all pain,
  Thy touch, thy power are evermore the
    same,
    O Man of Galilee!

3 Lord of my life, I dare step out to thee
  Who stilled the waves and stayed the toss-
    ing sea;
  When floods o'erwhelm, my safety thou
    wilt be;
  When nightfall comes, O Lord, abide with
    me;
    O Man of Galilee!

4 Pilot of souls, I trust thy guiding hand;
  Take thou the helm and, at thy blest
    command,
  I sail straight on until, the harbor won,
  I reach the glory of thy sweet well done;
    O Man of Galilee!
                    Robert Hoggard (1861-1935)

629 Darwells, 221; Samuel, 229

6.6.6.6.8.8.

SAVIOUR, we know thou art
  In every age the same;
Now, Lord, in ours exert
  The virtue of thy name;
And daily, through thy word, increase
Thy blood-besprinkled witnesses.

2 Thy people, saved below
    From every sinful stain,
  Shall multiply and grow
    If thy command ordain;
  And one into a thousand rise,
  And spread thy praise through earth and
    skies.

3 In many a soul, and mine,
    Thou hast displayed thy power;
  But to thy people join
    Ten thousand thousand more,
  Saved from the guilt and strength of sin,
  In life and heart entirely clean.
                    Charles Wesley (1707-88)

630 Fellowship with thee, 642

SPIRIT of eternal love,
  Guide me, or I blindly rove;
Set my heart on things above,
  Draw me after thee.
Earthly things are paltry show,
Phantom charms, they come and go;
Give me constantly to know
  Fellowship with thee.

Fellowship with thee,
Fellowship with thee,
Give me constantly to know
Fellowship with thee.

2 Come, O Spirit, take control
  Where the fires of passion roll;
  Let the yearnings of my soul
    Center all in thee.
  Call into thy fold of peace
  Thoughts that seek forbidden ways;
  Calm and order all my days,
    Hide my life in thee.

3 Thus supported, even I,
Knowing thee forever nigh,
Shall attain that deepest joy,
  Living unto thee.
No distracting thoughts within,
No surviving hidden sin,
Thus shall Heaven indeed begin
  Here and now in me.
Albert Orsborn (1886-1967)

631 Mendelssohn, 547; Still with thee, 549
11.10.11.10.

SPIRIT of God, thou art the bread of
  Heaven
  Come for my need in Jesus Christ the
  Lord;
Broken in him whose life was freely given
In deathless love he only could afford.

2 Thou art the bread that satisfies forever,
  The inward health that overcomes
  disease,
The love that lives through death, subsid-
  ing never,
  My secret fortress and my soul's release.

3 O Bread from God, I choose thee now with
  gladness,
  Though sweet the taste of earthly gain
  may be;
My spirit pines in poverty and sadness
  Unless my sustenance be found in thee.

4 Lord God, I come, thy life in mine is
  waking,
  Whate'er I am I bring into thy care.
Thy loving hands will bless me in the
  breaking
  Of bread thou gavest and I long to share.
Catherine Baird (1895-1984)

632 Still with thee, 549; Mendelssohn, 547
11.10.11.10.

STILL, still with thee, when purple morning breaketh,
  When the bird waketh, and the shadows
  flee;
Fairer than morning, lovelier than daylight,
  Dawns the sweet consciousness, I am
  with thee.

2 Still, still with thee! As to each newborn
  morning
  A fresh and solemn splendor still is
  given,
So does this blessèd consciousness,
  awaking,
  Breathe each day nearness unto thee
  and Heaven.

3 When sinks the soul, subdued by toil to
  slumber,
  Its closing eye looks up to thee in prayer;
Sweet the repose beneath thy wings
  o'ershading,
  But sweeter still, to wake and find thee
  there.

4 So shall it be at last, in that bright
  morning,
  When the soul waketh, and life's shadows flee;
O in that hour, fairer than daylight
  dawning,
  Shall rise the glorious thought, I am with
  thee!
Harriet Beecher Stowe (1811-96)

633 Sweet hour of prayer, 66
D.L.M.

SWEET hour of prayer, sweet hour of
  prayer,
  That calls me from a world of care,
And bids me at my Father's throne
Make all my wants and wishes known;
In seasons of distress and grief
My soul has often found relief,
And oft escaped the tempter's snare
By thy return, sweet hour of prayer.

2 Sweet hour of prayer, sweet hour of prayer,
Thy wings shall my petition bear
To him whose truth and faithfulness
Engage the waiting soul to bless;
And since he bids me seek his face,
Believe his word, and trust his grace,
I'll cast on him my every care
And wait for thee, sweet hour of prayer.

3 Sweet hour of prayer, sweet hour of prayer,
May I thy consolation share,
Till from Mount Pisgah's lofty height
I view my home, and at the sight
Put off this robe of flesh, and rise
To gain the everlasting prize,
And realize forever there
The fruits of the sweet hour of prayer.
W.W. Walford

Means of Grace

634
Sardis, 397; In me, Lord, 383*
8.7.8.7. Troch.

SWEET the moments, rich in blessing,
  Which before the cross I spend,
Life and health and peace possessing
  From the sinner's dying friend.

*In me, Lord, in me, Lord,
Thy will fulfil in me, Lord.*

2 Here it is I find my Heaven,
    While upon the Lamb I gaze;
  Love I much? I'm much forgiven,
    I'm a miracle of grace.

3 Love and grief my heart dividing,
    With my tears his feet I'll bathe;
  Constant still in faith abiding,
    Life deriving from his death.

4 May I still enjoy this blessing,
    In all need to Jesus go;
  Prove his death each day more healing,
    And himself more fully know.

*William Walter Shirley (1725-86) (verses),
Hugh Alfred Lambart Sladen (1878-1962)
(chorus)*

635
Take thou my hand, 806

TAKE thou my hand and guide me
  Till life be o'er,
To rest with thee beside me
  For evermore.
My Saviour, do not leave me
  One single day;
In Heaven with thee receive me
  To dwell alway.

2 When faint my heart with sadness,
    Bid cares all cease;
  Grant me in pain or gladness
    Thy perfect peace.
  In lowliness I bend me
    Before thy throne;
  O let thine eyes defend me,
    For blind my own!

3 E'en though my weak endeavor
    Feel not thy might,
  Yet thou wilt lead me ever
    All through the night.
  Then, take my hand and guide me
    Till life be o'er,
  To rest with thee beside me
    For evermore.

*Julie Katharine von Hausmann (1826-1901),
trs F.S. Cooper*

636
Irish, 99; Bishopthorpe, 77; Sawley, 132
C.M.

TALK with me, Lord, thyself reveal,
  While here o'er earth I rove;
Speak to my heart and let me feel
  The kindling of thy love.

2 With thee conversing, I forget
    All time and toil and care;
  Labor is rest, and pain is sweet,
    If thou, my God, art here.

3 Here then, my God, vouchsafe to stay,
    And bid my heart rejoice;
  My longing heart shall own thy sway
    And echo to thy voice.

4 Thou callest me to seek thy face;
    'Tis all I wish to seek;
  To attend the whispers of thy grace,
    And hear thee inly speak.

5 Let this my every hour employ
    Till I thy glory see,
  Enter into my Master's joy,
    And find my Heaven in thee.

Charles Wesley (1707-88)

637
Showers of blessing, 456
8.7.8.7. Dact.

THERE shall be showers of blessing:
  This is the promise of love;
There shall be seasons refreshing,
  Sent from the Saviour above.

*Showers of blessing,
  Showers of blessing we need;
Mercy drops round us are falling,
  But for the showers we plead.*

2 There shall be showers of blessing:
    Precious reviving again;
  Over the hills and the valleys,
    Sound of abundance of rain.

3 There shall be showers of blessing:
    Send them upon us, O Lord!
  Grant to us now a refreshing;
    Come, and now honor thy word.

4 There shall be showers of blessing:
    O that today they might fall,
  Now as to God we're confessing,
    Now as on Jesus we call!

Daniel Webster Whittle (1840-1901)

638 Carey's, 489; Euphony, 493; Stella, 503
8.8.8.8.8.8. Iambic

THOU Lamb of God, whose precious
blood
For every guilty sinner flows,
A cleansing, efficacious flood,
A healing stream for human woes,
Now let us feel its quickening power,
O cleanse our souls this very hour!

2 Assembled here with one accord,
We claim thy promised blessing now,
And dare believe thy precious word
While humbly at thy throne we bow.
O fill us with thy mighty power,
And save, O Lord, this very hour!

3 O solemnize each waiting heart,
And let us feel thy presence now!
Subdue, dear Lord, the stubborn heart,
That all in penitence may bow.
Convict us by thy mighty power,
And save, dear Lord, this very hour.

Harry Davis (1854-1918)

639 Thou Shepherd of Israel, 487; Israel's
Shepherd, 694   8.8.8.8. D. Amph.

THOU Shepherd of Israel, and mine,
The joy and desire of my heart,
For closer communion I pine,
I long to reside where thou art.
The pastures I languish to find
Where all who their shepherd obey
Are fed, on thy bosom reclined,
And screened from the heat of the day.

2 Ah! show me that happiest place,
The place of thy people's abode,
Where saints in true happiness gaze
And hang on a crucified God.
Thy love for a sinner declare,
Thy passion and death on the tree;
My spirit to Calvary bear,
To suffer and triumph with thee.

3 'Tis there, with the lambs of thy flock,
There only, I covet to rest,
To lie at the foot of the rock,
Or rise to be hid in thy breast.
'Tis there I would always abide,
And never a moment depart,
Concealed in the cleft of thy side,
Eternally held in thy heart.

Charles Wesley (1707-88)

640 Montgomery, 535; St Denio, 569;
Foundation, A.S. 976;   11.11.11.11.

TO God be the glory, a Saviour is mine,
Whose power is almighty, whose grace
is divine;
My heart he hath cleansed, he is dwelling
within,
So wondrously saving from sinning and
sin.

2 O wonder of wonders, to God be the praise,
I joy in his will, I delight in his ways!
And through every conflict, without and
within,
He saves me and keeps me from sinning
and sin.

3 No longer in bondage, my freedom I'll use
My Master to serve in the way he shall
choose;
To work or to witness, to go or remain,
His smile of approval my infinite gain.

4 Earth's pleasures and treasures no longer
allure,
My spirit aspires to the things which
endure;
To walk with my Saviour in garments of
white,
My highest ambition, my constant delight.

5 The world overcoming by limitless grace,
I worship the Lord in the light of his face;
So with him communing, like him I shall
grow,
And life everlasting enjoy here below.

Charles Coller (1863-1935)

641 Shepherd, hear my prayer! 784

UNTO thee will I cry,
Shepherd, hear my prayer!
Poor and needy am I,
Shepherd, hear my prayer!
Deep is calling unto deep,
Rugged are the heights, and steep;
Guide my steps and keep;
Hear, O hear my prayer!
Hear, O hear my prayer!

2 Where the tempest is loud,
Shepherd, hear my prayer!
'Mid the darkness and cloud,
Shepherd, hear my prayer!
Let me hear thy voice afar,

Coming with the morning star;
True thy mercies are!
   Hear, O hear my prayer!
   Hear, O hear my prayer!

3 Let the foe not prevail,
   Shepherd, hear my prayer!
My resources would fail,
   Shepherd, hear my prayer!
Order all my steps aright,
Carry me from height to height;
Yonder shines the light!
   Shepherd, lead me there!
   Lead me safely there!

Albert Orsborn (1886-1967)

642 Stella, 503; St Catherine, 499
8.8.8.8.8.8. Iambic

WE thank thee, Lord, for answered prayer,
For every token of thy care;
Since our requests to thee we brought,
We have received more than we sought.
More than we ask, thy word declares,
Shall be thy answer to our prayers.

2 We thank thee that our cry was heard,
And that, according to thy word,
Before thy promise we could plead,
Thou hadst begun to meet our need.
More than we ask, and greater far
Than we can think, thy mercies are.

3 As in this place our hearts are made
To bless thee for thy mighty aid,
Help us, as more for thee we dare,
To prove still more the strength of prayer.
Thy word is sure, thou canst not fail
To bless those who in prayer prevail.

Leslie Rusher

643 Near the cross, 272;
7.6.7.6. Troch.

WE the people of thy host,
   Standing here before thee,
For thy power, O Holy Ghost,
   We, as one, implore thee!

Send the power, send the power,
   Send it, we implore thee.
Fill us with the Holy Ghost,
   As we bow before thee.

2 God of ages, God of grace,
   Search these hearts before thee;
With thy power come fill this place,
   We, as one, implore thee.

3 Let not self hold any part,
   All we lay before thee;
Be thou conqueror of each heart,
   We, as one, implore thee.

4 Thine for time, and thine for aye,
   Battling, conquering for thee,
Till, when ended life's short day,
   We in Heaven adore thee.

Emma Moss Booth-Tucker (1860-1903)

644 Saved by grace, 47; Harton-Lea, 20
L.M.

WEAVER divine, thy matchless skill
   Hath planned the pattern of my ways;
Within the fabric of thy will
   I yield my residue of days.

I dwell in thy abiding care,
And find my soul's refreshment there;
Content to trust my way to thee
Thy overruling plan I see.

2 Somber the colors are and gay,
   Varied the workings of thy hand;
I would not wish to know the way,
   Nor seek thy will to understand.

3 Human design may cause me pain,
   And test my faith through doubt and fear,
Grant me to feel thy touch again,
   Thy reassuring voice to hear.

4 Christ of the loom, thy loving hand
   Doth thread the pattern for my good;
I too would weave at thy command
   Until thy will be understood.

Brindley Boon

645 What a friend, 451; Hyfrydol, 438;
Blaenwern, 430   8.7.8.7. D. Troch.

WHAT a friend we have in Jesus,
   All our sins and griefs to bear!
What a privilege to carry
   Everything to God in prayer!
O what peace we often forfeit,
   O what needless pain we bear,
All because we do not carry
   Everything to God in prayer!

2 Have we trials and temptations?
   Is there trouble anywhere?
We should never be discouraged:
   Take it to the Lord in prayer.
Can we find a friend so faithful,
   Who will all our sorrows share?
Jesus knows our every weakness:
   Take it to the Lord in prayer.

Prayer

3 Are we weak and heavy laden,
   Cumbered with a load of care?
Precious Saviour, still our refuge:
   Take it to the Lord in prayer.
Do thy friends despise, forsake thee?
   Take it to the Lord in prayer;
In his arms he'll take and shield thee,
   Thou wilt find a solace there.
Joseph Scriven (1819-86)

646
Armadale, 8; Whitburn, 58
L.M.

WHAT various hindrances we meet
   In coming to the mercy seat!
Yet who that knows the worth of prayer
But wishes to be often there!

2 Prayer makes the darkest cloud withdraw,
Prayer climbs the ladder Jacob saw,
Gives exercise to faith and love,
Brings every blessing from above.

3 Restraining prayer, we cease to fight;
Prayer makes the soldier's armor bright;
And Satan trembles when he sees
The weakest saint upon his knees.

4 O Lord, increase our faith and love,
So shall we all thy goodness prove
And gain from thine own boundless store
The fruits of prayer for evermore.
William Cowper (1731-1800)

647
At thy feet I fall, 613

WHEN shall I come unto the healing
   waters?
   Lifting my heart, I cry to thee my
   prayer.
Spirit of peace, my Comforter and healer,
   In whom my springs are found, let my
   soul meet thee there.

From a hill I know,
Healing waters flow;
O rise, Immanuel's tide,
And my soul overflow!

2 Wash from my hands the dust of earthly
   striving;
   Take from my mind the stress of secret
   fear;
Cleanse thou the wounds from all but thee
   far hidden.
   And when the waters flow let my healing
   appear.

3 Light, life and love are in that healing
   fountain,
   All I require to cleanse me and restore;
Flow through my soul, redeem its desert
   places,
   And make a garden there for the Lord I
   adore.
Albert Orsborn (1886-1967)

648
Nuttall, 192
6.4.6.4.6.6.6.4.

WHERE lowly spirits meet
   Instant in prayer,
All at one mercy seat,
   One plea to share,
With thee we intercede,
Leader of those who lead,
Heart of our Army's need,
   Make us thy care.

2 Let not thy people boast,
   Empty are we,
Martial and mighty host
   Though we may be.
Naught of our own we claim,
Forth from thy heart we came,
Thou art our altar-flame;
   We live by thee.

3 Where secret rivers rise,
   Lead us to grace;
Even through clouded skies
   Show us thy face.
Own us thy people still,
Seal us within thy will,
And in thy holy hill
   Stablish our place.
Albert Orsborn (1886-1967)

649
Lord, fill my craving heart, 108
C.M.

WHILE here before thy cross I kneel,
   To me thy love impart;
With a deep, burning love for souls,
   Lord, fill my craving heart.

Lord, fill my craving heart,
Lord, fill my craving heart,
   With a deep, burning love for souls,
Lord, fill my craving heart.

2 Deepen in me thy work of grace,
   Teach me to do thy will,
Help me to live a spotless life,
   Thy holy laws fulfil.

3 With mighty power my soul baptize,
   My longing heart inspire,
That I may from this moment rise
   A living flame of fire.

4 I want in this dark world to shine,
   And ever faithful be,
That all around shall know I'm thine
   In blest reality.

William Henry Hutchings (c 1870-1945)

* * *

see also: 32 God who touchest earth with
               beauty
          181 O Christ, who came to share our
               human life
          295 Lord, I hear of showers of
               blessing
          458 Take time to be holy
          827 Peace in our time, O Lord
          839 Hushed was the evening hymn
          971 I come to the Garden
          973 Near to the heart of God

The Scriptures

650 Lathbury, 713

BREAK thou the bread of life,
   O Lord, to me,
As thou didst break the loaves
   Beside the sea;
Beyond the sacred page
   I seek thee, Lord;
My spirit pants for thee,
   O living Word!

2 Thou art the bread of life,
   O Lord, to me,
Thy holy word the truth
   That saveth me;
Give me to eat and live
   With thee above;
Teach me to love thy truth,
   For thou art love.

3 O send thy Spirit, Lord,
   Now unto me,
That he may touch my eyes
   And make me see;
Show me the truth concealed
   Within thy word,
And in thy book revealed
   I see the Lord.

Mary Artemisia Lathbury (1841-1913)
(verse 1),
Alexander Groves (1842-1909)
(verses 2 and 3)

651 Richmond, 125; St Stephen, 130;
        Azmon, A.S. 988   C.M.

COME, Holy Ghost, our hearts inspire,
   Let us thine influence prove,
Source of the old prophetic fire,
   Fountain of light and love.

2 Come, Holy Ghost, for moved by thee
   The prophets wrote and spoke;
Unlock the truth, thyself the key,
   Unseal the sacred book.

3 Expand thy wings, celestial Dove,
   Brood o'er our nature's night;
On our disordered spirits move,
   And let there now be light.

4 God, through himself, we then shall know,
   If thou within us shine,
And sound, with all thy saints below,
   The depths of love divine.

Charles Wesley (1707-88)

652 Buckland, 275; Weber, 301
                           7.7.7.7.

HOLY Bible, book divine,
   Precious treasure, thou art mine;
Mine, to tell me whence I came;
Mine, to teach me what I am.

2 Mine, to call me when I rove;
Mine, to show a Saviour's love;
Mine art thou to guide my feet;
Mine, to judge, condemn, acquit.

3 Mine, to comfort in distress,
If the Holy Spirit bless;
Mine, to show by living faith
Man can triumph over death.

4 Mine, to tell of joys to come,
And the rebel sinner's doom;
Holy Bible, book divine,
Precious treasure, thou art mine.

John Burton, Sr. (1773-1822)

653 St Denio, 569; *No, never alone, 566;
        Foundation, A.S. 976   11.11.11.11.

HOW firm a foundation, ye saints of the
      Lord,
Is laid for your faith in his excellent word!
What more can he say than to you he hath
      said,
To you who for refuge to Jesus have fled:

*No, never alone, no, never alone,
He promised he never would leave me,
Never, no never, alone.*

2 Fear not, I am with thee, O be not
　　dismayed,
For I am thy God, I will still give thee aid!
I'll strengthen thee, help thee, and cause
　　thee to stand,
Upheld by my gracious, omnipotent hand.

3 When through the deep waters I call thee
　　to go,
The rivers of grief shall not thee overflow,
For I will be with thee thy trials to bless,
And sanctify to thee thy deepest distress.

4 When through fiery trials thy pathway
　　shall lie,
My grace all-sufficient shall be thy supply;
The flames shall not hurt thee; I only
　　design
Thy dross to consume, and thy gold to
　　refine.

5 The soul that on Jesus hath leaned for
　　repose,
I will not, I will not desert to its foes;
That soul, though all Hell should en-
　　deavor to shake,
I'll never, no never, no never forsake.

Anon

654 Abridge, 69; Westminster, 142;
Down in the garden, 84　　C.M.

LAMP of our feet, whereby we trace
　Our path when wont to stray,
Stream from the fount of heavenly grace,
　Brook by the traveler's way;

2 Bread of our souls, whereon we feed,
　True manna from on high,
Our guide and chart, wherein we read
　Of realms beyond the sky;

3 Pillar of fire through watches dark,
　And radiant cloud by day,
When waves would whelm our tossing
　　bark,
　Our anchor and our stay;

4 Word of the ever-living God,
　Will of his glorious Son,
Without thee how could earth be trod,
　Or Heaven itself be won?

5 Lord, grant that we aright may learn
　The wisdom it imparts,
And to its heavenly teaching turn
　With simple, childlike hearts.

Bernard Barton (1784-1849)

655 Ravenshaw, 774

LORD, thy word abideth,
　And our footsteps guideth;
Who its truth believeth
Light and joy receiveth.

2 When our foes are near us,
Then thy word doth cheer us,
Word of consolation,
Message of salvation.

3 When the storms are o'er us,
And dark clouds before us,
Then its light directeth,
And our way protecteth.

4 Who can tell the pleasure,
Who recount the treasure,
By thy word imparted
To the simple-hearted?

5 Word of mercy, giving
Succor to the living;
Word of life, supplying
Comfort to the dying.

6 O that we, discerning
Its most holy learning,
Lord, may love and fear thee,
Evermore be near thee!

Henry Williams Baker (1821-77)

656 Turner, 504; St Matthias, 500;
Solid Rock, 501　　8.8.8.8.8.8. Iambic

SET forth within the sacred word
　The path of life is plainly shown;
The ways of God its lines record,
　For every soul of man made known.
The truth, of all our hopes the ground,
Is here within its pages found.

2 God's ample grace for fallen man,
　His care for our eternal good,
The depth of his salvation plan,
　The doctrine of atoning blood,
The Scriptures' living words express
And point the way to holiness.

3 But how shall we that truth declare,
　Thy grace, thy love, thy beauty show?
Only as we thy nature wear
　Shall men that nature truly know;
And as we walk with thee abroad
They shall perceive the mind of God.

Means of Grace

4 So teach us, Lord, to use each power
  As we the doctrine shall adorn,
That truth and grace shall spring to flower
  In lives renewed and souls reborn;
As we to all the world unfold
  The glory of the faith we hold.
                    Will J. Brand (1889-1977)

657 Rest, 124; St Peter, 129
                                    C.M.

THE Spirit breathes upon the word,
  And brings the truth to sight;
Precepts and promises afford
  A sanctifying light.

2 A glory gilds the sacred page,
  Majestic, like the sun;
It gives a light to every age;
  It gives, but borrows none.

3 Let everlasting thanks be thine
  For such a bright display
As makes a world of darkness shine
  With beams of heavenly day.

4 My soul rejoices to pursue
  The steps of him I love,
Till glory breaks upon my view
  In brighter worlds above.
                    William Cowper (1731-1800)

658 Lakeside, 104; Westminster, 142;
       Belmont, 76   C.M.

THY word is like a garden, Lord,
  With flowers bright and fair;
And everyone who seeks may pluck
  A lovely garland there.

2 Thy word is like a deep, deep mine;
  And jewels rich and rare
Are hidden in its mighty depths,
  For every searcher there.

3 Thy word is like a starry host;
  A thousand rays of light
Are seen, to guide the traveler
  And make his pathway bright.

4 Thy word is like an armory,
  Where soldiers may repair,
And find for life's long battle-day
  All needful weapons there.

5 O may I love thy precious word,
  May I explore the mine,
May I its fragrant flowers glean,
  May light upon me shine!

6 O may I find my armor there,
  Thy word my trusty sword!
I'll learn to fight with every foe
  The battle of the Lord.
                    Edwin Hodder (1837-1904)

* * *

see also: 95 Blessèd are the poor in spirit
          856 For your holy book we thank you

Family Worship: Home

659 Sawley, 132; French, 88
                                    C.M.

BLEST be the dear uniting love
  That will not let us part;
Our bodies may far off remove,
  We still are one in heart.

2 Joined in one spirit to our head,
  Where he appoints we go;
And still in Jesus' footsteps tread,
  And show his praise below.

3 O may we ever walk in him,
  And nothing know beside,
Nothing desire, nothing esteem,
  But Jesus crucified.

4 Closer and closer let us cleave,
  To his beloved embrace;
Expect his fulness to receive,
  And grace to answer grace.

5 Partakers of the Saviour's grace,
  The same in mind and heart,
Nor joy, nor grief, nor time, nor place,
  Nor life, nor death can part.
                    Charles Wesley (1707-88)

660 Dennis, 165; Carlisle, 164
                                    S.M.

BLEST be the tie that binds
  Our hearts in Christian love;
The fellowship of kindred minds
  Is like to that above.

2 Before our Father's throne
  We pour our ardent prayers;
Our fears, our hopes, our aims are one,
  Our comforts and our cares.

3 We share our mutual woes,
   Our mutual burdens bear;
And often for each other flows
   The sympathizing tear.

4 When we asunder part,
   It gives us inward pain;
But we shall still be joined in heart
   And hope to meet again.

5 From sorrow, toil and pain,
   And sin, we shall be free;
And perfect love and friendship reign
   Through all eternity.

John Fawcett (1740-1817)

661 Nativity New, 117; Fewster, 86
C.M.

HAPPY the home when God is there
   And love fills every breast,
Where one their wish, and one their prayer,
   And one their heavenly rest.

2 Happy the home where Jesus' name
   Is sweet to every ear,
Where children early lisp his fame
   And parents hold him dear.

3 Happy the home where prayer is heard
   And praise is wont to rise,
Where parents love the sacred word,
   And live but for the skies.

4 Lord! let us in our homes agree
   This blessèd peace to gain;
Unite our hearts in love to thee,
   And love to all will reign.

Henry Ware (1794-1843)

662 My Shepherd, 115; Bedford, 74
C.M.

HELP us to help each other, Lord,
   Each other's cross to bear;
Let each his friendly aid afford,
   And feel his brother's care.

2 Help us to build each other up,
   Our little stock improve;
Increase our faith, confirm our hope,
   And perfect us in love.

3 Up into thee, our living head,
   Let us in all things grow,
Till thou hast made us free indeed
   And spotless here below.

Charles Wesley (1707-88)

663 Bethany, 429; Whither Pilgrims? 453;
What a friend, 451   8.7.8.7. D. Troch.

HOME is home, however lowly,
   Home is sweet when love is there,
Home is home when hearts are holy,
   Earth has ne'er a spot so fair.
Jesus makes our home a heaven,
   Sacred in the fireside warm;
After battling through the long day,
   Home's a shelter from the storm.

2 To a little home in Bethany
   Jesus loved to wend his way;
Tender hearts were waiting for him
   In the evening of the day.
Jesus there dispelled the sadness,
   There the humble meal he blessed;
There they worshiped him with gladness;
   There his sacred form would rest.

3 Let us make our home the threshold
   Of the city bright and fair,
Each the other's joy possessing,
   Each the other's burden share.
In the storm of deep affliction
   Let us seek the heavenly balm,
In life's tempest just remember
   Prayer will make the storm a calm.

Arthur Smith Arnott (1870-1941)

664 Love at home, 237
7.5.7.5.7.7.7.5.

O THERE'S joy in every heart
   When there's love at home;
There's a smile on every face
   When there's love at home!
Voices have a kindly sound,
Happiness beams all around,
Peace and gentleness abound
   When there's love at home.

Love at home! Love at home!
There's an angel in the house
When there's love at home.

2 O there's sunshine on the hearth
   When there's love at home,
And there's music in the air
   When there's love at home!
Faces at the door are sweet,
Laughter echoes in the street,
Paths are smooth for little feet
   When there's love at home.

3 When there's Jesus in the midst,
   There is love at home;
He will teach you what to do
   When there's love at home;
Help you in life's busy mart;
Whisper softly in your heart
Of the bright and better part,
   When there's love at home.
Anon

3 Each day is a round of duty,
   A pressing, absorbing quest;
Each evening the Lord will question:
   Today have you done your best?

4 Each night-time the glittering starlight
   Stands watch at the day's closed door;
Each morning anew God calls me
   To rise and to try once more.
Mads Nielsen, (1879-1958)
trs Flora Larsson

Morning

665 Tallis, 52; Morning Hymn, 35   L.M.

AWAKE, my soul, and with the sun
   Thy daily stage of duty run;
Shake off dull sloth, and joyful rise
To pay thy morning sacrifice.

2 Let all thy converse be sincere,
   Thy conscience as the noonday clear;
For God's all-seeing eye surveys
Thy secret thoughts, thy words and ways.

3 All praise to thee, who safe has kept
And hast refreshed me while I slept;
Grant, Lord, when I from death shall wake
I may of endless life partake.

4 Lord, I my vows to thee renew;
Disperse my sins as morning dew;
Guard my first springs of thought and will,
And with thyself my spirit fill.

5 Direct, control, suggest, this day,
All I may think, or do, or say;
That all my powers, with all their might,
In thy sole glory may unite.

6 Praise God, from whom all blessings flow;
Praise him, all creatures here below;
Praise him above, ye heavenly host;
Praise Father, Son and Holy Ghost.
Thomas Ken (1637-1711)

666 Each day is a gift, 639

EACH day is a gift supernal,
   A shining new chance to live;
Each day brings a heavenly challenge
To all that I have to give.

2 Each day is a golden treasure,
   Whose riches I cannot guess,
A store of created beauty
That humbly I may possess.

667 Melcombe, 34; Morning Hymn, 35;
Job, 30; Duke Street, 17   L.M.

FORTH in thy name, O Lord, I go
   My daily labor to pursue,
Thee, only thee, resolved to know
   In all I think, or speak, or do.

2 Thee may I set at my right hand,
   Whose eyes my inmost purpose see;
And labor on at thy command,
   And offer all my works to thee.

3 Give me to bear thy easy yoke,
   And every moment watch and pray,
And still to things eternal look,
   And hasten to thy glorious day.

4 For thee delightfully employ
   Whate'er thy bounteous grace hath
      given,
And run my course with even joy,
   And closely walk with thee to Heaven.
Charles Wesley (1707-88)

668 Melcombe, 34; Morning Hymn, 35;
Ernan, 19   L.M.

NEW every morning is the love
   Our wakening and uprising prove,
Through sleep and darkness safely
      brought,
Restored to life and power and thought.

2 If on our daily course our mind
Be set to hallow all we find,
New treasures still of countless price
God will provide for sacrifice.

3 Old friends, old scenes, will lovelier be
As more of Heaven in each we see;
Some softening gleam of love and prayer
Shall dawn on every cross and care.

4 The trivial round, the common task,
  Will furnish all we ought to ask;
  Room to deny ourselves, a road
  To bring us daily nearer God.

5 Only, O Lord, in thy great love,
  Fit us for perfect rest above;
  And help us, this and every day,
  To live more nearly as we pray.

John Keble (1792-1866)

669 Carlisle, 164; Lascelles, 170;
  Southport, 178   S.M.

THIS is the day of light:
  Let there be light today;
O Dayspring, rise upon our night,
  And chase its gloom away.

2 This is the day of rest:
  Our failing strength renew;
On weary brain and troubled breast
  Shed thou thy freshening dew.

3 This is the day of peace:
  Thy peace our spirits fill;
Bid thou the blasts of discord cease,
  The waves of strife be still.

4 This is the day of prayer:
  Let earth and Heaven draw near;
Lift up our hearts to seek thee there,
  Come down to meet us here.

5 This is the first of days:
  Send forth thy quickening breath,
And wake dead souls to love and praise,
  Thou vanquisher of death!

John Ellerton (1826-93)

Evening

670 Abide with me, 517; Sunset, 522;
  Emerson, 520   10.10.10.10. Iambic

ABIDE with me; fast falls the eventide;
  The darkness deepens; Lord, with me
  abide!
When other helpers fail, and comforts flee,
Help of the helpless, O abide with me!

2 Swift to its close ebbs out life's little day;
  Earth's joys grow dim, its glories pass
  away;
Change and decay in all around I see;
O thou who changest not, abide with me!

3 I need thy presence every passing hour;
  What but thy grace can foil the tempter's
  power?
Who like thyself my guide and stay can
  be?
Through cloud and sunshine, O abide with
  me!

4 I fear no foe, with thee at hand to bless;
  Ills have no weight, and tears no
  bitterness.
Where is death's sting? Where, grave, thy
  victory?
I triumph still if thou abide with me.

5 Hold thou thy cross before my closing
  eyes;
Shine through the gloom, and point me to
  the skies;
Heaven's morning breaks, and earth's vain
  shadows flee;
In life, in death, O Lord, abide with me!

Henry Francis Lyte (1793-1847)

671 Tallis, 52; Hursley, 26
                              L.M.

GLORY to thee, my God, this night,
  For all the blessings of the light;
Keep me, O keep me, King of kings,
Beneath thine own almighty wings.

2 Forgive me, Lord, for thy dear Son,
  The ill that I this day have done;
That with the world, myself and thee,
I, ere I sleep, at peace may be.

3 If in the night I sleepless lie,
  My soul with heavenly thoughts supply;
Let no ill dreams disturb my rest,
No powers of darkness me molest.

4 O may my soul on thee repose,
  And with sweet sleep mine eyelids close,
Sleep that may me more vigorous make
To serve my God when I awake.

Thomas Ken (1637-1711)

672 St Luke, 46; Deep Harmony, 16
                              L.M.

MY God, how endless is thy love!
  Thy gifts are every evening new,
And morning mercies from above
Gently distil like early dew.

2 Thou spread'st the curtains of the night,
   Great Guardian of my sleeping hours;
Thy sovereign word restores the light,
   And quickens all my drowsy powers.

3 I yield my powers to thy command,
   To thee I consecrate my days;
Perpetual blessings from thy hand
   Demand perpetual songs of praise.

Isaac Watts (1674-1748)

673 Eudoxia, 197; Barnby, 195
6.5.6.5.

NOW the day is over,
   Night is drawing nigh,
Shadows of the evening
   Steal across the sky.

2 Now the darkness gathers,
   Stars begin to peep,
Birds and beasts and flowers
   Soon will be asleep.

3 Jesus, give the weary
   Calm and sweet repose;
With thy tenderest blessing
   May their eyelids close.

4 When the morning wakens,
   Then may I arise
Pure and fresh and sinless
   In thy holy eyes.

Sabine Baring-Gould (1834-1924)

674 Ellers, 519; Bartholomew, 518
10.10.10.10. Iambic

SAVIOUR, again to thy dear name we raise
   With one accord our parting hymn of praise;
We stand to bless thee ere our worship cease,
Then, lowly kneeling, wait thy word of peace.

2 Grant us thy peace upon our homeward way;
With thee begun, with thee shall end the day;
Guard thou the lips from sin, the hearts from shame,
That in this house have called upon thy name.

3 Grant us thy peace, Lord, through the coming night,
Turn thou for us its darkness into light;
From harm and danger keep thy children free,
For dark and light are both alike to thee.

4 Grant us thy peace throughout our earthly life,
Our balm in sorrow, and our stay in strife;
Then, when thy voice shall bid our conflict cease,
Call us, O Lord, to thine eternal peace.

John Ellerton (1826-93)

675 Marshall, 189
6.4.6.4.6.6.6.4.

SOFTLY the shadows fall o'er land and sea,
Voices of evening call, speaking to me,
   Busy my hands this day,
   Small time to think or pray;
Now at the close of day I come to thee.

Lord, 'tis thy tender touch now we implore;
Day with its toil is done, labor is o'er;
Now in the evening while shadows fall,
Grant us thy peace, who give to thee our all.

2 What can I bring to thee, fruit of today?
Have I walked worthily in work and play,
   Lightened my brother's load,
   Walking life's toilsome road,
New strength and love bestowed, Master, I pray?

3 As the birds homeward wend, seeking their nest,
Thou who hast called me friend knowest me best;
   Forgive if I should roam,
   And grant that I may come
To find at last my home safe in thy breast.

Ivy Mawby (1903-83)

676 Hursley, 26; Abends, 2
L.M.

SUN of my soul, thou Saviour dear,
   It is not night if thou be near;
O may no earth-born cloud arise
To hide thee from thy servant's eyes!

2 When the soft dews of kindly sleep
My wearied eyelids gently steep,
Be my last thought: How sweet to rest
Forever on my Saviour's breast.

3 Abide with me from morn till eve,
For without thee I cannot live;
Abide with me when night is nigh,
For without thee I dare not die.

4 If some poor wandering child of thine
  Have spurned today the voice divine,
  Now, Lord, the gracious work begin;
  Let him no more lie down in sin.

5 Watch by the sick; enrich the poor
  With blessings from thy boundless store;
  Be every mourner's sleep tonight,
  Like infant's slumbers, pure and light.

6 Come near and bless us when we wake,
  Ere through the world our way we take,
  Till in the ocean of thy love
  We lose ourselves in Heaven above.
John Keble (1792-1866)

677 St Clements, 44

THE day thou gavest, Lord, is ended,
  The darkness falls at thy behest;
To thee our morning hymns ascended,
  Thy praise shall sanctify our rest.

2 We thank thee that thy Church unsleeping,
  While earth rolls onward into light,
  Through all the world her watch is keeping,
  And rests not now by day or night.

3 As o'er each continent and island
  The dawn leads on another day,
  The voice of prayer is never silent,
  Nor dies the strain of praise away.

4 The sun that bids us rest is waking
  Our brethren 'neath the western sky,
  And hour by hour fresh lips are making
  Thy wondrous doings heard on high.

5 So be it, Lord; thy throne shall never,
  Like earth's proud empires, pass away;
  Thy Kingdom stands, and grows forever,
  Till all thy creatures own thy sway.
John Ellerton (1826-93)

* * *

see also: 558 At even, ere the sun was set

THE SALVATION SOLDIER
Calling

678 A soldier of the cross, 68; Gerontius, 89
C.M.

AM I a soldier of the cross,
  A follower of the Lamb,
And shall I fear to own his cause,
  Or blush to speak his name?

In the name, the precious name
Of him who died for me,
Through grace I'll win the promised
  crown,
Whate'er my cross may be.

2 Must I be carried to the skies
  On flowery beds of ease,
While others fight to win the prize,
  And sail through stormy seas?

3 Are there no foes for me to face?
  Must I not stem the flood?
Is this vile world a friend to grace,
  To help me on to God?

4 Since I must fight if I would reign,
  Increase my courage, Lord!
I'll bear the toil, endure the pain,
  Supported by thy word.
Isaac Watts (1674-1748) (verses)

679 Be glad in the Lord, 481
8.8.8.8. Amph.

BE strong in the grace of the Lord,
  Be noble and upright and true,
Be valiant for God and the right,
  Live daily your duty to do.
    Be strong! Be strong!
  And God will your courage renew.

2 Be strong in the grace of the Lord,
  For wholehearted service prepare;
Be thoughtful for all who are weak,
  And hasten their burdens to share.
    Be strong! Be strong!
  Be eager to do and to dare.

3 Be strong in the grace of the Lord,
  Be armed with the power of his might;
Be daring when dangers abound,
  Courageous and brave in the fight.
    Be strong! Be strong!
  And victory will be your delight.
Walter Henry Windybank (1872-1952)

The Salvation Soldier

680 Follow thou me, 645

BY the peaceful shores of Galilee,
  Mending their nets by the silvery sea,
The fishermen toiled at their tasks each
      day,
Till the Master walkèd along that way.

Follow thou me, he calls again,
And I will make you fishers of men;
As in the days by Galilee,
Jesus is calling you and me.

2 And they left their nets when they heard
      his voice,
  Making the Master's call their choice;
  And they toiled with him for the world
      astray,
  To bring men back to the Father's way.

3 And the self-same voice is heard today,
  Calling to men in the self-same way
  As the fishermen heard by Galilee:
  Leave now your nets and follow me.
              Sidney Edward Cox (1887-1975)

681 Ring the bell, watchman, 776

COME, join our Army, to battle we go,
  Jesus will help us to conquer the foe;
Fighting for right and opposing the wrong,
The Salvation Army is marching along.

Marching along, marching along,
The Salvation Army is marching along;
Soldiers of Jesus, be valiant and strong;
The Salvation Army is marching along.

2 Come, join our Army, the foe must be
      driven;
  To Jesus, our captain, the world shall be
      given;
  Foes may surround us, we'll press through
      the throng;
  The Salvation Army is marching along.

3 Come, join our Army, the foe we defy,
  True to our colors, we'll fight till we die;
  Saved from all sin is our war cry and song;
  The Salvation Army is marching along.

4 Come, join our Army, and do not delay,
  The time for enlisting is passing away;
  Fierce is the battle, but victory will come;
  The Salvation Army is marching along.
              William James Pearson (1832-92)

682 Forward! be our watchword, 203;
Princethorpe, 206   6.5.6.5. D.

FORWARD! be our watchword,
  Steps and voices joined;
Seek the things before us,
  Not a look behind.
Burns the fiery pillar
  At our army's head;
Who shall dream of shrinking,
  By our captain led?
    Forward through the desert,
      Through the toil and fight;
    Jordan flows before us,
      Zion beams with light.

2 Forward, flock of Jesus,
    Salt of all the earth,
  Till each yearning purpose
    Springs to glorious birth.
  Sick, they ask for healing,
    Blind, they grope for day;
  Pour upon the nations
    Wisdom's loving ray.
      Forward, out of error,
        Leave behind the night;
      Forward through the darkness,
        Forward into light.

3 Glories upon glories
    Hath our God prepared,
  By the souls that love him
    One day to be shared.
  Eye hath not beheld them,
    Ear hath never heard,
  Nor of these hath uttered
    Thought or speech a word.
      Forward, ever forward,
        Where the heaven is bright;
      Till the veil be lifted,
        Till our faith be sight.
              Henry Alford (1810-71)

683 Warrington, 56; Truro, 54; Ernan, 19
                                    L.M.

GO, labor on, spend and be spent,
  Thy joy to do the Father's will;
It is the way the Master went;
  Should not the servant tread it still?

2 Go, labor on, 'tis not for naught,
  Thy earthly loss is heavenly gain;
  Men heed thee, love thee, praise thee not;
  The Master praises; what are men?

Calling

3 Go, labor on, enough while here
   If he shall praise thee; if he deign
Thy willing heart to mark and cheer,
   No toil for him shall be in vain.

4 Go, labor on while it is day,
   The world's dark night is hastening on;
Speed, speed thy work, cast sloth away,
   'Tis only thus that souls are won.

5 Men die in darkness at your side,
   Without a hope to cheer the tomb;
Take up the torch and wave it wide,
   The torch that lights time's thickest
     gloom.

6 Toil on, faint not, keep watch, and pray;
   Be wise the sinning soul to win;
Go forth into the world's highway,
   Compel the wanderer to come in.
Horatius Bonar (1808-89)

684 Stand like the brave, 570; St Denio, 569; Foundation, A.S. 976 11.11.11.11.

GOD'S trumpet is sounding: To arms! is
   the call;
More warriors are wanted to help on the
   war;
My King's in the battle, he's calling for me,
A salvation soldier for Jesus I'll be.

*Stand like the brave! Stand like the
   brave!*
*Stand like the brave, with thy face to
   the foe!*

2 On land and on water my colors I'll show,
   Through ten thousand battles with Jesus
     I'll go,
In danger I'm certain he'll take care of me,
His blood and fire soldier forever I'll be.

3 I'll fight to the last with the Lord's sword
     and shield,
And count it an honor to die in the field;
In death and the grave there is victory for
     me,
A salvation soldier in Glory I'll be.

4 The war will go on till the world is
     possessed,
The Salvation Army Jehovah has blessed;
More heroes of faith on the roll we shall
     see;
The Salvation Army's the Army for me.
William James Pearson (1832-92) (verses),
Fanny Crosby (1820-1915) (chorus)

685 Monks Gate, 212; Pilgrim Song, 213
6.5.6.5.6.6.6.5.

HE who would valiant be
   'Gainst all disaster,
Let him in constancy
   Follow the Master!
There's no discouragement
Shall make him once relent
His first avowed intent
   To be a pilgrim.

2 Who so beset him round
   With dismal stories,
Do but themselves confound,
   His strength the more is.
No foes shall stay his might,
Though he with giants fight;
He will make good his right
   To be a pilgrim.

3 Since, Lord, thou dost defend
   Us with thy Spirit;
We know we at the end
   Shall life inherit.
Then fancies flee away,
I'll fear not what men say,
I'll labor night and day
   To be a pilgrim.
John Bunyan (1628-88),
alt Percy Dearmer (1867-1936)

686 Gird on the armour, 651

I HAVE read of men of faith
   Who have bravely fought till death,
     Who now the crown of life are wearing;
Then the thought comes back to me,
   Can I not a soldier be,
     Like to those martyrs bold and daring?

*I'll gird on the armor and rush to the
     field,*
*Determined to conquer, and never to
     yield;*
   So the enemy shall know,
   Wheresoever I may go,
That I am fighting for Jehovah.

2 I, like them, will take my stand
   With the sword of God in hand,
     Smiling amid opposing legions;
I the victor's crown will gain,
And at last go home to reign
     In Heaven's bright and sunny regions.

The Salvation Soldier

3 I will join at once the fight,
Leaning on my Saviour's might,
  He is almighty to deliver;
From my post I will not shrink,
Though of death's cup I should drink;
  Hell to defeat is my endeavor.

4 Will you not enlist with me,
And a valiant soldier be?
  Vain 'tis to waste your time in slumber;
Jesus calls for men of war
Who will fight and ne'er give o'er,
  Routing the foe in fear and wonder.
Mark William Sanders (1862-1943)

687 I'll stand for Christ, 686

IN the Army of Jesus we've taken our
    stand
  To fight 'gainst the forces of sin,
To the rescue we go, Satan's power to
    o'erthrow,
  And his captives to Jesus we'll win.

I'll stand for Christ, for Christ alone
  Amid the tempest and the storm.
Where Jesus leads I'll follow on;
  I'll stand, I'll stand for Christ alone.

2 We go forth not to fight 'gainst the sinner,
    but sin;
  The lost and the outcast we love;
And the claims of our King we before them
    will bring
  As we urge them his mercy to prove.

3 Jesus pitied our case, and he died for our
    race,
  To save a lost world he was slain;
But he rose and now lives, and his pardon
    he gives
  Unto all who will call on his name.

4 Though our trials be great and God's
    enemies strong,
  To battle undaunted we go,
For our warfare's the Lord's and to him
    we belong,
  In his strength we shall conquer the foe.
Frederick William Fry (1859-1939), alt

688 Armadale, 8; Maryton, 33
                          L.M.

LORD, as we take our chosen way
  In commerce, industry or art,
The state or science, we would pray
  To serve with singleness of heart.

2 Thou, Lord, a craftsman's tools hast plied,
  A craftsman's excellence hast shown,
And honest labor sanctified
  By making human toil thine own.

3 In works or office, field or mart,
  Where our appointments, Lord, may be,
Grant that with mind and hand and heart
  We labor as we would for thee.

4 So shall our light be shed abroad
  And we, as Christians truly named,
Shall strive to be approved of God,
  His workmen, not to be ashamed.
Will J. Brand (1889-1977)

689 Stand like the brave, 570
                          11.11.11.11.

O SOLDIER, awake, for the strife is at
    hand,
With helmet and shield, and a sword in
    thy hand,
To meet the bold tempter, go, fearlesssly
    go,
And stand like the brave, with thy face to
    the foe.

Stand like the brave! Stand like the
    brave!
Stand like the brave, with thy face to
    the foe!

2 Whatever thy danger take heed and
    beware,
But turn not thy back, for no armor is
    there;
If thou wouldst the legions of darkness
    o'erthrow,
Then stand like the brave with thy face to
    the foe.

3 Press on, never doubting, thy captain is
    near
With grace to support, and with comfort
    to cheer;
His love like a stream in the desert will
    flow;
Then stand like the brave, with thy face to
    the foe.
Fanny Crosby (1820-1915)

Calling

690 Onward, Christian soldiers, 205;
Armageddon, 200   6.5.6.5. D.

ONWARD, Christian soldiers,
  Marching as to war,
With the cross of Jesus
  Going on before!
Christ, the royal Master,
  Leads against the foe;
Forward into battle
  See his banners go.

Onward, Christian soldiers,
  Marching as to war,
With the cross of Jesus
  Going on before!

2 At the sign of triumph
    Satan's host doth flee;
  On then, Christian soldiers,
    On to victory!
  Hell's foundations quiver
    At the shout of praise;
  Brothers, lift your voices,
    Loud your anthems raise.

3 Like a mighty army
    Moves the Church of God;
  Brothers, we are treading
    Where the saints have trod.
  We are not divided,
    All one body we,
  One in hope, in doctrine,
    One in charity.

4 Crowns and thrones may perish,
    Kingdoms rise and wane,
  But the Church of Jesus
    Constant will remain.
  Gates of Hell can never
    'Gainst the Church prevail;
  We have Christ's own promise,
    And that cannot fail.

5 Onward then, ye people!
    Join our happy throng,
  Blend with ours your voices
    In the triumph song.
  Glory, laud and honor
    Unto Christ the King,
  This through countless ages
    Men and angels sing.
                    Sabine Baring-Gould (1834-1924)

691 Rescue the perishing, 775

RESCUE the perishing, care for the dying,
  Snatch them in pity from sin and the
    grave;
Weep o'er the erring one, lift up the fallen,
  Tell them of Jesus, the mighty to save.

Rescue the perishing, care for the dying,
  Jesus is merciful, Jesus will save.

2 Though they are slighting him, still he is
    waiting,
  Waiting the penitent child to receive;
  Plead with them earnestly, plead with them
    gently,
  He will forgive if they on him believe.

3 Down in the human heart, crushed by the
    tempter,
  Feelings lie buried that grace can
    restore;
  Touched by a loving hand, wakened by
    kindness,
  Chords that were broken will vibrate
    once more.

4 Rescue the perishing, duty demands it;
  Strength for thy labor the Lord will
    provide;
  Back to the narrow way patiently win them;
  Tell the poor wanderer a Saviour has
    died.
                    Fanny Crosby (1820-1915)

692 Armadale, 8; Arizona, 7
                                    L.M.

SAVIOUR and Lord, we pray to thee,
  Thy people ever would we be;
To thee whose love our lives has sealed,
To thee our lives we gladly yield.

2 A people called by thee to fight,
  We stand united in thy sight,
  One in our aim to vanquish sin,
  And bring thy glorious Kingdom in.

3 In this glad moment while we sing,
  Thy Army, we salute our King;
  By thee we live, on thee rely,
  By thee we'll conquer or we'll die.

4 Our strength for warfare is thy might,
  Our hope of guidance is thy light;
  Pour out thy Spirit while we wait,
  And let thy love thy will dictate.

The Salvation Soldier

5 Beneath thy standard still we'll stay;
　Thy cause shall every purpose sway;
　Nor will we lay our armor down
　Till we exchange it for a crown.
Thomas Hodgson Mundell (1849-1934)

693 Men of Harlech, 732

SOLDIER, rouse thee! War is raging,
　God and fiends are battle waging;
Every ransomed power engaging,
　Break the tempter's spell.
Dare ye still lie fondly dreaming,
Wrapped in ease and worldly scheming,
While the multitudes are streaming
　Downwards into Hell?

Through the world resounding,
Let the gospel sounding,
Summon all, at Jesus' call,
His glorious cross surrounding.
Sons of God, earth's trifles leaving,
Be not faithless but believing;
To your conquering captain cleaving,
　Forward to the fight.

2 Lord, we come, and from thee never
　Self nor earth our hearts shall sever;
　Thine entirely, thine for ever,
　　We will fight and die.
　To a world of rebels dying,
　Heaven and Hell and God defying,
　Everywhere we'll still be crying:
　　Will ye perish, why?

3 Hark! I hear the warriors shouting;
　Now the hosts of Hell we're routing;
　Courage! onward! never doubting
　　We shall win the day.
　See the foe before us falling,
　Sinners on the Saviour calling,
　Throwing off the bondage galling,
　　Join our glad array.
Attr George Scott Railton (1849-1913)

694 All hail, I'm saved! 600

SOLDIERS fighting round the cross,
　Fight for your Lord;
Reckon all things else but loss,
　Fight for your Lord.

All hail, I'm saved!
O come and join our conquering band.
All hail, I'm saved!
We'll conquer if we die.

2 In the name of Christ, your friend,
　Fight for your Lord;
With the powers of Hell contend,
　Fight for your Lord.

3 Fight the fight of faith with me,
　Fight for your Lord;
Jesus gives the victory,
　Fight for your Lord.

4 Be thou faithful, hear him cry,
　Fight for your Lord;
In my service fight and die,
　Fight for your Lord.

5 Faithfully your weapons wield,
　Fight for your Lord;
Stand your ground, and win the field,
　Fight for your Lord.
Anon

695 Falcon Street, 167; From strength to strength, 184; St Ethelwald, 174　S.M.

SOLDIERS of Christ, arise,
　And put your armor on,
Strong in the strength which God supplies
　Through his eternal Son.

2 Strong in the Lord of hosts,
　And in his mighty power,
Who in the strength of Jesus trusts
　Is more than conqueror.

3 Leave no unguarded place,
　No weakness of the soul;
Take every virtue, every grace,
　And fortify the whole.

4 To keep your armor bright
　Attend with constant care,
Still walking in your captain's sight
　And watching unto prayer.

5 That, having all things done,
　And all your conflicts past,
Ye may o'ercome through Christ alone,
　And stand complete at last.

6 From strength to strength go on,
　Wrestle and fight and pray;
Tread all the powers of darkness down,
　And win the well-fought day.
Charles Wesley (1707-88) (verses)

Calling

696
Storm the forts of darkness, 802

SOLDIERS of our God, arise!
   The day is drawing nearer;
Shake the slumber from your eyes,
   The light is growing clearer.
Sit no longer idly by,
While the heedless millions die,
Lift the blood-stained banner high,
   And take the field for Jesus.

Storm the forts of darkness,
Bring them down, bring them down!
Storm the forts of darkness,
Bring them down, bring them down!
Pull down the devil's kingdom,
Where'er he holds dominion;
Storm the forts of darkness, bring
      them down!
Glory, honor to the Lamb,
Praise and power to the Lamb,
Glory, honor, praise and power,
Be forever to the Lamb!

2 See the brazen hosts of Hell,
   Their art and power employing,
More than human tongue can tell,
   The blood-bought souls destroying.
Hark! from ruin's ghastly road
Victims groan beneath their load;
Forward, O ye sons of God,
   And dare or die for Jesus.

3 Warriors of the risen King,
   Great Army of salvation,
Spread his fame, his praises sing
   And conquer every nation.
Raise the glorious standard higher,
Work for victory, never tire;
Forward march with blood and fire,
   And win the world for Jesus.
                    Robert Johnson

697
Monkland, 286; University College, 300;
Michael, row the boat ashore
(with hallelujahs), 285   7.7.7.7.

SOLDIERS of the cross, arise,
   Gird you with your armor bright;
Mighty are your enemies,
   Hard the battle ye must fight.

2 O'er a faithless, fallen world
   Raise your banner in the sky;
Let it float there wide unfurled;
   Bear it onward; lift it high.

3 'Mid the homes of want and woe,
   Strangers to the living word,
Let the Saviour's herald go,
   Let the voice of hope be heard.

4 Where the shadows deepest lie,
   Carry truth's unsullied ray;
Where are crimes of blackest dye,
   There the saving sign display.

5 To the weary and the worn
   Tell of realms where sorrows cease;
To the outcast and forlorn
   Speak of mercy and of peace.

6 Be the banner still unfurled,
   Still unsheathed the Spirit's sword,
Till the kingdoms of the world
   Are the Kingdom of the Lord.
          William Walsham How (1823-97)

698
Sound the battle cry! 794

SOUND the battle cry!
   See, the foe is nigh,
Raise the standard high
   For the Lord.
Gird your armor on;
Stand firm every one;
Rest your cause upon
   His holy word.

Rouse, then, soldiers, rally round the
      banner!
Ready, steady, pass the word along;
Onward, forward, shout aloud hosanna!
   Christ is captain of the mighty
      throng.

2 Strong to meet the foe,
   Marching on we go,
While our cause we know
   Must prevail.
Shield and banner bright,
Gleaming in the light,
Battling for the right,
   We ne'er can fail.

3 O thou God of all,
   Hear us when we call,
Help us one and all
   By thy grace!
When the battle's done,
And the victory won,
May we wear the crown
   Before thy face.
          William Fiske Sherwin (1826-88)

The Salvation Soldier

699 Stand up for Jesus, 264; Geibel, 251;
God bless the Prince of Wales, 252
7.6.7.6. D. Iambic

STAND up, stand up for Jesus,
Ye soldiers of the cross!
Lift high his royal banner,
It must not suffer loss.
From victory unto victory
His army he shall lead
Till every foe is vanquished,
And Christ is Lord indeed.

2 Stand up, stand up for Jesus!
The trumpet call obey;
Forth to the mighty conflict
In this his glorious day.
Ye that are men now serve him
Against unnumbered foes;
Let courage rise with danger,
And strength to strength oppose.

3 Stand up, stand up for Jesus!
Stand in his strength alone;
The arm of flesh will fail you,
Ye dare not trust your own.
Put on salvation armor,
And watching unto prayer,
Where duty calls or danger,
Be never wanting there.

4 Stand up, stand up for Jesus!
The strife will not be long;
This day the noise of battle,
The next the victor's song.
To him that overcometh
A crown of life shall be,
He with the King of Glory
Shall reign eternally.

George Duffield (1818-88)

700 On we march, 763

THE Lord's command to go into the world
and preach the gospel unto all,
Is just as true today as when his first disciples heard this mighty call;
So let us gird ourselves and go to battle
'gainst the powers of sin and wrong,
Join the fight for the right, in his everlasting might, and sing our marching
song:

*On we march with the blood and the
fire,
To the ends of the earth we will go;
And the Saviour's love will be the
theme of our song
Because we love him so.*

2 O'er land and sea the Saviour shows the
way to every soul sunk deep in sin;
From Calvary's rugged cross there flows
a stream to make the foulest sinner
clean;
We'll fill the ranks and, trusting in the God
of hosts to lead our mighty throng,
Join the fight for the right, in his everlasting might, and sing our marching
song:

3 The victory's sure; we're trusting in the
promise of our Saviour, Lord and King;
Lo, I am with you, keeps us free from
doubting; to the heavens our praises
ring;
The whole wide world shall come beneath
the sway of Christ; proclaim it loud and
long,
Join the fight for the right, in his everlasting might, and sing our marching
song:

Charles Mehling (1889-1969)

701 Ellacombe, 147; St Matthew, 157;
The voice of Jesus, 159* D.C.M.

THE Son of God goes forth to war,
A kingly crown to gain,
His blood-red banner streams afar;
Who follows in his train?
Who best can drink his cup of woe,
Triumphant over pain,
Who patient bears his cross below,
He follows in his train.

*We shall not lose the fight of faith,
For Jesus is our Lord,
We lay all carnal weapons down
To take his shining sword.*

2 The martyr first, whose eagle eye
Could pierce beyond the grave,
Who saw his Master in the sky,
And called on him to save;
Like him, with pardon on his tongue
In midst of mortal pain,
He prayed for them that did the wrong;
Who follows in his train?

3 A glorious band, the chosen few
On whom the Spirit came,
Twelve valiant saints, their hope they knew,
And mocked the cross and flame;
They met the tyrant's brandished steel,
The lion's gory mane,
They bowed their necks the death to feel;
Who follows in their train?

Calling

4 A noble army, men and boys,
   The matron and the maid,
Around the Saviour's throne rejoice,
   In robes of light arrayed;
They climbed the steep ascent of Heaven,
   Through peril, toil and pain;
O God, to us may grace be given
   To follow in their train!
Reginald Heber (1783-1826),
Catherine Baird (1895-1984) (chorus)

702   Victory for me, 841

To the front! the cry is ringing;
   To the front! your place is there;
In the conflict men are wanted,
   Men of hope and faith and prayer.
Selfish ends shall claim no right
   From the battle's post to take us;
Fear shall vanish in the fight,
   For triumphant God will make us.

No retreating, Hell defeating,
   Shoulder to shoulder we stand;
God, look down, with glory crown
   Our conquering band.
    Victory for me
Through the blood of Christ, my
    Saviour;
    Victory for me
Through the precious blood.

2 To the front! the fight is raging;
   Christ's own banner leads the way;
Every power and thought engaging,
   Might divine shall be our stay.
We have heard the cry for help
   From the dying millions round us,
We've received the royal command
   From our dying Lord who found us.

3 To the front! no more delaying,
   Wounded spirits need thy care;
To the front! thy Lord obeying,
   Stoop to help the dying there.
Broken hearts and blighted hopes,
   Slaves of sin and degradation,
Wait for thee, in love to bring
   Holy peace and liberation.
Herbert Howard Booth (1862-1926)

703   Fighting On, 557

To the war! to the war! loud and long
   sounds the cry;
To the war! every soldier who fears not to
   die;
See the millions who're drifting to Hell's
   endless woe,
O who in the name of Jehovah will go?

Fighting on, fighting on;
Fighting on, fighting on;
   With the blood and fire
   We will never tire,
We'll fight until the Master calls.

2 To the war! to the war! who'll the war cry
   obey?
'Tis the great God who calls you to fight
   while 'tis day;
Though the battle be fierce, and though
   mighty the foe,
The Salvation Army to victory must go.

3 To the war! to the war! louder rings out
   the cry;
Who'll enlist in this Army all Hell to defy?
All the armor of Heaven our God will
   bestow,
O who in the might of Jehovah will go?

4 To the war! to the war! every man to his
   post;
Go, care for the dying; go, seek for the
   lost;
Hark! converts are singing, their bright
   faces glow,
As they joyfully shout: To the war we will
   go!
M. Stark

704   Meet me at the fountain, 440;
Hyfrydol, 438; Salvator, 443
8.7.8.7. D. Troch.

WANTED, hearts baptized with fire,
   Hearts completely cleansed from sin,
Hearts that will go to the mire,
   Hearts that dare do aught for him;
Hearts that will be firmer, braver,
   Hearts like heroes gone before,
Hearts enjoying God's full favor,
   Hearts to love him more and more.

Hearts to hoist the colors bravely,
   Hearts to share the hardest fight,
Hearts that know their duty clearly,
   Hearts to dare and do the right.

2 Wanted, hearts that beat true ever,
  Hearts that can for others feel,
Hearts that prove the traitor never,
  Hearts that will the wounded heal;
Hearts o'erflowing with compassion,
  Hearts renewed by grace divine,
Hearts aglow with full salvation,
  Hearts to say: Thy will, not mine!

3 Wanted, hearts to love the masses,
  Hearts to help him seek the lost,
Hearts to help him save all classes,
  Hearts to help him save the worst;
Hearts to share with him the weeping,
  Hearts to bear with him the cross,
Hearts to help him with the reaping,
  Hearts to trust through gain or loss.

4 Wanted, hearts like thine, Lord, holy,
  Hearts that in thine image shine,
Hearts that turn from sin and folly,
  Hearts to know no way but thine;
Hearts that unto thee are given,
  Hearts possessed with dying love,
Hearts on earth but filled with Heaven,
  Hearts inspirèd from above.
                    John Lawley (1859-1922)

705 The voice of Jesus, 159
                    D.C.M.

WE'RE in God's Army and we fight
  Wherever wrong is found;
A lowly cot or stately home
  May be our battleground.
We own no man as enemy,
  Sin is our challenged foe;
We follow Jesus, Son of God,
  As to the war we go.

We shall not lose the fight of faith,
  For Jesus is our Lord,
We lay all carnal weapons down
  To take his shining sword.

2 When our invading forces march,
  In every tongue we sing;
We are of every class and race,
  Yet one in Christ, the King.
Our Master's darkest battlefield,
  Upon a lonely height,
Reveals God's sword to everyone,
  A cross of love and light.

3 His Kingdom cometh not by force
  But, by the gentle power
Of righteousness and truth and grace,
  He triumphs every hour.

Sometimes his happy people march
  With banners floating high,
Though often in secluded ways,
  They fight that self may die.

4 The good fight is the fight of faith,
  Heaven's victories are won
By men unarmed, save with the mind
  That was in Christ, the Son.
As morning overwhelms the night,
  So truth shall sin o'erthrow,
And love at last shall vanquish hate
  As sunshine melts the snow.
                    Catherine Baird (1895-1984)

706 Just where he needs me, 546
                    11.10.11.10.

WHAT can I say to cheer a world of
    sorrow?
How bring back hope where men have
    sorely failed?
Just where I am I'll speak the word of
    comfort,
  Tell how for me Christ's sacrifice availed.

Just where he needs me, my Lord has
    placed me,
Just where he needs me, there would I
    be!
And since he found me, by love he's
    bound me
  To serve him joyfully.

2 What can I do to ease life's heavy burdens?
  What can I do to help mankind in need?
Just where I am I'll share my neighbor's
    hardship,
  Lighten his load, and prove a friend
    indeed.

3 What can I do to justify my living?
  What can I be to make this life
    worthwhile?
I'll be a voice to call men to the Saviour,
  Just where I am, and win my Father's
    smile.
                    Miriam M. Richards (1911-89)

707 Armageddon, 200; Rachie, 207
                    6.5.6.5. D.

WHO is on the Lord's side?
  Who will serve the King?
Who will be his helpers
  Other lives to bring?
Who will leave the world's side?
  Who will face the foe?
Who is on the Lord's side?
  Who for him will go?

By thy grand redemption,
By thy grace divine,
We are on the Lord's side;
Saviour, we are thine.

2 Not for weight of glory,
Not for crown and palm,
Enter we the army,
Raise the warrior psalm;
But for love that claimeth
Lives for whom he died;
He whom Jesus nameth
Must be on his side.

3 Jesus, thou hast bought us,
Not with gold or gem,
But with thine own life-blood
For thy diadem.
With thy blessing filling
Each who comes to thee,
Thou hast made us willing,
Thou hast made us free.

4 Fierce may be the conflict,
Strong may be the foe,
But the King's own army
None can overthrow.
Round his standard ranging,
Victory is secure,
For this truth unchanging
Makes the triumph sure.

Master, thou wilt keep us,
By thy grace divine,
Always on the Lord's side,
Saviour, always thine.
Frances Ridley Havergal (1836-79)

708 The home over there, 483; We speak of the realms, 484   8.8.8.8. Amph.

WHO'LL fight for the Lord everywhere,
Till we march by the river of light,
Where the Lamb leads his hosts free from care,
All robed in their garments of white?

Everywhere, everywhere, who'll fight
for the Lord everywhere?

2 O think of the sin everywhere,
And how grievous man's darkness and loss,
Of the burden of shame he must bear
Till, repentant, he kneels at the cross.

3 O Lord, lead us forth everywhere
Till each sin-burdened soul knows thy rest,
Till thy name and thy nature they share,
And with peace all the nations are blessed.

4 I'll fight for the Lord everywhere,
For the need of the lost I can see;
Many dying in sin everywhere,
My Jesus alone can set free.
George Scott Railton (1849-1913), alt

see also: 564 Come ye yourselves apart
749 Oft have I heard thy tender voice
977 Lead on O King eternal
979 Are ye able
980 Truehearted, whole hearted

Faith and Trust

709 Down in the garden, 84   C.M.

A FRIEND of Jesus! O what bliss
That one, so vile as I,
Should ever have a friend like this
To lead me to the sky!

Friendship with Jesus, fellowship
divine,
O what blessèd sweet communion,
Jesus is a friend of mine!

2 A friend when other friendships cease,
A friend when others fail,
A friend who gives me joy and peace,
A friend who will prevail.

3 A friend when sickness lays me low,
A friend when death draws near,
A friend as through the vale I go,
A friend to help and cheer.

4 A friend when life's short race is o'er,
A friend when earth is past,
A friend to meet on Heaven's shore,
A friend when home at last.
Joseph C. Ludgate (d 1947)

710 He hideth my soul, 537;
Behold Him! 536   11.8.11.8.

A WONDERFUL Saviour is Jesus, my Lord,
A wonderful Saviour to me;
He hideth my soul in the cleft of the rock,
Where rivers of pleasure I see.

*He hideth my soul in the cleft of the
  rock
That shadows a dry, thirsty land;
He hideth my life in the depths of his
  love,
And covers me there with his hand.*

2 A wonderful Saviour is Jesus, my Lord,
     He taketh my burden away;
   He holdeth me up and I shall not be moved,
     He giveth me strength as my day.

3 With numberless blessings each moment
     he crowns,
   And, filled with his goodness divine,
   I sing in my rapture: O glory to God
   For such a redeemer as mine!
                Fanny Crosby (1820-1915)

711 Trust in God, 838

AS the varied way of life we journey,
  Come the plains and then the
    mountainside,
Come the days of joy when birds are
    singing,
  And the world is fair and sweet and wide;
Then a deeper joy comes, overfilling,
  From the everlasting throne of love,
And all other joy is but an echo
  From the ever-blessèd heights above.

2 There are shadows on the earthly pathway
     Where, at times uncertainly, we tread;
   In perplexity we halt and linger
     Till our faith again is upward led.
   For the heights of truth are ever calling,
     And celestial radiance from afar
   On our pilgrim way is gently falling
     For our comfort where the shadows are.

3 In the days of peace and golden sunshine,
     In the days of joy, or days of woe,
   There is confidence in him who holds us;
     There is light to guide us here below.
   And beyond await the heights of rapture
     Where all earthly joys, transcended, fade
   In the glory of the Saviour's presence,
     In the home eternal he has made.
                          Lily Sampson

712 Montgomery, 535; Houghton, 533;
Begone, Unbelief, 530 10.10.11.11.

BEGONE, unbelief,
  My Saviour is near,
And for my relief
  Will surely appear;
By prayer let me wrestle,
  And he will perform;
With Christ in the vessel,
  I smile at the storm.

2 Though dark be my way,
     Since he is my guide,
   'Tis mine to obey,
     'Tis his to provide;
   Though cisterns be broken
   And creatures all fail,
   The word he has spoken
   Will surely prevail.

3 His love in time past
     Forbids me to think
   He'll leave me at last
     In trouble to sink;
   Each sweet Ebenezer
     I have in review
   Confirms his good pleasure
     To help me quite through.

4 Since all that I meet
     Shall work for my good,
   The bitter is sweet,
     The medicine food;
   Though painful at present,
     'Twill cease before long,
   And then O how pleasant
     The conqueror's song!
                John Newton (1725-1807)

713 Blessèd Lord, 410; Helmsley, 417
8.7.8.7.8.7. Troch.

BLESSÈD Lord, in thee is refuge,
  Safety for my trembling soul,
Power to lift my head when drooping
  'Midst the angry billows' roll.
    I will trust thee,
  All my life thou shalt control.

2 In the past too unbelieving
     'Midst the tempest I have been,
   And my heart has slowly trusted
     What my eyes have never seen.
       Blessèd Jesus,
     Teach me on thy arm to lean.

3 O for trust that brings the triumph
When defeat seems strangely near!
O for faith that changes fighting
Into victory's ringing cheer;
Faith triumphant,
Knowing not defeat or fear!
Herbert Howard Booth (1862-1926)

714 Pembroke, 467; He Lives, 466*
8.8.6.8.8.6.

BUT can it be that I should prove
Forever faithful to thy love,
From sin forever cease?
I thank thee for the blessèd hope;
It lifts my drooping spirit up,
It gives me back my peace.

*He lives, He lives,
I know that my redeemer lives.*

2 In thee, O Lord, I put my trust,
Mighty and merciful and just;
Thy sacred word is passed;
And I, who dare thy word receive,
Without committing sin shall live,
Shall live to God at last.

3 I rest in thine almighty power;
The name of Jesus is a tower
That hides my life above;
Thou canst, thou wilt my helper be;
My confidence is all in thee,
The faithful God of love.

4 Wherefore, in never-ceasing prayer,
My soul to thy continual care
I faithfully commend;
Assured that thou through life shalt save,
And show thyself beyond the grave
My everlasting friend.
Charles Wesley (1707-88)

715 St Michael, 175; Silchester, 177
S.M.

COMMIT thou all thy griefs
And ways into his hands,
To his sure trust and tender care
Who Heaven and earth commands.

2 Who points the clouds their course,
Whom winds and seas obey,
He shall direct thy wandering feet,
He shall prepare thy way.

3 Thou on the Lord rely,
So safe shalt thou go on;
Fix on his work thy steadfast eye,
So shall thy work be done.

4 No profit canst thou gain
By self-consuming care;
To him commend thy cause, his ear
Attends the softest prayer.

5 Thy everlasting truth,
Father, thy ceaseless love
Sees all thy children's wants, and knows
What best for each will prove.
*Paulus Gerhardt (1607-76),
trs John Wesley (1703-91)*

716 Courage, Brother, 432; Bethany, 429
8.7.8.7. D. Troch.

COURAGE, brother, do not stumble,
Though thy path be dark as night;
There's a star to guide the humble:
Trust in God and do the right.
Let the road be long and dreary,
And its end far out of sight,
Foot it bravely, strong or weary:
Trust in God and do the right.

2 Simple rule and safest guiding,
Inward peace and inward light,
Star upon our path abiding:
Trust in God and do the right.
Courage, brother, do not stumble,
Though thy path be dark as night;
There's a star to guide the humble:
Trust in God and do the right.
Norman Macleod (1812-72)

717 Wiltshire, 143; Ellacombe, 147
C.M.

DEAR Lord, I lift my heart to thee,
My helplessness I own;
The way before I cannot see,
I dare not walk alone.

2 More clearly would I realize
Thy presence and thy power,
Not only under summer skies,
But in the darkest hour.

3 Not only when I sense thee near
Art thou most surely nigh,
Nor hast thou, Lord, a quicker ear
Because my faith is high.

4 My changing moods do not control
Thy covenanted aid;
Thou hast the guarding of my soul,
And I am not afraid.

5 So often in the pleasant place
Our faith depends on sight;
The temper of my trust must face
Its trial in the night.

The Salvation Soldier

6 Then quietness and confidence
  And waiting on the Lord
Shall be my strength, my sure defense,
And peace be my reward.

John Izzard

718 Duke Street, 17; Pentecost, 40
L.M.

FIGHT the good fight with all thy might,
  Christ is thy strength, and Christ thy
    right;
Lay hold on life, and it shall be
Thy joy and crown eternally.

2 Run the straight race through God's good
    grace,
Lift up thine eyes and seek his face;
Life with its way before us lies,
Christ is the path, and Christ the prize.

3 Cast care aside, lean on thy guide,
  His boundless mercy will provide;
Lean, and the trusting soul shall prove
Christ is thy life, and Christ thy love.

4 Faint not, nor fear, his arms are near,
  He changeth not, and thou art dear;
Only believe, and thou shalt see
That Christ is all in all to thee.

John Samuel Bewley Monsell (1811-75)

719 Troyte, 470
8.8.8.4.

FOR thy sweet comfort in distress,
  For aid when heavy burdens press,
My love for thee I will confess,
  And thank thee, Lord.

2 For strength to tread a lonely way,
For darkness changed to shining day,
For burdens lifted when I pray,
  I thank thee, Lord.

3 For ease which comes swift after pain,
For peace which follows after strain,
For seeming loss now turned to gain,
  I thank thee, Lord.

4 When shadows fall and dark the night,
When clouds hang low, no ray of light,
Thy loveliness breaks on my sight,
  I thank thee, Lord.

5 Lord, grant me courage, make me strong,
However steep the way, and long,
That I may sing the conqueror's song,
  And thank thee, Lord.

Doris N. Rendell (1896-1990)

720 Stella, 503; Eaton, 491
8.8.8.8.8.8. Iambic

GIVE me the faith which can remove
  And sink the mountain to a plain;
Give me the childlike praying love
  Which longs to build thy house again;
Thy love let it my heart o'erpower,
And all my simple soul devour.

2 I want an even, strong desire,
  I want a calmly fervent zeal,
To save poor souls out of the fire,
  To snatch these from the verge of Hell,
And turn them to a pardoning God,
And quench the brands in Jesus' blood.

3 I would the precious time redeem,
  And longer live for this alone,
To spend, and to be spent for them
  Who have not yet my Saviour known;
Fully on them my labors prove,
And only breathe to breathe thy love.

4 My talents, gifts, and graces, Lord,
  Into thy blessèd hands receive;
And let me live to preach thy word,
  And let me to thy glory live;
My every sacred moment spend
In publishing the sinner's friend.

5 Enlarge, inflame and fill my heart
  With boundless charity divine;
So shall I all my strength exert,
  And love them with a zeal like thine,
And lead them to thy open side,
The sheep for whom their shepherd died.

Charles Wesley (1707-88)

721 Lascelles, 170; Franconia, 168;
Southport, 178
S.M.

GIVE to the winds thy fears;
  Hope, and be undismayed;
God hears thy sighs and counts thy tears,
  God shall lift up thy head.

2 Through waves and clouds and storms
  He gently clears thy way;
Wait thou his time, so shall this night
  Soon end in joyous day.

3 What though thou rulest not?
  Yet Heaven and earth and Hell
Proclaim God sitteth on the throne,
  And ruleth all things well.

4 Far, far above thy thought
  His counsel shall appear,
When fully he the work hath wrought
  That caused thy needless fear.

Faith and Trust

5   Let us in life, in death,
      Thy steadfast truth declare,
  And publish with our latest breath
      Thy love and guardian care.

Paulus Gerhardt (1607-76),
trs John Wesley (1703-91)

722
Happy People, 416; Praise, my soul, 422
8.7.8.7.8.7. Troch.

HAPPY we who trust in Jesus,
    Sweet our portion is and sure;
When despair or doubt would seize us,
    By his grace we shall endure.
      Happy people,
    Happy, in his love secure!

2 God in love and mercy found us,
    We are precious in his sight;
  And though Satan's hosts surround us,
    They shall all be put to flight,
      For our Father
    Keeps us safe by day and night.

3 Lo! our Father never slumbers,
    Ever watchful is his care;
  We rely not on our numbers,
    In his strength secure we are.
      Sweet our portion
    Who the Father's kindness share.

4 As the bird beneath her feathers
    Guards the objects of her care,
  So the Lord his children gathers,
    Spreads his wings, and hides us there;
      Thus protected,
    All our foes we boldly dare.

Thomas Kelly (1769-1855), alt

723
Dennis, 165; Southport, 178
S.M.

HAVE faith in God, my heart,
    Trust and be unafraid;
God will fulfil in every part
    Each promise he has made.

2 Have faith in God, my mind,
    Though oft thy light burns low;
  God's mercy holds a wiser plan
    Than thou canst fully know.

3 Have faith in God, my soul,
    His cross for ever stands;
  And neither life nor death can pluck
    His children from his hands.

4 Lord Jesus, make me whole;
    Grant me no resting place,
Until I rest, heart, mind and soul,
    The captive of thy grace.

Bryn Austin Rees (1911-83)

724
Kitching, 710

HAVE we not known it, have we not heard
    it?
    Power unto God belongs.
Yet do we daily find in his mercy
    Themes for the sweetest songs;
Healing the wounded, raising the fallen,
    Making the blind to see,
Saying to all who seek his face
These precious words of redeeming grace:

No more! No more!
He remembers sins no more,
They are pardoned for ever,
And he will never
Bring them up against me any more.
I'll hear no more
Of the evil days of yore;
I'm a pardoned offender,
And God will remember them no more.

2 Joy-bursts of singing gaily are springing
    With every day that starts;
  If we were silent then would the stones
      cry
    Shame on our fainting hearts.
  O banish sadness, sing now for gladness!
    Glory in Christ, the Lord!
  Who is a God like unto thee,
  One who can pardon iniquity?

3 Safe in the dark day; safe in the bright
      day;
    Safe till my latest breath;
  There is endurance in this assurance,
    Stronger than fear of death.
  When the accuser comes to the judgment,
    Seeking my soul to claim,
  I have a token in the blood,
  I have the word of a pardoning God.

Albert Orsborn (1886-1967)

725
He leadeth me! 21;
He wipes the tear, 63
L.M.

HE leadeth me! O blessèd thought!
    O words with heavenly comfort fraught!
Whate'er I do, where'er I be,
Still 'tis God's hand that leadeth me.

The Salvation Soldier

He leadeth me, he leadeth me!
By his own hand he leadeth me;
His faithful follower I will be,
For by his hand he leadeth me.

2 Sometimes 'mid scenes of deepest gloom,
Sometimes where Eden's bowers bloom,
By waters still, o'er troubled sea,
Still 'tis his hand that leadeth me.

3 Lord, I would clasp thy hand in mine,
Nor ever murmur or repine,
Content, whatever lot I see,
Since 'tis my God that leadeth me.

4 And when my task on earth is done,
When by thy grace the victory's won,
E'en death's cold wave I will not flee,
Since God through Jordan leadeth me.

Joseph Henry Gilmore (1834-1918)

726 Hold thou my hand! 543
11.10.11.10.

HOLD thou my hand! so weak I am, and helpless,
   I dare not take one step without thy aid;
Hold thou my hand! for then, O loving Saviour,
   No dread of ill shall make my soul afraid.

2 Hold thou my hand! and closer, closer draw me
   To thy dear self, my hope, my joy, my all;
Hold thou my hand, lest haply I should wander,
   And, missing thee, my trembling feet should fall.

3 Hold thou my hand! the way is dark before me
   Without the sunlight of thy face divine;
But when by faith I catch its radiant glory,
   What heights of joy, what rapturous songs are mine.

4 Hold thou my hand! that when I reach the margin
   Of that lone river thou didst cross for me,
A heavenly light may flash across its waters,
   And every wave like crystal bright shall be.

Fanny Crosby (1820-1915)

727 Bullinger, 342; Stephanos, 343
8.5.8.3.

I AM trusting thee, Lord Jesus,
   Trusting only thee;
Trusting thee for full salvation,
   Great and free.

2 I am trusting thee for pardon,
   At thy feet I bow;
For thy grace and tender mercy
   Trusting now.

3 I am trusting thee for cleansing
   In the crimson flood;
Trusting thee to make me holy
   By thy blood.

4 I am trusting thee to guide me;
   Thou alone shalt lead,
Every day and hour supplying
   All my need.

5 I am trusting thee for power,
   Thine can never fail;
Words which thou thyself shalt give me
   Must prevail.

6 I am trusting thee, Lord Jesus,
   Never let me fall;
I am trusting thee for ever,
   And for all.

Frances Ridley Havergal (1836-79)

728 Mozart, 496
8.8.8.8.8.8. Iambic

I DWELL within the secret place
Where refuge from my foes I find;
And leaving cumbering cares with him
   Ensures for me an even mind.
The guest of God! O thought sublime,
That he my host should be through time!

2 While in his dwelling place I stay,
   A favored and contented guest,
His angels hold a charge divine
   To keep my feet in ways of rest.
The guest of God! What ecstasy
That I should share his sanctuary!

3 No fears can wake my darkest nights,
   No clouds can spoil my brightest days;
While sheltering 'neath his holy roof
   His guardian care evokes my praise.
The guest of God, below, above!
My life surrounded is by love!

200

4 But more is he than host to me
    And I am more to him than guest;
    He is my Saviour and my friend,
    Eternal love made manifest.
    The guest of God! Such happiness
    My simple tongue fails to express!
        Arch R. Wiggins (1893-1976)

729   Thou art enough for me, 53   L.M.

I KNEEL beside thy sacred cross,
    And count for thee my life as dross;
O satisfy my soul this hour
With thy dear love, my healing power.

Thou art enough for me,
Thou art enough for me;
O precious, living, loving Lord,
Yes, thou art enough for me!

2 My helpless soul, rest thou in God
    And lean upon his faithful word,
    So in my heart, Lord, thou shalt find
    That I am to thy will resigned.

3 At times 'tis hard for flesh and blood
    To say: Thy will be done, my God;
    But if my grief means others' gain,
    O what to me are loss and pain!

4 Through every fear my soul doth climb
    Above the things of passing time,
    And to my eyes the sight is given
    Which makes my earth a present Heaven.
        William Elwin Oliphant (1860-1941)

730   I know whom I have believed, 97   C.M.

I KNOW not why God's wondrous grace
    To me he hath made known;
Nor why, unworthy of such grace,
    He claimed me for his own.

But I know whom I have believèd,
And am persuaded that he is able
To keep that which I've committed
Unto him against that day.

2 I know not how this saving faith
    To me he did impart,
Nor how believing in his word
    Wrought peace within my heart.

3 I know not how the Spirit moves,
    Convincing men of sin;
Revealing Jesus through the word,
    Creating faith in him.

4 I know not what of good or ill
    May be reserved for me,
Of weary ways or golden days,
    Before his face I see.
        Daniel Webster Whittle (1840-1901)

731   I must have the Saviour with me, 376   8.7.8.7. Troch.

I MUST have the Saviour with me,
    For I dare not walk alone;
I must feel his presence near me,
    And his arm around me thrown.

Then my soul shall fear no ill;
Let him lead me where he will,
I will go without a murmur,
And his footsteps follow still.

2 I must have the Saviour with me,
    For my faith at best is weak;
He can whisper words of comfort
    That no other voice can speak.

3 I must have the Saviour with me
    In the onward march of life;
Through the tempest and the sunshine,
    Through the battle and the strife.
        Fanny Crosby (1820-1915)

732   I'm in his hands, 687

I SHALL not fear though darkened clouds
    may gather round me;
    The God I serve is one who cares and
      understands.
Although the storms I face would threaten
    to confound me,
    Of this I am assured: I'm in his hands.

I'm in his hands, I'm in his hands;
Whate'er the future holds
  I'm in his hands,
The days I cannot see
Have all been planned for me;
His way is best, you see;
  I'm in his hands.

2 What though I cannot know the way that
    lies before me?
    I still can trust and freely follow his
      commands;
My faith is firm since it is he that watches
    o'er me;
    Of this I'm confident: I'm in his hands.

3 In days gone by my Lord has always
    proved sufficient,
  When I have yielded to the law of love's
    demands;
  Why should I doubt that he would ever-
    more be present
    To make his will my own? I'm in his
    hands!

Stanley E. Ditmer

733 Trentham, 180; Silchester, 177
S.M.

I WANT the faith of God,
  Great mountains to remove,
Full confidence in Jesus' blood,
  The faith that works by love.

2 The faith that will rejoice,
  To saints by Jesus given,
That turns the key of Paradise
  And saves from earth to Heaven.

3 I want the faith that wears,
  That can Jehovah see,
That glad life's heaviest burden bears,
  That grips eternity.

4 The faith that cannot fail,
  That makes salvation sure,
Anchored within the heavenly veil,
  The faith that will endure.

5 I want the faith that fires,
  And gives me heat and light,
That all my soul with zeal inspires,
  That makes me love to fight.

6 The faith that saves from sin,
  That will for victory strive,
That brings the power of God within
  And keeps my soul alive.

William James Pearson (1832-92)

734 Thou Shepherd of Israel, 487;
In the strength of the Lord, 485*
8.8.8.8. D. Amph.

I'LL go in the strength of the Lord,
  In paths he has marked for my feet;
I'll follow the light of his word,
  Nor shrink from the dangers I meet.
His presence my steps shall attend,
  His fulness my wants shall supply;
On him, till my journey shall end,
  My unwavering faith shall rely.

I'll go, (I'll go,) I'll go in the strength,
I'll go in the strength of the Lord,
I'll go, (I'll go,) I'll go in the strength,
I'll go in the strength of the Lord.

[repeat last line after third verse]

2 I'll go in the strength of the Lord
  To work he appoints me to do;
In joy which his smile doth afford
  My soul shall her vigor renew.
His wisdom shall guard me from harm,
  His power my sufficiency prove;
I'll trust his omnipotent arm,
  And prove his unchangeable love.

3 I'll go in the strength of the Lord
  To conflicts which faith will require,
His grace as my shield and reward,
  My courage and zeal shall inspire.
Since he gives the word of command,
  To meet and encounter the foe,
With his sword of truth in my hand,
  To suffer and triumph I'll go.

Edward Turney (1816-72)

735 Gerontius, 89; Colne, 79
C.M.

I'M not ashamed to own my Lord,
  Or to defend his cause,
Maintain the honor of his word,
  The glory of his cross.

2 Jesus, my God! I know his name,
  His name is all my trust;
Nor will he put my soul to shame,
  Nor let my hope be lost.

3 Firm as his throne his promise stands,
  And he can well secure
What I've committed to his hands
  Till the decisive hour.

4 Then will he own my worthless name
  Before his Father's face,
And in the new Jerusalem
  Appoint my soul a place.

Isaac Watts (1674-1748)

736 Penlan, 259; Rutherford, 260
7.6.7.6. D. Iambic

IN heavenly love abiding,
  No change my heart shall fear;
And safe is such confiding,
  For nothing changes here.
The storm may roar without me,
  My heart may low be laid;
But God is round about me,
  And can I be dismayed?

2 Wherever he may guide me,
  No want shall turn me back;
My shepherd is beside me,
  And nothing can I lack.
His wisdom ever waketh,
  His sight is never dim;
He knows the way he taketh,
  And I will walk with him.

3 Green pastures are before me
  Which yet I have not seen;
Bright skies will soon be o'er me,
  Where the dark clouds have been.
My hope I cannot measure,
  My path to life is free;
My Saviour has my treasure,
  And he will walk with me.

Anna Laetitia Waring (1823-1910)

737 Hollingside, 323; Aberystwyth, 320;
Ramsgate, 312   7.7.7.7. D.

JESUS, lover of my soul,
  Let me to thy bosom fly,
While the nearer waters roll,
  While the tempest still is high.
Hide me, O my Saviour, hide,
  Till the storm of life be past;
Safe into the haven guide;
  O receive my soul at last!

2 Other refuge have I none,
  Hangs my helpless soul on thee;
Leave, ah! leave me not alone,
  Still support and comfort me.
All my trust on thee is stayed,
  All my help from thee I bring;
Cover my defenseless head
  With the shadow of thy wing.

3 Thou, O Christ, art all I want,
  More than all in thee I find;
Raise the fallen, cheer the faint,
  Heal the sick, and lead the blind.
Just and holy is thy name,
  I am all unrighteousness;
False and full of sin I am,
  Thou art full of truth and grace.

4 Plenteous grace with thee is found,
  Grace to cover all my sin;
Let the healing streams abound,
  Make and keep me pure within.
Thou of life the fountain art,
  Freely let me take of thee;
Spring thou up within my heart,
  Rise to all eternity.

Charles Wesley (1707-88)

738 St Matthias, 500; Solid Rock, 501
8.8.8.8.8.8. Iambic

LEAVE God to order all thy ways,
  And hope in him whate'er betide;
Thou'lt find him in the evil days
  Thy all-sufficient strength and guide;
Who trusts in God's unchanging love
Builds on the rock that naught can move.

2 Only thy restless heart keep still,
  And wait in cheerful hope, content
To take whate'er his gracious will,
  His all-discerning love, hath sent;
Nor doubt our inmost wants are known
To him who chose us for his own.

3 Sing, pray, and swerve not from his ways,
  But do thine own part faithfully;
Trust his rich promises of grace,
  So shall they be fulfilled in thee;
God never yet forsook at need
The soul that trusted him indeed.

Georg Christian Neumark (1621-81),
trs Catherine Winkworth (1827-78)

739 Brahms' Lullaby, 623

LET thy heart be at rest,
  For the Father is shown
In the love of our Master
  Whose work is made known;
Only walk in his way
  And thy soul shall be free,
For the peace of the Lord
  Shall be laid upon thee.

2 Let thy heart be at rest
  When life's pathway runs steep,
And with death there's a tryst
  That the body must keep;
Though the future is veiled
  Thou shalt not be afraid,
For the peace of the Lord
  On thy heart has been laid.

3 He has journeyed before thee,
  A place to prepare;
Now the Comforter guides thee
  To be with him there;
In the heart of the Father
  Thy dwelling shall be,
For the peace of the Lord
  Has been laid upon thee.

Catherine Baird (1895-1984)

740 Hammond, 524; Love's old sweet song, 525*   10.10.10.10.10.10.

LIKE to a lamb who from the fold has
    strayed
Far on the mountain, of the dark afraid,
Seeking a shelter from the night's alarm,
Longing for comfort of the shepherd's arm,
So Jesus found me on sin's mountain
    drear,
Gathered me close and banished all my
    fear.

*In the love of Jesus there is all I need,
While I follow closely where my Lord
    may lead;
    By his grace forgiven,
    In his presence blest,
    In the love of Jesus,
In the love of Jesus, is perfect rest.*

**In the love of Jesus there is all I need,
While I follow closely where my Lord
    may lead;
    By his grace forgiven,
    In his presence blest,
    In the love of Jesus, is perfect rest,
    Is perfect rest.*

2 Like to a pilgrim in an unknown land
Seeking the comfort of a guiding hand,
Fearing the perils of the winding way,
Pleading for strength sufficient every day,
I met my Lord; and, though the path be
    dim,
He knows the way and I will walk with
    him.

3 Like to a child who, when the night may
    fall,
Out of the darkness hears his father call,
Far and a-weary though his feet may roam,
Sees in the distance shining lights of
    home,
So at the last the music of his voice
Will calm my fears and make my heart
    rejoice.

                 Ivy Mawby (1903-83)

741 Pembroke, 467; Praise, 468; Christ is all, 463*   8.8.6.8.8.6.

LORD Jesus, thou dost keep thy child
    Through sunshine or through tempest
    wild;
    Jesus, I trust in thee.
Thine is such wondrous power to save;
Thine is the mighty love that gave
    Its all on Calvary.

**Christ is all, yes, all in all,
My Christ is all in all.*

2 O glorious Saviour, thee I praise!
To thee my new glad song I raise,
    And tell of what thou art.
Thy grace is boundless in its store;
Thy face of love shines evermore;
    Thou givest me thy heart.

3 Upon thy promises I stand,
Trusting in thee; thine own right hand
    Doth keep and comfort me.
My soul doth triumph in thy word;
Thine, thine be all the praise, dear Lord,
    As thine the victory.

4 Love perfecteth what it begins;
Thy power doth save me from my sins;
    Thy grace upholdeth me.
This life of trust, how glad, how sweet;
My need and thy great fulness meet,
    And I have all in thee.

             Jean Sophia Pigott (1845-82)
             W. H. Williams (chorus)

742 Chalvey, 181; Diademata, 182   D.S.M.

MY faith looks up to thee,
    My faith so small, so slow;
It lifts its drooping eyes to thee,
    And claims the blessing now.
    Thy wondrous gift, O Lord,
    By faith it sees afar,
Thy perfect love it claims to share;
    It doth not, cannot fear.

2   My faith takes hold of thee,
    My faith so weak, so faint;
It lifts its trembling hands to thee,
    Trembling, but violent.
    The Kingdom of thy love,
    E'en now, it takes by force,
And waits till thou, its last resource,
    Shall seal and sanctify.

3   My faith holds fast on thee,
    My faith still small, but sure;
Its anchor holds alone to thee,
    Whose presence keeps me pure.
    And thou, all-conquering Lord,
    Always to see and hear,
By night, by day, art ever near,
    Art ever near to me.

             Bramwell Booth (1856-1929)

Faith and Trust

743 Harlan, 215; Light, 216
6.6.4.6.6.6.4.

MY faith looks up to thee,
Thou Lamb of Calvary,
Saviour divine;
Now hear me while I pray,
Take all my guilt away,
O let me from this day
Be wholly thine!

2 May thy rich grace impart
Strength to my fainting heart,
My zeal inspire;
As thou hast died for me,
O may my love to thee
Pure, warm and changeless be,
A living fire!

3 While life's dark maze I tread,
And griefs around me spread,
Be thou my guide;
Bid darkness turn to day,
Wipe sorrow's tears away,
Nor let me ever stray
From thee aside.

4 When ends life's transient dream,
When death's cold, sullen stream
Shall o'er me roll,
Blest Saviour, then in love,
Fear and distrust remove;
O bear me safe above,
A ransomed soul!

Ray Palmer (1808-87)

744 Almsgiving, 469; Troyte, 470
8.8.8.4.

MY God, my Father, make me strong,
When tasks of life seem hard and long,
To greet them with this triumph-song:
Thy will be done.

2 Draw from my timid eyes the veil,
To show, where earthly forces fail,
Thy power and love must still prevail,
Thy will be done.

3 With confident and humble mind,
Freedom in service I would find,
Praying through every toil assigned,
Thy will be done.

4 Things deemed impossible I dare,
Thine is the call and thine the care;
Thy wisdom shall the way prepare,
Thy will be done.

5 All power is here and round me now,
Faithful I stand in rule and vow,
While 'tis not I, but ever thou:
Thy will be done.

6 Heaven's music chimes the glad days in,
Hope soars beyond death, pain and sin,
Faith shouts in triumph, love must win,
Thy will be done.

Frederic Mann (1846-1928)

745 Will your anchor hold? 60;
Solid Rock, 501   L.M.

MY hope is built on nothing less
Than Jesus' blood and righteousness,
I dare not trust the sweetest frame,
But wholly lean on Jesus' name.

On Christ, the solid rock, I stand,
All other ground is sinking sand.

2 When darkness seems to veil his face,
I rest on his unchanging grace;
In every high and stormy gale,
My anchor holds within the veil.

3 His oath, his covenant and blood,
Support me in the 'whelming flood;
When all around my soul gives way,
He then is all my hope and stay.

Edward Mote (1797-1874)

746 Euphony, 493; Solid Rock, 501
8.8.8.8.8.8. Iambic

NOW I have found the ground wherein
Sure my soul's anchor may remain,
The wounds of Jesus, for my sin
Before the world's foundation slain;
Whose mercy shall unshaken stay
When Heaven and earth are fled away.

2 O Love, thou bottomless abyss,
My sins are swallowed up in thee!
Covered is my unrighteousness,
Nor spot of guilt remains on me,
While Jesus' blood, through earth and
skies:
Mercy, free, boundless mercy, cries.

3 With faith I plunge me in this sea,
Here is my hope, my joy, my rest;
Hither, when Hell assails, I flee,
I look into my Saviour's breast;
Away, sad doubt and anxious fear!
Mercy is all that's written there.

The Salvation Soldier

4 Though waves and storms go o'er my head,
  Though strength and health and friends
    be gone,
  Though joys be withered all and dead,
  Though every comfort be withdrawn,
  On this my steadfast soul relies:
  Father, thy mercy never dies.

5 Fixed on this ground will I remain,
  Though my heart fail and flesh decay;
  This anchor shall my soul sustain,
  When earth's foundations melt away;
  Mercy's full power I then shall prove,
  Loved with an everlasting love.
        Johann Andreas Rothe (1688-1758),
        trs John Wesley (1703-91)

747 Pembroke, 467;
                            8.8.6.8.8.6.

O LORD, how often should we be
  Defeated, were it not for thee;
    Cast down, but for thy grace!
  When all the arts of Hell oppose,
  We find a refuge from our foes
    Within the holy place.

2 We dare not boast, O Lord of light,
  In human wisdom, or in might,
    To keep us pure within.
  Do thou assist, we humbly pray,
  Lest in our blindness we should stray
    Into the toils of sin.

3 Thee will we serve, and thee alone,
  No other ruler will we own,
    But with a godly fear
  Redeem the time at thy command,
  Then, with the saints at thy right hand,
    Triumphantly appear.
            Albert Orsborn (1886-1967)

748 Carey's, 489; Eaton, 491
                    8.8.8.8.8.8. Iambic

O LORD, we long to see your face,
  To know you risen from the grave;
  But we have missed the joy and grace
  Of seeing you, as others have.
  Yet in your company we'll wait,
  And we shall see you, soon or late.

2 O Lord, we do not know the way,
  Nor clearly see the path ahead;
  So often, therefore, we delay
  And doubt your power to raise the dead.
  Yet with you we will firmly stay;
  You are the truth, the life, the way.

3 We find it hard, Lord, to believe;
  All habit makes us want to prove;
  We would with eye and hand perceive
  The truth and person whom we love.
  Yet, as in fellowship we meet,
  You come yourself each one to greet.

4 You come to us, our God, our Lord;
  You do not show your hands and side;
  But faith has its more blest reward;
  In love's assurance we confide.
  Now we believe, that we may know,
  And in that knowledge daily grow.
        John Raphael Peacey (1896-1971)

749 Land of pure delight, 154;
        Ellacombe, 147   D.C.M.

OFT have I heard thy tender voice
  Which calls, dear Lord, to me,
  And asks a quick yet lasting choice
  'Twixt worldly joys and thee;
  It stirs my heart's deep fountain springs,
  And breaks the barriers down;
  It bids me rise on faith's strong wings,
  And cries: No cross, no crown!

2 And yet, alas! a storm-tossed sea
  Of care and doubt and fear
  Still parts me, Saviour Lord, from thee,
  Although thou art so near.
  O speak again and bid me come,
  From every fear set free,
  In spite of self and sin and storm,
  Upon the waves to thee.

3 O Lord, I dare to trust in thee,
  Who maketh all things new,
  My sins to slay, my tears to stay,
  My sorrows to subdue;
  And in the battle's blazing heat,
  When flesh and blood would quail,
  I'll fight and trust, and still repeat
  That Jesus cannot fail.
        Bramwell Booth (1856-1929)

750 Yesterday, today, forever, 349;
        Hold the fort, 344   8.5.8.5.

OFT our trust has known betrayal,
  Oft our hopes were vain,
  But there's one in every trial
  Constant will remain.

Yesterday, today, forever,
  Jesus is the same;
We may change, but Jesus never;
  Glory to his name!

2 Like a rock 'midst dashing billows
 Holding fast its place,
 Jesus is in all life's sorrows
 When we trust his grace.

3 Do your duty, shirk it never,
 Leave the rest with God;
 Stand your ground, today, forever;
 Victory through the blood!
   Richard Slater (1854-1939) (verses),
Albert Benjamin Simpson (1843-1919) (chorus)

751   Leidzén, 716

PEACE, perfect peace, far beyond all
 understanding;
 Peace, perfect peace, left with us by
 Christ, our Lord;
 Peace, perfect peace, through eternities
 expanding;
 Peace, perfect peace! Peace, perfect
 peace!

2 Peace, perfect peace, in each trial and
 disaster;
 Peace, perfect peace, fresh and sweet
 with every dawn;
 Peace, perfect peace, is the greeting of the
 Master:
 Peace, perfect peace! Peace, perfect
 peace!

3 Peace, perfect peace, though the tempest
 round me rages;
 Peace, perfect peace, stronger than the
 powers of Hell;
 Peace, perfect peace, still unchanging
 through the ages;
 Peace, perfect peace! Peace, perfect
 peace!

4 Peace, perfect peace, when at last death
 shall o'ertake me;
 Peace, perfect peace, shall surround my
 lowly grave;
 Peace, perfect peace, when the songs of
 angels wake me;
 Peace, perfect peace! Peace, perfect
 peace!
     Erik Leidzén (1894-1962)

752   Pax Tecum, 516
           10.10.

PEACE, perfect peace, in this dark world
 of sin?
The blood of Jesus whispers peace within.

2 Peace, perfect peace, by thronging duties
 pressed?
 To do the will of Jesus, this is rest.

3 Peace, perfect peace, with sorrows surging round?
 On Jesus' bosom naught but calm is
 found.

4 Peace, perfect peace, with loved ones far
 away?
 In Jesus' keeping we are safe, and they.

5 Peace, perfect peace, our future all
 unknown?
 Jesus we know, and he is on the throne.

6 Peace, perfect peace, death shadowing us
 and ours?
 Jesus has vanquished death and all its
 powers.

7 It is enough: earth's struggles soon shall
 cease,
 And Jesus call us to Heaven's perfect
 peace.
    Edward Henry Bickersteth (1825-1906)

753   I will guide thee, 379; Bethany, 429
           8.7.8.7. Troch.

PRECIOUS promise God hath given
 To the weary passerby,
All the way from earth to Heaven;
 I will guide thee with mine eye.

I will guide thee, I will guide thee,
I will guide thee with mine eye;
All the way from earth to Heaven,
I will guide thee with mine eye.

2 When temptations almost win thee,
 And thy trusted watchers fly,
Let this promise ring within thee:
 I will guide thee with mine eye.

3 When thy secret hopes have perished
 In the grave of years gone by,
Let this promise still be cherished:
 I will guide thee with mine eye.

4 When the shades of life are falling,
 And the hour has come to die,
Hear thy trusted leader calling:
 I will guide thee with mine eye.
     Nathaniel Niles (1835-1917)

The Salvation Soldier

754 Trusting as the moments fly, 299
7.7.7.7.

SIMPLY trusting every day,
 Trusting through a stormy way,
Even when my faith is small,
Trusting Jesus, that is all.

Trusting as the moments fly,
Trusting as the days go by,
Trusting him whate'er befall,
Trusting Jesus, that is all.

2 Brightly doth his Spirit shine
Into this poor heart of mine;
While he leads I need not fall,
Trusting Jesus, that is all.

3 Singing, if my way be clear,
Praying, if the path be drear,
If in danger, for him call;
Trusting Jesus, that is all.

4 Trusting him while life shall last,
Trusting him till earth be past,
Till within the jasper wall;
Trusting Jesus, that is all.

Edgar Page Stites (1836-1921)

755 Count your blessings, 202
6.5.6.5. D.

SINCE the Lord redeemed us from the
 power of sin,
Since his Spirit sealed us other lives to
 win,
Grace enough is given that we may endure,
And we prove the promises of God are
 sure.

All the promises of God are sure,
Through the ages shall their truth
 endure;
Hallelujah! To the heart that's pure
All the gracious promises of God are
 sure.

2 What the Lord ordaineth will be for the
 best,
Just to trust and follow him is perfect rest;
Never will he fail us if our faith is pure,
For we know the promises of God are sure.

3 Hope will give us courage in the darkest
 night,
Faith and love will make the heavy burden
 light;
Let us then be cheerful and our hearts
 assure
That the gracious promises of God are
 sure.

Albert Orsborn (1886-1967)

756 Dennis, 165; St Ethelwald, 174
S.M.

SPIRIT of faith, come down,
 Reveal the things of God,
And make to us the Godhead known,
 And witness with the blood.

2 'Tis thine the blood to apply,
 And give us eyes to see
Who did for every sinner die
 Hath surely died for me.

3 Then, only then, we feel
 Our interest in his blood,
And cry, with joy unspeakable:
 Thou art my Lord, my God!

4 Inspire the living faith,
 Which whosoe'er receives,
The witness in himself he hath
 And consciously believes;

5 The faith that conquers all,
 And doth the mountain move,
And saves whoe'er on Jesus call,
 And perfects them in love.

Charles Wesley (1707-88)

757 Standing on the promises, 797

STANDING on the promises of Christ my
 King,
Through eternal ages let his praises ring;
Glory in the highest, I will shout and sing,
 Standing on the promises of God.

Standing, standing,
 Standing on the promises of God my
 Saviour;
Standing, standing,
 I'm standing on the promises of God.

2 Standing on the promises that cannot fail,
When the howling storms of doubt and
 fear assail;
By the living word of God I shall prevail,
 Standing on the promises of God.

3 Standing on the promises of Christ my
 Lord,
Bound to him eternally by love's strong
 cord,
Overcoming daily with the Spirit's sword,
 Standing on the promises of God.

4 Standing on the promises I cannot fall,
Listening every moment to the Spirit's call,
Resting in my Saviour as my all in all,
 Standing on the promises of God.

Faith and Trust

5 Standing on the promises I now can see,
  Perfect, present cleansing in the blood for
    me;
  Standing in the liberty where Christ makes
    free,
  Standing on the promises of God.
                    Russell Kelso Carter (1849-1926)

758 The cross is not greater than his grace,
        814

THE cross that he gave may be heavy,
  But it ne'er outweighs his grace;
The storm that I feared may surround me,
  But it ne'er excludes his face.

  *The cross is not greater than his
    grace,
  The storm cannot hide his blessèd
    face;
  I am satisfied to know, that with Jesus
    here below,
  I can conquer every foe.*

2 The thorns in my path are not sharper
    Than composed his crown for me;
  The cup which I drink not more bitter
    Than he drank in Gethsemane.

3 The scorn of my foes may be daring,
    For they scoffed and mocked my God;
  They'll hate me for my holy living,
    For they crucified my Lord.

4 The light of his love shines the brighter
    As it falls on paths of woe;
  The toil of my work will grow lighter
    As I stoop to raise the low.
                    Ballington Booth (1857-1940)

759 Casting all your care on him, 365
        8.7.8.7. Troch.

THERE is strength in knowing Jesus
  When your heart is bowed with care,
'Mid the problems that distress you;
  O what joy to feel him there!

  *Casting all your care on him,
  Casting all your care on him,
  In his promises confiding
  In his mighty love abiding,
  Casting all your care on him.*

2 When the darkness round you gathers,
    When your path seems hid from sight,
  Jesus then in love is watching,
    And he always leads aright.

3 There is peace which passes knowledge
    And a joy no tongue can tell,
  When we bring our cares to Jesus,
    Hear him whisper: All is well.
                    Ivy Mawby (1903-83)

760 Saved by grace, 47
                              L.M.

THOSE first disciples of the Lord
  Received the promise of his word
And in their lives such power did dwell
To speed the message they should tell
To all mankind, that Jesus lives,
And grace to each believer gives;
May that same grace inspire today
To live for Christ, the life and way.

2 Revival is our present need,
  And can be ours if we will heed
  That promise ratified by grace,
  Declared in Christ for every race;
  For power from God is very sure
  To men of faith who will endure,
  And love will triumph over sin
  To bring God's glorious Kingdom in.

3 The powers of evil long have sought
  To ruin man in deed and thought;
  His longings for the true and good
  Have been frustrated, though he would
  Desire to conquer; yet we know
  God wills, indeed, this should be so.
  The promise now we may receive;
  'Tis sure for all who dare believe.

4 Our deeds must ever match our creed,
  Then God our way will truly lead
  As when those first disciples heard
  And boldly trusted God's great word.
  If we believed as they believed,
  Great grace would hallow every deed,
  Light would be ours his truth to know
  And send us forth his love to show.
                    John Hunt (1897-1982)

761 Sandon, 511
                    10.4.10.4.10.10.

THOUGH thunders roll and darkened be
    the sky,
  I'll trust in thee!
Though joys may fade and prospects droop
    and die,
  I'll trust in thee!
No light may shine upon life's rugged way,
Sufficient is thy grace from day to day.

209

2   I'm not outside thy providential care,
    I'll trust in thee!
I'll walk by faith thy chosen cross to bear,
    I'll trust in thee!
Thy will and wish I know are for the best,
This gives to me abundant peace and rest.

3   Thy word is sure, thy promise never fails,
    I'll trust in thee!
A hiding place thou art when Hell assails,
    I'll trust in thee!
I conquer all while hiding 'neath thy wing,
And in the storm sweet songs of triumph
    sing.

4   I'm pressing on towards my home in
    Heaven,
    I'll trust in thee!
Where crowns of life to faithful ones are
    given,
    I'll trust in thee!
This hope is mine, through Jesus
    crucified,
And all through grace I shall be glorified.
John Lawley (1859-1922)

762   Trust in God, 838

THOUGH thy waves and billows are gone
    o'er me,
    Night and day my meat has been my
        tears,
Fain I would pour out my soul before thee,
    At whose hand my advocate appears.
Only thou art still my soul's defender,
    Hand of strength, and all-prevenient
        grace;
Frail am I, but thou art my befriender,
    And I trust the shining of thy face.

2   As the hart that panteth for the fountain,
    So I long for thee, the living God;
To the spring that flows from out the
    mountain,
    Lead me forth with thine unerring rod.
From the depths my soul has called upon
    thee,
    From the hill shall make thy praises
        known,
For my foes shall not prevail upon me,
    By thy strength shall they be
        overthrown.

3   By thy loving-kindness so unfailing,
    Never once hast thou forsaken me;
  O for grace that I, by prayer prevailing,
    May in faithful love remember thee!

Lo! my soul before thine altar kneeling,
    Renders up the sacrifice of praise;
Place thy hand upon me for my sealing,
    Thine alone, throughout my length of
    days.
Albert Orsborn (1886-1967)

763   Houghton, 533; Hanover, 531
10.10.11.11.

THOUGH troubles assail,
    And dangers affright,
Though friends should all fail,
    And foes all unite,
Yet one thing secures us,
    Whatever betide,
The Bible assures us
    The Lord will provide.

2   The birds without barn
    Or storehouse are fed,
From them let us learn
    To trust for our bread;
His saints what is fitting
    Shall ne'er be denied,
So long as 'tis written:
    The Lord will provide.

3   His call we obey,
    Like Abr'ham of old,
Not knowing our way,
    But faith makes us bold;
For though we are strangers,
    We have a good guide,
And trust, in all dangers,
    The Lord will provide.

4   No strength of our own
    Or goodness we claim;
Yet, since we have known
    The Saviour's great name,
In this our strong tower
    For safety we hide,
The Lord is our power,
    The Lord will provide.

5   When life sinks apace,
    And death is in view,
The word of his grace
    Shall comfort us through;
No fearing or doubting
    With Christ on our side,
We hope to die shouting:
    The Lord will provide!
John Newton (1725-1807)

Faith and Trust

764 All through the night, 339; Caritas, 340
8.4.8.4.8.8.8.4.

THROUGH the love of God our Saviour
  All will be well;
Free and changeless is his favor,
  All, all is well.
Precious is the blood that healed us,
Perfect is the grace that sealed us,
Strong the hand stretched forth to shield
   us,
  All must be well.

2 Though we pass through tribulation,
  All will be well;
Ours is such a full salvation,
  All, all is well.
Happy, still in God confiding,
Fruitful, if in Christ abiding,
Holy, through the Spirit's guiding,
  All must be well.

3 We expect a bright tomorrow,
  All will be well;
Faith can sing through days of sorrow,
  All, all is well.
On our Father's love relying,
Jesus every need supplying,
Or in living, or in dying,
  All must be well.
          Mary Peters (1813-56)

765 Marching, 387; St Oswald, 396
8.7.8.7. Troch.

THROUGH the night of doubt and sorrow
  Onward goes the pilgrim band,
Singing songs of expectation,
  Marching to the promised land.

2 Clear before us through the darkness
  Gleams and burns the guiding light;
Brother clasps the hand of brother,
  Stepping fearless through the night.

3 One the light of God's own presence
  O'er his ransomed people shed,
Chasing far the gloom and terror,
  Brightening all the path we tread.

4 One the object of our journey,
  One the faith which never tires,
One the earnest looking forward,
  One the hope our God inspires.

5 One the strain that lips of thousands
  Lift as from the heart of one;
One the conflict, one the peril,
  One the march in God begun.

6 One the gladness of rejoicing
  On the far eternal shore,
Where the one almighty Father
  Reigns in love for evermore.
    Bernhardt Severin Ingemann (1789-1862),
    trs Sabine Baring-Gould (1834-1924)

766 Ochills, 762

TO the hills I lift my eyes,
  The distant hills before me;
Hills that rise to reach the skies,
  And spread their glory o'er me.
Planted by omnipotent hand,
  By divine appointment they stand,
To the hills I lift my eyes,
  The beckoning hills before me.

2 Eyes may scan the dizzy height,
  And human feet stand on it;
Only faith, in mystic flight,
  Can see the realms beyond it.
Steeper than the mountains of time,
  Higher than the loftiest climb,
O'er the hills I lift my eyes;
  From thence my help is coming.

3 To the hills I'll turn again,.
  Away from earthly slumber,
There to gain the topmost plain;
  May naught my way encumber.
On the highest summit I'll stand,
  There to view the long-promised land;
Though my eyes look to the skies,
  I lift my heart to Heaven.
        Ernest Rance (1896-1988)

767 Sandon, 511
10.4.10.4.10.10.

UNTO the hills around do I lift up
  My longing eyes;
O whence for me shall my salvation come,
  From whence arise?
From God, the Lord, does come my cer-
  tain aid,
From God, the Lord, who Heaven and earth
  hath made.

2 He will not suffer that thy foot be moved,
  Safe shalt thou be;
No careless slumber shall his eyelids close
  Who keepeth thee.
Behold, he sleepeth not; he slumbereth
  ne'er
Who keepeth Israel in his holy care.

3 Jehovah is himself thy keeper true,
    Thy changeless shade;
Jehovah thy defense on thy right hand
    Himself hath made.
And thee no sun by day shall ever smite,
No moon shall harm thee in the silent
    night.

4 From every evil shall he keep thy soul,
    From every sin.
Jehovah shall preserve thy going out,
    Thy coming in.
Above thee watching, he whom we adore
Shall keep thee henceforth, yea, for
    evermore.
        John Douglas Sutherland Campbell
        (1845-1914)

768 Leaning on the everlasting arms, 715

WHAT a fellowship, what a joy divine,
    Leaning on the everlasting arms;
What a blessèdness, what a peace is mine,
    Leaning on the everlasting arms.

    Leaning, leaning,
Safe and secure from all alarms;
Leaning, leaning,
Leaning on the everlasting arms.

2 O how sweet to walk in this pilgrim way,
    Leaning on the everlasting arms!
O how bright the path grows from day to
    day,
    Leaning on the everlasting arms!

3 What have I to dread, what have I to fear,
    Leaning on the everlasting arms?
I have blessèd peace with my Lord so near,
    Leaning on the everlasting arms.
        Elisha Albright Hoffman (1839-1929)

769 Love at home, 237
7.5.7.5.7.7.7.5.

WHAT a work the Lord has done
    By his saving grace;
Let us praise him, every one,
    In his holy place.
He has saved us gloriously,
Led us onward faithfully,
Yet he promised we should see
    Even greater things.

    Greater things! Greater things!
Give us faith, O Lord, we pray,
Faith for greater things.

2 Sanctify thy name, O Lord,
    By thy people here,
For the altar or the sword!
    Save us from our fear
When the battle rages fast;
Help us in the fiery blast,
Let us not be overcast,
    Prove thy greater things.

3 Every comrade, Lord, we pray,
    Thou wilt richly bless;
Lead us forth into the fray,
    One in holiness,
One in faith and harmony,
One in perfect charity;
Then we know that we shall see
    Even greater things.
        Albert Orsborn (1886-1967)

770 A Perfect Trust, 459
8.7.8.7.7.7. Troch.

WHEN I ponder o'er the story
    Of my life's defeat and grief,
How much misery and blindness
    I can trace to unbelief!
O how many fights I've lost,
    All for want of faith to trust!

    O for a deeper, O for a greater,
O for a perfect trust in the Lord!

2 Can I wonder I have faltered?
    Can I be surprised to fall?
When my faith could most have saved me,
    I have trusted least of all.
When my own resources fail,
    Then his power should most prevail.

3 If to grace there is no limit,
    Why should I be slow to plead?
If thy power is not restricted,
    Why not speak my every need?
All the treasures of his throne,
    Faith will make them all my own.

4 Yes, dear Saviour, I will trust thee,
    Live by faith and not by sight,
Knowing thou art close beside me,
    Giving victory in the fight.
Jesus, while thou art so near,
    I will never, never fear.
        Cornelie Booth (1864-1920)

Faith and Trust

771 It is well with my soul, 695

WHEN peace like a river attendeth my
way,
When sorrows like sea billows roll,
Whatever my lot, thou hast taught me to
know
It is well, it is well with my soul.

It is well with my soul,
It is well, it is well with my soul.

2 Though Satan should buffet, though trials
should come,
Let this blest assurance control,
That Christ hath regarded my helpless
estate,
And hath shed his own blood for my
soul.

3 For me be it Christ, be it Christ hence to
live;
If Jordan above me shall roll,
No pang shall be mine, for in death as in
life,
Thou wilt whisper thy peace to my soul.

4 But Lord, 'tis for thee, for thy coming we
wait,
The sky, not the grave, is our goal;
O trump of the angel! O voice of the Lord!
Blessèd hope, blessèd rest of my soul!
Horatio Gates Spafford (1828-88)

772 Theodora, 297;
St Bees, 293   7.7.7.7.

WHEN we cannot see our way,
Let us trust and still obey;
He who bids us forward go,
Cannot fail the way to show.

2 Though the sea be deep and wide,
Though a passage seem denied,
Fearless let us still proceed,
Since the Lord vouchsafes to lead.

3 Though it be the gloom of night,
Though we see no ray of light,
Since the Lord himself is there,
'Tis not meet that we should fear.

4 Night with him is never night,
Where he is, there all is light;
When he calls us, why delay?
They are happy who obey.

5 Be it ours, then, while we're here,
Him to follow without fear,
Where he calls us, there to go,
What he bids us, that to do.
Thomas Kelly (1769-1855)

773 Keep on believing, 708;
Blessèd Assurance, 621

WHEN you feel weakest, dangers
surround,
Subtle temptations, troubles abound,
Nothing seems hopeful, nothing seems
glad,
All is despairing, everything sad:

Keep on believing, Jesus is near;
Keep on believing, there's nothing to
fear;
Keep on believing, this is the way;
Faith in the night as well as the day.

2 If all were easy, if all were bright,
Where would the cross be, and where the
fight?
But in the hardness, God gives to you
Chances of proving that you are true.

3 God is your wisdom, God is your might,
God's ever near you, guiding aright;
He understands you, knows all you need;
Trusting in him you'll surely succeed.

4 Let us press on then, never despair,
Live above feeling, victory's there;
Jesus can keep us so near to him
That nevermore our faith shall grow dim.
Lucy Milward Booth-Hellberg (1868-1953)

＊   ＊   ＊

see also: 47 God's love is as high as the
heavens
397 When we walk with the Lord
485 Father, I know that all my life
556 All scenes alike engaging prove
559 Awake, our souls; away, our fears
579 He giveth more grace
653 How firm a foundation
790 When you find the cross is heavy
917 My times are in thy hand
918 O God of Bethel, by whose hand
974 Dwelling in Beulah Land
976 How firm a foundation
987 Life is great
991 'Tis so sweet to trust in Jesus

The Flag

774 Haste away to Jesus, 151;
Ellacombe, 147   D.C.M.

ABOVE the world-wide battlefield through
long and warring years,
A flag of many victories triumphantly
appears;
And as we fight beneath its folds for all
that most we prize,
O God of battles, in thy name our flag un-
hindered flies.

*'Neath our colors, waving, we will fight,
nor will we tire
While our God is saving the world by
blood and fire.*

2 O flag of hallowed memories a thousand
times retold,
The chronicles of twice-born men beneath
thy shade enrolled;
Glad trophies won from Satan's power who
fight nor count the odds,
Contented that the wounds be theirs, they
claim the victory God's.

3 And when, in solemn covenant, its folds
hung over me,
I promised God most earnestly his soldier
I would be;
I pray that when the trumpet calls, my last
great battle won,
The Army flag shall cover all that death
can seize upon.

4 A standard for the multitude uplifted
everywhere;
For this and nothing less than this, thine
Army, Lord, prepare;
'Gainst sin and darkness still to fight to
bring that day to birth
When folded lies the blood and fire, thy
Kingdom come on earth.
Will J. Brand (1889-1977)

775 Poor old Joe, 769

ALL round the world the Army chariot
rolls,
All round the world the Lord is saving
souls,
All round the world our soldiers will be
brave,
Around our colors we will rally,
Wave, soldiers, wave.

*Keep waving, keep waving, keep every
flag unfurled,
We soon shall have our colors waving
all round the world.*

2 All round the world with music and with
song,
All round the world we'll boldly march
along,
All round the world to free each sin-bound
slave,
We'll wave our Army flags for Jesus,
Wave, soldiers, wave.

3 All round the world redeeming grace shall
flow,
All round the world we will to battle go,
All round the world the universe to save,
With blood and fire, with faith and feeling,
Wave, soldiers, wave.
William James Pearson (1832-92)

776 Austria, 408
8.7.8.7. D. Troch.

ARMY flag! Thy threefold glory
Greets the rising of the sun;
Radiant is the way before thee,
Rich the trophies to be won;
Onward in the cause of Jesus!
Witness where the dawning glows,
Flying on the wings of morning,
Follow where the Saviour goes.

2 Slowly sinks the reign of darkness,
Yielding to the Saviour's day,
When the slaves of sinful bondage
Cast their evil chains away.
Upward, Christward, homeward, Godward!
Millions who are now afar
Shall be brought into the Kingdom,
Where the Father's children are.

3 Army flag! We too will follow,
Follow as with willing heart,
Honored in the cause we fight for,
Glad to take a soldier's part,
Until men confess Christ's Kingdom
Vaster than the world has seen,
Crown with glory and dominion
Christ, the lowly Nazarene.
Albert Orsborn (1886-1967)

777 Bethany, 429; Europe, 435
8.7.8.7. D. Troch.

EMBLEM of a thousand battles,
In the war for truth and right,
Leading onward through the darkness
To the everlasting light.

The Flag

Proudly we salute the colors,
    For this flag our love confess,
Which, when flown o'er all the nations,
    Stands for peace and righteousness.

2 Red reveals the love of Calvary,
    Where the healing fountains flow,
Richness of our Saviour's giving
    To mankind in need and woe,
Proof supreme of heavenly pity
    For a lost and sinning race,
Over which our heavenly Father
    Poured his tenderness and grace.

3 Blue, the sign of holy living,
    Speaks of inward purity,
Yellow stands for fire from Heaven,
    Healing, cleansing, setting free.
First the cross to bear for Jesus,
    Bearing shame for his dear sake;
Then the crown of fadeless glory
    Which we from his hands shall take.

4 Lo! the flag again is lifted
    So that all may plainly see
Red and blue and yellow gleaming,
    Proof of final victory.
We will pledge a fresh allegiance
    To the cause of Christ, our King;
Offer him our heart's devotion,
    Dearest treasures to him bring.
Doris N. Rendell (1896-1990), alt

778   I'll be true, 684

'NEATH our standard, we're engaging
  Foes of God around us raging,
And the battle we are waging
    'Neath the yellow, red and blue.

I'll be true! I'll be true!
True to my colors, the yellow, red and
    blue;
I'll be true! I'll be true!
True to my Saviour in the Army.

2 In this warfare we're delighting,
  For our Saviour we are fighting;
'Gainst the host of Hell uniting,
    'Neath the yellow, red and blue.

3 Onward! each success repeating,
  Never from the foe retreating,
All our enemies defeating,
    'Neath the yellow, red and blue.
Gustave Adolph Alexander Augustine Grozinsky
(c 1870-1937)

779   Yellow star and red and blue, 162
D.C.M.

THE flag is yours, the flag is mine,
  That flies o'er lands and seas;
From north to south, from east to west,
  Unfurled by every breeze.
The blood-stained flag, the fiery flag,
  The flag of purity,
That brings new life, new hope, new joy,
  And tells of victory.

Yellow star and red and blue,
Blood and fire, through and through;
That's the flag for me and you,
The flag of the dear old Army.

2 The flag is yours, the flag is mine,
  With all its colors mean;
The Saviour's blood, the Holy Ghost,
  A love that's pure and clean.
That heart of yours, this heart of mine,
  Must beat for ever true
To the flag of God's great Army,
  The yellow, red and blue.
Arch R. Wiggins (1893-1976)

780   We'd better bide a wee, 161·
D.C.M.

THEY bid me choose an easier path,
  And seek a lighter cross;
They bid me mingle with Heaven's gold
  A little of earth's dross;
They bid me, but in vain, once more
  The world's illusions try;
I cannot leave the dear old flag,
  'Twere better far to die.

2 They say the fighting is too hard,
  My strength of small avail,
When foes beset and friends are fled,
  My faith must surely fail.
But, O how can I quit my post
  While millions sin-bound lie?
I cannot leave the dear old flag,
  'Twere better far to die.

3 They say I can a Christian be,
  And serve God quite as well,
And reach Heaven just as surely by
  The music of church bell;
But, O the drum and clarion call
  Of band make my pulse fly!
I cannot leave the dear old flag,
  'Twere better far to die.

The Salvation Soldier

4 I answer, life is fleeting fast,
    I cannot, cannot wait;
For me my comrades beckoning stand
    Beyond the pearly gate;
I hear their hallelujahs grand,
    I hear their battle cry:
O do not leave the dear old flag,
    'Twere better far to die!
        Frederick Booth-Tucker (1853-1929)

781   Stand up for Jesus, 264
              7.6.7.6. D. Iambic

UNFURL the Army banner,
    The yellow, red and blue;
Its colors so resplendent
    Display for all to view.
Its message is eternal,
    Inspired from Heaven above,
Bright emblem of salvation,
    Of holiness and love.

2 Lift high the Army banner
    In every land and clime;
It calls to deeds of valor,
    It speaks of grace divine.
Salvation, O salvation!
    For every sinner free,
For every tribe and nation,
    To all eternity.

3 Beneath this glorious banner
    By Jesus' grace we stand
In bonds of love eternal,
    A holy, blood-washed band.
To arms, Salvation Army!
    Loud rings the clarion call,
Nor weary in the conflict
    Till Christ is Lord of all.
        William Drake Pennick (1884-1944)

782   Lift up the banner, 106
              C.M.

WE'LL shout aloud throughout the land
    The praises of our God,
We'll fight beneath our flag unfurled,
    Kept by his precious blood.

So we'll lift up the banner on high,
    The salvation banner of love;
We'll fight beneath its colors till we die,
    Then go to our home above.

2 Salvation full shall be our cry,
    Whatever men may say;
We'll fight for God until we die;
    We're bound to win the day.

3 Salvation soldiers, fighting on,
    Be more courageous still;
To God the world shall yet belong,
    And bend its stubborn will.
    James Conner Bateman (1854-88) (verses),
    William Thomas Giffe (b 1848) (chorus)

783   Lift up the Army banner, 718

WOULD you of our banner know the
        meaning,
    With its yellow, red and blue?
In the breeze, its crimson glory streaming,
    Waves a message grand and true.

Lift up the Army banner, blood and fire,
    Blood and fire, lift it higher;
Lift up the Army banner, blood and fire,
    For it tells of full salvation.

2 Blood-red crimson tells of God's salvation,
    Bids us think of Christ who died
For the sins of every tribe and nation,
    When the blood flowed from his side.

3 Fiery yellow, emblem of the Spirit,
    Leads us back to Pentecost;
He was sent to plead the Saviour's merit,
    And to help us save the lost.

4 Heavenly blue suggests we may be holy,
    Purified from inbred sin;
Evil tempers, pride, and worldly folly,
    Nevermore to dwell within.
        William Drake Pennick (1884-1944)

           *   *   *

see also: 382 Salvation! O the joyful sound

Swearing-in of Soldiers

784   French, 88; Martyrdom, 113
              C.M.

COME, let us use the grace divine,
    And all, with one accord,
In a perpetual covenant join
    Ourselves to Christ the Lord;

2 Give up ourselves, through Jesus' power,
    His name to glorify;
And promise in this sacred hour
    For God to live and die.

3 The covenant we this moment make
    Be ever kept in mind:
We will no more our God forsake,
    Or cast his words behind.

Swearing-in of Soldiers

4 We never will throw off his fear
Who hears our solemn vow;
And if thou art well pleased to hear,
Come down and meet us now.

Charles Wesley (1707-88)

785 Pembroke, 467;
8.8.6.8.8.6.

FOR every rule of life required
Our heavenly Father has inspired
The Scriptures, we believe.
Preserver through our length of days,
He is the object of our praise,
Creator, we believe.

2 With God the Father dwell the Son
And Holy Spirit, Three in One,
The Godhead, we believe.
While Christ the Son as man is known,
He still is God, and thus are shown
Two natures, we believe.

3 When tempted our first parents strayed
From God (and thus the world) though
made
Quite sinless, we believe.
Atoning for a whole world's sin
By love that we might pardon win,
Christ suffered, we believe.

4 We must repent before God's face
If we would have by his full grace
Salvation, we believe.
The covenant is ratified
And we by grace are justified
Through Jesus, we believe.

5 Continuance in this state demands
That we obey divine commands
And constantly believe.
We may be wholly sanctified,
Kept by the Spirit, and abide
All blameless, we believe.

6 As we have lived, so shall we gain
Eternal joy or lasting pain;
God judges, we believe.
He is our maker, Saviour, friend;
We give him worship without end,
And now his grace receive.

Dorothy Olive Joy (1903-82)

786 Showers of blessing, 456; Jesus is
looking for thee, 457*   8.7.8.7. Dact.

I WOULD be thy holy temple,
Sacred and indwelt by thee;
Naught then could stain my commission,
'Tis thy divine charge to me.

*Take thou my life, Lord,
In deep submission I pray,
My all to thee dedicating,
Accept my offering today.*

**Take thou my life, Lord, I pray;
Take thou my life, Lord, I pray;
My all to thee dedicating,
Accept my offering today.*

2 Seeking to mirror thy glory,
Living to answer thy call,
Each faithful vow now renewing,
Gladly I yield thee my all.

3 Time, health and talents presenting,
All that I have shall be thine;
Heart, mind and will consecrating,
No longer shall they be mine.

4 O for a heart of compassion,
Moved at the impulse of love,
Lost ones to bring to thy footstool,
Thy gracious riches to prove!

Brindley Boon

787 Pass me not, 347; My humble cry, 346
8.5.8.5.

IN this hour of dedication,
As we kneel to pray,
Holy Spirit, come upon us,
Fit us for the fray.

*Jesus, Saviour,
Hear us as we pray;
Keep us, Lord, thy faithful soldiers
Till the crowning day.*

2 Christ has need of dauntless soldiers;
Teach us how to fight,
Keep us ever in the vanguard
For the cause of right.

3 'Tis a war 'gainst Hell we're waging,
Mighty is the foe;
In the conquering name of Jesus
We to victory go.

4 Ours a life of self-denial,
But of glory, too,
As each day in dedication
We our vows renew.

Doris N. Rendell (1896-1990)

The Salvation Soldier

788 Anything for Jesus, 199; Forward! be our watchword, 203   6.5.6.5. D.

JESUS, thou hast won us,
　Saved us, set us free;
Now thy hand upon us
　Bids us follow thee;
Sin's dark ways forsaking,
　Filled with new desire,
We our vows are making
　'Neath the blood and fire.

Lord, our vow performing,
　We will fight for thee;
Hell's dominions storming,
　Other souls to free.

2 Comrades here remind us
　We are not alone,
Thou to them dost bind us,
　They and we are one;
All, our vows observing,
　One great Army make;
Praying, fighting, serving
　For thy Kingdom's sake.

3 On to full salvation,
　This shall be our goal;
Thine in consecration,
　Body, mind and soul;
On to holy living,
　Weakness left behind;
Perfect service giving,
　Perfect joy to find.
Will J. Brand (1889-1977)

789 Buckland, 275; Theodora, 297; Last Hope, 284   7.7.7.7.

LORD of life and love and power,
　In this sacrificial hour,
We would dedicate to thee
All we are for days to be.

2 We are eager to obey,
Send us, Lord, into the fray;
Fearless in thy name we go
Forth to battle 'gainst the foe.

3 Mighty are the tasks ahead,
But by our commander led,
When temptations fierce assail,
In thy strength we shall prevail.

4 Sin is rampant, fear and shame
Blight men's souls, their bodies maim;
Joyous tidings we proclaim,
That for such our Saviour came.

5 Saints of old obeyed the call;
At thy word they gave up all;
Where they trod so valiantly,
May we follow fearlessly.

6 Mighty Captain of the host,
Fill us with the Holy Ghost;
Suffer not our feet to stray
From this new and living way.
Doris N. Rendell (1896-1990)

790 When the mists have rolled away, 452; Heavenly Mansions, 437; Ellan Vannin, 434   8.7.8.7. D. Troch.

WHEN you find the cross is heavy,
　And you feel like giving in,
Take your weakness straight to Jesus,
　He will strengthen you within;
He will give you grace and power,
　He will bring you safely through;
Countless hosts he leads to victory,
　He will do the same for you.

He will bring you safely through,
He will bring you safely through;
He will give you grace and power
In temptation's darkest hour;
He is with his hosts in battle,
He will surely be with you.

2 Foes may scoff and friends may wound you
　As you tread the narrow way,
When they spurn or misinterpret
　All the kindly words you say,
As you daily strive to lead them
　From the paths of sin and shame,
Pointing them unto the Saviour
　Who for sinners once was slain.

3 You will find that trusting Jesus
　Makes your daily pathway bright,
And the glory of believing
　Turns your darkness into light;
There's a gladness which increases
　As to serve him you aspire,
And a peace which comes with trusting
　When his will is your desire.
Frederick Alfred Trevillian (1858-1925), alt

Dedication of Children

791 Horsley, 95; Colne, 79   C.M.

FATHER, we for our children plead,
　The children thou hast given;
Where shall we go in time of need
　But to the God of Heaven?

Dedication of Children

2 We ask for them not wealth or fame
   Amid the worldly strife:
But, in the all-prevailing name,
   We ask eternal life.

3 We seek the Spirit's quickening grace
   To make them pure in heart,
That they may stand before thy face
   And see thee as thou art.
Thomas Hastings (1784-1872)

792 Ruth, 208; Anything for Jesus, 199
                        6.5.6.5. D.

GENTLE arms of Jesus
   Take this little child,
Fold him (her) in your comfort
   'Neath your glance so mild;
In your care and shelter
   Let him (her) lie at rest,
Knowing that you hold him (her)
   Feeling safe and blest.

2 Loving arms of Jesus,
   Shield this baby small
From the many dangers
   Threatening us all.
But above all other,
   Earnestly we pray:
Keep his (her) heart from evil,
   Let him (her) walk your way.

3 Sacred arms of Jesus,
   Bless this baby dear,
In your heavenly Kingdom
   Let his (her) name appear.
As he (she) grows in knowledge,
   Seal him (her) as your own,
Let your guiding presence
   In his (her) life be shown.
Flora Larsson

793 Innocents, 283; Buckland, 275;
       Prayer of childhood, 291   7.7.7.7.

GENTLE Jesus, meek and mild,
   Look upon a little child,
Pity my simplicity,
Suffer me to come to thee.

2 Fain I would to thee be brought,
Gracious Lord, forbid it not;
In the Kingdom of thy grace
Give a little child a place.

3 Loving Jesus, gentle Lamb,
In thy gracious hands I am;
Make me, Saviour, what thou art,
Live thyself within my heart.

4 Lamb of God, I look to thee,
Thou shalt my example be;
Thou art gentle, meek and mild;
Thou wast once a little child.

5 Now I would be as thou art;
Give me an obedient heart;
Thou art pitiful and kind,
Let me have thy loving mind.

6 I shall then show forth thy praise,
Serve thee all my happy days;
Then the world shall always see
Christ, the holy child, in me.
Charles Wesley (1707-88)

794 I think when I read, 538
                      11.8.11.8. D.

I THINK, when I read that sweet story of
   old,
   When Jesus was here among men,
How he called little children as lambs to
   his fold,
   I should like to have been with them
     then.
I wish that his hands had been placed on
   my head,
   That his arm had been thrown around
     me,
And that I might have seen his kind look
   when he said:
   Let the little ones come unto me!

2 Yet still to his footstool in prayer I may
   go,
   And ask for a share in his love;
And if I now earnestly seek him below,
   I shall see him and hear him above,
In that beautiful place he is gone to
   prepare
   For all who are washed and forgiven;
And many dear children are gathering
   there,
   For of such is the Kingdom of Heaven.

3 But thousands and thousands who wan-
   der and fall
   Never heard of that heavenly home;
I should like them to know there is room
   for them all,
   And that Jesus has bid them to come.
I long for the joys of that glorious time,
   The sweetest and brightest and best,
When the dear little children of every clime
   Shall crowd to his arms and be blessed.
Jemima Luke (1813-1906)

795

South Shields, 444
8.7.8.7. D. Troch.

LORD, with joyful hearts we worship,
  Eager to express our praise;
For each blessing you have granted
  We would thank you all our days.
At this moment we're rejoicing,
  Conscious you are very near,
As these parents, for your blessing
  Bring their baby boy (girl) so dear.

2 Lord, we pray that you will grant them
  Strength and wisdom from above,
Patience too, with understanding,
  As they raise this child they love.
Grant the pledges they're now making
  Will forever be held true,
And as baby grows, discerning,
  He (she) will choose them to pursue.

3 May the love that here surrounds him (her)
  Be his (her) portion through the years,
And our prayers for him (her) continue
  As he (she) learns earth's joys and fears;
May your Spirit fall upon him (her)
  In this dedication hour,
Keep him (her), Lord, from all that's evil,
  Fill him (her) now with grace and power.
                    Marjorie Beryl Davies

796

Alstone, 4; Melcombe, 34
L.M.

O FATHER, friend of all mankind,
  Our prayer with thankful hearts we sing
As joyfully our little child,
  In Jesus' name, to thee we bring.

2 O guide us that we too may guide,
  And teach us faithfully to share
The wealth of God, more bountiful
  Than this world's bidders have to spare.

3 We dedicate to Heaven's cause
  Thy gift; O may he (she) early choose
To heed thy voice, and for thy sake
  The passing gains of earth to lose!

4 Receive and bless our child, great God;
  When to full stature he (she) is grown
May his (her) devotion to thy word
  In ceaseless love for men be shown.
                    Catherine Baird (1895-1984)

797

Mothers of Salem, 737

WHEN mothers of Salem
  Their children brought to Jesus,
The stern disciples drove them back,
  And bade them depart;
But Jesus saw them ere they fled,
And sweetly smiled and kindly said:
Suffer little children to come unto me.

2 For I will receive them
  And fold them to my bosom;
I'll be a shepherd to these lambs,
  O drive them not away!
For if their hearts to me they give,
They shall with me in Glory live;
Suffer little children to come unto me.

3 How kind was our Saviour
  To bid these children welcome!
But there are many thousands who
  Have never heard his name;
O shine upon them from above,
And show thyself a God of love!
Teach the little children to come unto thee.
        William Medlen Hutchings (1827-76)

Warfare

798

Come, shout and sing, 633

COME, shout and sing, make Heaven ring
  With praises to our King,
Who bled and died, was crucified,
  That he might pardon bring.
  His blood doth save the soul,
  Doth cleanse and make it whole,
The blood of Jesus cleanses white as
  snow.

O the blood of Jesus cleanses white as
  snow, yes, I know!
The blood of Jesus cleanses white
  as snow,
  I bless the happy day,
  When he washed my sins away,
The blood of Jesus cleanses white as
  snow.

2 Come, join our band, and make a stand
  To drive sin from our land;
To do or die, our battle cry,
  We fight at God's command.
  With banner wide unfurled,
  We tell to all the world:
The blood of Jesus cleanses white as
  snow.

3 The Lord is near when foes appear,
  With him we shall not fear,
But fight the fight for God and right,
  Nor count the cost too dear.
Then when we come to die,
  We'll shout our battle cry:
The blood of Jesus cleanses white as
  snow.

James Conner Bateman (1854-88)

799 Titchfield, 327; Maidstone, 325;
Ramsgate, 312   7.7.7.7. D.

EARTHLY kingdoms rise and fall,
  Kings and nations come and go,
Thou, O God, art over all,
  None thine empire shall o'erthrow.
Of thy grace are we enrolled
  In the train of thy dear Son,
Pledged our faith undimmed to hold
  Until victory is won.

2 High o'er rampart, tower and wall,
  Faith her standard proudly flies;
Youth obeys her trumpet call,
  Marching forth to grand emprise.
In each hand uplifted high
  Gleams a consecrated sword;
Hark! they shout their battle cry:
  Rise and fight for Christ, our Lord.

3 Seasoned in a hundred fights,
  Warriors lend their strength and skill;
Time but deepens their delights
  In the conquest over ill.
With unceasing war grown wise,
  None will on himself depend;
Each upon his Lord relies,
  Now, and till the war shall end.

4 Thine, O faith, the victory!
  Thou shalt overcome the world;
In that day thy foes shall be
  Down to final darkness hurled.
Thine it is our hearts to cheer,
  Thine to make us brave and strong;
Ours to press the battle here,
  Then to swell the triumph song.

Will J. Brand (1889-1977)

800 God is keeping his soldiers fighting, 655

GOD is keeping his soldiers fighting,
  Evermore we shall conquerors be;
All the hosts of Hell are uniting,
  But we're sure to have victory.

Though to beat us they've been trying,
Our colors still are flying,
And our flag shall wave forever,
  For we never will give in.

*No, we never, never, never will give in,
  No we won't! No we won't!
No, we never, never, never will give in,
  For we mean to have the victory for
  ever.*

2 We will follow our conquering Saviour,
  From before him Hell's legions shall fly;
Our battalions never shall waver,
  They're determined to conquer or die.
From holiness and Heaven
We never will be driven;
We will stand our ground forever,
  For we never will give in.

3 With salvation for every nation,
  To the ends of the earth we will go,
With a free and full salvation,
  All the power of the cross we'll show.
We'll tear Hell's throne to pieces,
And win the world for Jesus,
We'll be conquerors forever,
  For we never will give in.

William James Pearson (1832-92)

801 God's Soldier, 62
                    D.L.M.

GOD'S soldier marches as to war,
  A soldier on an alien shore,
A soldier true, a soldier who
Will keep the highest aims in view.
God's soldier goes where sin is found;
Where evil reigns, his battleground;
A cunning foe to overthrow
And strike for truth a telling blow.

*We're going to fill, fill, fill the world with
  glory;
We're going to smile, smile, smile and
  not frown;
We're going to sing, sing, sing the
  gospel story;
We're going to turn the world upside
  down.*

2 God's soldier has to stand alone,
Accepting burdens not his own;
A lonely work he cannot shirk,
Where dark and deadly dangers lurk.
God's soldier must be courageous be,
And from his duties never flee,
For millions wait, whose need is great,
And he must not God's plan frustrate.

Harry Read

The Salvation Soldier

802 Hark, hark, my soul, 542; Pilgrims, 548
11.10.11.10.

HARK, hark, my soul, what warlike songs
  are swelling
  Through all the land and on from door
  to door;
How grand the truths those burning
  strains are telling
Of that great war till sin shall be no
  more.

Salvation Army, Army of God,
Onward to conquer the world with fire
  and blood.
Onward to conquer the world with fire
  and blood.

2 Onward we go, the world shall hear our
  singing:
  Come guilty souls, for Jesus bids you
  come;
And through the dark its echoes, loudly
  ringing,
Shall lead the wretched, lost and wandering home.

3 Far, far away, like thunder grandly pealing,
  We'll send the call for mercy full and
  free,
And burdened souls, by thousands humbly kneeling,
Shall yield, dear Lord, their contrite
  hearts to thee.

4 Conquerors at last, though long the fight
  and dreary!
  Bright days shall dawn and sin's dark
  night be past;
Our battles end in saving sinners weary,
And Satan's kingdom down shall fall at
  last.
  Frederick William Faber (1814-63),
  alt George Scott Railton (1849-1913)

803 Rachie, 207; Armageddon, 200
6.5.6.5. D.

HARK! the sounds of singing
  Coming on the breeze,
Notes of triumph winging
  Over lands and seas.
Martial hosts assemble,
  Flushed with victory,
Hell's battalions tremble
  And prepare to flee.

Army of salvation!
  Army of the Lord!
Christ our inspiration,
  Christ our great reward.

2 Whence have come these legions,
  Valiant, free and strong?
Worldwide are the regions
  Where they combat wrong.
Gathering 'neath our banner
  While the trumpets blend,
Here in fervent manner
  Let our praise ascend.

3 Plucked as brands from burning,
  Saved by Jesus' might,
Earth's allurement spurning,
  We for Christ will fight.
He who found and freed us
  From our captive chain,
Surely he shall lead us
  To eternal gain.

4 Wondrous, wondrous story
  Of our God-made host,
Unto Jesus glory,
  'Tis in him we boast.
Out of every nation,
  By his might restored,
Army of salvation,
  Army of the Lord.
  Charles Coller (1863-1935)

804 Hold the fort, 344
8.5.8.5.

HO, my comrades, see the signal
  Waving in the sky!
Reinforcements now appearing,
  Victory is nigh.

Hold the fort, for I am coming,
  Jesus signals still;
Wave the answer back to Heaven:
  By thy grace we will.

2 See the mighty host advancing,
  Satan leading on;
Mighty men around us falling,
  Courage almost gone.

3 See the glorious banner waving,
  Hear the trumpet blow;
In our leader's name we'll triumph
  Over every foe.

4 Fierce and long the battle rages,
  But our help is near;
Onward comes our great commander;
  Cheer, my comrades, cheer!
  Philip Paul Bliss (1838-76)

805 Never mind, go on! 746

IN the fight, say, does your heart grow
     weary?
Do you find your path is rough and thorny,
And above the sky is dark and stormy?
     Never mind, go on!
Lay aside all fear, and onward pressing,
Bravely fight and God will give his
     blessing;
Though the war at times may prove
     distressing,
     Never mind, go on!

When the road we tread is rough,
  Let us bear in mind,
In our Saviour strength enough
  We may always find;
Though the fighting may be tough
  Let our motto be:
Go on, go on to victory!

2 Faithful be, delaying not to follow
  Where Christ leads, though it may be
       through sorrow;
  If the strife should fiercer grow tomorrow,
       Never mind, go on!
  Cheerful be, it will your burdens lighten,
  One glad heart will always others brighten;
  Though the strife the coward's soul may
       frighten,
       Never mind, go on!

3 When downhearted, look away to Jesus,
  Who for you did shed his blood most
       precious;
  Let us say, though all the world should
       hate us:
       Never mind, go on!
  Do your best in fighting for your Saviour,
  For his sake fear not to lose men's favor;
  If beside you should a comrade waver,
       Never mind, go on!
                    Richard Slater (1854-1939)

806 Maryland, 64
                              D.L.M.

I'VE found the secret of success,
     'Tis holding on, 'tis holding on;
The way to every blessedness,
     'Tis holding on, 'tis holding on.
Our warfare may be hard and fierce,
Oft Satan's arrows wound and pierce,
But still we get more smiles than tears
     By holding on, by holding on.

2 Have you your fighting just begun?
     Keep holding on, keep holding on;
  The hardest battles have been won
     By holding on, by holding on.
  Though you may meet with runaways
  Who mourn their weakness half their days,
  Yet you can gain eternal praise
     By holding on, by holding on.

3 If full salvation you would gain,
     Keep holding on, keep holding on;
  To conquer sins that bring you pain,
     Keep holding on, keeping holding on.
  God loves to give the better part,
  Not unto those who only start,
  But those who seek with all their heart,
     And then in faith keep holding on.
                         Ruth Tracy (1870-1960)

807 Joy in The Salvation Army, 706

JOY! joy! joy! there is joy in The Salva-
     tion Army,
     Joy! joy! joy! in the Army of the Lord.
  Sing to God, sing to God, with loud joyful
     songs of praise;
  Beat the drums, beat the drums, while sal-
     vation music plays.
  Play the music, play, sing the happy song,
  Loud hosannas shout with the happy
     throng,
  To the happy land we'll march along,
     And be joyful all the way.

2 Joy! joy! joy! there is joy in The Salvation
     Army,
     Joy! joy! joy! in the Army of the Lord.
  Blood and fire, blood and fire, is the Army
     soldier's might;
  Blood and fire, blood and fire, is our vic-
     tory in the fight.
  'Tis the blood and fire gives the battle cry,
  'Tis the blood and fire makes the foe to
     fly,
  'Tis the blood and fire gives the Army joy
     And victory all the way.

3 Joy! joy! joy! there is joy in The Salvation
     Army,
     Joy! joy! joy! in the Army of the Lord.
  We will sing, we will sing, till the world is
     full of joy;
  We will shout, we will shout, till glad voices
     rend the sky.
  With a thousand bands and a thousand
     drums

We will praise the Lord in bright, happy homes,
We will sing and shout till the Master comes,
We will ever praise the Lord.

William James Pearson (1832-92)

808 We shall win, 508
9.9.9.9.

LET us sing of his love once again,
Of the love that can never decay,
Of the blood of the Lamb who was slain,
Till we praise him again in that day.

I believe Jesus saves,
And his blood makes me whiter than
snow.

2 There is cleansing and healing for all
Who will wash in the life-giving flood;
There is perfect deliverance and joy
To be had in this world through the blood.

3 Even now while we taste of his love,
We are filled with delight through his name;
But what will it be when above
We shall join in the song of the Lamb!

4 Then we'll march in his name, till we come
At his bidding to cease from the fight;
And our Saviour shall welcome us home
To the mansions of glory and light.

5 So with banners unfurled to the breeze,
Our motto shall holiness be,
Till the crown from his hand we shall seize,
And the King in his glory we see.

Francis Bottome (1823-94)

809 Over Jordan, 768

MAKE the world with music ring,
While with heart and voice we sing
Praises to our God and King,
Hallelujah!
Tell with no uncertain sound,
To the nations all around,
Of the Saviour we have found,
Hallelujah!

Hallelujah! Hallelujah!
We shall conquer through the blood,
Give the glory all to God;
Hallelujah! Hallelujah!
We shall conquer through the blood,
Hallelujah!

2 Through the blood we shall prevail,
Though both earth and Hell assail,
God in man can never fail,
Hallelujah!
Keep your weapons sharp and bright,
Buckle on the armor tight,
Fighting is our great delight,
Hallelujah!

3 Everlasting arms are round,
Walls of fire the saints surround,
Enemies we shall confound,
Hallelujah!
Forward with the sword and shield,
Victory waits us on the field,
Stand your ground and never yield,
Hallelujah!

4 Sing your songs, ye saints of light,
Soon we shall escape from night,
Up to glory wing our flight,
Hallelujah!
Face to face we then shall see
Him who died upon the tree,
Crowned with glory we shall be,
Hallelujah!

John Lawley (1859-1922)

810 The day of victory's coming, 815

MARCH on, salvation soldiers,
March forward to the fight,
With Jesus as our leader,
We'll put the foe to flight;
In spite of men and devils
We'll raise our banner high,
For the day of victory's coming by and by.

The day of victory's coming, 'tis coming
by and by,
When to the cross of Calvary all
nations they will fly;
We're soldiers in the Army, we'll fight
until we die,
For the day of victory's coming by
and by.

2 Hell's forces may be mighty,
A strong opposing band,
Yet never be discouraged,
For Jesus boldly stand;
With blood and fire we'll conquer,
Our every foe defy,
For the day of victory's coming by and by.

224

3   Though some would try to crush us,
    We're rising every day,
    And soon o'er every land and sea
    Our flag shall have the sway;
    Salvation free to all men
    Shall be our battle cry,
For the day of victory's coming by and by.
James Conner Bateman (1854-88)

811   A robe of white, 598

MARCHING on in the light of God,
    Marching on, I am marching on;
Up the path that the Master trod,
    Marching, marching on.

A robe of white, a crown of gold,
    A harp, a home, a mansion fair,
A victor's palm, a joy untold,
    Are mine when I get there.

For Jesus is my Saviour, he's washed
    my sins away,
Died for me on Calvary's mountain;
I'm happy in his wondrous love, singing
    all the day,
I'm living, yes, I'm living in the
    fountain.

2 Marching on through the hosts of sin,
    Marching on, I am marching on;
Victory's mine while I've Christ within;
    Marching, marching on.

3 Marching on in the Spirit's might,
    Marching on, I am marching on;
More than conqueror in every fight;
    Marching, marching on.

4 Marching on with the flag unfurled,
    Marching on, I am marching on;
Preaching Christ to a dying world;
    Marching, marching on.
Robert Johnson

812   Carlisle, 164; St Michael, 175   S.M.

MY soul, be on thy guard!
    Ten thousand foes arise,
The hosts of sin are pressing hard
    To draw thee from the skies.

2   O watch and fight and pray,
    The battle ne'er give o'er!
Renew it boldly every day,
    And help divine implore.

3   Ne'er think the victory won,
    Nor lay thine armor down;
The work of faith will not be done
    Till thou obtain the crown.
George Heath (1750-1822)

813   War Cry, 843

ON to the conflict, soldiers, for the right,
    Arm you with the Spirit's sword and
    march to fight;
Truth be your watchword, sound the ring-
    ing cry:
    Victory, victory, victory!

Ever is the war cry,
    Victory, victory!
Ever is the war cry,
    Victory!
Write it on your banners,
    Get it on your knees,
Victory, victory, victory!

2 Fiercely it rages, deadly is the strife,
But the prize that you shall win is endless
    life;
Jesus shall crown you, your reward shall
    be
    Victory, victory, victory!

3 Valiant and cheerful, marching right along,
Every foe shall quit the field, though proud
    and strong;
Fear shall oppress them; truth shall make
    them flee;
    Victory, victory, victory!

4 Soon shall the warfare and the conflict
    cease,
Soon shall dawn the welcome day of last-
    ing peace;
Foes all subdued, we'll raise the joyful cry:
    Victory, victory, victory!
William Howard Doane (1832-1915)

814   Steadily forward march! 799

SALVATION is our motto,
    Salvation is our song,
And round the wide, wide world,
    We'll send the cry along.
Yes, Jesus is the sinners' friend,
    The Bible tells us so;
Their many sins he will forgive,
    And wash them white as snow.

The Salvation Soldier

Steadily forward march! to Jesus we
will bring
Sinners of every kind, and he will take
them in.
Rich and poor as well, it does not
matter who,
Bring them in with all their sin;
He'll wash them white as snow.

2 Though all the world oppose us,
Yet we will never fear,
With Jesus as our leader
His presence ever near;
A wall of fire around us,
We'll never doubt his power,
But forward go the lost to save,
Yes, from this very hour.

3 Then forward to the conflict,
As through the world we go
Rejoicing in the blood
That washes white as snow.
Yes, we will fight for Jesus,
Though fierce the battle be;
O'er sin and Satan he will give
His soldiers victory.
James Slack (c 1888)

815 Shout aloud salvation, 785

SHOUT aloud salvation, and we'll have
another song;
Sing it with a spirit that will start the world
along;
Sing it as our comrades sang it many a
thousand strong,
As they were marching to Glory.

March on, march on! we bring the
jubilee;
Fight on, fight on! salvation makes us
free;
We'll shout our Saviour's praises over
every land and sea
As we go marching to Glory.

2 How the anxious shout it when they hear
the joyful sound!
How the weakest conquer when the Saviour they have found!
How our grand battalions with triumphant power abound,
As we go marching to Glory.

3 So we'll make a thoroughfare for Jesus
and his train;
All the world shall hear us as fresh con-
verts still we gain;
Sin shall fly before us for resistance is in
vain,
As we go marching to Glory.
George Scott Railton (1849-1913)

816 Theodora, 297; Hendon, 282
7.7.7.7.
STRIVE, when thou art called of God,
When he draws thee by his grace,
Strive to cast away the load
That would hinder in the race.

2 Fight, though it may cost thy life;
Storm the kingdom, but prevail;
Let not Satan's fiercest strife
Make thee, warrior, faint or quail.

3 Art thou faithful? Wake and watch.
Love with all thy heart Christ's ways;
Seek not worldly ease to snatch,
Look not for reward or praise.

4 Soldiers of the cross, be strong!
Watch and war through fear or pain,
Daily conquering sin and wrong,
Till our King o'er earth shall reign.
Johann Joseph Winckler (1670-1722),
trs Catherine Winkworth (1827-78)

817 Keep in step, 707

VALIANT soldier, marching to the fray,
Keep in step all the time.
Do not lag or falter by the way,
Keep in step all the time.
You may find the way is long and drear,
Many dangers may cause you to fear;
Do not give in but strive and persevere
And keep in step all the time.

Keep in step all the time,
Keep in step all the time;
Don't fall out and rest for a while,
Follow Jesus all the way, and smile.
Keep in step all the time,
Keep in step all the time;
You will find each day your pathway
easy
If you keep in step all the time.

2 Valiant soldier, you must not despair,
   Keep in step all the time.
Follow Jesus gladly everywhere,
   Keep in step all the time.
March on bravely o'er the battlefield,
In the mighty conflict never yield,
But trust in Jesus, he's your guide and
   shield,
   So keep in step all the time.

3 Valiant soldier, fighting for the Lord,
   Keep in step all the time;
Don your armor, take your shield and
   sword,
   Keep in step all the time.
Forward, forward, 'tis the Lord's command,
In the cause of right now take your stand,
Go marching forward to the promised land,
And keep in step all the time.
Alfred Herbert Vickery (1894-1976)

818 Happy Song, 661

WE are marching on with shield and
   banner bright,
We will work for God and battle for the
   right,
We will praise his name, rejoicing in his
   might,
   And we'll work till Jesus calls.

Then awake, then awake, happy song,
   happy song;
Shout for joy, shout for joy, as we
   gladly march along.
We are marching onward, singing as
   we go,
To the promised land where living
   waters flow;
Come and join our ranks as soldiers
   here below,
   Come and work till Jesus calls.

2 In the open air our Army we prepare,
   As we rally round our blessèd standard
      there;
And the Saviour's cross we gladly learn to
   share
   While we work till Jesus calls.

3 We are marching on; our captain, ever
   near,
Will protect us still, his guiding voice we
   hear;
Let the foe advance, we'll never, never fear,
But we'll work till Jesus calls.

4 We are marching on and pressing t'wards
   the prize,
To a glorious crown beyond the glowing
   skies,
To the radiant fields where pleasure never
   dies,
   And we'll work till Jesus calls.
Fanny Crosby (1820-1915), alt

819 With the conquering Son of God, 862

WE are sweeping through the land,
   With the sword of God in hand,
We are watching and we're praying while
   we fight;
   On the wings of love we'll fly
   To the souls about to die,
And we'll lead them to behold the pre-
   cious light.

With the conquering Son of God
Who has washed us in his blood,
Dangers braving, sinners saving,
We are sweeping through the land.

2 O the blessèd Lord of light,
   We will serve him with our might,
And his arm shall bring salvation to the
   poor!
   They shall lean upon his breast,
   Know the sweetness of his rest;
Of his pardon he the vilest will assure.

3 We are sweeping on to win
   Perfect victory over sin,
And we'll shout the Saviour's praises
   evermore;
   When the strife on earth is done,
   And the final victory's won,
We'll rejoin our conquering comrades gone
   before.
George Scott Railton (1849-1913)

820 We shall win, 508
                                    9.9.9.9.

WE'RE a band that shall conquer the foe,
   If we fight in the strength of the King;
With the sword of the Spirit, we know,
   We sinners to Jesus shall bring.

I believe we shall win,
If we fight in the strength of the King.

2 We have conquered in times that are past,
   And scattered the foe from the field;
So we'll fight for the King to the last,
   And the sword of the Spirit we'll wield.

The Salvation Soldier

3 Our foe may be mighty and brave,
   And the fighting be hard and severe;
But the King is the mighty to save,
   And in conflict he always is near.

4 In the name of the King we will fight,
   With our banners unfurled to the breeze;
We will battle for God and the right,
   And the kingdom of Satan we'll seize.

5 Ever true to the Army and God,
   We will fight in the name of the King;
We shall win with the fire and the blood,
   And the world to his feet we shall bring.
        William Hodgson (1853-1926)

821   Happy Song, 661

WE'RE an Army fighting for a glorious King;
We will make the world with hallelujahs ring;
With victorious voices we will ever sing:
   There's salvation for the world.

For the world, for the world, Jesus died, Jesus died,
For the world, for the world, there is room in Jesus' side.
All the world to save, to battle we will go,
And we ever will our colors boldly show,
With a trumpet voice we'll let the millions know
   There's salvation for the world.

2 We're an Army brave, arrayed in armor bright;
We will turn the world from darkness into light;
As we march along we'll shout with all our might:
   There's salvation for the world.

3 We're an Army saved, by blood and fire made strong;
And with righteousness we mean to conquer wrong;
This shall be our universal battle song:
   There's salvation for the world.
        William James Pearson (1832-92)

822   We're the Army, 848

WE'RE the soldiers of the Army of salvation,
   That God is raising now to save the world;
And we won't lay down our arms till every nation
   Shall have seen the flag of blood and fire unfurled.

We're the Army that shall conquer,
As we go to seek the lost and to bring them back to God;
And his salvation to every nation
We will carry with the fire and the blood.

2 Though the hosts of Hell and darkness all surround us,
   By suffering and temptation we are tried,
But we know that not a foe can e'er confound us
   While Jehovah's mighty power is on our side.

3 So we'll put our trust in God who ne'er will fail us,
   We know that his salvation we shall see;
And through all the fighting, those who shall assail us
   Shall be conquered through the blood of Calvary.
        Thomas Charles Marshall (1854-1942)

823   Yield not to temptation, 579
        11.11.11.11.

YIELD not to temptation, for yielding is sin;
Each victory will help you some other to win.
Fight manfully onward, dark passions subdue;
Look ever to Jesus, he will carry you through.

Ask the Saviour to help you,
Comfort, strengthen and keep you;
He is willing to aid you,
He will carry you through.

2 Shun evil companions, bad language disdain,
God's name hold in reverence, nor take it in vain.

Be thoughtful and earnest, kind-hearted
and true;
Look ever to Jesus, he will carry you
through.

3 To him that o'ercometh God giveth a
crown;
Through faith we shall conquer though
often cast down.
He who is our Saviour our strength will
renew;
Look ever to Jesus, he will carry you
through.
Horatio Richmond Palmer (1834-1907)

* * *

see also: 700 The Lord's command to go into
the world
859 Jesus, with what gladness
866 Soldiers of King Jesus

The World for God

824 Whosoever will may come, 860

ALL have need of God's salvation,
If with him they'd live forever;
But a promise he has given,
It is written: Whosoever.

*Whosoever will may come,
And who comes to him shall never
Disappointed turn away;
Praise the Lord! 'tis whosoever.*

2 And this word it reaches nations;
Not the rich or learned or clever
Only shall by him be rescued,
O praise God! 'tis whosoever.

3 For the poor and brokenhearted
There's a hope, and they need never
Have a fear about their coming,
For the book says: Whosoever.

4 To all kingdoms and all peoples
'Tis the same, and shall be ever;
There's no difference in the message,
But to all 'tis whosoever.
William John McAlonan (1863-1925)

825 Harlan, 215; Moscow, 217
6.6.4.6.6.6.4.

CHRIST for the world, we sing;
The world to Christ we bring
With loving zeal;
The poor and those who mourn,
The faint and overborne,
Sin-sick and sorrow-worn,
Whom Christ doth heal.

2 Christ for the world, we sing;
The world to Christ we bring
With fervent prayer;
The wayward and the lost
By restless passions tossed,
Redeemed at countless cost
From dark despair.

3 Christ for the world, we sing;
The world to Christ we bring
With joyful song;
The new-born souls, whose days
Reclaimed from sin's dark ways,
Inspired with hope and praise,
To Christ belong.

4 Christ for the world, we sing;
The world to Christ we bring
With one accord;
With us the work to share,
With us reproach to dare,
With us the cross to bear,
For Christ our Lord.
Samuel Wolcott (1813-86)

826 Westminster, 142; St Peter, 129
C.M.

IN Christ there is no east or west,
In him no south or north,
But one great fellowship of love
Throughout the whole wide earth.

2 In him shall true hearts everywhere
Their high communion find;
His service is the golden cord
Close-binding all mankind.

3 Join hands then, brothers of the faith,
Whate'er your race may be;
Who serves my Father as a son
Is surely kin to me.

4 In Christ now meet both east and west,
In him meet south and north;
All Christly souls are one in him
Throughout the whole wide earth.
John Oxenham (1852-1941)

827 Peace, 185; Diademata, 182
D.S.M.

PEACE in our time, O Lord,
To all the peoples—peace!
Peace surely based upon thy will
And built in righteousness.
Thy power alone can break
The fetters that enchain
The sorely stricken soul of life,
And make it live again.

2   Too long mistrust and fear
     Have held our souls in thrall;
  Sweep through the earth, keen Breath of
      Heaven,
     And sound a nobler call!
     Come, as thou didst of old,
     In love so great that men
  Shall cast aside all other gods
     And turn to thee again.

3   O shall we never learn
     The truth all time has taught,
  That without God as architect
     Our building comes to naught?
     Lord, help us, and inspire
     Our hearts and lives that we
  May build, with all thy wondrous gifts,
     A Kingdom meet for thee.

4   Peace in our time, O Lord,
     To all the peoples—peace!
  Peace that shall build a glad new world,
     And make for life's increase.
     O living Christ, who still
     Dost all our burdens share,
  Come now and dwell within the hearts
     Of all men everywhere.

John Oxenham (1852-1941)

828   Alford, 245; St Theodulph, 262
                       7.6.7.6. D. Iambic

SALVATION! Shout salvation,
   We who God's gifts enjoy;
Let sanctified elation
   Our grateful songs employ.
The sweet redemption story
   To us is ever new;
To Jesus be the glory,
   Our Saviour strong and true.

2 Salvation! Sing salvation;
   Was e'er so grand a theme?
  Sing on till every nation
   Shall hear of Calvary's stream.
  Sing out the tidings glorious
   That God so loved the world,
  Till Christ shall be victorious
   And Hell be backward hurled.

3 Salvation! Speak salvation
   In every sinner's ear;
  It carries consolation,
   It stanches sorrow's tear.
  The sad, the sick, the dying,
   In Christ are fully blest;
  Yea, all on him relying
   In him find perfect rest.

4 Salvation! Shout salvation
   Till Jesus comes again
  To claim each blood-bought nation
   And o'er his Kingdom reign.
  Soon we in realms of Glory
   Shall join the ransomed throng,
  And sing the deathless story,
   Redemption's endless song.

Charles Coller (1863-1935)

829   Christ for the whole wide world, 628

TELL them in the east and in the west,
  Tell them of the one you love the best.
Tell them how to find the sweetest rest
Leaning on the loving Saviour's breast.
Tell them all about the dear old book,
Tell them there is life just for a look;
  Let this banner be unfurled:
  Christ for the whole wide world.

*Tell them of the baby in the manger
    laid,
    Sent from Heaven above;
Tell them how for them he was a
    ransom paid,
    Just because of love.
Tell them with your lips and by your
    actions too,
    And with flag unfurled,
Tell it out with a shout, tell it out with
    a shout:
    Christ for the whole wide world.*

2 To the beat of Army drums, make known
  That the Saviour-King has sin o'erthrown;
  Tell the rich and poor, the sad and lone,
  Till his power to everyone is shown.
  Tell it to the people you may meet,
  Tell it in the hall and in the street;
    Let this banner be unfurled:
    Christ for the whole wide world.

3 Tell it to the young and to the old,
  Tell them they may all be warriors bold,
  Tell them of the shepherd and the fold,
  Tell them of the heavenly harps of gold.
  Tell it with a clarion voice so clear,
  Let the story ring out far and near,
    Let this banner be unfurled:
    Christ for the whole wide world.

Arthur Smith Arnott (1870-1941), alt

The World for God

830 The world for God, 827

THE world for God! The world for God!
There's nothing else will meet the hunger of my soul.
I see forsaken children, I see the tears that fall
From women's eyes, once merry, now never laugh at all;
I see the sins and sorrows of those who sit in darkness;
I see in lands far distant, the hungry and oppressed.
But behold! On a hill, Calvary! Calvary!

The world for God! The world for God!
I give my heart! I'll do my part!
The world for God! The world for God!
I give my heart! I will do my part!

2 The world for God! The world for God!
I call to arms the soldiers of the blood and fire:
Go with the Holy Bible. Its words are peace and life
To multitudes who struggle with crime and want and strife.
Go with your songs of mercy, show Christ in loving kindness,
Make known the sufferings of the cross, the sacrifice of God;
For behold! On a hill, Calvary! Calvary!

3 The world for God! The world for God!
For this, dear Lord, give to my soul consuming fire.
Give fire that makes men heroes, turns weakness into might,
The fire that gives the courage to suffer for the fight,
The fire that changes fearing to pentecostal daring,
The fire that makes me willing for Christ to live or die;
For behold! On a hill, Calvary! Calvary!
Evangeline Booth (1865-1950)

831 Give to Jesus glory, 354
8.7.8.7. Iambic

TO save the world the Saviour came;
It was for this in mercy
He gave his life; the news proclaim
And give to Jesus glory.

Give to Jesus glory,
Give to Jesus glory,
Proclaim redemption's wondrous plan
And give to Jesus glory.

2 What matchless grace, how rich, how free!
Our Saviour calls all to him;
A Saviour he to all would be;
O give to Jesus glory!

3 In every land where man is found,
Let us make known the story
Of love divine; its praises sound
And give to Jesus glory.

4 There pardon is for all who come
Their sins confessing truly;
Then pardon claim, O guilty one,
And give to Jesus glory.
Richard Slater (1854-1939) (verses),
W. H. Clark (chorus)

832 When the mists have rolled away, 452
8.7.8.7. D. Troch.

WE are witnesses for Jesus
In the haunts of sin and shame,
In the underworld of sorrow
Where men seldom hear his name;
For to bind the brokenhearted
And their liberty proclaim,
We are witnesses for Jesus
In the haunts of sin and shame.

Tell the world, O tell the world!
Make salvation's story heard;
In the highways, in the byways,
And in lands beyond the sea,
Do some witnessing for Jesus
Wheresoever you may be.

2 We are witnesses for Jesus
In the lands beyond the sea,
Where the millions bound by evil
Have no hope of liberty;
As we tell the gospel tidings,
Lo! the captives are set free;
We are witnesses for Jesus
In the lands beyond the sea.

3 We are witnesses for Jesus
In the home and in the mart,
Where the cares of life and fashion
Crowd the Saviour from the heart;
When we urge his claims with wisdom
Many choose the better part;
We are witnesses for Jesus
In the home and in the mart.
William Drake Pennick (1884-1944)

833
Austria, 408; Blaenwern, 430
8.7.8.7. D. Troch.

WE have caught the vision splendid
Of a world which is to be,
When the pardoning love of Jesus
Freely flows from sea to sea,
When all men from strife and anger,
Greed and selfishness are free,
When the nations live together
In sweet peace and harmony.

2 We would help to build the city
Of our God, so wondrous fair;
Give our time, bring all our talents,
And each gift of beauty rare,
Powers of mind, and strength of purpose,
Days of labor, nights of strain,
That God's will may be accomplished,
O'er the kingdoms he shall reign.

3 Founded on the rock of ages,
Built upon God's promise sure,
Strengthened by the cords of service,
We shall stand firm and secure;
When the Father, Son and Spirit
Crown our labors with success,
Men and angels then uniting
Shall God's mighty love confess.

Doris N. Rendell (1896-1990)

see also: 160 Jesus shall reign where'er the sun
981 We've a story to tell to the nations

THE YOUNG SALVATIONIST
Childhood

834
Children of Jerusalem, 276
7.7.7.7.

CHILDREN of Jerusalem
Sang the praise of Jesus' name;
Children, too, of modern days,
Join to sing the Saviour's praise.

*Hark, hark, hark, while children's
voices sing!
Hark, hark, hark, while children's
voices sing
Loud hosannas, loud hosannas, loud
hosannas to our King!*

2 We are taught to love the Lord,
We are taught to read his word,
We are taught the way to Heaven,
Praise for all to God be given.

3 Parents, teachers, old and young,
All unite to swell the song,
Higher and yet higher rise
Till hosannas reach the skies.
John Henley (1800-42) alt

835
Strike for victory, 211; Ruth, 208
6.5.6.5. D.

CHILDREN, sing for gladness,
Tell the world in song
Of the Saviour's goodness,
Who forgives the wrong;
Spread the tidings everywhere,
Tell it all around,
What a loving Saviour
May by all be found.

*Sing, sing for gladness,
Children, sing;
Sing, sing in sweetness
For your King;
Sound out the praises
Everywhere,
Of a loving Saviour
Ever near.*

2 Sing about the mercy
Of our heavenly King,
Shout aloud the victories
He for us did bring,
How he left his throne above,
Pain and death to bear,
To reveal Heaven's glory
And to lead us there.

3 Sing aloud of Heaven,
Where the holy go,
Who through Jesus' power
Conquer every foe;
There in songs unbroken,
Bowed before his face,
Sing 'mid bliss unspoken
Of his wondrous grace.

Anon

Childhood

836 Come with happy faces, 196
6.5.6.5. D.

COME with happy faces
  To the place of prayer;
Jesus now is waiting,
  We shall find him there.

With a grateful spirit,
  Now our voices raise;
Thank him for his goodness
  In a song of praise.

2 Come with happy faces;
  Jesus rose today;
Leave the world behind us,
  Seek the narrow way.

3 Come with happy faces,
  Come with hearts sincere;
God our thought is reading,
  He is ever near.

4 Come with happy faces,
  Learn the words of truth;
Jesus loves his children;
  Trust him in your youth.
      Fanny Crosby (1820-1915)

837 Buckland, 275; Monkland, 286;
Last Hope, 284   7.7.7.7.

FATHER, lead me day by day,
  Ever in thine own sweet way;
Teach me to be pure and true,
Show me what I ought to do.

2 When in danger make me brave,
  Make me know that thou canst save,
Keep me safe by thy dear side,
Let me in thy love abide.

3 When I'm tempted to do wrong,
  Make me steadfast, wise and strong;
And when all alone I stand,
Shield me with thy mighty hand.

4 When my heart is full of glee,
  Help me to remember thee;
Happy most of all to know
That my Father loves me so.

5 When my work seems hard and dry,
  May I press on cheerily;
Help me patiently to bear
Pain and hardship, toil and care.

6 May I do the good I know,
  Be thy loving child below;
Then at last go home to thee,
Evermore thy child to be.
      John Page Hopps (1834-1911)

838 Horsley, 95; Sawley, 132
C.M.

GOD make my life a little light
  Within the world to glow;
A little flame that burneth bright
  Wherever I may go.

2 God make my life a little flower
  That giveth joy to all,
Content to bloom in native bower
  Although the place be small.

3 God make my life a little song
  That comforteth the sad,
That helpeth others to be strong,
  And makes the singer glad.

4 God make my life a little staff
  Whereon the weak may rest,
That so what strength and health I have
  May serve my neighbors best.
      Matilda Barbara Betham-Edwards
      (1836-1919)

839 Samuel, 229; Evening, 222
6.6.6.6.8.8.

HUSHED was the evening hymn,
  The temple courts were dark,
  The lamp was burning dim
    Before the sacred ark;
When suddenly a voice divine
Rang through the silence of the shrine.

2 The old man, meek and mild,
    The priest of Israel, slept;
  His watch the temple child,
    The little Levite, kept;
And what from Eli's sense was sealed,
The Lord to Hannah's son revealed.

3 O give me Samuel's ear,
    The open ear, O Lord,
  Alive and quick to hear
    Each whisper of thy word;
Like him to answer at thy call
And to obey thee first of all.

4 O give me Samuel's heart,
    A lowly heart, that waits
  Where in thy house thou art,
    Or watches at thy gates
By day and night, a heart that still
Moves at the breathing of thy will.

233

5   O give me Samuel's mind,
     A sweet unmurmuring faith,
    Obedient and resigned
      To thee in life and death;
That I may read with childlike eyes
Truths that are hidden from the wise.
James Drummond Burns (1823-64)

840
Festive Carol, 250; Tyrolese, 268;
I love to tell the story, A.S. 969
7.6.7.6. D. Iambic

I LOVE to hear the story
   Which angel voices tell,
How once the King of Glory
   Came down on earth to dwell;
I am both weak and sinful,
   But this I surely know:
The Lord came down to save me
   Because he loved me so.

2 I'm glad my blessèd Saviour
   Was once a child like me,
To show how pure and holy
   His little ones might be;
And if I try to follow
   His footsteps here below,
He never will forsake me
   Because he loves me so.

3 To sing his love and mercy
   My sweetest songs I'll raise;
For though I cannot see him,
   I know he hears my praise;
And mine his loving promise
   That even I may go
To sing among the angels,
   Because he loves me so.
Emily Huntington Miller (1833-1913)

841
Jesus bids us shine, 698

JESUS bids us shine with a clear, pure
   light,
Like a little candle burning in the night;
In the world is darkness, so we must shine,
You in your small corner and I in mine.

2 Jesus bids us shine first of all for him;
   Well he sees and knows it if our light is
     dim.
   He looks down from Heaven to see us
     shine;
   You in your small corner and I in mine.

3 Jesus bids us shine, then, for all around
   Many kinds of darkness in this world
     abound:
   Sin and want and sorrow; so we must
     shine,
   You in your small corner and I in mine.
Susan Bogart Warner (1819-85)

842
Stephanos, 343; Bristow, 341;
Bullinger, 342   8.5.8.3.

JESUS, friend of little children,
   Be a friend to me;
Take my hand and ever keep me
   Close to thee.

2 Show me what my love should cherish,
   What, too, it should shun,
Lest my feet for poison flowers
   Swift should run.

3 Teach me how to grow in goodness,
   Daily as I grow;
Thou hast been a child, and surely
   Thou dost know.

4 Step by step, O lead me onward,
   Upward into youth;
Wiser, stronger, still becoming
   In thy truth.
Walter John Mathams (1853-1931)

843
Yes, Jesus loves me, 304; Bowes, 274
7.7.7.7.

JESUS loves me! This I know,
   For the Bible tells me so;
Little ones to him belong;
   They are weak, but he is strong.

Yes, Jesus loves me;
The Bible tells me so.

2 Jesus loves me, he who died
   Heaven's gate to open wide;
He will wash away my sin,
   Let his little child come in.

3 Jesus loves me! He will stay
   Close beside me all the way;
If I love him, when I die
   He will take me home on high.
Anna Bartlett Warner (1827-1915)

844
A Sunbeam, 350
8.6.8.6.

JESUS wants me for a sunbeam,
   To shine for him each day,
In every way try to please him,
   At home, at school, at play.

Childhood

A sunbeam, a sunbeam,
Jesus wants me for a sunbeam;
A sunbeam, a sunbeam,
I'll be a sunbeam for him.

2 Jesus wants me to be loving
   And kind to all I see,
Showing how pleasant and happy
   His little one may be.

3 I will ask Jesus to help me
   To keep my heart from sin;
Ever reflecting his goodness,
   And always shine for him.

4 I'll be a sunbeam for Jesus,
   I can if I but try,
Serving him moment by moment,
   Then live with him on high.
   Nellie Talbot

845 Saviour, like a shepherd, 424;
Shepherd, 425   8.7.8.7.8.7. Troch.

SAVIOUR, like a shepherd lead us,
   Much we need thy tender care;
In thy pleasant pastures feed us,
   For our use thy folds prepare.
Blessèd Jesus, blessèd Jesus,
   Thou hast bought us, thine we are.

2 We are thine; do thou befriend us;
   Be the guardian of our way;
Keep thy flock, from sin defend us,
   Seek us when we go astray.
Blessèd Jesus, blessèd Jesus,
   Hear, O hear us when we pray!

3 Thou hast promised to receive us,
   Poor and sinful though we be;
Thou hast mercy to relieve us,
   Grace to cleanse and power to free.
Blessèd Jesus, blessèd Jesus,
   Let us early turn to thee.

4 Early let us seek thy favor;
   Early let us do thy will;
Gracious Lord, our only Saviour,
   With thyself our hearts now fill.
Blessèd Jesus, blessèd Jesus,
   Thou hast loved us, love us still.
   Attr Dorothy Ann Thrupp (1779-1847)

846 Buckland, 275; University College, 300
7.7.7.7.

SAVIOUR, teach me day by day
   Love's sweet lesson to obey;
Sweeter lesson cannot be,
Loving him who first loved me.

2 How shall I my life employ?
Love will be my only joy;
Ever new that joy will be,
Loving him who first loved me.

3 Teach me, Lord, thy steps to know,
By the way which thou didst go;
Ever keeping close to thee,
Loving him who first loved me.

4 So will I rejoice to show
All the love I feel and owe;
Ever serving, ever free,
Loving him who first loved me.
   Jane Eliza Leeson (1808-81)

847 Dare to be a Daniel, 635

STANDING by a purpose true,
   Heeding God's command,
Honor them, the faithful few;
   All hail to Daniel's band!

Dare to be a Daniel,
   Dare to stand alone,
Dare to have a purpose firm,
   Dare to make it known.

2 Many mighty men are lost,
   Daring not to stand,
Who for God had been a host
   By joining Daniel's band.

3 Many giants, great and tall,
   Stalking through the land,
Headlong to the earth would fall
   If met by Daniel's band.

4 Hold the gospel banner high;
   On to victory grand;
Satan and his host defy
   And shout for Daniel's band.
   Philip Paul Bliss (1838-76)

848 Stories of Jesus, 801

TELL me the stories of Jesus
   I love to hear;
Things I would ask him to tell me
   If he were here:
Scenes by the wayside,
   Tales of the sea,
Stories of Jesus,
   Tell them to me.

235

2 First let me hear how the children
    Stood round his knee;
And I shall fancy his blessing
    Resting on me;
Words full of kindness,
    Deeds full of grace,
All in the love-light
    Of Jesus' face.

3 Tell me, in accents of wonder,
    How rolled the sea,
Tossing the boat in a tempest
    On Galilee;
And how the Master,
    Ready and kind,
Chided the billows
    And hushed the wind.

4 Into the city I'd follow
    The children's band,
Waving a branch of the palm tree
    High in my hand;
One of his heralds,
    Yes, I would sing
Loudest hosannas:
    Jesus is King!

5 Show me that scene, in the garden,
    Of bitter pain;
And of the cross where my Saviour
    For me was slain;
Sad ones or bright ones,
    So that they be
Stories of Jesus;
    Tell them to me.

William Henry Parker (1845-1929)

849   Festive Carol, 250; Tyrolese, 268
                    7.6.7.6. D. Iambic

THE wise may bring their learning,
    The rich may bring their wealth,
And some may bring their greatness,
    And some bring strength and health.
We, too, would bring our treasures
    To offer to the King;
We have no wealth or learning,
    What shall we children bring?

2 We'll bring him hearts that love him,
    We'll bring him thankful praise,
And young souls meekly striving
    To walk in holy ways;
And these shall be the treasures
    We offer to the King,
And these are gifts that even
    The poorest child may bring.

3 We'll bring the little duties
    We have to do each day;
We'll try our best to please him
    At home, at school, at play;
And better are these treasures
    To offer to our King
Than richest gifts without them;
    Yet these a child may bring.

Anon

850   Hundreds and thousands, 672

THERE are hundreds of sparrows, thou-
    sands, millions,
They're two a penny, far too many there
    must be;
There are hundreds and thousands, mil-
    lions of sparrows,
But God knows every one and God
    knows me.

2 There are hundreds of flowers, thou-
    sands, millions,
And flowers fair the meadows wear for
    all to see;
There are hundreds and thousands, mil-
    lions of flowers,
But God knows every one and God
    knows me.

3 There are hundreds of planets, thou-
    sands, millions,
Way out in space each has a place by
    God's decree;
There are hundreds and thousands, mil-
    lions of planets,
But God knows every one and God
    knows me.

4 There are hundreds of children, thou-
    sands, millions,
And yet their names are written on God's
    memory;
There are hundreds and thousands, mil-
    lions of children,
But God knows every one and God
    knows me.

John Gowans

851   Carlisle, 164; Franconia, 168
                          S.M.

WE are the hands of Christ;
    He uses us each day
To show his love to everyone
    In every kind of way.

Childhood

2 We are the feet of Christ;
   His errands we must run
To fetch, to carry and to help
   In every way we can.

3 We are the eyes of Christ;
   All beauty we must share,
And hope one day to bring to you
   All those who do not care.

4 We are the lips of Christ;
   He speaks through us to men,
To cheer, to comfort and to tell
   Of his great love for them.

5 We are the friends of Christ;
   We love his work to do;
His friendship is so wonderful
   Will you not share it too?

David Rutherford Fraser

2 And since the Lord retaineth
   His love for children still,
Though now as King he reigneth
   On Zion's heavenly hill,
We'll serve beneath his banner
   Till victory is won,
And sing aloud: Hosanna
   To David's royal Son!

3 For should we fail proclaiming
   Our great redeemer's praise,
The stones, our silence shaming,
   Would their hosannas raise;
But shall we only render
   The tribute of our words?
No, while our hearts are tender,
   They, too, shall be the Lord's.

John King (1789-1858)

852 When he cometh, 578

WHEN he cometh, when he cometh
   To make up his jewels,
All his jewels, precious jewels,
   His loved and his own;

Like the stars of the morning,
His bright crown adorning,
They shall shine in their beauty
Bright gems for his crown.

2 He will gather, he will gather
   The gems for his Kingdom;
All the pure ones, all the bright ones,
   His loved and his own.

3 Little children, little children
   Who love their redeemer,
Are his jewels, precious jewels,
   His loved and his own.

William Orcutt Cushing (1823-1902)

853 Day of rest, 248; Hosanna, 255
7.6.7.6. D. Iambic

WHEN, his salvation bringing,
   To Zion Jesus came,
The children all stood singing
   Hosanna to his name;
Nor did their zeal offend him,
   But, as he rode along,
He bade them still attend him,
   And smiled to hear their song.

854 You can't stop God from loving you, 361
8.7.8.7. D. Iambic

YOU can't stop rain from falling down,
   Prevent the sun from shining,
You can't stop spring from coming in,
   Or winter from resigning,
Or still the waves or stay the winds,
   Or keep the day from dawning,
You can't stop God from loving you,
   His love is new each morning.

2 You can't stop ice from being cold,
   You can't stop fire from burning,
Or hold the tide that's going out,
   Delay its sure returning,
Or halt the progress of the years,
   The flight of fame or fashion,
You can't stop God from loving you,
   His nature is compassion.

3 You can't stop God from loving you
   Though you may disobey him,
You can't stop God from loving you,
   However you betray him;
From love like this no power on earth
   The human heart can sever,
You can't stop God from loving you,
   Not God—not now, nor ever.

John Gowans

* * *

see also: **323 I am so glad that our Father in Heaven**

237

The Young Salvationist

Youth

855 Alstone, 4
L.M.

A BOY was born in Bethlehem
With tiny hands and downy head;
The shepherds came to worship him
Asleep within a manger bed.

2 A boy grew up in Nazareth,
A sturdy lad and full of grace;
He laughed and ran and studied too,
And God smiled through his glowing
face.

3 A young man walked by Galilee,
He talked about a Kingdom fair
Where love alone can reign and rule,
And God was speaking through him
there.

4 On Calvary a young man died,
In sorrow bowed beneath the skies
He grieved for every child of man
While love beamed through his suffer-
ing eyes.

5 On Easter morning Jesus came
To hail the friends who mourned him
dead;
And lo, with bright, unclouded eyes,
They looked upon their living head.
Catherine Baird (1895-1984)

856 Ottawa, 462
8.7.8.7.7.7.

FOR your holy book we thank you,
And for all who served you well,
Writing, guarding and translating,
That its pages might forthtell
Your strong love and tender care
For your people everywhere.

2 For your holy book we thank you,
And for those who work today,
That the people of all nations,
Reading it, and following, may
Know your love and tender care
For your people everywhere.

3 For your holy book we thank you;
May its message be our guide,
May we understand the wisdom
Of the laws it will provide;
And your love and tender care
For your people everywhere.

4 For your holy book we thank you;
May its message in our hearts
Lead us now to see in Jesus
All the grace your word imparts;
All your love and tender care
For your people everywhere.
Ruth Carter (1900-82)

857 Happy Service, 660

GREATEST joy is found in serving Jesus
In the glad days of youth;
He alone can know the way, and lead me
Into the paths of truth.

*Lasting happiness and peace unending
Does the Saviour bestow on his
children;
Greatest joy is found in serving Jesus
In the glad days of youth.*

2 There's no other friend to help and cheer
me,
None else to be my guide;
I can tread the road of life in triumph
With Jesus by my side.

3 He has saved me, he will surely keep me
Free from the power of sin;
My desire is now to love him always,
Others for him to win.
*Jarl Wahlström,
versification by Brindley Boon*

858 A miracle of grace, 597

I'M going to make my life into a melody,
I'm going to praise my Saviour all day
long,
I'm going to make my life into a symphony,
A glorious symphony of song.

*For God will fill me with his power,
My pathway trace;
He's going to make my life into a
miracle,
A mighty miracle of grace.*

2 I'm going to set my face to climb the high-
est heights,
I'm going to conquer all the foes ahead,
I'm going to tread the noble way the saints
have trod,
Those warrior saints whom God has led.

238

3 I'm going to turn my life into an active
      quest,
   I'm going to plumb the depths of God's
      design,
   I'm going to taste the riches of his won-
      drous love,
   His gracious gifts of love divine.
                           Flora Larsson

859 Song of the highway, 210;
       Camberwell, 201   6.5.6.5. D.

JESUS, with what gladness I can truly
      sing:
Thou art my redeemer, friend and guide
   and King;
Thou art mine for ever; I will give to thee
All my life and treasure; thine alone I'll
   be.
   *All I have I give thee, though my powers
      are small,*
   *Life and time and talents, Jesus, take
      them all.*
   *All I have I give thee, though my powers
      are small,*
   *Life and time and talents, Jesus, take
      them all.*

2 I will be a warrior, fighting the good fight,
   Battling 'gainst all evil in the cause of right;
   Jesus, give me courage, make me true and
      brave
   That the lost and dying I may help to save.

3 I will be a pilgrim in the great crusade,
   Following thy footsteps, ever unafraid;
   Thou wilt lead me upward on the narrow
      way,
   Though it be through darkness, to thy
      glorious day.
                        Gladys M. Taylor

860 Misericordia, 475; Childhood, 471;
       Just as thou art, 474   8.8.8.6.

JUST as I am, thine own to be,
   Friend of the young who lovest me,
To consecrate myself to thee,
   O Jesus Christ, I come.

2 In the glad morning of my day,
   My life to give, my vows to pay,
   With no reserve, and no delay,
      With all my heart, I come.

3 Just as I am, young, strong and free,
   To be the best that I can be
   For truth and righteousness and thee,
      Lord of my life, I come.

4 With many dreams of fame and gold,
   Success and joy to make me bold;
   But dearer still my faith to hold,
      For my whole life, I come.

5 And for thy sake to win renown,
   And then to take my victor's crown,
   And at thy feet to cast it down,
      O Master, Lord, I come.
                  Marianne Farningham (1834-1909)

861 Harton-Lea, 20; Rimington, 42
                                  L.M.

LORD of my youth, teach me thy ways
   That I may serve thee all my days;
Naught to withhold from thee who gave
Thy greatest gift the world to save.

2 Lord of my youth, this heart of mine
   Enfold within thy love divine;
   With each emotion sanctified,
   Thy life in me be glorified.

3 Lord of my youth, in thought and deed
   I would from sin be ever freed;
   Pure be my tongue and clean my mind,
   In service bold, in action kind.

4 Lord of my youth, take thou my hands,
   Use them as thy great love demands;
   Swift be my feet to stay the pace
   Of running in the heavenly race.

5 Lord of my youth, I bring to thee
   All the blest gifts thou lendest me;
   Treasures of earth shall have no place
   Beside the riches of thy grace.
                           Brindley Boon

862 Day of rest, 248; Aurelia, 246
                        7.6.7.6. D. Iambic

O JESUS, I have promised
      To serve thee to the end,
Be thou for ever near me,
      My Master and my friend.
I shall not fear the battle
      If thou art by my side,
Nor wander from the pathway,
      If thou wilt be my guide.

2 O let me feel thee near me;
      The world is ever near;
   I see the sights that dazzle,
      The tempting sounds I hear.
   My foes are ever near me,
      Around me and within;
   But, Jesus, draw thou nearer
      And shield my soul from sin.

The Young Salvationist

3 O let me hear thee speaking
  In accents clear and still,
Above the storms of passion,
  The murmurs of self-will.
O speak to reassure me,
  To chasten or control;
O speak to make me listen,
  Thou Guardian of my soul.

4 O Jesus, thou hast promised
  To all who follow thee,
That where thou art in Glory,
  There shall thy servant be;
And, Jesus, I have promised
  To serve thee to the end;
O give me grace to follow,
  My Master and my friend.

John Ernest Bode (1816-74)

863 Sardis, 397; Stainer, 400; Galilee, 371
8.7.8.7. Troch.

PLAN our life, O gracious Saviour,
  Call upon us in our youth;
May we be, with high endeavor,
  Bearers of thy love and truth.

2 Hear us, Lord, our faults confessing,
  We would be renewed within,
Then, when armed with inward blessing,
  Shall our outward work begin.

3 Fill us with thy inspiration,
  All our works confirmed by thee;
Let them be thy revelation,
  Pure as thou wouldst have them be.

4 Give us courage when we falter,
  Balance thought before the act,
Placing talents on thine altar,
  Facing up to sternest fact.

5 With thy plan before us ever,
  Keep us loyal to our aim;
Then shall all our life's endeavor
  Glorify our Father's name.

Wilfrid Bayliss (1882-1952)

864 Pilgrims, 548; Hark, hark, my soul, 542
11.10.11.10.

RISE up, O youth! for mighty winds are
    stirring,
  Men's hearts grow faint through all the
    earth today;
Evil, with evil everywhere conferring,
  Summons its legions forth in dread
    array.

*Hear then our answer: Lord, lead us on
Fighting nor resting until thy war is
  won.*

2 Deep in our hearts another voice is calling,
  Urgent, insistent sounds the voice
    divine;
Out in the darkness men are thickly
    falling;
  Go with the cross, it is thy battle sign.

3 Forward, O youth! but first, in true sub-
    mission,
  Bring all thou hast and art to Christ, thy
    Lord;
Take from his hand his glorious
    commission,
  Rise then, and in his name unsheathe
    thy sword.

4 Arm then, O youth! the battle front in-
    creases,
  Leaping the frontiers of a stricken world;
Strive till the foes of God are dashed to
    pieces,
  Back with their armies into darkness
    hurled.

Will J. Brand (1889-1977)

865 South Shields, 444; Whither Pilgrims?
453   8.7.8.7. D. Troch.

SAVIOUR, while my heart is tender,
  I would yield that heart to thee;
All my powers to thee surrender,
  Thine and only thine to be.
Take me now, Lord Jesus, take me,
  Let my youthful heart be thine;
Thy devoted servant make me,
  Fill my soul with love divine.

2 Send me, Lord, where thou wilt send me,
  Only do thou guide my way;
May thy grace through life attend me,
  Gladly then shall I obey.
Let me do thy will, or bear it,
  I would know no will but thine;
Shouldst thou take my life, or spare it,
  I that life to thee resign.

3 May this solemn consecration
  Never once forgotten be;
Let it know no alteration,
  Registered, confirmed by thee.
Thine I am, O Lord, forever,
  To thy service set apart;
Suffer me to leave thee never,
  Seal thine image on my heart.

John Burton, Jr. (1803-77)

866 Song of the highway, 210

6.5.6.5. D.

SOLDIERS of King Jesus
  Fought in days of yore,
Mighty was their courage,
  Great the name they bore;
Valiantly they suffered,
  Gloriously they died,
Proud to serve their leader,
  Christ, the crucified.

Soldiers in the Army,
  Soldiers of the King,
Faith and dauntless courage
  To his cause we bring.
May we never waver,
  Strengthened by his might,
In his steps we follow,
  In his name we fight.

2 Jesus is our captain,
    Holy is his name;
  In his cause enlisted,
    Freedom we proclaim;
  'Gainst the powers of evil
    We will take our stand,
  Marching ever forward
    To Immanuel's land.

3 We will be his warriors,
    Soldiers of the cross,
  We will fight his battles,
    Fear not shame or loss;
  All the world his Kingdom,
    Every race his own,
  We will help to lead them
    To his royal throne.
          Doris N. Rendell (1896-1990)

867 Whitburn, 58; Llangollen, 32;
    Duke Street, 17; Simeon, 49   L.M.

THE Lord is King! I own his power,
  His right to rule each day and hour;
I own his claim on heart and will,
And his demands I would fulfil.

2 He claims my heart, to keep it clean
  From all defiling taint of sin;
  He claims my will, that I may prove
  How swift obedience answers love.

3 He claims my hands for active life
  In noble deeds and worthy strife;
  He claims my feet, that in his ways
  I may walk boldly all my days.

4 He claims my lips, that purest word
  In all my converse may be heard;
  My motives, passions, thoughts, that
    these,
  My inner life, my King may please.

5 He claims the brightness of my youth,
  My earnest strivings after truth;
  My joys, my toil, my craftsman's skill,
  All have their place, and serve his will.

6 O Lord, my King, I turn to thee!
  Thy loyal service makes me free;
  My daily task thou shalt assign,
  For heart and will and life are thine.
          Darley Terry (1847-1933)

868 The pathway of duty, 448

8.7.8.7. D. Troch.

THERE'S a road of high adventure,
  There's a Kingdom fair to gain,
There's a cross to follow bravely,
  And a warfare to maintain.
For the splendor of his service
  To the youth of every land,
God's own trumpeters are sounding;
  Who will heed the great command?

By the pathway of duty
  Flows the river of God's grace;
By the pathway of duty
  Flows the river of God's grace.

2 There's a city of the future
    Which the Lord will surely build,
  Where the hopes of all the ages
    Shall with glory stand fulfilled;
  And the master builder calleth;
    Hands are wanted, hear him say,
  Youthful hands to build my city;
    Who will offer them today?

3 There are multitudes in darkness,
    Where the light may never shine
  Till the torch of youth, uplifted,
    Beams with radiance divine;
  There's a world at random drifting,
    Which belongs to Christ the Lord;
  He is claiming youth's allegiance
    Till his Kingdom is restored.
          Will J. Brand (1889-1977) (verses),
          Sidney Edward Cox (1887-1975) (chorus)

The Young Salvationist

869 Marianina, 420

WE find pleasure in the Army;
 Gladly we our tuneful tribute pay;
Launched upon a high adventure,
 Learning both to work and pray,
 Youth is learning how to pray,
 How to work and fight and pray,
Turning leisure into treasure
 That shall time itself outstay.

2 In the Army there is service;
 Youth is called upon its part to play;
We may build a grand tomorrow
 If we heed the call today,
 Yes, 'tis ours, this call today,
 Youth's most urgent call today;
Full employment brings enjoyment;
 Join us then without delay.

3 There is witness in the Army,
 Like a lamp of clear and living flame
That is fed by saints unnumbered
 Telling of the Saviour's name,
 Of the wonder of his name,
 Of salvation in his name;
Living, dying, testifying,
 They his saving grace proclaim.

4 There's a future for the Army
 Till this great and glorious war is won;
Girding on salvation armor,
 Youth proclaims its fight begun;
 Yes, we truly have begun;
 And our warfare once begun,
God reliant, Hell defiant,
 We will earn the King's: Well done.
                                   Will J. Brand (1889-1977)

870 St Theodulph, 262; Tyrolese, 268;
Festive Carol, 250   7.6.7.6. D. Iambic

WE praise thee, heavenly Father,
 For all thy tender care;
Rich tokens of thy mercy
 And love are everywhere,
Thou art from everlasting,
 And ever shalt endure;
Throughout unending ages
 Thy promises are sure.

2 We praise thy name, Lord Jesus,
 Thou art the Christ divine;
No sacrificial offering
 Can e'er compare with thine,
Living thy life for others,
 Then dying on the tree,
To rise again triumphant
 In glorious majesty.

3 We praise thee, Holy Spirit,
 Revealer of the truth;
Seal us thine own, we pray thee,
 In these glad days of youth.
Equip for joyful service,
 Arm us with holy might,
Give victory in temptation
 And courage for the fight.

4 We worship and adore thee,
 Blest Trinity above;
Our lives we gladly yield thee
 As tokens of our love.
Thine own we now restore thee,
 Our wills to thee resign;
Accept our grateful offerings
 And make us fully thine.
                          Walter Henry Windybank (1872-1952)

871 Mozart, 496
                                    8.8.8.8.8.8. Iambic

WHAT wondrous gifts are in my care,
 Of body, intellect and will,
Of time and place to think and plan
 And to employ my every skill;
My great creator's power to bless
In silent worship I confess.

2 O holy Jesus, come from God,
 I blend my wak'ning thought with thine,
Who found amid the fields and hills
 Deep secrets of the flower and vine;
And in the quiet Temple heard,
With eager mind, the sacred word.

3 O Jesus, Master, teach me now
 My various energies to use;
I would be humbly questioning
 Nor any gleam of light refuse,
That I, at last, with glad surprise,
May share the virtue of the wise.

4 The grandeur of the universe
 In awful majesty unfolds,
And far beyond our keenest sight
 Are mysteries no man beholds;
Still God, whose might must yet appear,
In thee, O Jesus, cometh near.
                              Catherine Baird (1895-1984)

THE LIFE TO COME

872 My beautiful home, 36; Job, 30
L.M.

ABOVE the waves of earthly strife,
  Above the ills and cares of life,
Where all is peaceful, bright and fair,
My home is there, my home is there.

My beautiful home, my beautiful home,
  In the land where the glorified ever
    shall roam,
Where angels bright wear crowns of
    light,
  My home is there, my home is there.

2 Away from sorrow, doubt and pain,
  Away from worldly loss and gain,
  From all temptation, tears and care,
  My home is there, my home is there.

3 Beyond the bright and pearly gates,
  Where Jesus, loving Saviour, waits,
  Where all is peaceful, bright and fair,
  My home is there, my home is there.
                    Mary Ann Kidder (1825-1905)

873 Beautiful Star, 273

BEAUTIFUL land, so bright, so fair,
  Untold glories linger there,
Crystal rivers and shining strand,
Home of the soldier, beautiful land!

Beautiful home, beautiful home,
Home of the soldier, beautiful,
    beautiful home.

2 Beautiful theme, the courts above
  Echo with redeeming love,
  Songs triumphant and music grand,
  Home of the soldier, beautiful land!

3 Beautiful prospect, converse sweet,
  Kindred souls each other greet;
  Blest are thy children, a holy band,
  Home of the soldier, beautiful land!

4 Beautiful thought, though earth decay,
  Stars grow pale and pass away,
  Firmly shall thy foundation stand,
  Home of the soldier, beautiful land!
                              R. Moorcock

874 Newcastle, 65; Maryland, 68
D.L.M.

BRIEF is our journey through the years,
  And fleeting are our longest days;
We cherish every laden hour
  And linger o'er familiar ways;
For toil and grief, or joy and gain,
  When blessed by God, are sanctified,
And friendships forged through serving
    him,
  With each new test, are purified.

2 Yet know we that the sun must set,
    The darkness of the night draws near
  When we, as all men, must obey
    The voice inaudible, but clear,
  That calls us from beyond the years,
    Away from all we feel and see;
  How shall we bear a last farewell,
    O beauteous world, how part from thee?

3 With Jesus' name upon their lips,
    The vale of death his servants tread;
  In him they dared believe; in him
    They dare depart; nor sigh, nor dread;
  To love committing all their loves,
    All counted good through peace or strife,
  Content to die believing still
    In Jesus, everlasting life.
                    Catherine Baird (1895-1984)

875 Calfaria, 412; Bithynia, 409
8.7.8.7.8.7. Troch.

DAY of judgment! Day of wonders!
  Hark the trumpet's awful sound,
Louder than a thousand thunders,
  Shakes the vast creation round!
    How the summons
  Will the sinner's heart confound!

2 See the judge, our nature wearing,
    Clothed in majesty divine!
  Ye who long for his appearing
    Then shall say: This God is mine.
      Gracious Saviour,
    Own us in that day as thine.

3 Now the powers of nature, shaken
    At his look, prepare to flee;
  Souls in sin's deep sleep must waken,
    Summoned now his wrath to see;
      Careless sinner,
    What will then become of thee?

4 But to those who have confessèd,
   Loved and served the Lord below,
He will say: Come near, ye blessèd,
   See the Kingdom I bestow.
     You forever
   Shall my love and glory know!
John Newton (1725-1807)

876   St Philip, 514; Sine Nomine, 515
10.10.10.8.

FOR all the saints who from their labors
   rest,
Who thee by faith before the world
   confessed,
Thy name, O Jesus, be forever blessed,
   Hallelujah! Hallelujah!

2 Thou wast their rock, their fortress and
   their might;
Thou, Lord, their captain in the well-fought
   fight;
Thou in the darkness drear their one true
   light,
   Hallelujah! Hallelujah!

3 O may thy soldiers, faithful, true and bold,
Fight as the saints who nobly fought of
   old,
And win, with them, the victor's crown of
   gold,
   Hallelujah! Hallelujah!

4 And when the strife is fierce, the warfare
   long,
Steals on the ear the distant triumph song,
And hearts are brave again, and arms are
   strong,
   Hallelujah! Hallelujah!

5 But lo! there breaks a yet more glorious
   day:
The saints triumphant rise in bright array;
The King of Glory passes on his way,
   Hallelujah! Hallelujah!
William Walsham How (1823-97)

877   Forever with the Lord, 183
D.S.M.

FOREVER with the Lord!
   Amen; so let it be!
Life from the dead is in that word,
   'Tis immortality.
   Here in the body pent,
   Absent from him I roam,
Yet nightly pitch my moving tent
   A day's march nearer home.

2 My Father's house on high,
   Home of my soul, how near
At times, to faith's foreseeing eye,
   Thy golden gates appear.
   Ah! then my spirit faints
   To reach the land I love,
The bright inheritance of saints,
   Jerusalem above.

3 Forever with the Lord!
   Father, if 'tis thy will,
The promise of that faithful word
   E'en here in me fulfil.
   Be thou at my right hand,
   Then can I never fail;
Uphold thou me, and I shall stand,
   Fight, and I must prevail.

4 So when my latest breath
   Shall rend the veil in twain,
By death I shall escape from death,
   And life eternal gain.
   Knowing as I am known,
   How shall I love that word,
And oft repeat before the throne:
   Forever with the Lord!
James Montgomery (1771-1854)

878   Troyte, 470; Almsgiving, 469
8.8.8.4.

FOR those we love within the veil,
   Who once were comrades of our way,
We thank thee, Lord; for they have gone
   To cloudless day.

2 And life for them is life indeed,
   The splendid goal of earth's strait race;
And where no shadows intervene
   They see thy face.

3 Free from the fret of mortal years,
   And knowing now thy perfect will,
With quickened sense and heightened joy
   They serve thee still.

4 O fuller, sweeter is that life,
   And larger, ampler is the air;
Eye cannot see nor heart conceive
   The glory there!

5 There are no tears within their eyes;
   With love they keep perpetual tryst;
And praise and work and rest are one
   With thee, O Christ.
William Charter Piggott (1872-1943)

The Life to Come

879 They'll sing a welcome home, 140
C.M.

GIVE me the wings of faith to rise
  Within the veil and see
The saints above, how great their joys,
  How bright their glories be.

They'll sing their welcome home to me,
They'll sing their welcome home to me;
  And the angels will stand
  On the hallelujah strand,
And sing me a welcome home.
Welcome, welcome home!
  And the angels will stand
  On the hallelujah strand,
And sing me a welcome home.

2 Once they were mourners here below
    And poured out cries and tears;
  They wrestled hard, as we do now,
    With sins and doubts and fears.

3 I ask them whence their victory came;
    They, with united breath,
  Ascribe their conquest to the Lamb,
    Their triumph to his death.

4 They marked the footsteps that he trod;
    His zeal inspired their breast;
  And, following their incarnate God,
    Possess the promised rest.

5 Our glorious leader claims our praise
    For his own pattern given,
  While the long cloud of witnesses
    Shows the same path to Heaven.
                Isaac Watts (1674-1748) (verses),
                Robert Lowry (1826-99) (chorus)

880 St Matthew, 157;
Land of pure delight, 154   D.C.M.

HOW happy every child of grace
  Who knows his sins forgiven!
This earth, he cries, is not my place,
  I seek my place in Heaven,
A country far from mortal sight;
  Yet, O by faith, I see
The land of rest, the saints' delight,
  The Heaven prepared for me!

2 A stranger in the world below,
    I calmly sojourn here;
  Nor can its happiness or woe
    Provoke my hope or fear.
  Its evils in a moment end,
    Its joys as soon are past;
  But O the bliss to which I tend
    Eternally shall last!

3 To that Jerusalem above
    With singing I repair;
  While in the flesh, my hope and love,
    My heart and soul, are there;
  There my exalted Saviour stands,
    My merciful high priest,
  And still extends his wounded hands
    To me, of saints the least.

4 Then let me joyfully remove
    That fuller life to share;
  I shall not lose my friends above,
    But more enjoy them there.
  There we in Jesus' praise shall join,
    His boundless love proclaim,
  And sing the everlasting song
    Of Moses and the Lamb.
                Charles Wesley (1707-88)

881 My home is in Heaven, 740

I HAVE a home that is fairer than day,
  And my dear Saviour has shown me the
    way;
Oft when I'm sad and temptations arise,
  I look to my home far away.

My home is in Heaven, there is no
    parting there,
All will be happy, glorious, bright and
    fair;
There'll be no sorrow, there will be no
    tears,
  In that bright home far away.

2 Friends I shall see who have journeyed
    before
  And landed safe on that beautiful shore;
  I shall see Jesus, that will be my joy
    In that bright home far away.

3 O who will journey to Heaven with me?
  Jesus has died that we all may be free;
  Come then to him who has laid up for you
    A crown in that home far away.
                Ada Mary Nisbett (c 1866-1931)

882 Nuttall, 192; Santa Lucia, 194
6.4.6.4.6.6.6.4.

I'M but a stranger here,
  Heaven is my home;
Earth is a desert drear,
  Heaven is my home.
Danger and sorrow stand
Round me on every hand;
Heaven is my fatherland,
  Heaven is my home.

The Life to Come

2 What though the tempest rage,
   Heaven is my home;
Short is my pilgrimage,
   Heaven is my home.
And time's wild wintry blast
Soon will be overpast,
I shall reach home at last,
   Heaven is my home.

3 There, at my Saviour's side,
   Heaven is my home,
I shall be glorified,
   Heaven is my home;
There, with the good and blest,
Those I loved most and best,
I shall forever rest,
   Heaven is my home.

Thomas Rawson Taylor (1807-35)

883 Kidder, 709

LORD, I care not for riches, neither silver
      nor gold;
I would make sure of Heaven, I would enter the fold.
In the book of thy Kingdom, with its pages
   so fair,
Tell me, Jesus, my Saviour, is my name
   written there?

Is my name written there,
On the page white and fair?
In the book of thy Kingdom,
Is my name written there?

2 Lord, my sins they are many, like the
      sands of the sea,
But thy blood, O my Saviour, is sufficient
   for me;
For thy promise is written in bright letters
   that glow:
Though your sins be as scarlet, I will make
   them like snow.

3 O that beautiful city with its mansions of
   light,
With its glorified beings in pure garments
   of white;
Where no evil thing cometh to despoil what
   is fair;
Where the angels are watching, yes, my
   name's written there.

Yes, my name's written there,
On the page white and fair,
In the book of thy Kingdom,
Yes, my name's written there.

Mary Ann Kidder (1825-1905)

884 Some glad, sweet day, 791

O HOW I'd like to see his face,
   My Lord beholding!
O how I'd like to take my place,
   His arms enfolding!
Someday I'll cross old Jordan's tide,
Someday the gates will open wide,
Then I shall at his feet abide,
   My Lord beholding.

Someday I'll see his blessèd face,
Someday I'll see his blessèd face,
I'll hear the music of his voice,
Some glad, sweet day.

2 There on the cross he died for me,
   My soul redeeming;
Up from the grave he rose for me,
   My pardon sealing.
Someday I'll cross old Jordan's tide,
Someday the gates will open wide,
Then I shall at his feet abide,
   My Lord beholding.

3 O'er all the hills and dales of life,
   With Jesus walking,
Amidst the noise of earthly strife,
   I hear him talking.
Someday I'll cross old Jordan's tide,
Someday the gates will open wide,
Then I shall at his feet abide,
   My Lord beholding.

Arthur Smith Arnott (1870-1941)

885 Euphony, 493; St Catherine, 499
8.8.8.8.8.8. Iambic

O SOUL, consider and be wise,
   And seek salvation while you may,
In this alone your safety lies
   Against the awful judgment day;
'Tis Heaven or Hell, the choice is yours
Which through eternity endures.

2 Satan has taught mankind to sin,
   And lures them from the heavenly goal;
Shall he a further triumph win,
   And doom your unrepenting soul
To travel an unending road,
Forever separate from God?

3 Where God is not! O awful thought,
   A realm deserted, cast aside,
With sin to full fruition brought
   And evil crowned and deified;
Where dread remorse and vain desire
Burn like an unconsuming fire.

4 God stoops from Heaven your soul to save,
   He calls you now from Calvary;
What hope have you beyond the grave,
   And who can give you hope but he?
Why longer in your sin remain?
For your redemption Christ was slain.
Will J. Brand (1889-1977)

886

The home over there,483; We speak of
the realms, 484   8.8.8.8. Amph.

O THINK of the home over there,
   By the side of the river of light,
Where the saints all immortal and fair
   Are robed in their garments of white.

Over there, over there, O think of the
   home over there.
Over there, over there, O think of the
   home over there.

2 O think of the friends over there,
   Who before us the journey have trod;
Of the song that they breathe on the air
   In their home in the palace of God.

3 My Saviour is now over there,
   Where my kindred and friends are at
      rest;
Then away from my sorrow and care
   Let me fly to the land of the blest.

4 I'll soon be at home over there,
   For the end of my journey I see;
Many dear to my heart over there
   Are waiting and watching for me.
De Witt Clinton Huntington (1830-1912)

887

Jordan's Banks, 102
      C.M.

ON Jordan's stormy banks I stand,
   And cast a wistful eye
To Canaan's fair and happy land,
   Where my possessions lie.

I am bound for the promised land,
I'm bound for the promised land;
O who will come and go with me?
I am bound for the promised land.

2 That bright, transporting, rapturous scene
   That rises to my sight,
Sweet fields arrayed in living green,
   And rivers of delight.

3 There generous fruits that never fail,
   On trees immortal grow;
There rocky hills, and brooks and vales,
   With milk and honey flow.

4 O'er all those wide extended plains
   Shines one eternal day;
There God, the Son, forever reigns
   And scatters night away.

5 Soon will the Lord my soul prepare
   For joys beyond the sky,
Where never-ceasing music rolls,
   And praises never die.
Samuel Stennett (1727-95) (verses)

888

In God's tomorrow, 689

ONE golden dawning, one glorious
      morning,
   When earth's dark shadows flee away,
Our voices blending in song unending,
   In brightest realms of fadeless day.

There'll be no sorrow in God's tomorrow,
   There'll be no sadness, doubt, or fears;
There'll be no sorrow in God's tomorrow,
   For he will wipe away all tears.

2 No sad repining; love's sun is shining
   Where Jesus dwells; O wondrous place!
Our praises voicing in glad rejoicing
   To him who saved us by his grace.

3 With Christ forever! No sin can sever
   A fellowship as blest, so sweet;
We'll sing in Glory salvation's story;
   Before his throne we'll stand complete.
Sidney Edward Cox (1887-1975)

889

Safe in the arms of Jesus, 261
      7.6.7.6. D. Iambic

SAFE in the arms of Jesus,
   Safe on his gentle breast,
There by his love o'ershaded,
   Sweetly my soul shall rest.
Hark! 'tis the voice of angels
   Borne in a song to me
Over the fields of glory,
   Over the jasper sea.

Safe in the arms of Jesus,
   Safe on his gentle breast,
There, by his love o'ershaded,
   Sweetly my soul shall rest.

2 Safe in the arms of Jesus,
   Safe from corroding care,
Safe from the world's temptations,
   Sin cannot harm me there.
Free from the blight of sorrow,
   Free from my doubts and fears;
Only a few more trials,
   Only a few more tears.

The Life to Come

3 Jesus, my heart's dear refuge,
   Jesus has died for me;
Firm on the rock of ages
   Ever my trust shall be.
Here let me wait with patience,
   Wait till the night is o'er,
Wait till I see the morning
   Break on the golden shore.

Fanny Crosby (1820-1915)

890
Dennis, 165; Southport, 178
S.M.

SERVANT of God, well done!
   Rest from thy loved employ;
The battle fought, the victory won,
   Enter thy Master's joy.

2 The heavenly summons came,
   He started up to hear;
A mortal arrow pierced his frame,
   He fell, but felt no fear.

3 His spirit, with a bound,
   Left its encumbering clay;
His tent, at sunrise, on the ground
   A darkened ruin lay.

4 The pains of death are past,
   Labor and sorrow cease;
And, life's long warfare closed at last,
   His soul is found in peace.

5 Soldier of Christ, well done!
   Praise be thy new employ;
And while eternal ages run,
   Rest in thy Saviour's joy.

James Montgomery (1771-1854)

891
Shall we gather at the river? 398
8.7.8.7. Troch.

SHALL we gather at the river,
   Where bright angel feet have trod,
With its crystal tide forever
   Flowing by the throne of God?

Yes, we'll gather at the river,
   The beautiful, the beautiful river,
Gather with the saints at the river
   That flows by the throne of God.

2 On the margin of the river
   Dashing up its silver spray,
We will walk and worship ever
   All the happy, golden day.

3 Ere we reach the shining river,
   Lay we every burden down;
Grace our spirits will deliver
   And provide a robe and crown.

4 At the shining of the river,
   Mirror of the Saviour's face,
Saints whom death will never sever
   Raise their song of saving grace.

Robert Lowry (1826-99)

892
When we all get to Heaven, 407
8.7.8.7. Troch.

SING the wondrous love of Jesus,
   Sing his mercy and his grace;
In the mansions bright and blessèd
   He'll prepare for us a place.

When we all get to Heaven,
   What a day of rejoicing that will be!
When we all see Jesus,
   We'll sing and shout the victory!

2 While we walk this pilgrim pathway,
   Clouds may overspread the sky;
But when traveling days are over,
   Not a shadow, not a sigh.

3 Let us then be true and faithful,
   Trusting, serving every day;
Just one glimpse of him in Glory
   Will the toils of life repay.

4 Onward to the prize before us,
   Soon his beauty we'll behold;
Soon the pearly gates will open,
   We shall tread the streets of gold.

Eliza Edmunds Hewitt (1851-1920)

893
While the light, 856

SINS of years are all numbered,
   Blackest stains brought to light,
Broken pledges uncovered,
   None escape from his sight.
Unwashed hearts are rejected,
   Guilty souls rise alone,
When you stand in the light
   Of his great judgment throne.

While the light from Heaven is falling,
Sins reproving, wants revealing,
While redeeming grace is flowing,
He can wash your sins away.

2 All the past with its chances,
   All the 'what might have been',
Each encounter with evil
   He had meant you should win;
How you'll wish you'd gone forward,
   Loving Jesus alone,
When you stand in the light
   Of his great judgment throne!

3 Ransomed sinners of all kinds,
Trembling followers as well,
With their robes surely blood-washed,
They shall come forth to tell
Of the battles fought bravely,
Of the victories won,
As they stand in the light
Of his great judgment throne.

*Lucy Milward Booth-Hellberg
(1868-1953), alt*

894 Promoted to Glory, 772

SUMMONED home! the call has sounded
Bidding a soldier his warfare cease;
And the song of angels resounding
Welcomes a warrior to eternal peace.
Praise the Lord! From earthly struggles
A comrade has found release.
Death has lost its sting, the grave its
victory,
Conflicts and dangers are over;
See him honored at the throne of glory,
Crowned by the hand of Jehovah.

*Strife and sorrow over,
The Lord's true faithful soldier
Has been called to go from the ranks
below
To the conquering host above.*

2 Once the sword, but now the scepter,
Once the fight, now the rest and fame;
Broken every earthly fetter,
Now the glory for the cross and shame;
Once the loss of all for Jesus,
But now the eternal gain.
Trials and sorrows here have now their
meaning found,
Mysteries their explanation;
Safe forever in the sunlight gleaming
Of his eternal salvation.

Herbert Howard Booth (1862-1926)

895 Homeland, 671

THE homeland! the homeland!
The land of the free-born;
There's no night in the homeland,
But aye the fadeless morn;
I'm sighing for the homeland,
My heart is aching here;
There's no pain in the homeland
To which I'm drawing near.

2 My Lord is in the homeland
With angels bright and fair;
There's no sin in the homeland,
And no temptation there;
The voices of the homeland
Are ringing in my ears,
And when I think of the homeland
My eyes are filled with tears.

3 For those I love in the homeland
Are calling me away
To the rest and peace of the homeland,
And the life beyond decay;
For there's no death in the homeland,
There is no grief above;
Christ bring us all to the homeland
Of his eternal love.

Hugh Reginald Haweis (1838-1901)

896 Rutherford, 260
7.6.7.6. D. Iambic

THE sands of time are sinking;
The dawn of Heaven breaks;
The summer morn I've sighed for,
The fair, sweet morn, awakes;
Dark, dark hath been the midnight,
But dayspring is at hand,
And glory, glory dwelleth
In Immanuel's land.

2 O Christ! He is the fountain,
The deep, sweet well of love;
The streams on earth I've tasted
More deep I'll drink above;
There to an ocean fulness
His mercy doth expand,
And glory, glory dwelleth
In Immanuel's land.

3 With mercy and with judgment
My web of time he wove,
And aye the dews of sorrow
Were lustered by his love;
I'll bless the hand that guided,
I'll bless the heart that planned,
When throned where glory dwelleth
In Immanuel's land.

Anne Ross Cousin (1824-1906)

The Life to Come

897 There is a happy land, 235;
Happy Land, 234   6.4.6.4.6.7.6.4.

THERE is a happy land,
  Far, far away,
Where saints in glory stand,
  Bright, bright as day.
O how they sweetly sing:
Worthy is our Saviour-King!
Loud let his praises ring,
  Praise, praise for aye.

2 Come to this happy land,
    Come, come away;
  Why will you doubting stand,
    Why still delay?
  O we shall happy be
  When, from sin and sorrow free,
  Lord, we shall live with thee,
    Blest, blest for aye.

3 Bright in that happy land
    Beams every eye;
  Kept by a Father's hand,
    Love cannot die.
  On, then, to glory run;
  Be a crown and kingdom won,
  And bright above the sun
    Reign, reign for aye.
                    Andrew Young (1807-89)

898 Land of pure delight, 154;
St Matthew, 157   D.C.M.

THERE is a land of pure delight,
  Where saints immortal reign;
Infinite day excludes the night,
  And pleasures banish pain.
There everlasting spring abides,
  And never-withering flowers;
Death, like a narrow sea, divides
  This heavenly land from ours.

2 Sweet fields beyond the swelling flood
    Stand dressed in living green;
  So to the Jews old Canaan stood,
    While Jordan rolled between.
  But timorous mortals start and shrink
    To cross this narrow sea,
  And linger, shivering on the brink,
    And fear to launch away.

3 O could we make our doubts remove,
    Those gloomy thoughts that rise,
  And see the Canaan that we love
    With unbeclouded eyes!

Could we but climb where Moses stood
  And view the landscape o'er,
Not Jordan's stream, nor death's cold
    flood,
  Could fright us from the shore.
                    Isaac Watts (1674-1748)

899 Heavenly Mansions, 437
                    8.7.8.7. D. Troch.

THERE'S a crown laid up in Glory,
  There's a robe for each to wear,
And we never need be sorry
  That we did life's troubles share;
For our crown will shine the brighter
  For the battles we have won,
And our robes will be the whiter
  When our traveling days are done.

When our fighting here is over,
  And our victories are all won,
There's a mansion up in Glory
  When our traveling days are done.

2 There's a golden harp in Glory,
    There's a welcome for the true,
  There's a rest for all the weary,
    There's a victor's palm for you.
  O we'll praise the Lamb forever
    When we stand before his throne,
  And our joys will end, no never,
    When our traveling days are done!

3 There will be no room for sadness,
    There will be no sorrow there,
  And unceasing songs of gladness
    Shall forever fill the air;
  There will be no death, no weeping
    In that land, and evermore
  We shall dwell in Jesus' keeping
    When our traveling days are o'er.
                    Arthur White Bovan (c 1869-1903)

900 We shall win, 508
                    9.9.9.9.

THERE'S a land that is fairer than day,
  And by faith we can see it afar;
For the Father waits over the way
  To prepare us a dwelling place there.

In the sweet by-and-by
We shall meet on that beautiful shore.

2 We shall sing on that beautiful shore
    The melodious songs of the blest;
  And our spirits shall sorrow no more,
    Not a sigh for the blessing of rest.

The Life to Come

3 To our bountiful Father above
    We will offer the tribute of praise
For the glorious gift of his love,
    And the blessings that hallow our days.
          Sanford Fillmore Bennett (1836-98)

901 Marching to Zion, 171;
To Zion's happy land, 179   S.M.

TO leave the world below,
    March upward with our band,
And step by step we mean to go
    To Zion's happy land.

We're marching to Zion, beautiful,
    beautiful Zion;
We're marching onward to Zion, that
    beautiful city of God.

2   The city we shall see,
        The heavenly music hear,
Marching to songs of victory,
        With all the Army there.

3   The pearly gates are wide,
        The streets are bright and fair;
We'll march together, side by side,
        Till safely landed there.

4   Beside the crystal stream,
        Led on by Zion's King,
We'll swell the great salvation theme
    And songs of victory sing.

5   With blood and fire unfurled
        We march to victory grand;
The Army means to lead the world
    To Zion's happy land.
        William James Pearson (1832-92) (verses),
        Robert Lowry (1826-99) (chorus)

902 Land beyond the blue, 385
8.7.8.7. Troch.

WE are marching home to Glory,
    Marching up to mansions bright,
Where bright golden harps are playing,
    Where the saints are robed in white.

There's a golden harp in Glory,
    There's a spotless robe for you;
March with us to the hallelujah city,
    To the land beyond the blue.

2 March to swell the heavenly chorus,
    With departed friends to stay,
Sweetest notes of hallelujah music
    On the golden harps to play.

3 March across death's swelling river,
    Jesus will the waves divide;
We shall have a hallelujah Heaven
    When we reach the other side.

4 March to see the living fountains,
    March to tread the golden street;
Every true salvation soldier
    We shall up in Glory meet.

5 Sinners, join our happy Army,
    March with us to Canaan's shore;
Robes of white and harps of glory
    May be yours for evermore.
      William James Pearson (1832-92) (verses),
               R. F. Hughes (chorus)

903 The Homeward Trail, 818

WE are marching up the hillside and the
    trail leads home;
    We are marching up the hillside and the
        winding trail leads home;
Yes, sometimes we're finding that the trail
    is a-winding,
    But we don't mind, no we don't mind,
        for the trail leads home.

We're on the homeward trail, we're on
    the homeward trail,
    Singing as we go, going home.
We're on the homeward trail, we're on
    the homeward trail,
    Singing, singing, singing, singing,
    going home.

2 We are marching on our journey and the
    trail leads home;
    We are marching on our journey and the
        winding trail leads home;
Jesus' feet were bleeding when he took
    the trail that's leading
    To the homeland, to the homeland, for
        the trail leads home.

3 By and by we'll strike the valley but the
    trail leads home;
    'Tis the shadow of the valley but the
        winding trail leads home;
Jesus will be with me when I'm walking
    through the valley,
    Through the valley, through the valley,
        for the trail leads home.
        Arthur Smith Arnott (1870-1941)

251

The Life to Come

904
We speak of the realms, 484
8.8.8.8. Amph.

WE speak of the realms of the blest,
  That country so bright and so fair,
And oft are its glories confessed;
  But what must it be to be there!

To be there, to be there!
O what must it be to be there!

2 We speak of its peace and its love,
  The robes which the glorified wear,
The songs of the blood-washed above;
  But what must it be to be there!

3 We speak of its freedom from sin,
  From sorrow, temptation and care,
From trials without and within;
  But what must it be to be there!

4 Do thou, Lord, in pleasure or woe,
  For Heaven our spirits prepare;
Then soon shall we joyfully know
  And feel what it is to be there.
Elizabeth Mills (1805-29)

905
The Eden Above, 593;
The Ash Grove, 592   12.11.12.11.

WE'RE bound for the land of the pure
    and the holy,
  The home of the happy, the Kingdom of
    love;
Ye wanderers from God in the broad road
    of folly,
  O say, will you go to the Eden above?

Will you go? Will you go?
Will you go? Will you go?
O say, will you go to the Eden above?

2 In that blessèd land neither sighing nor
    anguish
  Can breathe in the fields where the glo-
    rified rove;
Ye heart-burdened ones, who in misery
    languish,
  O say, will you go to the Eden above?

3 Each saint has a mansion, prepared and
    all furnished,
  Ere from this small house he is sum-
    moned to move;
Its gates and its towers with glory are
    burnished;
  O say, will you go to the Eden above?

4 March on, happy soldiers, the land is be-
    fore you,
  And soon its ten thousand delights we
    shall prove;
Yes, soon we'll be massed on the hills of
    bright Glory,
  And drink the pure joys of the Eden
    above.

We will go! We will go!
We will go! We will go!
O yes, we will go to the Eden above!
William Hunter (1811-77)

906
The Glory Song, 529
10.10.10.10. Dact.

WHEN all my labors and trials are o'er,
  And I am safe on that beautiful shore,
Just to be near the dear Lord I adore,
  Will through the ages be Glory for me.

O that will be Glory for me,
Glory for me, Glory for me,
When by his grace I shall look on his
  face,
That will be Glory, be Glory for me!

2 When by the gift of his infinite grace,
  I am accorded in Heaven a place,
Just to be there, and to look on his face,
  Will through the ages be Glory for me.

3 Friends will be there I have loved long ago,
  Joy like a river around me will flow,
Yet just a smile from my Saviour, I know,
  Will through the ages be Glory for me.
Charles Hutchison Gabriel (1856-1932)

907
When the roll is called up yonder, 853

WHEN the trumpet of the Lord shall
    sound, and time shall be no more,
  And the morning breaks, eternal, bright
    and fair,
When the saved of earth shall gather over
    on the other shore,
  And the roll is called up yonder, I'll be
    there.

When the roll is called up yonder, I'll
  be there.

2 On that bright and cloudless morning,
    when the dead in Christ shall rise,
  And the glory of his resurrection share,
When his chosen ones shall gather to their
    home beyond the skies,
  And the roll is called up yonder, I'll be
    there.

The Life to Come

3 Let us labor for the Master from the dawn
    till setting sun,
  Let us tell of all his wondrous love and
    care;
  Then, when all of life is over, and our work
    on earth is done,
  And the roll is called up yonder, we'll be
    there.
James Milton Black (1856-1938)

908   Numberless as the sands, 753

WHEN we gather at last over Jordan,
  And the ransomed in Glory we see,
As the numberless sands of the seashore,
  What a wonderful sight that will be!

*Numberless as the sands of the
    seashore,*
Numberless as the sands of the shore!
  O what a sight 'twill be
  When the ransomed host we see,
*As numberless as the sands of the
    seashore!*

2 When we see all the saved of the ages,
  Who from sorrow and trials are free,
Meeting there with a heavenly greeting,
  What a wonderful sight that will be!

3 When we stand by the beautiful river,
  'Neath the shade of the life-giving tree,
Gazing over the fair land of promise,
  What a wonderful sight that will be!

4 When at last we behold our redeemer,
  And his glory unclouded we see,
While as King of all kingdoms he reigneth,
  What a wonderful sight that will be!
Francis Augustus Blackmer (1855-1930)

909   Maidstone, 325; Titchfield, 327
                      7.7.7.7. D.

WHO are these arrayed in white,
  Brighter than the noonday sun,
Foremost of the sons of light,
  Nearest the eternal throne?
These are they that bore the cross,
  Nobly for their Master stood,
Sufferers in his righteous cause,
  Followers of the dying God.

2 Out of great distress they came,
  Washed their robes by faith below
In the blood of yonder Lamb,
  Blood that washes white as snow;
Therefore are they next the throne,
  Serve their Master day and night;
God resides among his own,
  God doth in his saints delight.

3 He that on the throne doth reign,
  Shall his saints forever feed,
With the tree of life sustain,
  To the living fountains lead;
He shall all their sorrows chase,
  All their wants at once remove,
Wipe the tears from every face,
  Fill up every soul with love.
Charles Wesley (1707-88)

910   Sweeping through the gates, 804

WHO, who are these beside the chilly
    wave,
Just on the borders of the silent grave,
Shouting Jesus' power to save,
  Washed in the blood of the Lamb?

*Sweeping through the gates of the new
    Jerusalem,*
  Washed in the blood of the Lamb.

2 These, these are they who in their youth-
    ful days,
Found Jesus early, and in wisdom's ways
Proved the fulness of his grace,
  Washed in the blood of the Lamb.

3 These, these are they who in affliction's
    woes
Ever have found in Jesus calm repose,
Such as from a pure heart flows,
  Washed in the blood of the Lamb.

4 These, these are they who in the conflict
    dire
Boldly have stood amid the hottest fire;
Jesus now says: Come up higher;
  Washed in the blood of the Lamb.
Tullius Clinton O'Kane (1830-1912)

911   Manchester, 111; A Little Ship, 67
                              C.M.

WITH steady pace the pilgrim moves
  Toward the blissful shore,
And sings with cheerful heart and voice:
  'Tis better on before.

The Life to Come

2 His passage through a desert lies,
   Where furious lions roar;
He takes his staff, and smiling says:
   'Tis better on before.

3 When tempted to forsake his God
   And give the contest o'er,
He hears a voice which says: Look up,
   'Tis better on before.

4 When stern affliction clouds his face,
   And death stands at the door,
Hope cheers him with her happiest note:
   'Tis better on before.

5 And when on Jordan's bank he stands,
   And views the radiant shore,
Bright angels whisper: Come away,
   'Tis better on before.

6 And so it is, for high in Heaven
   They never suffer more;
Eternal calm succeeds the storm,
   'Tis better on before.
                    Richard Jukes (1804-67)

913 Ere the sun goes down, 641

YOU must have your sins forgiven,
   Ere the sun, ere the sun goes down,
If you wish to go to Heaven
   When the sun, when the sun goes down.
O now to God be crying,
For your time is swiftly flying,
In the grave you'll soon be lying
   When the sun goes down!

Ere the sun, ere the sun goes down,
Ere the sun, ere the sun goes down,
   O sinner, come to Jesus
   Ere the sun goes down!

2 Every chance will soon be past,
   When the sun, when the sun goes down;
Even this may be the last,
   When the sun, when the sun goes down.
If this offer be rejected,
And salvation still neglected,
Death may come when least expected,
   When the sun goes down.
                 Frederick William Fry (1859-1939)

912 Bright Crowns, 78; Coronation, 352
C.M.

YE valiant soldiers of the cross,
   Ye happy praying band,
Though in this world we suffer loss,
   We'll reach fair Canaan's land.

Bright crowns there are, bright crowns
      laid up on high,
For you and me there's a palm of
      victory;
   There's a palm of victory.

2 All earthly pleasures we'll forsake,
   While Heaven appears in view;
In Jesus' strength we'll undertake
   To fight our passage through.

3 O what a glorious shout there'll be
   When Heaven at last is won;
Jesus, and all our friends, we'll see,
   And God shall say: Well done.
                                Anon

914 Prepare Me, 121
C.M.

YOUR garments must be white as snow,
   Prepare to meet your God;
For to his throne you'll have to go;
   Prepare to meet your God.

Prepare me, prepare me, Lord,
Prepare me to stand before thy throne.

2 Prepare me now, prepare me here,
   To stand before thy throne,
That I, without a doubt or fear,
   May stand before thy throne.

3 Lord, cleanse my heart and make me pure,
   To stand before thy throne;
My pride and self and temper cure,
   To stand before thy throne.
                                Anon

SPECIAL OCCASIONS
New Year

915 Chalvey, 181; From strength to strength, 184   D.S.M.

AND are we yet alive,
  And see each other's face?
Glory and praise to Jesus give
  For his redeeming grace!
Preserved by power divine
  To full salvation here,
Again in Jesus' praise we join,
  And in his sight appear.

2 What troubles we have seen,
     What conflicts we have passed,
Fightings without and fears within,
  Since we assembled last!
But out of all the Lord
  Has brought us by his love;
And still he doth his help afford,
  And hides our life above.

3 Then let us make our boast
     Of his redeeming power,
Which saves us to the uttermost,
  Till we shall sin no more.
Let us take up the cross,
  Till we the crown obtain,
And gladly reckon all things loss,
  So we may Jesus gain.
                    Charles Wesley (1707-88)

916 Love at home, 237   7.5.7.5.7.7.7.5.

FATHER, let me dedicate,
  This new year to thee,
In whatever worldly state
  Thou wilt have me be;
Not from sorrow, pain, or care
Would I ask that thou shouldst spare;
This alone shall be my prayer,
    Glorify thy name.

  Thy great name! Thy great name!
Let my life, O Lord, each day
    Glorify thy name.

2 If in mercy thou wilt spare
     Joys that yet are mine,
If on life serene and fair
  Brighter rays may shine,
Let my glad heart, while it sings,
Rise by faith's exultant wings,
And, whate'er the future brings,
    Glorify thy name.

3 If thou callest to the cross,
     And its shadow come
Turning all my gain to loss,
  Shrouding heart and home,
Let me think how thy dear Son
His eternal glory won,
And in steadfast faith pray on:
    Glorify thy name.
            Lawrence Tuttiett (1825-97) (verses), alt

917 St Michael, 175; Silchester, 177   S.M.

MY times are in thy hand,
  My God, I wish them there;
My life, my friends, my soul I leave
  Entirely to thy care.

2 My times are in thy hand,
     Whatever they may be,
Pleasing or painful, dark or bright,
  As best may seem to thee.

3 My times are in thy hand,
     Why should I doubt or fear?
A Father's hand will never cause
  His child a needless care.

4 My times are in thy hand,
     Jesus, the crucified;
The hand my cruel sins had pierced
  Is now my guard and guide.

5 My times are in thy hand,
     I'll always trust in thee;
And after death at thy right hand
  I shall forever be.
            William Freeman Lloyd (1791-1853)

918 French, 88; Salzburg, 131   C.M.

O GOD of Bethel, by whose hand
  Thy people still are fed,
Who through this weary pilgrimage
  Hast all our fathers led;

2 Our vows, our prayers, we now present
     Before thy throne of grace;
God of our fathers, be the God
  Of their succeeding race.

3 Through each perplexing path of life
     Our wandering footsteps guide;
Give us each day our daily bread,
  And raiment fit provide.

Special Occasions

4 O spread thy covering wings around,
    Till all our wanderings cease,
And at our Father's loved abode
    Our souls arrive in peace.

5 Such blessing from thy gracious hand
    Our humble prayers implore;
And thou shalt be our chosen God
    And portion, evermore.

Philip Doddridge (1702-51)

919 Sovereignty, 502; Melita, 495
8.8.8.8.8.8. Iambic

O SAVIOUR, now to thee we raise
    With thankful hearts a song of praise,
For all that thou for us hast done,
For sinners saved, for victories won;
That more may thy salvation see,
We dedicate ourselves to thee.

2 O bring the vilest and the worst,
Whose lives are most by sin accurst,
That they may know there's mercy still
And hope for whosoever will;
That sinners changed to saints may be,
We dedicate ourselves to thee.

3 That soldiers may be trained to fight,
And daily walk with thee in white,
That they thy purpose more may know,
And do thy perfect will below,
That all through thee may victors be,
We dedicate ourselves to thee.

Anon

* * *

see also: 12 Now thank we all our God
13 O God, our help in ages past

Self-Denial

920 Shall we meet? 399; Bethany, 429
8.7.8.7. Troch.

BRING your tithes into the storehouse,
    Lay your best at Jesus' feet;
Bring an offering to the altar,
    Make your sacrifice complete.

Bring your dearest and your best,
Bring your dearest and your best,
Join with us in self-denial,
Bring your dearest and your best.

2 Bring your time and bring your talents,
    Bring the gift which costs you pain;
Bring your best, your dearest treasure,
    Let God have his own again.

3 Though your all is very little,
    Cast it in God's treasury;
Jesus always recognizes
    What is given cheerfully.

4 Prove the Lord, for he has promised
    That his blessings he will send;
Heaven's windows shall be opened,
    Mercies shall on you descend.

Barbara Stoddart (1865-1915)

921 Princethorpe, 206; Look away to
Jesus, 204; Count your blessings, 202
6.5.6.5. D.

CHRIST of self-denial
    Who for help dost call,
We have given little,
    Thou hast given all;
Offerings and thanksgivings
    Thou wilt not despise;
While our best we bring thee,
    Bless our sacrifice.

2 Having food and clothing,
    We will be content,
Thou hast needful blessings
    In abundance sent;
Freely by thy bounty
    Thou dost let us live,
More and more receiving,
    More and more to give.

3 From thy thankful people,
    From each grateful home,
As thy hand hath given,
    To thy hand shall come;
Love for help is seeking,
    Knocking at each door,
All thy children gladly
    Give thee more and more.

William James Pearson (1832-92)

922 Govaars, 373; Hyfrydol, 438
8.7.8.7. D. Troch.

THIS, our time of self-denial
    We as faithful soldiers keep;
By our consecrated giving
    Wider fields our comrades reap.
Souls in darkness yet are calling,
    Come and help us, still they cry;
With our gifts our hearts outpouring,
    We will help them lest they die.

Harvest

2 Laying now our gifts before thee,
  We toward thine altar move;
Lord, accept these simple tokens
  Of our deep, unswerving love.
None can estimate their measure
  When within thy hands they lie;
All that we sincerely offer
  Thou wilt use and multiply.

3 Naught we hold save by surrender;
  Nothing keep but that we give;
Loving life too much, we lose it;
  Dead to self, we truly live.
Jesus, grant us understanding,
  Gain is found through sacrifice;
For thy gift of life eternal
  Thou didst pay love's greatest price.

Will J. Brand (1889-1977)

* * *

see also: 475 And is it so? A gift from me
482 Dear Lord, I do surrender
514 Not my own, but saved by Jesus
516 O God, what offering shall I give
525 Take my life, and let it be

Harvest

923 St Matthew, 157; Ellacombe, 147
D.C.M.

AT harvest time our eyes behold
  Full sheaves of ripened grain,
But whence have come these fields of gold
  To beautify the plain?
Ere man could reap the rich supply
  Which meets a country's need,
Into the ready ground to die
  There fell the tiny seed.

2 Through storm and rain, 'neath darken-
      ing skies,
  After the seed is sown,
Deep buried in the earth it lies,
  Abiding yet alone;
And men the precious fruits await,
  Long patience follows toil,
Before the harvest rich and great
  Bursts from the furrowed soil.

3 O in the morning sow thy seed,
  At eve stay not thy hand;
Though tears may fall, and hearts may
      bleed
  Obey thy Lord's command.

Part with thy best; unless it die
  It must abide alone;
But God is pledged to multiply
  Seed for his Kingdom sown.

Ruth Tracy (1870-1960)

924 Come, ye thankful people, 321
7.7.7.7. D.

COME, ye thankful people, come,
  Raise the song of harvest home;
All is safely gathered in
Ere the winter storms begin.
God, our maker, doth provide
For our wants to be supplied;
Come to God's own temple, come,
Raise the song of harvest home.

2 All the world is God's own field,
Fruit unto his praise to yield;
Wheat and tares together sown,
Unto joy or sorrow grown;
First the blade and then the ear,
Then the full corn shall appear;
Lord of harvest, grant that we
Wholesome grain and pure may be!

3 For the Lord our God shall come,
And shall take his harvest home;
From his field shall in that day
All offenses purge away,
Give his angels charge at last
In the fire the tares to cast,
But the fruitful ears to store
In his garner evermore.

4 Even so, Lord, quickly come,
Bring thy final harvest home;
Gather thou thy people in,
Free from sorrow, free from sin;
There, forever purified,
In thy garner to abide;
Come, with all thine angels, come,
Raise the glorious harvest home!

Henry Alford (1810-71)

925 Truro, 54; Morning Hymn, 35
L.M.

ETERNAL source of every joy,
  Well may thy praise our lips employ,
While in thy temple we appear,
Whose goodness crowns the circling year.

2 The flowery spring at thy command
Embalms the air and paints the land;
The summer rays with vigor shine,
To raise the corn, and cheer the vine.

257

3 Thy hand in autumn richly pours
Through all our coasts abundant stores,
And winters, softened by thy care,
No more their barren aspect wear.

4 Seasons and months and weeks and days
Demand successive songs of praise;
Still be the cheerful homage paid
With opening light and evening shade.

5 To thee by every right belongs
The sweetest note in all our songs,
But also what must please thee more:
Our lives to serve, our hearts to adore.

Philip Doddridge (1702-51)

926 Praise, 468; Christ is all, 463
8.8.6.8.8.6.

OUR thankful hearts need joyful songs
To tell thee how all praise belongs
By right, dear Lord, to thee.
Thy power has worked to meet our wants,
Thy love has silenced all complaints,
Thy goodness, Lord, we see.

2 The sower's scattered seed has grown;
In rain and snow and sun is shown
Thy hand unfailing, strong,
Who quickened into life the seed;
The harvest is thy work indeed
And thine shall be the song.

3 The reaper's sickle work has found;
The gathered fruits from tree and ground
With thankfulness we store.
Thy truth, O Lord, thy works declare,
A Father's love forbids all fear;
We'll trust and serve thee more.

4 O help us at this harvest time
To test ourselves, by help divine,
To see what fruit we bear,
What promise are we making thee,
As ripened souls we wish to be
When harvest home draws near.

Richard Slater (1854-1939)

927 Morning has broken, 735

PRAISE and thanksgiving,
Father, we offer,
For all things living
Thou madest good:
Harvest of sown field,
Fruits of the orchard,
Hay from the mown field,
Blossom and wood.

2 Bless thou our labor
We bring to serve thee,
That with our neighbor
We may be fed.
Sowing or tilling,
We would work with thee,
Harvesting, milling
For daily bread.

3 Father, providing
Food for thy children,
Thy wisdom guiding
Teaches us share
One with another,
So that, rejoicing
With us, our brother
May know thy care.

4 Then will thy blessing
Reach every people,
All men confessing
Thy gracious hand.
Where thy will reigneth
No man will hunger:
Thy love sustaineth,
Fruitful the land.

Albert Frederick Bayly (1901-84)

928 Take time to be holy, 571; Go, bury thy
sorrow, 559   11.11.11.11.

SEEDS now we are sowing, and fruit they
must bear,
For blessing or cursing, for joy or despair;
Though we may forget them, the things of
the past
Will work out God's sentence upon us at
last.

2 Seeds now we are sowing, each day that
we live,
That must to our future its character give;
When God sends his reapers, our gladness or woe
Will spring from the nature of seeds we
now sow.

3 O sinner, remember you're sowing such
seed,
By wishing and thinking, by word and by
deed,
As will in the future bear evil or good,
Make tares or ripe wheat for the garner of
God.

Richard Slater (1854-1939)

Harvest

929
St Theodulph, 262; Hosanna, 255
7.6.7.6. D. Iambic

SING to the Lord of harvest,
　Sing songs of love and praise,
With joyful hearts and voices,
　Your hallelujahs raise;
By him the rolling seasons
　In fruitful order move;
Sing to the Lord of harvest
　A song of grateful love.

2　By him the clouds drop fatness,
　　The deserts bloom and spring,
The hills leap up in gladness,
　　The valleys laugh and sing;
He filleth with his fulness
　　All things with large increase;
He crowns the year with goodness,
　　With plenty and with peace.

3　Heap on his sacred altar
　　The gifts his goodness gave,
The golden sheaves of harvest,
　　The souls he died to save;
Your hearts lay down before him,
　　When at his feet ye fall,
And with your lives adore him
　　Who gave his life for all.
John Samuel Bewley Monsell (1811-75)

930
Bringing in the sheaves, 624

SOWING in the morning, sowing seeds of
　　kindness,
　Sowing in the noontide and the dewy
　　eves;
Waiting for the harvest and the time of
　　reaping,
　We shall come rejoicing, bringing in the
　　sheaves.

_Bringing in the sheaves, bringing in
　　the sheaves,
We shall come rejoicing, bringing in
　　the sheaves._

2　Sowing in the sunshine, sowing in the
　　shadows,
　Fearing neither clouds nor winter's
　　chilling breeze,
By and by the harvest and the labor ended,
　We shall come rejoicing, bringing in the
　　sheaves.

3　Go then, though with weeping, sowing for
　　the Master,
　Though the loss sustained our spirit
　　often grieves;
When our labor's over, he will bid us
　　welcome;
　We shall come rejoicing, bringing in the
　　sheaves.
Knowles Shaw (1834-78)

931
Sowing the seed, 795

SOWING the seed by the dawn-light fair,
　Sowing the seed by the noonday glare,
Sowing the seed by the fading light,
Sowing the seed in the solemn night:
　O what shall the harvest be?

_Sown in the darkness or sown in the
　　light,
Sown in our weakness or sown in our
　　might,
Gathered in time or eternity,
Sure, ah! sure, will the harvest be._

2　Sowing the seed by the wayside high,
Sowing the seed on the rocks to die,
Sowing the seed where the thorns will
　　spoil,
Sowing the seed in the fertile soil:
　O what shall the harvest be?

3　Sowing the seed with an aching heart,
Sowing the seed while the teardrops start,
Sowing in hope, till the reapers come,
Gladly to gather the harvest home:
　O what shall the harvest be?
Emily Sullivan Oakey (1829-83)

932
Soon the reaping time will come, 50;
Beethoven, 9　　　　　　　　L.M.

THIS is the field, the world below,
　In which the sower came to sow;
Jesus, the wheat; Satan, the tares;
For so the word of God declares.

_And soon the reaping time will come,
And angels shout the harvest home._

2　Most awful truth, and is it so?
Must all the world the harvest know?
Must all before the judge appear?
Then for the harvest, O prepare!

3　To love my sins, a saint appear,
To grow with wheat and be a tare,
May serve me while on earth below,
Where tares and wheat together grow.

4 But all who are from sin set free,
Their Father's Kingdom soon shall see,
Shine like the sun forever there;
He that hath ears, then let him hear.
Joseph Hinchsliffe (1760-1807)

933 Turner, 504; Mozart, 496
8.8.8.8.8.8. Iambic

To thee, O Lord of earth and sky,
With grateful hearts we now draw nigh,
For all the fruits thy generous soil
Hath yielded in return for toil;
We want henceforth our lives to be
All fruitful in good work for thee.

2 We thank thee that thou takest heed
To all thy creatures' daily need;
That over us, on sea or land,
Has daily been thy bounteous hand;
We want henceforth our lives to be
Filled up with grateful work for thee.

3 While heartfelt thanks to thee ascend,
With them new vows for war we blend,
Determined in thy strength to go
And live for thee 'gainst every foe;
Henceforth each day our lives shall be
Filled with both work and war for thee.

4 Make us more earnest souls to save
As hourly we approach the grave;
So that, if ere this time next year
We should before thy throne appear,
With joy we may thy glory see
Because till death we fought for thee.
Thomas Charles Marshall (1854-1942)

934 Bishopgarth, 358; Vicar of Bray, 360
8.7.8.7. D. Iambic

To thee, O Lord, our hearts we raise
In hymns of adoration,
To thee bring sacrifice of praise
With shouts of exultation;
Bright robes of gold the fields adorn,
The hills with joy are ringing,
The valleys stand so thick with corn
That even they are singing.

2 And now, on this thanksgiving day,
Thy bounteous hand confessing,
Upon thine altar, Lord, we lay
The first fruits of thy blessing.
By thee the souls of men are fed
With gifts of grace supernal;
Thou who dost give us earthly bread,
Give us the bread eternal.

3 We bear the burden of the day,
And often toil seems dreary;
But labor ends with sunset ray,
And rest comes for the weary.
May we, at last, our labors o'er,
No task for thee neglected,
Stand in thy sight for evermore,
Our offerings accepted.

4 O blessèd is that land of God
Where saints abide forever,
Where golden fields spread far and broad,
Where flows the crystal river.
The strains of all its holy throng
With ours today are blending;
Thrice blessèd is that harvest song
Which never hath an ending.
William Chatterton Dix (1837-98)

935 We plough the fields, 269
7.6.7.6. D. Iambic

We plough the fields, and scatter
The good seed on the land,
But it is fed and watered
By God's almighty hand;
He sends the snow in winter,
The warmth to swell the grain,
The breezes and the sunshine,
The soft refreshing rain.

*All good gifts around us
Are sent from Heaven above;
Then thank the Lord, O thank the Lord
For all his love!*

2 He only is the maker
Of all things near and far;
He paints the wayside flower,
He lights the evening star;
The winds and waves obey him,
By him the birds are fed;
Much more to us, his children,
He gives our daily bread.

3 We thank thee then, O Father,
For all things bright and good,
The seed time and the harvest,
Our life, our health, our food.
Accept the gifts we offer
For all thy love imparts,
And, what thou most desirest,
Our humble, thankful hearts.
*Matthias Claudius (1740-1815),
trs Jane Montgomery Campbell (1817-78)*

936
Covenant, 81; Coronation, 352
C.M.

WE praise thee, Lord, with heart and
    voice,
  While with first-fruits we come;
We bring thank offerings and rejoice,
  And shout the harvest home.

2 For crops made ripe by golden fire,
  For all thy power has done,
We'll lift thy praises higher and higher,
  And shout the harvest home.

3 Rich fruits of holiness we see
  Where men in grace have grown;
Salvation reapers we will be,
  And shout the harvest home.

4 Seed sown with tears thy life receives,
  Making thy goodness known;
Reapers return with golden sheaves,
  And shout the harvest home.
William James Pearson (1832-92)

*   *   *

see also: 2 All creatures of our God and King
         12 Now thank we all our God
         16 O worship the King, all glorious
            above
         25 All things bright and beautiful
         28 For the beauty of the earth
         34 Let us with a gladsome mind
         40 Summer suns are glowing
      983 Great is thy faithfulness

Corps Anniversaries

937
Monkland, 286; Trusting as the moments
fly, 299
7.7.7.7.

FOR thy mercy and thy grace,
  Faithful through another year,
Hear our song of thankfulness;
  Jesus, our redeemer, hear.

2 Veiled the future; let thy light
  Guide us, Bright and Morning Star;
Fierce our foes and hard the fight,
  Arm us, Saviour, for the war.

3 In our weakness and distress,
  Rock of strength, be thou our stay;
In the pathless wilderness
  Be our true and living way.

4 Keep us faithful, keep us pure,
  Keep us evermore thine own;
Help, O help us to endure;
  Fit us for the promised crown.
Henry Downton (1818-85)

938
Salvator, 443; Vesper Hymn, 450
8.7.8.7. D. Troch.

HEAVENLY Father, thou hast brought us
  Safely to the present day,
Gently leading on our footsteps,
  Watching o'er us all the way.
Friend and guide through life's long
    journey,
  Grateful hearts to thee we bring;
But for love so true and changeless
  How shall we fit praises sing?

2 Mercies new and never-failing
  Brightly shine through all the past,
Watchful care and loving kindness,
  Always near from first to last,
Tender love, divine protection
  Ever with us day and night;
Blessings more than we can number
  Strew the path with golden light.

3 Shadows deep have crossed our pathway;
  We have trembled in the storm;
Clouds have gathered round so darkly
  That we could not see thy form;
Yet thy love hath never left us
  In our griefs alone to be,
And the help each gave the other
  Was the strength that came from thee.

4 Many that we loved have left us,
  Reaching first their journey's end;
Now they wait to give us welcome,
  Brother, sister, child and friend.
When at last our journey's over,
  And we pass away from sight,
Father, take us through the darkness
  Into everlasting light.
Hester Periam Hawkins (1846-1928)

939
Regent Square, 423; Love Divine, 418
8.7.8.7.8.7. Troch.

SING we many years of blessing
  Since the Army opened fire,
Led by valiant hearts possessing
  Love's unquenchable desire;
Hallelujah! Hallelujah!
  Still their lives our own inspire.

2 Bold they lifted high their banner,
  Braving sin's hostility;
Strange their word, their song, their
    manner,
  Wondering, men drew near to see;
Hallelujah! Hallelujah!
  Many found salvation free.

3 For the faithful who have striven
 In the fight so well begun,
For the years so gladly given
 By the saints whose race is run,
Hallelujah! Hallelujah!
 For the last great conflict won.

4 When elate with joy unspoken,
 Or beneath the chastening rod,
Still his promises, unbroken,
 Speak the faithfulness of God;
Hallelujah! Hallelujah!
 We will sound his name abroad.

5 Father, Son and Spirit, raising
 Heart and voices now to thee,
Thine eternal goodness praising,
 Holy, blessèd Trinity,
Hallelujah! Hallelujah!
 Thine our years, our lives shall be.

Will J. Brand (1889-1977)

* * *

see also: 158 God is with us, God is with us
 163 Not unto us, O Lord
 173 Yet once again, by God's
  abundant mercy
 552 Thank you, Lord, for all your
  goodness
 769 What a work the Lord has done

New Buildings

940 Darwalls, 221; Southampton, 231
6.6.6.6.8.8.

CHRIST is our cornerstone,
 On him alone we build;
With his true saints alone
 The courts of Heaven are filled.
Our hopes we place on his great love
For present grace and joys above.

2 O then with songs of praise
 Make earth and Heaven ring;
Our voices we will raise
 The Three in One to sing;
In joyful song we will proclaim
Both loud and long that glorious name.

3 Here, gracious God, do thou
 For evermore draw nigh;
Accept each faithful vow,
 And mark each suppliant sigh;
On all who pray, in copious shower,
Thy wonder-working blessings pour.

---

4 Here may we gain from Heaven
 The grace which we implore;
And may that grace, once given,
 Be with us evermore,
Until that day when all the blest
Shall find in thee eternal rest.

Sixth- or seventh-century Latin hymn,
trs John Chandler (1806-76)

941 Hollingside, 323; Titchfield, 327
7.7.7.7. D.

LORD of Heaven and earth and sea,
 We would render thanks to thee
For the blessing thou hast given,
Joys of earth and hopes of Heaven.
Grateful for thy loving care,
We have built this house of prayer,
And with hearts sincere, we pray
For thy presence here this day.

2 Help us, Lord, each one to be
Consecrated unto thee;
Make each heart a living stone
In a temple all thine own.
Holy Spirit, fill this place
With thy pentecostal grace;
Dwell with us, and from this hour
Manifest thy mighty power.

3 Generations yet to be
In this house may worship thee;
Work, which now we gladly share,
Will be then in other care.
Grant, O Lord, whate'er may be,
That thy word, from error free,
May be cherished, true and pure,
While this fabric shall endure.

Frank Samuel Turney (1863-1932)

942 Arizona, 7; Morning Hymn, 35
L.M.

O GOD, in whom alone is found
 The strength by which all toil is blest,
Upon this consecrated ground
 Now bid thy cloud of glory rest.

2 In thy great name we place this stone;
 To thy great truth these walls we rear;
Long may they make thy glory known,
 And long our Saviour triumph here.

3 And while thy sons, from earth apart,
 Here seek the truth from Heaven that
  sprung,
Fill with thy Spirit every heart,
 With living fire touch every tongue.

New Buildings

4 Lord, grant our souls thy peace and love;
  Let sin and error pass away,
Till truth's full influence from above
  Rejoice the earth with cloudless day.
  Henry Ware (1794-1843)

943
The Crimson Stream, 266;
Aurelia, 246   7.6.7.6. D. Iambic

O GOD of love eternal,
  Be present here we pray,
Accept the gift we offer
  This celebration day,
Make of this place your temple,
  Let all who enter here
Be one with us in purpose,
  Your love and joy to share.

2 Except you build the house, Lord,
  Our work is all in vain,
Except your Spirit fill it
  But blocks of stone remain;
But if our hearts are open
  And you in power come down,
The glory of your presence
  Will all our labors crown.

3 Here may the lost find refuge,
  The striving saint find grace;
Let youth obey your calling
  And children see your face;
May every word here spoken
  Direct men to your throne,
And every note of music
  Be for your praise alone.

4 Then sanctify, our Father,
  This offering we have made,
Here let your Son be honored,
  Your Spirit be obeyed;
Our lives be cleansed for service
  In Christ's atoning blood,
And every true believer
  Become the house of God.
  Maureen Elsa Jarvis

944
St Theodulph, 262; Aurelia, 246
7.6.7.6. D. Iambic

O LORD, regard thy people,
  Whose love designs to frame
This house of glad remembrance,
  And here inscribe thy name.
To thee, the sure foundation,
  Our witness would we raise,
Her walls to speak salvation,
  Her gates to tell thy praise.

2 We thank thee for our birthright,
  Secured at such a price;
Forbid that we despise it,
  Or shrink from sacrifice.
Inspire our hearts to serve thee,
  Thy chosen path to tread,
That we may follow boldly
  Where nobler hearts have led.
  Albert Orsborn (1886-1967)

945
Truro, 54; Wareham, 55   L.M.

THIS stone to thee in faith we lay;
  To thee this temple, Lord, we build;
Thy power and goodness here display,
  And be it with thy presence filled.

2 Here, when thy people seek thy face,
  And dying sinners pray to live,
Hear thou in Heaven, thy dwelling place,
  And when thou hearest, Lord, forgive.

3 Here, when thy messengers proclaim
  The blessèd gospel of thy Son,
Still, by the power of his great name,
  Be mighty signs and wonders done.

4 Thy glory never hence depart;
  Yet choose not, Lord, this house alone;
Thy Kingdom come to every heart,
  In every nation fix thy throne.
  James Montgomery (1771-1854)

946
Colne, 79; Salzburg, 131   C.M.

THY presence and thy glories, Lord,
  Fill all the realms of space;
O come, and at thy people's prayer
  Now consecrate this place.

2 Sacred to thine eternal name,
  Behold, these walls we raise;
Let heralds here thy truth proclaim
  And saints show forth thy praise.

3 Eternal Spirit, heavenly dove!
  Thou author of all grace,
Come and reveal a Saviour's love
  To many in this place.

4 May thousands in the realms of day,
  Who shall with Jesus reign,
Point here, and each rejoicing say:
  There I was born again.
  Samuel Medley (1738-99), alt

see also: 575 Give us a day of wonders

263

Special Occasions

Weddings

947 Childhood, 471; St Margaret, 477
8.8.8.6.

O GOD of love, to thee we bow,
  And pray for these before thee now,
That, closely knit in holy vow,
  They may in thee be one.

2 When days are filled with pure delight,
  When paths are plain and skies are bright,
Walking by faith and not by sight,
  May they in thee be one.

3 When stormy winds fulfil thy will,
  And all their good seems turned to ill, ·
Then, trusting thee completely, still
  May they in thee be one.

4 Whate'er in life shall be their share
  Of quickening joy or burdening care,
  In power to do and grace to bear,
  May they in thee be one.
William Vaughan Jenkins (1868-1920)

948 Mendelssohn, 547; Hold thou my
hand! 543
11.10.11.10.

O PERFECT Love, all human thought
    transcending,
  Lowly we kneel in prayer before thy
    throne,
That theirs may be the love which knows
    no ending,
  Throughout their life divinely joined in
    one.

2 O perfect Life, be thou their full assurance
  Of tender charity and steadfast faith,
Of patient hope, and quiet brave
    endurance,
  With childlike trust that fears nor pain
    nor death.

3 Grant them the joy which brightens
    earthly sorrow,
  Grant them the peace which calms all
    earthly strife;
And to life's day the glorious unknown
    morrow
  That dawns upon eternal love and life.
Dorothy Frances Gurney (1858-1932)

949 St Alphege, 243; Aurelia, 246
7.6.7.6. Iambic

THE voice that breathed o'er Eden,
  That earliest wedding day,
The primal marriage blessing,
  It hath not passed away.

2 Be present, gracious Saviour,
  To join their loving hands,
As thou didst bind two natures
  In thine eternal bands.

3 O spread thy pure wing o'er them!
  Let no ill power find place,
When onward through life's journey
  The hallowed path they trace.

4 Till to the home of gladness,
  With Christ's own bride they rise,
And cast their crowns before thee
  In endless Paradise.
John Keble (1792-1866)

see also: 28 For the beauty of the earth
           438 Love divine, all loves excelling
           611 Lord of all hopefulness

Benedictions

950 My soul is now united, 257
7.6.7.6. D. Iambic

AND now to thee we render
  Our thanks for mercies past,
With grateful hearts imploring
  Thy favor to the last.
And at the great awakening
  May we be found above,
With saints and angels praising
  Thy providence and love.
James Frederick Swift (1847-1931)

951 For thine is the Kingdom, 647

FOR thine is the Kingdom, and thine is
    the power,
  And thine is the glory forever and ever;
For thine is the Kingdom and thine is the
    power,
  And thine is the glory forever and ever.

Matthew 6:13

952 Give to Jesus glory, 354
8.7.8.7. Iambic

GIVE to Jesus glory,
  Give to Jesus glory,
Proclaim redemption's wondrous plan
  And give to Jesus glory.
W. H. Clark

264

Benedictions

953
God be in my head, 589; Esher, 588;
Invocation, 590   12.10.10.10.11.

GOD be in my head,
    And in my understanding;
God be in my eyes,
And in my looking;
God be in my mouth,
And in my speaking;
God be in my heart,
And in my thinking;
God be at my end,
And at my departing.

From a book of hours, 1514

954
God be with you, 506; Randolph, 292
9.8.8.9.

GOD be with you till we meet again,
    By his counsels guide, uphold you,
With his sheep securely fold you;
God be with you till we meet again.

Till we meet, till we meet,
Till we meet at Jesus' feet;
Till we meet, till we meet,
God be with you till we meet again.

2 God be with you till we meet again,
    'Neath his wings protecting hide you,
    Daily manna still provide you;
God be with you till we meet again.

3 God be with you till we meet again,
    When life's perils thick confound you,
    Put his arm unfailing round you;
God be with you till we meet again.

4 God be with you till we meet again,
    Keep love's banner floating o'er you,
    Smite death's threatening wave before
        you;
God be with you till we meet again.

Jeremiah Eames Rankin (1828-1904)

955
As we pray, 610

JESUS, so dear to us,
    Jesus, be near to us,
Jesus, give ear to us
    Each as we pray;
Jesus, whate'er betide,
Jesus, be friend and guide,
Jesus, be by our side
    Now and for aye.

V. Hill

956
St Teresa, 780

LET nothing disturb thee,
    Nothing affright thee;
    All things are passing,
        God never changeth!
Patient endurance attaineth to all things;
Who God possesseth in nothing is
        wanting;
    Alone God sufficeth.

Teresa of Avila (1515-82),
trs Henry Wadsworth Longfellow (1807-82)

957
Old Hundredth, 38

L.M.

LORD of all glory and of grace;
    Lord of all nations, worlds and space,
Lord God o'er all eternity,
Reign thou—O reign thou over me.

Harry Read

958
Benediction, 11

L.M.

O FATHER, let thy love remain,
    O Son, may I thy likeness gain,
O Spirit, stay to comfort me,
O triune God, praise be to thee.

Hendrik Ghysen (1660-93),
trs William Frederic Palstra (1904-73)

959
Old Hundredth, 38

L.M.

PRAISE God, from whom all blessings
    flow;
Praise him, all creatures here below;
Praise him above, ye heavenly host;
Praise Father, Son and Holy Ghost.

Thomas Ken (1637-1711)

960
Praise God, I'm saved! 770

PRAISE God, I'm saved!
    Praise God, I'm saved!
All's well, all's well,
    He sets me free!

Thomas Henry Collett Leighton

961 The Lord bless thee, 820

THE Lord bless thee, and keep thee:
  The Lord make his face shine upon thee,
  And be gracious unto thee:
The Lord lift up his countenance upon
    thee,
  And give thee peace.

Numbers 6:24-26

962 Thou Shepherd of Israel, 487
8.8.8.8. D. Amph.

THIS, this is the God we adore,
  Our faithful, unchangeable friend,
Whose love is as great as his power,
  And knows neither measure nor end.
'Tis Jesus, the first and the last,
  Whose Spirit shall guide us safe home;
We'll praise him for all that is past,
  And trust him for all that's to come.

Joseph Hart (1712-68)

American Supplement

The Song Book

of

The Salvation Army

963 St Catherine, 499; Solid Rock, 501
8.8.8.8.8.8 Iambic

FAITH of our fathers! living still
  In spite of dungeon, fire, and sword;
O how our hearts beat high with joy
  Whene'er we hear that glorious word!
Faith of our fathers, holy faith!
We will be true to thee till death.

2 Faith of our fathers! we will strive
    To win all nations unto thee;
  And through the truth that comes from
      God
    Mankind shall then be truly free.
  Faith of our fathers, holy faith!
  We will be true to thee till death.

3 Faith of our fathers! we will love
    Both friend and foe in all our strife;
  And preach thee, too, as love knows how
    By kindly words and virtuous life.
  Faith of our fathers, holy faith!
  We will be true to thee till death.

Frederick William Faber (1814-63)

964 Duke Street, 17;
Truro, 54 (A.S. 986)   L.M.

O GOD, beneath thy guiding hand
  Our exiled fathers crossed the sea;
And when they trod the wintry strand,
  With prayer and psalm they worshiped
      thee.

2 Thou heard'st, well pleased, the song, the
      prayer;
    Thy blessing came, and still its power
  Shall onward through all ages bear
    The memory of that holy hour.

3 Laws, freedom, truth, and faith in God
    Came with those exiles o'er the waves;
  And where their pilgrim feet have trod,
    The God they trusted guards their
        graves.

4 And here thy name, O God of love,
    Their children's children shall adore,
  Till these eternal hills remove,
    And spring adorns the earth no more.

Leonard Bacon (1802-81)

965

The Star-spangled Banner

Francis Scott Key (1779-1843)

John Stafford Smith (1750-1836)

Maestoso ♩ = 96

1. O___ say, can you see by the dawn's ear - ly light, What so proud - ly we hailed at the twi - light's last gleam - ing, Whose broad stripes and bright stars, through the per - i - lous fight, O'er the ram - parts we watched were so gal - lant - ly stream - ing? And the rock - ets' red glare, the bombs

2. On the shore dim - ly seen through the mists of the deep, Where the foe's haught - y host in dread si - lence re - pos - es, What is that which the breeze, o'er the tow - er - ing steep As it fit - ful - ly blows, half con - ceals, half dis - clos - es? Now it catch - es the gleam of the

3. O___ thus be it ev - er, when free - men shall stand Be - tween their loved homes and the war's des - o - la - tion! Blest with vic - t'ry and peace, may the heav'n - res - cued land Praise the Pow'r that hath made and pre - served us a na - tion! Then___ con - quer we must, when our

burst - ing in air, Gave __ proof through the night that our flag was still
morn - ing's first beam, In full glo - ry re - flect - ed now shines on the
cause it is just, And __ this be our mot - to: In God is our

there; O __ say, does the __ star - span - gled ban - ner __ yet __
stream; 'Tis the star - span - gled __ ban - ner, O long may __ it __
trust; And the star - span - gled __ ban - ner in tri - umph __ shall __

wave __ O'er the land __ of the free and the home of the brave?
wave __ O'er the land __ of the free and the home of the brave.
wave __ O'er the land __ of the free and the home of the brave.

966

God of our fathers

10.10.10.10.
NATIONAL HYMN

Daniel C. Roberts (1841-1907)

George W. Warren (1828-1902)

Maestoso ♩ = 100

Trumpets before each verse

1. God of our fa - thers, whose al - might - y
2. Thy love di - vine hath led us in the
3. From war's a - larms, from dead - ly pes - ti -
4. Re - fresh thy peo - ple on their toil - some

hand Leads forth in beau - ty all the star - ry band
past, In this free land by thee our lot is cast;
lence, Be thy strong arm our ev - er - sure de - fense;
way, Lead us from night to nev - er - end - ing day;

Of shin - ing worlds in splen - dor through the skies,
Be thou our rul - er, guard - ian, guide and stay,
Thy true re - li - gion in our hearts in - crease,
Fill all our lives with love and grace di - vine,

Our grate - ful songs be - fore thy__ throne a - rise.
Thy word our law, thy paths our__ cho - sen way.
Thy boun - teous good - ness nour - ish__ us in peace.
And glo - ry, laud and praise be__ ev - er thine.

967 O beautiful for spacious skies

D.C.M.
MATERNA

Katherine Lee Bates (1859-1929)

Samuel A. Ward (1847-1903)

Moderato ♩ = 96

1. O beau - ti - ful for spa - cious skies, For am - ber waves of grain,__ For pur - ple moun - tain maj - es - ties A - bove the fruit - ed plain!__ A - mer - i - ca, A - mer - i - ca, God shed his grace on thee, __ And crown thy good with broth - er - hood From sea to shin - ing sea.

2. O beau - ti - ful for pil - grim feet Whose stern, im - pas - sioned stress__ A thor - ough - fare for free - dom beat A - cross the wil - der - ness! __ A - mer - i - ca, A - mer - i - ca, God mend thine ev - 'ry flaw,__ Con - firm thy soul in self - con -trol, Thy lib - er - ty in law.

3. O beau - ti - ful for he - roes proved In lib - er - at - ing strife, Who more than self their coun - try loved, And mer - cy more than life! __ A - mer - i - ca, A - mer - i - ca, May God thy gold re - fine, __ Till all suc - cess be no - ble -ness, And ev - 'ry gain di - vine.

4. O beau - ti - ful for pa - triot dream That sees, be - yond the years,__ Thine al - a - bas - ter cit - ies gleam Un - dimmed by hu - man tears!__ A - mer - i - ca, A - mer - i - ca, God shed his grace on thee, __ And crown thy good with broth - er - hood From sea to shin - ing sea.

271

968

My country 'tis of thee

6.6.4.6.6.6.4.
AMERICA

Samuel F. Smith (1808-95)

from *Thesaurus Musicus*, 1745

Andante ♩ = 84

1. My coun - try 'tis of thee, Sweet land of lib - er - ty
2. My na - tive coun - try, thee, Land of the no - ble free,
3. Let mu - sic swell the breeze, And ring from all the trees
4. Our fa - thers' God, to thee, Au - thor of lib - er - ty,

Of thee I sing; Land where my fa - thers died, Land of the
Thy name I love; I love thy rocks and rills, Thy woods and
Sweet free - dom's song; Let mor - tal tongues a - wake; Let all that
To thee we sing; Long may our land be bright With free - dom's

pil - grim's pride, From ev - 'ry moun - tain side, Let free - dom ring!
tem - pled hills; My heart with rap - ture thrills, Like that a - bove.
breathe par - take; Let rocks their si - lence break, The sound pro - long.
ho - ly light; Pro - tect us by thy might, Great God our King.

969

I love to tell the story

7.6.7.6. Iambic

Katherine Hankey (1834-1911)

William G. Fischer (1835-1912)

Moderato ♩ = 96

1. I love to tell the sto - ry Of un - seen things a - bove, Of
2. I love to tell the sto - ry, 'Tis pleas - ant to re - peat What
3. I love to tell the sto - ry, For those who know it best Seem

272

Je - sus and his glo - ry, Of __ Je - sus and __ his love. I
seems, each time I tell it, More __ won - der - ful - ly sweet. I
hun - ger - ing and thirst - ing To __ hear it like __ the rest. And

love to tell the sto - ry Be - cause I know 'tis __ true, __ It
love to tell the sto - ry, For some have nev - er __ heard __ The
when, in scenes of glo - ry, I sing the new, new __ song, __ 'Twill

sat - is - fies my long - ings As noth - ing else can do.
mes - sage of sal - va - tion From God's own ho - ly word.
be the old, old sto - ry That I have loved so long.

Chorus:

I love to tell the sto - ry, 'Twill be my theme in glo - ry, To

tell the old, __ old __ sto - ry Of Je - sus and his love.

273

970

We gather together

Netherlands Folk Hymn
trs Theodore Baker (1851-1934)

from *Nederlandtsch Gedenckelanck*, 1626
arr Edward Kremser (1838-1914)

971   I come to the garden alone

C. Austin Miles (1868-1946)

1. I come to the gar-den a - lone, _____ While the dew is still on the
2. He speaks, and the sound of his voice _____ Is so sweet the birds hush their
3. I'd stay in the gar-den with him _____ Though the night a - round me be

ros - es, And the voice I hear, fall - ing on my ear, The
sing - ing, And the mel - o - dy that he gave to me With-
fall - ing, But he bids me go; through the voice of woe, His

Chorus:

Son of God dis - clos - es.
in my heart is ring - ing. And he walks with me, and he
voice to me is call - ing.

talks with me, and he tells me I am his own; _____ And the

joy we share as we tar - ry there, None oth-er has ev - er _____ known. _____

275

972   The way of the Cross leads home

Jessie Brown Pounds (1861-1921)

Charles H. Gabriel (1856-1932)

Allegro moderato ♩ = 104

1. I must needs go home by the way of the cross. There's
2. I must needs go on in the blood - sprin - kled way, The
3. Then I bid fare - well to the way of the world, To

no oth - er way but this; I shall ne'er get sight of the
path that the Sav - iour trod, If I ev - er climb to the
walk in it nev - er - more; For my Lord says: Come! and I

Gates of Light, If the way of the cross I miss. ___
heights sub - lime, Where the soul is at home with God. ___
seek my home, Where he waits at the o - pen door. ___

Chorus:

The way of the cross leads home, (leads home,) The___ way of the cross leads home, (leads home,) It is

sweet to know, as I on - ward go, The way of the cross leads home.

276

973 Near to the heart of God

C.M.

Cleland B. McAfee (1866-1944)   Cleland B. McAfee (1866-1944)

Andante ♩ = 84

1. There is a place of qui - et rest, Near to the heart of God; A
2. There is a place of com - fort sweet, Near to the heart of God; A
3. There is a place of full re - lease, Near to the heart of God; A

place where sin can - not mo - lest, Near to the heart of God.
place where we our Sav - iour meet, Near to the heart of God.
place where all is joy and peace, Near to the heart of God.

Chorus:

O Je - sus, blest re - deem - er, Sent from the heart of God, Hold

us, who wait be - fore thee, Near to the heart of God.

974 Dwelling in Beulah Land

C. Austin Miles (1868-1946)

C. Austin Miles (1868-1946)

Allegro moderato ♩ = 112

1. Far a-way the noise of strife up-on my ear is fall-ing, Then I know the
2. Far be-low the storm of doubt up-on the world is beat-ing, Sons of men in
3. Let the storm-y breez-es blow, their cry can-not a-larm me; I am safe-ly
4. View-ing here the works of God, I sink in con-tem-pla-tion, Hear-ing now his

sins of earth be-set on ev-'ry hand; Doubt and fear and things of earth in
bat-tle long the en-e-my with-stand; Safe am I with-in the cas-tle
shel-tered here, pro-tect-ed by God's hand; Here the sun is al-ways shin-ing,
bless-ed voice, I see the way he planned; Dwell-ing in the Spir-it, here I

vain to me are call-ing, None of these shall move me from Beu-lah Land.
of God's word re-treat-ing, Noth-ing then can reach me, 'tis Beu-lah Land.
here there's naught can harm me, I am safe for-ev-er in Beu-lah Land.
learn of full sal-va-tion, Glad-ly will I tar-ry in Beu-lah Land.

Chorus:

I'm liv-ing on the moun-tain, un-der-neath a cloud-less sky, — I'm

drink-ing at the foun-tain that nev-er shall run dry; O yes! I'm feast-ing on the

man - na from a boun - ti - ful sup - ply, For I am dwell-ing in Beu - lah Land.

975   **Spirit of God, descend**   10.10.10.10.

George Croly (1780-1860)   Frederick C. Atkinson (1841-97)

Moderato ♩ = 96

1. Spir - it of God, de - scend up - on my heart;
2. Hast thou not bid me love thee, God and King?
3. Teach me to feel that thou art al - ways nigh;
4. Teach me to love thee as thine an - gels love,

Wean it from earth, through all its puls - es move.
All, all thine own, soul, heart and strength and mind.
Teach me the strug - gles of the soul to bear,
One ho - ly pas - sion fill - ing all my frame;

Stoop to my weak - ness, might - y as thou art,
I see thy cross; there teach my heart to cling:
To check the ris - ing doubt, the reb - el sigh;
The bap - tism of the heav'n - de - scend - ed Dove,

And make me love thee as I ought to love.
O let me seek thee, and O let me find!
Teach me the pa - tience of un - an - swered prayer.
My heart an al - tar and thy love the flame.

279

976

How firm a foundation

"K" in Rippon's *Selections*, 1787

11.11.11.11.
FOUNDATION

Early American Melody

Moderato ♩ = 76

1. How___ firm a foun - da - tion, ye saints of the
2. Fear___ not, I am with thee, O be not dis -
3. When___ through the deep wa - ters I call thee to
4. When___ through fie - ry tri - als thy path - way shall
5. The___ soul that on Je - sus hath leaned for re -

Lord, Is___ laid for your faith in his ex - cel - lent
mayed, For___ I am thy God, I will still give thee
go, The___ riv - ers of grief shall not thee o - ver -
lie, My___ grace all - suf - fi - cient shall be thy sup -
pose, I___ will not, I will not de - sert to its

word! What more can he say than to you he hath
aid! I'll strength - en thee, help thee, and cause thee to
flow, For I will be with thee thy tri - als to
ply; The flames shall not hurt thee; I on - ly de -
foes; That soul, though all Hell should en - deav - or to

said, To___ you who for ref - uge to Je - sus have fled?
stand, Up - held by my gra - cious om - nip - o - tent hand.
bless, And___ sanc - ti - fy to thee thy deep - est dis - tress.
sign Thy___ dross to con - sume, and thy gold to re - fine.
shake, I'll___ nev - er, no nev - er, no nev - er for - sake.

280

977   Lead on, O King eternal

Ernest W. Shurtleff (1862-1917)

7.6.7.6. D. Iambic

Henry Smart (1813-79)

1. Lead on, O King e - ter - nal, The day of march has come;___ Hence - forth in fields of con - quest Thy tents shall be our home.___ Through days of prep - a - ra - tion Thy grace has made us strong,___ And now, O King e - ter - nal, We lift our bat - tle song.

2. Lead on, O King e - ter - nal, Till sin's fierce war shall cease,___ And ho - li - ness shall whis - per The sweet a - men of peace;___ For not with swords loud clash - ing, Nor roll of stir - ring drums, With deeds of love and mer - cy, The heav'n - ly king - dom comes.

3. Lead on, O King e - ter - nal, We fol - low, not with fears,___ For___ glad - ness breaks like morn - ing Wher - e'er thy face ap - pears.___ Thy cross is lift - ed o'er___ us; We jour - ney in its light;___ The crown a - waits the con - quest; Lead on, O God of might.

978 Take up thy cross

Alfred Henry Ackley (1887-1960)

Alfred Henry Ackley (1887-1960)

10.8.10.8.

[G♭] Andante ♩ = 80

1. I walked one day a - long a coun - try road, And there a stran - ger jour - neyed too; Bent low be - neath the bur - den of his load; It was a cross, a cross I knew.

2. I cried: Lord Je - sus! and he spoke my name; I saw his hands all bruised and torn; I stooped to kiss a - way the marks of shame, The shame for me that he had borne.

3. O let me bear thy cross dear Lord, I cried, And lo, a cross for me ap - peared; The one, for - got - ten, I had cast a - side, The one so long that I had feared.

Chorus:

Take up thy cross and fol - low me, I hear the bless - ed Sav - iour call; How can I make a less - er sac - ri - fice When Je - sus gave his all?

979

Are ye able?

Earl Marlatt (1892-1976)

8.7.8.7. Troch.

Harry S. Mason (1881-1964)

Allegro moderato ♩ = 104

1. Are ye a - ble, said the Mas - ter, To be cru - ci - fied with
2. Are ye a - ble to re - mem - ber, When a thief lifts up his
3. Are ye a - ble? still the Mas - ter Whis - pers down e - ter - ni -

me? Yea, the stur - dy dream - ers an - swered, To the death we fol - low thee.
eyes, That his par - doned soul is wor - thy Of a place in par - a - dise?
ty, And he - ro - ic spir - its an - swer Now, as then, in Gal - i - lee:

Chorus:

Lord, we are a - ble, our spir - its are thine; Re - mold them,

make us ____ like thee di - vine. Thy guid - ing ra - diance a -

bove us shall be A bea - con to God, to love and loy - al - ty.

283

980 Truehearted, wholehearted

Frances Ridley Havergal (1836-79)

George Cole Stebbins (1846-1945)

11.10.11.10. Dact.

Andante moderato ♩. = 66

1. True - heart - ed, whole - heart - ed, faith - ful and loy - al, King of our
2. True - heart - ed, whole - heart - ed, full - est al - le - giance, Yield - ing hence -
3. True - heart - ed, whole - heart - ed, Sav - iour all - glo - rious! Take thy great

lives, by thy grace we will be; Un - der the stan - dard ex -
forth to our glo - ri - ous King; Val - iant en - deav - or and
pow - er and reign there a - lone, O - ver our wills and af -

alt - ed and roy - al, Strong in thy strength we will bat - tle for thee.
lov - ing o - be - dience, Free - ly and joy - ous - ly now would we bring.
fec - tions vic - to - rious, Free - ly sur - ren - dered and whol - ly thine own.

Chorus:

Peal out the watch - word! Si - lence it nev - er! Song of our

spir - its, re - joic - ing and free; Peal out the watch - word!

Loy - al for - ev - er! King of our lives, By thy grace we will be.

284

981

We've a story to tell to the nations

H. Ernest Nichol (1862-1928)

H. Ernest Nichol (1862-1928)

Allegro moderato ♩ = 112

1. We've a sto-ry to tell to the na - tions That shall turn their hearts to the right,— A sto-ry of truth and— mer-cy, A sto-ry of peace and light,— A sto-ry of peace and light.

2. We've a song to be sung to the na - tions That shall lift their hearts to the Lord,— A song that shall con-quer— e-vil And shat-ter the spear and sword,— And shat-ter the spear and sword.

3. We've a mes-sage to give to the na - tions, That the Lord who reign-eth a-bove— Hath sent us his Son to— save us, And show us that God is love,— And show us that God is love.

4. We've a Sav-iour to show to the na - tions Who the path of sor-row hath trod,— That all of the world's great— peo-ples Might come to the truth of God,— Might come to the truth of God.

Chorus:

For the dark-ness shall turn to dawn-ing, And the dawn-ing to noon-day bright,— And Christ's great king-dom shall come to earth, The King-dom of love and light.

285

982 Rejoice, ye pure in heart

Edward H. Pluptree (1821-91)

Arthur H. Messiter (1831-1916)

S.M.

[G♭] Moderato ♩ = 96

1. Re - joice, ye __ pure in heart, Re - joice, give __ thanks and sing; Your glo - rious __ ban - ner wave __ on __ high, The cross of Christ your __ King.
2. Bright youth and __ snow-crowned age, Strong men and __ maid - ens fair, Raise high your __ free, ex - ult - ing __ song, God's won - drous praise de - clare.
3. Yes, on through life's long path, Still chant - ing __ as ye go; From youth to __ age, by night __ and __ day, In glad - ness and in __ woe.
4. Still lift your __ stan - dard high, Still march in __ firm ar - ray, As war - riors __ thru the dark - ness __ toil Till dawns the gold - en __ day.

Chorus:

Re - joice, re - joice, re - joice, give __ thanks and sing!
Re - joice, re - joice,

983 Great is thy faithfulness

Thomas O. Chisholm (1866-1960)

William M. Runyan (1870-1957)

Moderato ♩ = 92

1. Great is thy faith - ful - ness, O God my Fa - ther, There is no
2. Sum - mer and win - ter, and spring-time and har - vest, Sun, moon and
3. Par - don for sin and a peace that en - dur - eth, Thy own dear

shad - ow of turn - ing with thee; Thou chang - est not, thy com -
stars in their cour - ses a - bove, Join with all na - ture in
pres - ence to cheer and to guide; Strength for to - day and bright

pas - sions they fail not; As thou hast been thou for - ev - er wilt be.
man - i - fold wit - ness To thy great faith - ful - ness, mer - cy and love.
hope for to - mor - row, Bless - ings all mine, with ten thou - sand be - side!

Chorus:

Great is thy faith - ful - ness! Great is thy faith - ful - ness! Morn - ing by

morn - ing new mer - cies I see; All I have need - ed thy

hand hath pro - vid - ed; Great is thy faith - ful - ness, Lord, un - to me!

287

984   In my heart there rings a melody

Elton M. Roth (1891-1951)

Elton M. Roth (1891-1951)

1. I have a song that Je - sus gave me, It was sent from Heav'n a - bove; There nev - er was a sweet - er mel - o - dy, 'Tis a mel - o - dy of love.
2. I love the Christ who died on Cal - v'ry, For he washed my sins a - way; He put with - in my heart a mel - o - dy, And I know it's there to stay.
3. 'Twill be my end - less theme in Glo - ry, With the an - gels I will sing; 'Twill be a song with glo - rious har - mo - ny, When the courts of Heav - en ring.

Chorus:

In my heart there rings a mel - o - dy, There rings a mel - o - dy with Heav-en's har - mo-ny; In my heart there rings a mel - o - dy; There rings a mel - o - dy of love.

985 Lead me to Calvary

C.M.

Jennie Evelyn Hussey (1874-1958)

William J. Kirkpatrick (1838-1921)

Andante ♩ = 84

1. King of my life, I crown thee now, Thine shall the glo - ry be;
2. Show me the tomb where thou wast laid, Ten - der - ly mourned and wept;
3. Let me, like Mar - y, through the gloom Come with a gift to thee;
4. May I be will - ing, Lord, to bear Dai - ly my cross for thee,

Lest I for - get thy thorn-crowned brow, Lead me to Cal - va - ry.
An - gels in robes of light ar - rayed Guard - ed thee whilst thou slept.
Show to me now the emp - ty tomb, Lead me to Cal - va - ry.
E - ven thy cup of grief to share; Thou hast borne all for me.

Chorus:

Lest I for - get Geth - sem - a - ne, Lest I for - get thine ag - o - ny;

Lest I for - get thy love for me, Lead me to Cal - va - ry.

986

Christ is alive!

L.M.
TRURO

Brian Wren

from *Psalmodia Evangelica*, 1789

1. Christ is a - live! Let Chris - tians sing. His
2. Christ is a - live! No long - er bound To
3. Not throned a - bove, re - mote - ly high, Un-
4. In ev - 'ry in - sult, rift and war, Where
5. Christ is a - live! His Spir - it burns Through

cross stands emp - ty to the sky. Let streets and homes with
dis - tant years in Pal - es - tine, He comes to claim the
touched, un - moved by hu - man pains, But dai - ly, in the
col - or, scorn or wealth di - vide, He suf - fers still, yet
this and ev - 'ry fu - ture age, Till all cre - a - tion

prais - es ring. His love in death shall nev - er die.
here and now And con - quer ev - 'ry place and time.
midst of life, Our Sav - iour with the Fa - ther reigns.
loves the more, And lives, though ev - er cru - ci - fied.
lives and learns His joy, his jus - tice, love and praise.

987 Life is great!

Brian Wren

8.7.8.7.8.7. Troch.
PRAISE, MY SOUL
John Goss (1800-80)

[D♭] Moderato ♩ = 92

1. Life is great! So sing a-bout it, As we can and
2. Life is great! What-ev-er hap-pens, Snow or sun-shine,
3. Love is great! The love of lov-ers, Whis-pered words and
4. Love is giv-ing and re-ceiv-ing: Boy and girl, and
5. God is great! In Christ he loved us, As we should but

as we should: Shops and bus-es, towns and peo-ple,
joy or pain, Hard-ship, grief, or dis-il-lu-sion,
long-ing eyes; Love that gaz-es at the cra-dle,
friend with friend. Love is bear-ing and for-giv-ing
nev-er can. Love that suf-fered, hoped and trust-ed,

Vil-lage, farm-land, field and wood. Life is great and
Suf-f'ring that I can't ex-plain. Life is great if
Where a child of lov-ing lies; Love that lasts when
All the hurts that hate can send. Love's the great-est
When dis-ci-ples turned and ran, Love that broke through

life is giv-en; Life is love-ly, free and good.
some-one loves me, Holds my hands and calls my name.
youth has fad-ed, Bends with age but nev-er dies.
way of liv-ing, Hop-ing, trust-ing to the end.
death for ev-er: Praise that lov-ing, liv-ing Man!

988   O for a thousand tongues

C.M.
AZMON

Charles Wesley (1707-88)

Carl G. Gläser (1784-1829)

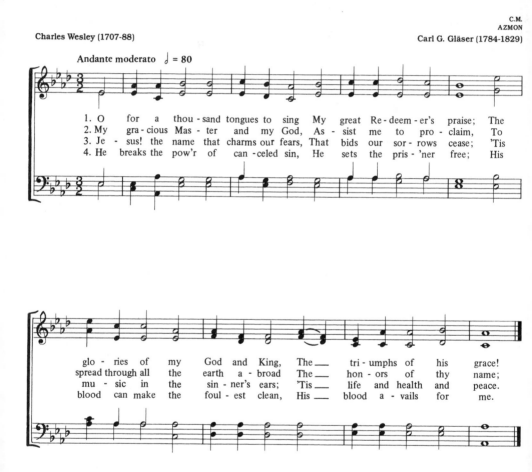

1. O for a thou - sand tongues to sing My great Re - deem - er's praise; The
2. My gra - cious Mas - ter and my God, As - sist me to pro - claim, To
3. Je - sus! the name that charms our fears, That bids our sor - rows cease; 'Tis
4. He breaks the pow'r of can - celed sin, He sets the pris - 'ner free; His

glo - ries of my God and King, The ___ tri - umphs of his grace!
spread through all the earth a - broad The ___ hon - ors of thy name;
mu - sic in the sin - ner's ears; 'Tis ___ life and health and peace.
blood can make the foul - est clean, His ___ blood a - vails for me.

989   Beneath the cross of Jesus

ST CHRISTOPHER

Elizabeth C. Clephane (1830-69)

Frederick C. Maker (1844-1927)

Andante moderato ♩ = 96

1. Be - neath the cross of Je - sus I fain would take my stand, The
2. Up - on that cross of Je - sus Mine eye at times can see The
3. I take, O cross, thy shad - ow For my a - bid - ing place; I

shad - ow of a might - y rock With - in a wea - ry land; A
ver - y dy - ing form of one Who suf - fered there for me; And
ask no oth - er sun - shine than The sun - shine of his face; Con -

home with - in the wil - der - ness, A rest up - on the way. From the
from my smit - ten heart, with tears, Two won - ders I con - fess: The
tent to let the world go by, To know no gain nor loss. My

burn - ing of the noon - tide heat And the bur - den of the day.
won - ders of his glo - rious love And my un - wor - thi - ness.
sin - ful self my on - ly shame, My glo - ry all the cross.

990   Victory in Jesus

Eugene M. Bartlett (1885-1941)

Eugene M. Bartlett (1885-1941)

[Gb] Moderato ♩ = 108

1. I heard an old, old sto - ry, how a Sav - iour came from glo - ry, How he
2. I heard a-bout his heal - ing, of his cleans-ing power re - veal - ing, How he
3. I heard a-bout a man - sion he has built for me in glo - ry, And I

gave his life on Cal - va - ry to save a wretch like me; I
made the lame to walk a - gain and caused the blind to see; And
heard a - bout the streets of gold be - yond the crys - tal sea; A -

heard a - bout his groan - ing, of his pre - cious blood's a - ton - ing, Then
then I cried: Dear Je - sus come and heal my bro - ken spir - it; And
bout the an - gels sing - ing and the old re - demp - tion sto - ry, And

I re - pent - ed of my sins and won the vic - to - ry.
some - how Je - sus came and brought to me the vic - to - ry.   O
some sweet day I'll sing up there the song of vic - to - ry.

Chorus:

vic - to - ry in Je - sus, my Sav - iour, for - ev - er! He sought me and

bought me with his re - deem - ing blood; He loved me ere I knew him, and

all my love is due him— He plunged me to vic - to - ry be - neath the cleans-ing flood.

991

'Tis so sweet to trust in Jesus

Louisa M.R. Stead (c. 1850-1917)

8.7.8.7. Troch.

William J. Kirkpatrick (1838-1921)

[Gb] Moderato ♩ = 108

1. 'Tis so sweet to trust in Je - sus, Just to take him at his word,
2. How I love to trust in Je - sus, Just to trust his cleans - ing blood,
3. Yes, I've learned to trust in Je - sus, And from sin and self to cease,
4. I'm so glad I learned to trust him, Pre - cious Je - sus, Sav - iour, Friend;

Just to rest up - on his prom - ise, Just to know: Thus saith the Lord.
Just in sim - ple faith to plunge me 'Neath the heal - ing, cleans - ing flood!
Now from Je - sus sim - ply tak - ing Life and rest and joy and peace.
And I know that he is with me, He'll be with me to the end.

Chorus:

Je - sus, Je - sus, how I trust him! How I've proved him o'er and o'er!

Je - sus, Je - sus, pre - cious Je - sus! O for grace to trust him more!

296

992

The Saviour is waiting

11.7.11.7.

Ralph Carmichael

Ralph Carmichael

Andante moderato ♩ = 96

1. The Sav - iour is wait - ing to en - ter your heart, Why don't you
2. If you'll take one step t'ward the Sav - iour my friend, You'll find his

let him come in?＿ There's noth - ing in this world to keep you a -
arms o - pen wide;＿ Re - ceive him, and all of your dark - ness will

part, What is your an - swer to him?＿
end, With - in your heart he'll a - bide.＿

Chorus:

Time af - ter time he has

wait - ed be - fore, And now he is wait - ing a - gain＿ To see＿ if you're

will - ing to o - pen the door:＿ O how he wants to come in.＿

993

How great thou art

Stuart K. Hine (1899-1989)

11.10.11.10.
Swedish Melody
arr Stuart K. Hine (1899-1989)

Andante ♩ = 72

1. O Lord my God, when I in awe-some won-der Con-sid-er all the worlds thy hands have made; ___ I see the stars, I hear the roll-ing thun-der, Thy pow'r through-out the u-ni-verse dis-played: ___

2. When through the woods and for-est glades I wan-der And hear the birds sing sweet-ly in the trees, ___ When I look down from loft-y moun-tain gran-deur, And hear the brook and feel the gen-tle breeze: ___

3. And when I think that God, his Son not spar-ing, Sent him to die, I scarce can take it in; ___ That on the cross, my bur-den glad-ly bear-ing, He bled and died to take a-way my sin: ___

4. When Christ shall come with shout of ac-cla-ma-tion, And take me home, what joy shall fill my heart! ___ Then I shall bow in hum-ble ad-o-ra-tion, And there pro-claim, my God, how great thou art! ___

*Author's original words are "works" and "mighty."

Copyright © 1953. Renewal 1981 by Manna Music, Inc., 2111 Kenmere Ave., Burbank, CA 91504. International Copyright Secured. All Rights Reserved. Used by Permission.

298

Chorus:

Then sings my soul, my Sav-iour God, to thee;⎯ How great thou art,⎯ how great thou art!⎯ Then sings my soul, my Sav-iour God, to thee:⎯ How great thou art,⎯ how great thou art!⎯

994

O Canada

Calixa Lavallée (1842-91)

Robert Stanley Weir (1856-1926)

1. O Can - a - da! our home and na - tive land! True_ pa - triot-love in all thy sons com - mand._____ With_ glow - ing hearts we_ see thee rise, The_ true North strong and free; From_ far and wide, O_
2. O Can - a - da! Where pines and ma - ples grow, Great_ prai - ries spread and lord - ly riv - ers flow,_____ How_ dear to us thy_ broad do - main, From_ east to west - ern sea! Thou_ land to hope for_
3. O Can - a - da! be - neath thy shin - ing skies May_ stal - wart sons and gen - tle maid - ens rise;_____ To _ keep thee stead - fast_ through the years From_ east to west - ern sea, Our_ own be - lov - ed
4. Ru - ler su - preme, who hear - est hum - ble prayer, Hold_ our Do-min - ion in thy lov - ing care._____ Help_ us to find, O_ God, in thee A _ last - ing, rich re - ward. As _ wait - ing for the_

Can - a - da, — We stand on guard for — thee.
all who toil! — Thou true north strong and — free!
na - tive land, Our true north strong and — free.
bet - ter day, We ev - er stand on — guard.

God keep our land —

glo - rious and free! — O Can - a - da, we stand on guard — for —

thee, — O Can - a - da, we stand on guard — for — thee.

CHORUS SECTION

CONTENTS

Many of these choruses are copyrighted and must not be reproduced without permission.

For index see pages 341–342.

Piano accompaniments are available in The Tune Book of The Salvation Army (piano edition). Recommended key signatures are supplied below.

Salvation and Invitation

1   C

Able to save, able to keep,
Yes, my Lord is able.
Giving me grace, giving me power,
Yes, my Lord is able.
He has turned the darkest night to day,
That's the reason I can say:
He's able to save, able to keep
Is Christ, my Saviour.

2   F

All that you need is a miracle,
And all that you need can be yours,
All that you need is available
The moment you turn to the Lord.

3   F

And yet he will thy sins forgive;
And yet he will thy sins forgive;
O come along, for Jesus is strong,
And he will thy sins forgive.

4   G

Are you coming home tonight?
Are you coming home tonight?
Are you coming home to Jesus
Out of darkness into light?
Are you coming home tonight?
Are you coming home tonight?
To your loving heavenly Father,
Are you coming home tonight?

5   B♭

Ask! Ask! Ask! and it shall be given;
Seek! Seek! Seek! and you're sure to find;
Knock! Knock! Knock! and the door will
    open,
For God! God! God! is so good and kind,
    O yes,
So ask! Ask! Ask! and it shall be given;
Seek! Seek! Seek! and you're sure to find;
Knock! Knock! Knock! and the door will
    open,
For God! God! God! is so good and kind.

6   F

Calling, calling, Jesus is calling,
    Calling me by my own name,
Through the avenues of wandering:
    Child of mine, come back again.

7   G

Calvary, so dear, so sweet, so precious;
    May its dark story ever in my memory
    dwell;
Jesus, so patient, so loving, so gracious,
    'Twas there his life he gave sin's sorrows
    to dispel.

8   E♭

Can a poor sinner come to Jesus?
Can he come? Can he come?
Can a poor sinner come to Jesus?
Can he come just now?

Chorus Section

Yes, O yes, he can come just now:
While the Saviour now is calling,
While the Holy Spirit's striving,
While the precious blood is flowing,
He can come just now.

9   F

Come with thy sin, come with thy sin,
Jesus is calling, come with thy sin.

10   G

Coming home, coming home,
Never more to roam;
Open wide thine arms of love;
Lord, I'm coming home.

11   G

Don't turn him away!
Don't turn him away!
He has come back to your heart again,
  Though you've gone astray;
O how you'll need him to plead your cause
  On that great judgment day!
Don't turn the Saviour away from your
  heart,
  Don't turn him away!

12   Bb

He is able, abundantly able to deliver, to
  deliver,
He is able, abundantly able to deliver all
  who trust in him.

13   G

I am coming to the Saviour who can wash
  away my sin,
Coming! Coming! Coming!
I am coming to the Saviour who can make
  my heart quite clean,
Coming! Coming! Coming!

14   Ab

I think of all his sorrow,
The garden and the morrow,
When cruel death did follow;
'Twas all for me, 'twas all for me.

15   Eb

Jesus is calling, is calling, is calling,
Jesus is calling,
Open your heart's door wide
And let him in.

16   F

Jesus said: He who comes to me shall
  never, never thirst again;
Jesus said: He who comes to me shall
  never, never thirst again;
Come ye who still are dry,
Come and drink a full supply.
Jesus said: He who comes to me shall
  never, never thirst again.

17   F

O Jesus, my Saviour, will welcome sinners
  home!
  Welcome sinners home!
  Welcome sinners home!
O Jesus, my Saviour, will welcome sinners
  home!
  Sinner, don't delay.

18   G

O let the dear Master come in,
His blood will cleanse you from sin;
He's knocking once more, now open the
  door,
And let the dear Master come in.

19   Eb

O the love of Christ, my Lord,
When he hung on Calvary's rugged tree;
O the love of Christ my Lord!
Sinner, 'twas for thy sake,
And he pleads still for thee.

20   C

O yes, there's salvation for you!
O yes, there's salvation for you!
For you on the cross Jesus suffered;
O yes, there's salvation for you!

21   Ab

Room, room, room at the cross,
  Room at the cross for thee.
Room, room, room at the cross,
  Room at the cross for thee.

22   D

Take Jesus to all the world,
  He'll put things right;
Take Jesus to all the world,
  He'll put things right.
Jesus died for all mankind,
So I know that you will find
If you take Jesus to all the world,
  He'll put things right.

Holiness

23 G

There is mercy in Jesus, there's mercy in
Jesus,
There's pardon for all who will come to the
blood.

24 E♭

They are nailed to the cross,
They are nailed to the cross,
O how much he was willing to bear!
With what anguish and loss
Jesus went to the cross,
And he carried my sins with him there.

25 B♭

To heal the broken heart he came,
To free the captive from his chain;
The blood he spilt when he was slain,
Brings guilty sinners home to God.

26 C

Travel along in the sunshine
On the King's highway;
Travel along, singing a song,
Follow Jesus day by day.
Never mind what lies before you,
Never mind what others do;
So travel along in the sunshine
On the King's highway.

27 G

Turn to the Lord and seek salvation,
Sound the praise of Jesus' name.
Glory, honor and salvation,
Christ, the Lord, is come to reign.

28 E♭

What shall the answer be?
What shall the answer be?
What will you do with Jesus,
O what shall the answer be?

29 F

Wonderful place called Calvary!
Wonderful place called Calvary!
Love, redeeming love, I see
At the place called Calvary.

30 F

You may be saved, O glorious thought!
Make haste, do not delay;
His precious blood salvation brought;
You may be saved today.

31 E♭

You've carried your burden, you've carried
it long;
Bring it to Jesus, he's loving and strong;
He'll take it away and your sorrows shall
cease,
He'll send you rejoicing with a heavenly
peace.

Holiness

32 G

All my days and all my hours,
All my will and all my powers,
All the passion of my soul,
Not a fragment but the whole
Shall be thine, dear Lord,
Shall be thine, dear Lord.

33 F

All my heart I give to thee;
Every moment to live for thee;
Daily strength to receive from thee
As I obey thy call.
While I bow to pray to thee,
I commit my way to thee;
Here, just now as I say to thee:
I dedicate my all.

34 F

All there is of me, Lord,
All there is of me,
Time and talents, day by day,
All I bring to thee;
All there is of me, Lord,
All there is of me,
On thine altar here I lay
All there is of me.

35 B♭

At thy feet I bow adoring,
Bending lower, lower still;
Giving up my all to follow,
Just to do my Master's will;
Giving up my all to follow,
Just to do my Master's will.

Chorus Section

36   C

Constantly abiding, Jesus is mine;
Constantly abiding, rapture divine;
He never leaves me lonely,
Whispers, O so kind:
I will never leave thee, Jesus is mine.

37   F

Dear Lord, at thy feet I still linger,
  'Tis sweet to rest here with thee;
O touch my life into beauty,
  Thy Spirit give to me.

38   E♭

Ever thine, thine alone,
  Henceforth, Saviour, I will be;
This my hope, my life's ambition,
  Day by day to grow like thee.

39   E♭

Give me a heart like thine,
Give me a heart like thine,
By thy wonderful power, by thy grace every
   hour,
Give me a heart like thine.

40   E♭

Go back to the old wells
  Where the waters are sweet;
Go back to the old wells
  Where joy and duty meet.
The waters of the old wells
  Will your spirit restore;
Go right back to the dear old wells,
  Leave them no more.

41   G

I give thee my best, nothing less, nothing
   less,
O gladly I give thee who loved me, my best.

42   G

I'm believing and receiving
  While I to the river go;
And my heart its waves are cleansing
  Whiter than the driven snow.

43   G

Jesus, Jesus, lily of the valley,
Bloom in all thy beauty in the garden of
   my heart;
Jesus, Jesus, lily of the valley,
Bloom in all thy beauty in the garden of
   my heart.

44   F

Much more hath God in store,
Much more, much more.
Greater glories we may yet behold,
Greater blessings as the days unfold,
Greater triumphs than have yet been told:
Much more! Much more hath God in store.

45   G

Nearer to thee, nearer to thee,
Blessèd Redeemer, to thee:
Only to know that the path I tread
Is bringing me nearer to thee.

46   G

Now the fruit of the Spirit is patience,
  And the fruit of the Spirit is peace,
The fruit of the Spirit is gentleness
  And joy that will never cease.
The gift of the Spirit is healing,
  And hope for the darkest hour,
The gift of the Spirit is love, yes, love and
   power, and power.

47   E♭

O I'm glad there is cleansing in the blood,
O I'm glad there is cleansing in the blood,
  Tell the world there is cleansing,
  All the world there is cleansing,
There is cleansing in the Saviour's blood.

48   F

Only one intention, only one ambition,
  Lord, at the cross I claim it mine.
Every treasure spending, in thy cause
   contending,
  Held by the power of a love like thine.

49   D

Reckon on me following thee,
Living for ever thy servant to be;
Cloudy or fine, Lord, I am thine
Until thy face I shall see.

50   D

Refining fire, go through my heart,
  Illuminate my soul;
Scatter thy life through every part,
  And sanctify the whole.

51   G

Reign, O reign, my Saviour,
Reign, O reign, my Lord!
  Send the sanctifying power
In the Army of the Lord;
  Send the sanctifying power
  in the Army.

Prayer

52   E♭

Sealed by thy Spirit, sealed by thy Spirit,
Sealed by thy Spirit, eternally thine;
Thus would I be to thy service devoted;
Sealed by thy Spirit, eternally thine.

53   F

Spirit of the living God,
  Fall afresh on me.
Spirit of the living God,
  Fall afresh on me.
Break me, melt me, mold me, fill me;
Spirit of the living God,
  Fall afresh on me.

54   C

Sweet Rose of Sharon, blooming for me,
Jesus, it is an emblem of thee;
Beautiful flower, fairest that grows,
I'm glad I've found thee,
Sweet Sharon's Rose.

55   E♭

There is not in my heart left one treasure,
  dear Lord,
  That I would not yield gladly to thee;
Only let, in thy mercy, thy pleadings be
  heard,
  They shall gladly be answered by me.

56   A♭

Whatsoever things are true,
Honest, just and lovely, too,
Pure in motive and in thought,
Things that are of good report,
  Think on these things!
  Think on these things!

57   F

Where he leads me I will follow,
Where he leads me I will follow,
Where he leads me I will follow,
I'll go with him, with him, all the way.

Prayer

58   G

Bless me now, bless me now,
Heavenly Father, bless me now;
Bless me now, bless me now,
Heavenly Father, bless me now.

59   G

Blessing through me, Lord, blessing
  through me,
Lord, send to others some blessing
  through me;
Living that all men thy glory shall see,
Lord, send to others some blessing
  through me.

60   G

Channels only, blessèd Master,
  But with all thy wondrous power
Flowing through me, thou canst use me
  Every day and every hour.

61   G

Come, beautiful Christ,
Radiate thy beauty in me.
  'Tis thee I adore,
  What can I ask more
Than to live for thee, beautiful Christ.

62   F

Come, Holy Spirit, and abide with me,
My heart is longing to confide in thee;
Such wondrous grace thou hast provided
  me,
Holy Spirit, abide with me.

63   G

Coming this way, yes, coming this way,
A mighty revival is coming this way;
Keep on believing, trust and obey,
A mighty revival is coming this way.

64   E♭

Enter, enter right into my heart, Lord,
  Enter now, enter now;
Enter, enter right into my heart, Lord,
  Enter now, enter now.

65   B♭

Fill the earthen vessel of my heart, Lord,
Fill the earthen vessel of my heart;
Let thy treasure, excelling in power,
Fill the earthen vessel of my heart.

Chorus Section

66   G

For they that wait upon the Lord
  Shall renew their strength;
They shall mount up with wings,
They shall mount up with wings as eagles;
They shall run and not be weary;
They shall walk and not faint:
They shall run and not be weary;
They shall walk and not faint:
They shall run and not be weary;
  Shall walk and not faint.

67   E♭

Here is the place for the lifting of burdens,
  Here is the place of freedom from care;
Here is the place where the sinner finds
    pardon,
  Here is the place where God answers
    prayer.

68   G

Holy Spirit, seal me I pray,
At the cross helpless I bow;
Only like Jesus I long to be,
Holy Spirit, seal me I pray.
Only like Jesus I long to be,
Holy Spirit, seal me I pray.

69   F

I am trusting, Lord, in thee,
Blessèd Lamb of Calvary,
Humbly at thy cross I bow;
Jesus saves me, saves me now:
Jesus saves me, Jesus saves me,
Saves me now.

70   C

I believe God answers prayer,
I believe God answers prayer,
I believe God answers prayer;
He's answered mine before.

71   G

I want to live right, that God may use me
  At any time and anywhere:
I want to live right, that God may use me
  At any time and anywhere.

72   C

If on my soul a trace of sin remaineth,
  If on my hands a stain may yet be seen;
If one dark thought a wearied mind
    retaineth,
  O wash me, Lord, till every part be clean.

For I would live that men may see thyself
  in me,
  I would in faith ascend thy holy hill,
And with my thoughts in tune with thy
    divinity,
  Would learn how best to do thy holy will.

73   E♭

In thee, O Lord, do I put my trust,
In thee, O Lord, do I put my trust,
In thee, O Lord, do I put my trust.

74   G

Jesus, hear my humble pleading,
  My great needs are known to thee,
Come, O come to me revealing
  All thy grace can do in me.

75   E♭

Jesus, thou lover of souls,
Jesus, thou lover of souls,
  O let me drink of thy Spirit,
Make me a lover of souls.

76   B♭

Keep the touch of God on your soul,
Keep the touch of God on your soul.
O wrestle, watch and pray,
Until the break of day,
And keep the touch of God on your soul.

77   E♭

Let the beauty of Jesus be seen in me,
All his wonderful passion and purity,
O thou Spirit divine, all my nature refine,
Till the beauty of Jesus be seen in me.

78   E♭

  Let the waves wash me,
  Let the waves cleanse me,
Lord, in thy power let them roll over me:
  Let the waves wash me,
  Let the waves cleanse me,
Lord, in thy power let them roll over me.

79   E♭

Lord, lay some soul upon my heart,
  And love that soul through me;
And may I humbly do my part
  To win that soul for thee.

80   G

Lord, lift me up and let me stand
By faith on Heaven's tableland:
A higher plane than I have found;
Lord, plant my feet on higher ground.

Prayer

81   B♭
Lord, make Calvary real to me;
Lord, make Calvary real to me,
Open mine eyes to see victory
  in Christ for me;
Lord, make Calvary real to me.

82   F
Lord, teach me how to pray,
Lord, teach me how to pray,
To tell my need, I know not how,
Lord, teach me how to pray.

83   F
Love I ask for, love I claim,
  A dying love like thine,
A love that feels for all the world,
  Saviour, give me a love like thine.

84   G
Make me a channel of blessing today,
Make me a channel of blessing I pray;
My life possessing, my service blessing,
Make me a channel of blessing today.

85   G
Make thyself known, Lord,
  In my life please be!
Make me thine own, Lord,
  Turn not from me!

86   E♭
Meet my need, Lord,
Meet my need, Lord,
Meet my need just now;
  I am waiting and thou art coming
To meet my need just now.

87   G
Never a prayer he will not answer,
Never a seeking soul to whom the Lord
  said nay;
Never a sin that his grace cannot cover,
Never a burden that he cannot roll away.

88   F
O come just now to me, my Lord!
O come just now to me, my Lord!
I give my all, I trust thy word,
O come just now to me!

89   G
O come to the cross where they nailed him,
  Raised high that the whole world might
  see;
Those wounds in his hands, in his feet and
  his side,
  Were made as he died there for me.

90   B♭
O Jesus, be thyself to me
  A living, bright reality;
O Jesus, be thyself to me
  A living, bright reality.

91   G
O pour it in my soul,
O pour it in my soul,
The spirit of Immanuel,
O pour it in my soul!

92   D♭
O touch me again, Lord, touch me again!
This moment I feel afresh thou canst heal,
So touch me again, Lord, O touch me
  again!

93   C
Power, power, power divine,
Power, power, Lord, be it mine;
Power thy promise, power my plea,
Lord, let thy power descend upon me.

94   B♭
Prayer gently lifts me to highest Heaven,
  From earth's confusion to Jesus' breast;
My sin and weakness, my doubt and
  sorrow,
  Are lost forever in sweetest rest.

95   G
Renew my will from day to day;
Blend it with thine, and take away
All that now makes it hard to say:
  Thy will be done.

96   C
Saviour, to me thy love impart,
  And let me now thy nature know;
O dwell within my glowing heart,
  Then shall my life thy beauty show.

Chorus Section

97   B♭

Send a new touch of power on my soul,
  Lord,
  Send it now, Lord; send it now, Lord;
Touch my lips with a coal from thine altar,
  Lord;
  Send a new touch of power on my soul.

98   E♭

Show us thy glory, Christ of the mount,
Thou art of light and wisdom the fount;
We would adore thee, make known thy
  power,
Stay with thy people, hallow this hour;
We would adore thee, make known thy
  power,
Stay with thy people, hallow this hour.

99   B♭

Silently now I wait for thee,
Ready my God thy will to see,
Open mine eyes, illumine me,
  Spirit divine.

100   G

Speak once again, Lord,
Speak once again, Lord,
I am listening at thy feet,
Speak to me again, Lord.

101   E♭

Spirit of God, O hear us pray;
  We would be wholly thine.
Now unto thee our souls aspire;
  Fill us with life divine.

102   E♭

Spirit of love, come and in me residing,
Show forth thy radiance glorious,
For evermore abiding.
Spirit of love, come and in me residing,
Show forth thy radiance glorious,
For evermore abiding.

103   E♭

Such as I have, Lord, I give unto thee,
Praying and waiting new visions to see;
Lord, wilt thou use me? Thy servant I'll be;
Such as I have, Lord, I give unto thee.

104   G

Sweet Spirit of Christ,
Make my poor heart thy dwelling,
Thy beauty adorning,
Other souls draw nigh to thee.

105   E♭

Teach me how to love thee,
  Teach me how to pray,
Teach me how to serve thee
  Better every day;
Teach me how to serve thee
  Better every day.

106   E♭

This is God's moment, God's moment
  for you;
A moment so solemn, yet joyous and new,
  Forgiven is all sinning,
  Real life is beginning,
For this is God's moment for you.

107   G

To be like Jesus!
This hope possesses me,
In every thought and deed,
This is my aim, my creed;
To be like Jesus!
This hope possesses me,
His Spirit helping me,
Like him I'll be.

108   C

To feel thy power, to hear thy voice,
To share thy cross be all my choice,
To feel thy power, to hear thy voice,
To share thy cross be all my choice.

109   G

To thy cross I come, Lord,
There for me is room, Lord,
  Poor unworthy me, even me.
Pardon every sin, Lord,
Place thy power within, Lord,
  Then I from this hour will follow thee.

110   F

Walk with me, walk with me,
Walk with me, walk with me,
All the way from earth to Heaven,
Blessèd Master, walk with me.

111   F

Wash me and cleanse me,
Wash me and cleanse me,
Take all my sin away.

Faith

112   F

We're all seeking the same Saviour,
We're all seeking the self-same Lord.
We're all claiming the same cleansing,
We're all finding our peace restored.

113   F

When I talk with Jesus,
  Bring to him my care,
With his own sweet comfort
  Jesus answers prayer.

114   G

Whisper a prayer in the morning,
  Whisper a prayer at noon,
Whisper a prayer in the evening,
  To keep your heart in tune.

Prayer changes things in the morning,
  Prayer changes things at noon,
Prayer changes things in the evening
  And keeps your heart in tune.

Faith

115   E♭

Clouds will change to sunshine,
  Night will turn to day,
If you will just remember
  God is not far away.

116   E♭

Don't stay in the valley,
  Where the shadows fall;
Climb up to the mountain top,
  'Tis the sweetest place of all;
Catch the heavenly breezes,
  Live in God's sunshine;
Doubts and fears will flee away,
  You'll be happy all the time.

117   E♭

Faith is the victory!
Faith is the victory!
O glorious victory
That overcomes the world.

118   G

Faith, mighty faith, the promise sees
  And looks to that alone;
Laughs at impossibilities
  And cries: It shall be done!
  And cries: It shall be done!
  And cries: It shall be done!
Laughs at impossibilities
  And cries: It shall be done!

119   A♭

Fully trusting in the battle's fray,
Fully trusting Jesus all the way,
Fully trusting, this the surest stay,
  Trusting alone in Jesus.

120   F

God can and will my every need supply,
If I by faith on his strong arm rely;
Sufficient is his love to satisfy;
  I know God can, I'm sure he will.

121   B♭

God is love,
I feel it in the air around me;
  God is love,
I see it in the heaven above me;
  God is love,
All nature doth agree;
But the greatest proof of his love to me
  Is Calvary.

122   B♭

God is still on the throne,
And he will remember his own;
  Though trials may press us
    and burdens distress us,
He never will leave us alone.
God is still on the throne,
And he will remember his own;
  His promise is true, he will
    not forget you;
God is still on the throne.

123   B♭

God is with us all the time,
In the morning when joybells chime,
In the evening when lights are low;
Our God is with us everywhere we go.

310

124   B♭

God will take care of you
  Through every day, o'er all the way;
He will take care of you,
God will take care of you.

125   E♭

He cannot forget me,
Though trials beset me,
  Forever his promise shall stand;
He cannot forget me,
Though trials beset me,
  My name's on the palm of his hand.

126   A♭

He is standing with us here in the plain;
Will you let him ease the load and the
    strain?
  He's a helper and a stay,
  Not a Saviour far away,
  But the Christ of every day,
Bless his name!

127   D♭

  He knows, he knows
The storms that would my way oppose;
  He knows, he knows
And tempers every wind that blows.

128   C

He writes the pardon on my heart,
  This moment I believe,
I can and I will and I do believe
  That Jesus died for me.

129   A♭

His Spirit answers to the blood
And tells me I am born of God,
And tells me I am born of God.

130   E♭

I believe in the word of God,
I believe in the word of God;
  Every promise is true,
  I believe it, do you?
I believe in the word of God.

131   B♭

I can see my pilot's face in every storm,
I can see my pilot's face in every storm;
  Though the billows round me roll,
  There is peace within my soul;
I can see my pilot's face in every storm.

132   G

I have a pilot who guides me
  Night and day;
Through cloud and sunshine I trust him,
  Come what may.
Dangers may threaten but I never fear;
I'm full of confidence while he is near;
I have a pilot who guides me
  Along life's way.

133   D

I know he cares for me, for me,
I know he cares for me, for me;
I'll trust my Father in Heaven
For I know that he cares for me.

134   C

If I take the wings of the morning,
  God is there;
Fly above the clouds of the dawning,
  Anywhere:
Even in the darkest night,
  I'm not beyond his care,
If I take the wings of the morning,
  God is there.

135   G

Jesus himself drew near,
Jesus himself drew near,
  When alone on the road
  oppressed by my load,
Jesus himself drew near and walked
  with me.

136   B♭

Keep on marching with a fighting faith,
  Fighting faith, fighting faith,
Keep on marching with a fighting faith
And win the world for Jesus.

137   D

  Launch out into the deep,
  O let the shoreline go!
Launch out, launch out in the ocean
  divine,
Out where the full tides flow.

138   G

Lean on his arm, trusting in his love,
Lean on his arm, all his mercies prove,
Lean on his arm, looking up above,
  Just lean on the Saviour's arm.

139   Eb

Now don't you let the troubles of tomorrow
  Bring sadness to your heart, and
    burdens too;
For if the Father's eye is on the sparrow,
  Then surely he will care for you.
He knoweth, he careth,
Each burden he beareth,
For if the Father's eye is on the sparrow,
  Then surely he will care for you.

140   Bb

Over and over, like a mighty, mighty sea,
Comes the love of Jesus rolling over me.

141   Bb

Over the sea, over the sea,
Jesus, Saviour, pilot me;
Over the sea, over the sea,
Over life's troubled sea.

142   Ab

Thou wilt keep him in perfect peace,
Thou wilt keep him in perfect peace,
Thou wilt keep him in perfect peace
Whose mind is stayed on thee.

143   G

'Tis wonderful to know the joy that cometh
  from above;
'Tis wonderful to walk with God in
  fellowship and love;
Though human hopes may vanish and
  earthly cares increase,
'Tis wonderful to dwell with him in
  confidence and peace.

144   F

Trusting thee ever, doubting thee never,
  Kept in thy hand to sin no more;
Trusting thee ever, doubting thee never,
  Thou hast my treasure and my store.

145   Ab

When tempted sore to worry,
And care my soul would flurry,
  I count, dear Lord, on thee,
  I count, dear Lord, on thee.
I let the storms pass o'er me,
I know they cannot harm me,
  I count, dear Lord, on thee,
  I count, dear Lord, on thee.
Hallelujah! Hallelujah!
  I count, dear Lord, on thee, on thee,
Hallelujah! Hallelujah!
  I count, dear Lord, on thee.

Experience and Testimony

146   G

A never-failing friend,
A never-failing friend
Is Christ to me, so rich and free,
  His favors never end.
A never-failing friend,
A never-failing friend,
Give up your sin and you shall win
  This never-failing friend.

147   D

All through the years his providence has
  led me,
  His abounding goodness has been all my
    song;
All through the years I tell his love and
  mercy,
  Singing Ebenezer as the years roll on.

148   F

Beauty for ashes my Lord doth prepare;
Garments of praise for my days of despair;
Gladness for sadness, and laughter for
  tears;
Oil for my woundings, and love for my
  fears.

149   C

Bless his name, he sets me free,
Bless his name, he sets me free,
O the blood, the precious blood,
I am trusting in the cleansing flood.
Bless his name, he sets me free.
Bless his name, he sets me free,
I know my sins are washed away,
And now in Jesus I am free.

Chorus Section

150   Ab

By the blood my Saviour shed upon the
   tree,
He redeemed me, he redeemed me;
By the blood my Saviour shed upon the
   tree,
I am now from sin set free.

151   Eb

Christ is the answer to my every need;
Christ is the answer, he is my friend
   indeed;
Problems of life my spirit may assail,
With Christ my Saviour, I shall never fail,
For Christ is the answer to my need.

152   Eb

Clear are the skies above me,
   Pure are the joys within,
Boundless the grace that keeps me
   Free from the power of sin;
Walking each hour with Jesus,
   Held by his mighty hand,
Pardoned, the past behind me,
   Before, the Gloryland.

153   Ab

Come along, come along to Beulah,
   There's a place for you;
Here the milk and honey flow,
Here we see the golden glow
   Of the Gloryland.
Come along, come along to Beulah,
   Keep a-marching on;
There are joybells ringing,
There are glad songs singing
   In the Beulah land.

154   Eb

Ever near to bless and cheer in the darkest
   hour,
When I'm tempted I can feel his power;
At his side I'll abide, never from him roam,
Till at last, fighting past, he will take me
   home.

155   Ab

Everybody should know;
Everybody should know;
I've found such a wonderful Saviour
That everybody should know.

156   G

For there is one God and one mediator
   'twixt God and man,
For there is one God and one mediator,
   the man Christ Jesus.
Who gave himself a ransom for us all,
Who gave himself a ransom for us all,
Who gave himself a ransom for us all,
   O what a wonderful Saviour!
For there is one God and one mediator
   'twixt God and man,
For there is one God and one mediator,
   the man Christ Jesus.

157   C

Glory to God, he has ransomed me,
   I am free, I am free!
Free from the bondage and power of wrong,
Now in my heart is a glad new song,
Free from the shame and sense of sin,
Out in the open I walk with him!
O praise his name, he has ransomed me,
   I am free, I am free!
No more the servant of sin to be,
   Now I am free!

158   D

God hath shined in our hearts,
God hath shined in our hearts,
To give the light of the knowledge of the
   glory of God
   In the face of Jesus Christ.

159   Ab

Gone is my burden, he rolled it away,
Opened my eyes to the light of the day;
Now in the fulness of joy I can say,
   I'm happy, I'm happy in Jesus.

160   G

He brought me out of darkness into light,
   Out of darkness into light;
He brought me out of darkness into light,
   The wondrous light of God.

161   Eb

He loved me, I cannot tell why,
He loved me, I cannot tell why;
   On Calvary's tree he suffered for me;
He loved me, I cannot tell why.

162   Ab

He's mine, he's mine, he's mine,
This wonderful Saviour, he's mine.

Experience and Testimony

163   E♭

He's the same today as yesterday,
  My great unchanging friend;
He's the same today as yesterday,
  Just the same unto the end.
By his mighty power he holds me,
In his arms of love enfolds me;
He's the same today as yesterday,
  My great unchanging friend.

164   C

I am not under law, but under grace;
  It is grace that rescued me,
  It is grace that keeps me free.
I have sought, I have found my
    hiding-place,
I am not under law, but under grace.

165   F

I have a Saviour who's mighty to keep,
  Mighty to keep evermore.

166   C

I have cast my burden on the Saviour
  And while I pray
I shall find in Jesus all the help I need
  On the upward way.
It is not in sorrow to defeat me,
  Nor the cheering ray of hope to dim,
For the present shows God's mercy,
  And the future is with him.

167   G

I know he's mine, this friend so dear,
He lives with me, he's ever near;
Ten thousand charms around him shine,
But best of all, I know he's mine.

168   A♭

I know, I know, I know, yes, I know,
  In Jesus' blood my heart is washed as
    white as driven snow.

169   B♭

I love him better every day,
I love him better every day,
Close by his side, there I'll abide;·
I love him better every day.

170   C

I want to sing it, I want to shout it,
I want to tell you all about it;
The love of Jesus, the love of Jesus;
  It brings the glory to my soul!
I can't compare it, I want to share it,
I feel I really must declare it,

The love of Jesus, the love of Jesus;
  It brings the glory to my soul!
I want to sing it, I want to shout it;
  It brings the glory to my soul!

171   C

I was wandering in the wilderness,
  Far away, far away,
But Jesus sought me in tenderness,
  Happy day, happy day.

172   C

If Jesus goes with me I'll go anywhere;
'Tis Heaven to me wherever I be, if he is
    there.
I count it a privilege here his cross to
    share;
If Jesus goes with me I'll go anywhere.

173   G

I'm living my life for Jesus,
  His love and grace I've seen;
And now that I live for Jesus,
  Life has a new-found theme.
My life has a new-found intention,
  I follow a purposeful aim,
And life has a new-found dimension,
  I witness that I'm born again.
I'm living my life for Jesus,
  His love and grace I've seen;
And now that I live for Jesus,
  Life has a new-found theme.

174   A♭

I'm satisfied with Jesus here,
  He's everything to me;
His dying love has won my heart,
  And now he sets me free.

175   C

I'm singing a glory song all day long;
All hail the power of Jesus' name,
His love for me is still the same
As the day when I was born again;
And that's why I'm singing a glory song
All day long.

176   C

In him abiding, my all confiding
  To the care of love divine;
His word believing, new life receiving
  As the branches from the vine;
His glory showing, I'm daily growing,
  While the rays of Heaven shine,
And I am singing, for joy is springing
  From this happy heart of mine.

Chorus Section

177   G

It's no longer I that liveth,
But Christ that liveth in me,
It's no longer I that liveth,
But Christ that liveth in me.
He lives! He lives!
Jesus is alive in me.
It's no longer I that liveth,
But Christ that liveth in me.

178   F

I've anchored my soul in the haven of rest,
  I sail the wide sea no more;
Now the tempest may sweep o'er the wild
    stormy deep,
  But in Jesus I'm safe evermore.

179   F

Jesus is able, Jesus is able,
  Able to save and to keep.
Jesus is able, Jesus is able,
  Able to save and to keep.

180   F

Jesus is all I need,
Jesus is all I need;
I'll follow where he leads:
Jesus is all I need.

181   F

Jesus is all I need,
My strength, my light, my Saviour,
  Jesus is all I need.

182   G

Jesus knows all about our struggles,
  He will guide till the day is done;
There's not a friend like the lowly Jesus,
  No, not one! No, not one!

183   C

Jesus saves, Jesus saves,
Saves and keeps me, hallelujah!
  Jesus saves, Jesus saves,
  Jesus saves me now.

184   B♭

Joy, joy, wonderful joy,
Peace, peace, naught can destroy,
Love, love so boundless and free,
All this my Lord gives to me.

185   D♭

Living, he loved me; dying, he saved me;
Buried, he carried my sins far away;
Rising, he justified, freely for ever;
One day he's coming, O glorious day!

186   G

Mine, mine, mine,
I know thou art mine;
Saviour, dear Saviour,
I know thou art mine.

187   D

My heart sings whenever I think of Jesus,
My heart sings whenever I think of him.
As I ponder his sweet grace,
And the glory of his face,
Then my heart sings whenever I think of
  him.

188   E♭

My sins, my sins are remembered no more,
My sins, my sins are remembered no more;
They are all gone, yes, every one;
My sins, my sins are remembered no more.

189   F

My sins rose as high as a mountain,
  They all disappeared in the fountain;
He wrote my name down for a palace and
    crown;
  Bless his dear name, I'm free:
He wrote my name down for a palace and
    crown;
  Bless his dear name, I'm free.

190   D

Never to be remembered any more,
Never to be remembered any more;
  He cast my record of sinfulness
  Into the sea of forgetfulness,
Never to be remembered any more.

191   F

Now my heart is glad,
  Gone is every fear;
How can I be sad
  When my Lord is near?
Gone is all my night,
  Breaks a light divine,
For my Saviour tells me I am his,
  And he is mine.

Experience and Testimony

192   D

O the blood of Jesus,
The precious blood of Jesus,
O the blood of Jesus,
It cleanses from all sin!

193   G

O the Lamb, the bleeding Lamb,
  The Lamb of Calvary;
The Lamb that was slain, but liveth again
  To intercede for me!

194   A♭

O what a loving Saviour,
  His love will ever fill my soul with praise;
O what a Saviour, and of his favor
  I'm determined my voice I'll raise.

195   C

On the road of happiness, on the road of
  love,
We're journeying together on to the realms
  above,
In the Master's footsteps we delight to
  walk:
Joy abounding we are finding on the road
  of happiness.

196   G

Peace is mine, I've naught to fear,
Trusting when dark clouds appear;
Joy is mine, I live each day
  'Neath my Saviour's smile.

197   G

Peace, peace, sweet peace,
  Wonderful gift from above;
O wonderful, wonderful peace,
  Sweet peace, the gift of God's love!

198   B♭

Rolled away, rolled away, rolled away,
O the burden of my heart rolled away;
Rolled away, rolled away, rolled away,
O the burden of my heart rolled away;
  Every sin had to go
  'Neath the cleansing flow,
Rolled away, rolled away, rolled away,
O the burden of my heart rolled away.

199   G

Saved and kept by the grace of God,
  Always happy are we,
Proud to tell of the cleansing blood,
And the power that sets us free.

200   G

Scatter a little sunshine,
  Scatter it far and near;
So many hearts are lonely,
  So many lives are drear;
Scatter a little sunshine,
  A little will go so far;
Scatter a little sunshine,
  Scatter it where you are.

201   D

Sing a song of happiness,
  Sing a song of love,
Sing a song of cheerfulness;
  Sing and you will prove
Life is not all bitterness,
  Life is not all wrong,
Life is full of hopefulness,
  Life's a happy song.

202   G

That old, old story is true,
That old, old story is true;
I've found out the reason they love it so
  well:
That old, old story is true.

203   A♭

The light of the world is Jesus,
The light of the world is Jesus,
  And if you come to him,
  He'll cleanse your soul from sin;
The light of the world is Jesus.

204   F

The Lord came down to save me,
The Lord came down to save me,
The Lord came down to save me
  Because he loved me so!

205   A♭

The path is very narrow but I'll follow,
  I'll follow, I'll follow;
The path is very narrow but I'll follow,
  I will follow in the footsteps of my Lord.

206   G

There's joy in following Jesus all the way;
There's joy in following Jesus every day;
His love is like a rainbow when earthly
  skies are gray;
There's joy in following Jesus all the way.

Chorus Section

207   B♭

There's no one like Jesus can cheer me
   today,
His love and his kindness can ne'er fade
   away;
In winter, in summer, in sunshine, in rain,
My Saviour's affections are always the
   same.

208   D

True happiness is love expressed in
   service,
True holiness, compassion deep and
   strong;
In giving of my best I find contentment,
And so forget how hard the way and long.

209   F

'Twas the suffering of Jesus,
   The dying of Jesus,
It broke my heart, won my heart;
   Wonderful Jesus!

210   F

We have a gospel that matches the hour,
We have discovered the true source of
   power,
Man is a weakling, but he can be strong,
Choosing the right and refusing the wrong.
Man has no meaning, no purpose, no soul,
Till he discovers that God is his goal.
This is the gospel that claims all our
   powers,
This is good news for this age of ours.

Praise

211   B♭

Can you wonder, can you wonder,
Can you wonder why it is I love him so?
   When I think of what he's done
   For me, the guilty one,
Can you wonder why it is I love him so?

212   B♭

His love passeth understanding,
His lifetime story my crowning glory;
His love passeth understanding,
His tender care is everything to me.

213   B♭

In life's early splendor
   Gladly would we bring
Hearts glowing and tender
   To our Saviour-King.
He gave all to save us;
   What have we to give?
Just a true devotion
   Every day we live.
Just a true devotion
   Every day we live.

214   A♭

Jesus of Galilee,
Jesus of Calvary,
Saviour for you and me;
Wonderful Jesus.

215   A♭

Life is a song when you walk with Jesus,
Talk with Jesus, work for Jesus;
Life is a song when you live for Jesus
And your heart's in tune with him.

216   A♭

O I love him, yes, I love him,
   Since for me he bled and died!
O I love him, yes, I love him
   More than all the world beside!

217   C

O the dearest, the fairest, is Jesus to me!
I'll praise his dear name that ever he came
To the cross, so to save a poor sinner like
   me!
I'll tell of his wonderful love.

218   A♭

O the love that sought me!
O the blood that bought me!
O the grace that brought me to the fold,
Wondrous grace that brought me to the
   fold.

219 Eb

O what a redeemer is Jesus, my Saviour!
Forgiving my sins and bearing all my
woe;
O what a redeemer is Jesus, my Saviour!
Proclaiming my liberty and washing me
white as snow.

220 Bb

Singing we go, our joy to show,
We want to fill the world with music;
This is the reason we sing:
Make Jesus King! Make Jesus King!
Singing we go, for this we know
With Jesus in the heart there's music,
This is the reason we sing:
Make Jesus King! Make Jesus King!

221 Bb

The heavenly gales are blowing,
The cleansing stream is flowing,
Beneath its waves I am going,
Hallelujah, praise the Lord!

222 Eb

We'll sing in the morning the songs of
salvation,
We'll sing in the noontide the songs of his
love,
And when we arrive at the end of our
journey
We'll sing the songs of Zion in the courts
above.

223 G

When the glory gets into your soul, my
brother;
When the glory gets into your soul, my
friend;
Then you'll shout the praises of your
heavenly Father,
When the glory gets into your soul.

Warfare

224 F

And we'll roll the old chariot along,
And we'll roll the old chariot along,
And we'll roll the old chariot along,
And we won't drag on behind.

225 D

Chosen to be a soldier,
Chosen by God;
Chosen to be a soldier,
Washed in his blood;
Chosen to be a soldier,
Lost ones to save,
Chosen to be a soldier
In the Army brave.

226 C

Christ for all! This is the Army's call,
Gospel of life, gospel of love, gospel of
light.
Hand in hand under the flag we stand
One in our faith, one in our hope, one in
our fight.
Bearers of a royal proclamation,
Heralding the coming of the King,
Hallelujah!
Christ shall reign, echo the glad refrain,
Till all the world praises to God shall sing.

227 C

Fighting, fighting on the narrow way;
The way is rough, the fighting tough,
But we shall win the day.
Fighting, fighting on the narrow way;
The way is rough, the fighting tough,
But we shall win the day.

228 F

Follow the flag, follow the flag,
Be a soldier brave and true;
Follow the flag, follow the flag,
Follow the yellow, red and blue.
March on bravely to victory;
Don't stay behind, joy you will find,
If you follow the Army flag.

229 G

I am a soldier, glory to God,
Fighting for Christ who bought me;
I am a soldier, washed in his blood,
Marching along to Glory.

Chorus Section

230   G

I love the dear old Army flag,
  Of the yellow, red and blue;
I love the dear old drum with its come,
    come, come,
  Calling, poor sinner, to you.
I love the songsters' song so grand,
  And the music of the band;
But the thing I love the best in the north,
    south, east and west,
  Is to fight in the ranks of the Army.

231   F

I want to be a soldier of the cross,
  Brave-hearted and true;
I want to be a soldier of the cross,
  I do, I do, I do, I do.
I want to be a soldier of the cross,
  Telling out the story,
  Walking with Jesus
  All the way to Glory.

232   E♭

I will make you fishers of men,
  Fishers of men, fishers of men,
I will make you fishers of men
  If you follow me.
If you follow me, if you follow me;
I will make you fishers of men
  If you follow me.

233   B♭

If the cross we boldly bear,
Then the crown we shall wear,
When we dwell with Jesus there
In his sight for evermore.

234   G

I'll be true, Lord, to thee,
I'll be true, Lord, to thee,
And whate'er may befall, I shall surely
    conquer all
If I'm only true to thee.

235   G

I'll try again, I'll try again,
I'll try again
  Thy true soldier to be!

236   B♭

In the Army ranks are we,
'Neath the flag, so dear, we've taken our
    stand;
We are marching forth a company grand,
  a conquering band to be.

We would battle, Lord, for thee;
Teach our hands to war, our fingers to
    fight,
That the souls who dwell in darkness and
    night
Thy Kingdom of light may see.

237   A♭

In the ranks of the dear old Army,
  'Neath the yellow, red and blue,
There's a place for every warrior,
  If to Jesus you'll be true.
Your reward will be a grand one
  In the sweet, sweet by-and-by,
There's a place for every warrior;
  Why don't you try? Why don't you try?

238   G

Stepping on together in the ranks of truth,
  Boldy the heroes tread,
Flushing with the courage and the hope of
    youth,
  God's blue sky o'erhead.
Whether in the desert or the star-lit north,
  Land of the ice or flame,
Soldiers of the cross are faring forth
  In God's great name.

239   G

The world is needing us,
Christ is leading us;
  Comrades, let us be true.
His love constraining us,
Prayer sustaining us,
  Faith will carry us through.
His service calling us,
None appalling us,
  Deeds of valor we'll do;
For souls are needing us,
Christ is leading us;
  Comrades, we will be true.

240   F

The yellow, red and blue shall fly
Above our heads until we die,
With blood and fire 'neath every sky,
We're sure to win, we're sure to win.

241   C

There's only one flag for me!
There's only one flag for me!
I'm going to march beneath the yellow, red
    and blue,

To its precious principles be true,
  There's only one flag for me!
  There's only one flag for me!
It speaks of power, pardon, peace and
  purity,
  There's only one flag for me!

242   E♭

We'll keep the old flag flying,
  Flying round the world;
We'll keep the old flag flying
  In every land unfurled;
We'll keep the old flag flying,
  Flying round the world,
Keep the old flag flying,
Keep the old flag flying,
  Flying round the world.

243   A♭

We'll never let the old flag fall,
For we love it the best of all;
We've taken the field for God and right,
We're in this war to fight! fight! fight!
We'll march to victory while we sing
The praises of our Lord and King;
To the end of the world our flag's unfurled.
We'll never let the old flag fall.

244   A♭

We're marching on, we're marching on,
  We're marching on together;
God bless our Army round the world,
  And keep us true forever.

Heaven

245   F

And I shall see him face to face,
And tell the story saved by grace;
And I shall see him face to face,
And tell the story saved by grace.

246   F

At the end of our journey
We shall wear a crown,
We shall wear a crown,
We shall wear a crown.
At the end of our journey
We shall wear a crown
  In the new Jerusalem.

247   F

Away over Jordan, with my blessèd Jesus,
Away over Jordan to wear a starry crown.

248   A♭

I shall know him, I shall know him,
  When redeemed by his side I shall stand;
I shall know him, I shall know him
  By the print of the nails in his hand.

249   D

Lay up treasure in Heaven,
  Life will pass away;
Lay up treasure in abundant measure
  For the great accounting day;
Lay up treasure in Heaven,
  Though men count thee poor,
Thou shalt reign with the sons of God
  For evermore.

250   G

There'll be no sorrow there,
There'll be no sorrow there,
In Heaven above, where all is love,
There'll be no sorrow there.

251   F

Wonderful Saviour, wonderful friend,
Wonderful love that never will end,
Wonderful home he has gone to prepare,
Wonder of wonders, I shall be there.

Index to the Song Section

Note: First lines of first verses are shown in **bold type**, first lines of successive verses in roman type and first lines of choruses in *italic type.*

Index to the Songs

Index to the Songs

Index to the Songs

Index to the Songs

Index to the Songs

Index to the Songs

Index to the Songs

Index to the Songs

Index to the Songs

Index to the Songs

Index to the Songs

Index to the Songs

Index to the Songs

Index to the Songs

Index to the Songs

Index to the Songs

Index to the Songs

Index to the Songs

Index to the Chorus Section

Index to the Choruses

Metrical Index
of tunes in
The Tune Book of
The Salvation Army
and the American Supplement

AN asterisk (*) indicates that the tune can be used for the meter under which it appears by making some small adjustment, such as tying two notes for one syllable, repeating lines, or using verse and chorus together.

When choosing an alternative tune it should be remembered that:

1. Even if the number of lines and syllables agree, the stresses may not. For instance, 8.7.8.7. Iambic has a different rhythmic stress from 8.7.8.7. Trochaic: the first is weak, strong; whereas the latter is strong, weak.
2. Tunes in the irregular meter are not interchangeable apart from a few exceptions.
3. The words of all verses, not just the first, should be checked for compatibility.
4. A tune should sensitively reflect the words of the song.

Long Meter

1 A little star peeps o'er the hill
2 Abends
3 Accrington
4 Alstone
5 And above the rest
6 Angelus
7 Arizona
8 Armadale
9 Beethoven
10 Behold me standing at the door
11 Benediction
12 Beulah Land
13 Boston
14 Calvary
15 Confidence
16 Deep Harmony
17 Duke Street
18 Eden
19 Ernan
20 Harton-Lea
21 He leadeth me!
22 Here at the cross
23 Hereford
24 Holly
25 *How much more
26 Hursley
27 I'll serve my Lord alone
28 It was on the cross
29 I've washed my robes
30 Job
31 Lambton Green
32 Llangollen
33 Maryton
34 Melcombe
35 Morning Hymn
36 My beautiful home
37 O happy day
38 Old Hundredth
39 On Calvary's brow
40 Pentecost
41 Retreat
42 Rimington
43 Rockingham
44 St Clements
45 *St Francis (with alleluias)
46 St Luke
47 Saved by grace
48 Silver Hill

49 Simeon
50 Soon the reaping time will come
51 Sounding Praise
52 Tallis
53 Thou art enough for me
54, 986 Truro
55 Wareham
56 Warrington
57 Was it for me?
58 Whitburn
59 Why not tonight?
60 *Will your anchor hold?
61 Winchester New

Double Long Meter

10 *Behold me standing at the door
62 God's Soldier
21 *He leadeth me (with chorus)
63 He wipes the tear
64 Maryland
65 Newcastle
47 *Saved by grace (with chorus)
66 Sweet hour of prayer
57 *Was it for me? (with chorus)

Common Meter

67 A Little Ship
68 A soldier of the cross
69 Abridge
70 Amazing Grace!
71 Arnold's
72 Around the throne
73 Auld Lang Syne
988 Azmon
74 Bedford
75 *Behold the Saviour
76 Belmont
77 Bishopthorpe
78 Bright Crowns
79 Colne
80 Congress
81 Covenant
82 Crimond
83 Diadem
84 Down in the garden
85 Evan
86 Fewster
87 Fountain

88 French
89 Gerontius
90 God loved the world
91 Grimsby
92 Hallelujah to the Lamb
93 Hardy Norseman
94 He loves me, too
95 Horsley
96 I feel like singing
97 I know whom I have believed
98 I love the Saviour's name
99 Irish
100 I've found the pearl
101 Jesus saves me now
102 Jordan's Banks
103 Joy to the world!
104 Lakeside
105, 985 Lead me to Calvary
106 Lift up the banner
107 Lloyd
108 Lord, fill my craving heart
109 Lover of the Lord
110 Lydia
111 Manchester
112 Margaret
113 Martyrdom
114 Miles Lane
115 My Shepherd
116 Nativity
117 Nativity New
973 Near to the heart of God
118 None but Christ can satisfy
119 O come to my heart
120 Only trust him
121 Prepare Me
122 Remember Me
123 *Repton
124 *Rest
125 Richmond
126 St Agnes
127 St Ann
128 St Magnus
129 St Peter
130 St Stephen
131 Salzburg
132 Sawley
133 Slater
134 Spirit Divine
135 *Spohr (repeat last two lines)

Metrical Index

Metrical Index

8.7.8.7.D. Dactylic
457 Jesus is looking for thee
458 Tell me the story of Jesus

8.7.8.7.7.7. Trochaic
459 A perfect trust
460 Irby
461 *None of self
462 Ottawa

8.8.6.8.8.6
463 Christ is all
464 Come, comrades dear
465 Come on, my partners
466 He Lives
467 Pembroke
468 Praise

8.8.8.4.
469 Almsgiving
470 Troyte

8.8.8.6.
471 Childhood
472 He lifted me
473 Jesus is good to me
474 Just as thou art
475 Misericordia
476 O live thy life in me!
477 *St Margaret (repeat third line)
478 Take all my sins away
479 Take me as I am

8.8.8.8 Amphibrachic
480 Almighty to save
481 Be glad in the Lord
482 O Speak
483 The home over there
484 We speak of the realms

8.8.8.8.D. Amphibrachic
485 In the strength of the Lord
486 *The Cross now covers my sins
487 Thou Shepherd of Israel

8.8.8.8.8.8. Iambic
488 Cardiff
489 Carey's
490 Credo
491 Eaton
492 Eternal God
493 Euphony
494 Make me aware of thee
495 Melita
496 Mozart
497 Old 23rd
498 Sagina
499 St Catherine
500 St Matthias
501 Solid Rock
502 Sovereignty
403 Stella
504 Turner
505 Ye banks and braes

9.8.8.9.
506 God be with you
292 Randolph

9.8.9.8.D.
507 Crugybar
486 The cross now covers my sins

9.9.9.9.
508 We shall win
509 Yes, O yes!

10.4.10.4.10.10.
510 Lux Benigna
511 Sandon

10.8.10.8.
978 Take up thy cross

10.8.10.8.10.10.10.8.
512 Cleansing for me
513 Long, long ago

10.10.10.8.
514 St Philip
515 Sine Nomine

10.10.
516 Pax Tecum

10.10.10.10. Iambic
517 Abide with me
518 Bartholomew
519 Ellers
520 Emerson
521 Motondo Hymn
966 National Hymn
975 Spirit of God, descend
522 Sunset

10.10.10.10.10.10.
523 Christians, Awake
524 Hammond
525 Love's old sweet song

10.10.10.10. Dactylic
526 Beautiful Christ
527 I am so glad
528 O for a heart whiter than snow
529 The Glory Song

10.10.11.11.
530 *Begone, Unbelief
531 Hanover
532 Harwich New
533 Houghton
534 Laudate Dominum
535 Montgomery

11.7.11.7.
992 The Saviour is waiting

11.8.11.8.
536 Behold Him!
537 He hideth my soul

11.8.11.8.D.
538 I think when I read
539 Sweet story of old
540 The old rustic bridge
541 Those endearing young charms

11.10.11.10.
542 Hark, hark, my soul
543 Hold thou my hand!
544, 993 How great thou art!
545 *I know a fount
546 Just where he needs me
547 Mendelssohn

548 Pilgrims (with refrain)
549 Still with thee

11.10.11.10. Dactylic
980 Truehearted, wholehearted

11.11.11.7.
550 Shout the sound
551 Whosoever Heareth

11.11.11.11.
552 *Adeste Fideles
553 Away in a manger
554 Caring for me
555 Come, children, come quickly
556 Cossar
557 *Fighting On
558 Flow gently, sweet Afton
976 Foundation
559 Go, bury thy sorrow
560 Hiding in thee
561 If ever I loved thee
562 I'm the child of a King
563 Lord Jesus, I long
564 Manger Scene
565 My Jesus, I love thee
566 No, never alone
567 Normandy Carol
568 O bliss of the purified
569 St Denio
570 Stand like the brave
571 Take time to be holy
572 The Conquering Saviour
573 The Lion of Judah
574 *The meeting of the waters (repeat last line)
575 *The wounds of Christ
576 To God be the glory
577 Unsworth
578 *When he cometh
579 Yield not to temptation

12.9.12.9.
580 At the cross
581 Home on the range
582 Is it nothing to you?
583 Life for a look
584 Sweet Heaven
585 The old rugged cross
586 Trust and obey
587 We'll all shout hallelujah

12.10.10.10.11.
588 Esher
589 God be in my head
590 Invocation

12.11.12.11.
552 *Adeste Fideles
591 Blacklands
592 The Ash Grove (repeat last two lines)
593 The Eden Above
575 *The wounds of Christ

12.12.
594 Hallelujah! 'tis done
595 I am saved

Irregular
596 A melody in my heart
597 A miracle of grace
598 A robe of white

Metrical Index

The Doctrines
of
The Salvation Army

1. We believe that the Scriptures of the Old and New Testaments were given by inspiration of God, and that they only constitute the Divine rule of Christian faith and practice.

2. We believe that there is only one God, who is infinitely perfect, the Creator, Preserver, and Governor of all things, and who is the only proper object of religious worship.

3. We believe that there are three persons in the Godhead—the Father, the Son and the Holy Ghost, undivided in essence and co-equal in power and glory.

4. We believe that in the person of Jesus Christ the Divine and human natures are united, so that He is truly and properly God and truly and properly man.

5. We believe that our first parents were created in a state of innocency, but by their disobedience they lost their purity and happiness, and that in consequence of their fall all men have become sinners, totally depraved, and as such are justly exposed to the wrath of God.

6. We believe that the Lord Jesus Christ has by His suffering and death made an atonement for the whole world so that whosoever will may be saved.

7. We believe that repentance towards God, faith in our Lord Jesus Christ, and regeneration by the Holy Spirit, are necessary to salvation.

8. We believe that we are justified by grace through faith in our Lord Jesus Christ and that he that believeth hath the witness in himself.

9. We believe that continuance in a state of salvation depends upon continued obedient faith in Christ.

10. We believe that it is the privilege of all believers to be wholly sanctified, and that their whole spirit and soul and body may be preserved blameless unto the coming of our Lord Jesus Christ.

11. We believe in the immortality of the soul; in the resurrection of the body; in the general judgment at the end of the world; in the eternal happiness of the righteous; and in the endless punishment of the wicked.

Mission Statement

The Salvation Army, founded in 1865, is an international religious and charitable movement organized and operated on a quasi-military pattern and is a branch of the Christian church. Its membership includes officers (clergy), soldiers/adherents (laity), members of varied activity groups and volunteers who serve as advisors, associates and committed participants in its service functions.

The motivation of the organization is love of God and a practical concern for the needs of humanity. This is expressed by a spiritual ministry, the purposes of which are to preach the Gospel, disseminate Christian truths, supply basic human necessities, provide personal counseling and undertake the spiritual and moral regeneration and physical rehabilitation of all persons in need who come within its sphere of influence regardless of race, color, creed, sex or age.